Interpreting
Popular M

Interpreting Popular Music

David Brackett

With a New Preface by the Author

University of California Press

Berkeley   Los Angeles   London

First published by the Press Syndicate of the University of Cambridge and printed in Great Britain at the University Press, Cambridge.

Cambridge University Press, 1995

University of California Press, Berkeley and Los Angeles, California

University of California Press, Ltd., London, England

© 1995, 2000 by David Brackett
First California Paperback, 2000

Library of Congress Cataloging-in-Publication Data
Brackett, David.
    Interpreting popular music / David Brackett.—1st Calif. pbk.
      p.   cm.
    Originally published: Cambridge ; New York : Cambridge University Press, 1995.
    Includes bibliographical references (p.), discography (p.), and index.
    ISBN 0-520-22541-4 (pbk. : alk. paper)
    1. Popular music—History and criticism. 2. Popular music—Analysis, appreciation.
    I. Title.

    ML3470 .B73 2000
    781.64—dc21   00-042611

Printed in the United States of America
08 07 06 05 04 03 02 01 00
10 9 8 7 6 5 4 3 2 1
The paper used in this publication is both acid-free and totally chlorine-free (TCF). It meets the minimum requirements of ANSI/NISO Z39.48-1984 (R 1997) (*Permanence of Paper*). ♾

For my parents, Stanley and Marion Brackett

Contents

Preface

This project began as an attempt to find language that could explain my continuing fascination with popular music in the face of a notable lack of encouragement within academia to pursue that fascination. Not only did popular music have no place in the music curriculum, but the training I received seemed to make defending the viability of popular music an impossibility. Somehow, I *knew* that the popular music I enjoyed was in no way less interesting than the classical music that both I and my teachers loved; yet the methods I was learning to describe, praise, discuss, and write about music gave me no vocabulary to describe the "interesting" qualities of popular music in the way that I could describe the counterpoint of J. S. Bach, the intricate harmonic plan and dramatic form of Beethoven, or the delicate orchestral nuances of Debussy, Mahler, and Stravinsky. The harmonic plan of the popular music I enjoyed was usually quite simple, consisting often of only three or four chords. If it did contain modulations, these occurred within a simple and repetitious structure. In terms of "orchestration," these songs didn't fare much better, as their instrumentation often remained relatively static throughout.

One unforeseen consequence of this search for a style-specific analytical terminology was an increasing dissatisfaction with the idea of merely finding the language to discuss popular music in terms of its musical processes, as I came to recognize the strong link between the idea of discussing the "music itself" and the very repertoire already enshrined in academic study. In the end, this study leaned further and further away from the idea that the most important components in musical meaning could be found in internal musical relationships; instead, it sought to come to terms with the idea that musical meaning is socially constructed – even the type of musical meaning that seems to derive from internal musical relationships. Nevertheless, I did not wish to dismiss the importance of musical syntax entirely, for, as a musician, I remain convinced that the *sounds* of music – the way they are produced, the way they differ from one another, the way they resemble each other, the relationship between specific gestures and their effects – are important. One of the great strengths of formal musical training is the ability to describe and analyze the sonic materials of music, and hence, this is the most obvious area where musicologists can contribute to the study of popular music. However, the tendency of the analytical techniques which I inherited to respond to certain sonic features while ignoring others challenged me to explore the idea of analytical pertinence, and thus, to emphasize how analytical metalanguage remains inextricable both from its socio-historical context and from any act of aesthetic evaluation.

In this book, I have tried to address students of music and those interested in the study of popular music who may not be trained musicians. Although any discussion of music in technical terms tends to create difficulties for those without specialized training in music, I have attempted to write the book in such a way that the main points will be clear to those from a variety of backgrounds. Issues are broached – such as the impact of race, gender, and class on musical interpretation, and the importance of history and genre to the social meaning of music – that I trust will be of interest to those outside the field of musicology. The stress here on ideas such as the musical code, and on music as a rhetorical practice, seeks to link the affective aspects of musical sounds with the perceptions of musical listeners who may not be musicians. At the same time, the emphasis on the socially and historically contingent nature of musical *meaning* and on the role of power relations in determining meaning shifts the emphasis away from that found in much other musicological work, although, as I mention in chapter one, the amount of work in musicology interested in these issues has increased considerably since I began this project in the late 1980s. I have chosen pieces of popular music from North America and Great Britain as my objects of study, primarily because of my interests and background, but also because I think that these particular songs raise interesting questions. While I do not propose an overarching method for the interpretation of popular music, the concern here with the way in which specific texts arise from (and contribute to) specific contexts to create different modalities of interpretation could, in principle, be applied to a broad range of musics, popular or otherwise.

With the changed perspective brought on by the reception of this book over the past five-plus years, it is increasingly clear that *Interpreting Popular Music* speaks to a particular moment in popular music studies when visions were rife of a synthesis between the sociological and musicological branches of the field. During the four or so years I was completing the manuscript for this book, works appeared – such as Richard Middleton's *Studying Popular Music* (1990), John Shepherd's *Music as Social Text* (1991), Sheila Whiteley's *The Space Between the Notes* (1992), Allan Moore's *Rock: The Primary Text* (1993), and Robert Walser's *Running with the Devil* (1993) – that struggled with the particular problems posed by popular music to the activity of music analysis, as well as with the general epistemological framework of music analysis itself.

It is also clearer in retrospect that *Interpreting Popular Music* remains part of the ongoing reevaluation of the field of musicology. Particularly contested in this reevaluation, along with notions of the possibility of objective distance and the like in historiography, has been the activity of musical analysis. The main dividing line still lies between those interested in understanding the conditions that enable the practice of music analysis and those who take those conditions for granted, a division that in many ways reproduces the line between those who are and are not interested in the institutional and discursive conditions of the canon. These differences – which cut across the study of various forms of music, be they popular, non-Western, art music, or jazz – have occasioned acrimonious exchanges, largely based on disciplinary or sub-disciplinary affiliations, which have managed to obscure both the larger recurring issues and the way in which such exchanges frequently respond to exigencies of institutional and professional power. In light of this, the discussion in chapter one about the particular challenges faced by musicologists who wish to study popular music is offered more as an analysis of how a particular conjunction of power and knowledge tends to steer students toward one particular type of music and away from others rather than as a wholesale dismissal of musicology.

The idea of "interpretation" in this book has also occasioned some confusion; it does not, in this case, refer specifically to hermeneutic activity, although occasionally I do slide into uncontextualized phenomenology (especially in chapter five) that may mistakenly, if understandably, create the impression that one of the goals of the book was to reify the meaning of these recorded musical performances. Rather, *Interpreting Popular Music* aims to explore the conditions under which certain types of interpretation become possible, to take seriously statements or concepts, and to understand them both in the context of the events that preceded and followed them and in light of the historical formation of genres. In this case, the specific concepts that it aims to take seriously include the relationship between jazz and pop, the discourses of authenticity surrounding Hank

Williams, the idea of irreducible difference and James Brown, and the paradoxical anti-intellectualism of a pop music intellectual. The problems encountered may indeed stem from the occasional tenuousness of the difference between musical events and musical practices, from the difficulty of studying events/practices as forms of "meaningful" activity, and from trying to understand musical gesture as social practice, but the solution surely lies neither in the vagaries of neo-structuralist formalism (resulting from either conventional musical analysis or theories that oppose "musical experience" to the mediated, always social realm of the symbolic), nor in a more rigorous approach to semiotics.

Another issue that the reception of *Interpreting Popular Music* raised for me is that of the intellectual frame and authorial identity. As a reaction to the tendency of much work in cultural studies of the early nineties to deploy citations in order to accrue intellectual capital, I may have effectively obscured the intellectual framework for my own undertaking. This work is a kind of "history of the present," as Foucault describes it: an attempt to work from questions generated by current issues toward historical events with a particular focus on the conditions that enable the discourses in which the events are embedded. Another important aspect of the intellectual context for this book, in addition to the debates discussed earlier pertaining to musicology, was debates within popular music studies about the relative importance of sociology and musicology. The resolution to this debate remains a chimera, made more difficult by the fact that music seems to be the one area of cultural practice in which cultural studies scholars seem to be content not to refer to the specific characteristics of the medium they are studying. While many have been quick to dismiss musicological description for its supposed formalism, they have also not been able to acknowledge the advantages that may derive from an ability to describe the sonic details of popular music. Although *Interpreting Popular Music* addresses this issue in chapters one and six, the problem is clearer to me than it was then, as (non-musicologist) popular music scholars continue to call for a "theory of sound" without engaging with "theories of sound" that may already exist.

I also consciously avoided questions of the relationship of my personal experiences to the music I was writing about. This is most problematic, obviously, when I address issues such as the reception of popular music recorded by African Americans in chapters two and four. Skepticism about the importance of an author's intentions influenced to some degree why I did not include more autobiographical information about why I, a white, straight, bourgeois male, would choose the objects for study that I did. Above all I wanted to avoid the self-justification that might trace my involvement with these artists and recordings to some originary, inspirational moment in my past, to anything that might smack of the "White Negro" or "Vanilla Ice" syndrome on the one hand, or of hand-wringing guilt on the other. Recognizing, as many have, that it requires a certain privilege to renounce the subject position of "author," I nonetheless felt that to dwell on questions of the relationship of my identity to the music I was writing about would shift the focus from the analytical issues to the elements of my biography. I dealt with this by trying both to diffuse any sense of mastery over the material and to avoid prescriptive formulations about what "black music" or "white music" is or is not, or how it should be studied. The main peril I see in white academics writing about "black music" is that they may be tempted to "speak for" black people, reproducing an odious historical power imbalance, or that they may ignore available evidence about what the music means and has meant to African Americans. No easy solution exists to this problem. Clearly, music scholarship on all subjects will benefit from hearing a greater variety of voices within its mix.

Although it is such an obvious point, I will risk stating it anyway: the relationship between music and identity is a complex, fascinating, and intensely personal one for musicians, fans, and scholars alike. Perhaps because of the intensity of this subject, chapter four (on James Brown) has elicited some surprising claims – to wit, that it argues for some sort of absolute difference between "black" and "white" musics. One reason I was reluctant to bring personal experiences into the book was my awareness of the fluid relationship between identity and musical style. That is, while various types of music may be historically associated with a certain group of people, that does not prevent people from outside that group from participating in it and enjoying it. Although I was not yet familiar with Paul Gilroy's theories advanced in *The Black Atlantic* (which appeared as I was completing the manuscript), the view espoused in chapter four on the relationship between identity and race is close to his idea of "anti-anti-essentialism." In other words, while there is no essential, natural difference between people belonging to different racial groups, and while even the idea of racial difference is not natural but always fluid and shifting due to political exigencies, the idea of racial difference is a social fact that affects the practice of popular music. Members of historically dominated groups may even choose to use (in the words of Gayatri Spivak) "strategic essentialism" as a means of asserting control over self-representation. At the same time – as the ongoing and ever more rapid adoption by white youth of African American and Latino style (in clothing, speech, and physical gestures, as well as music) indicates – we may use these categories as ways of making sense of the world, and as a way of referring to large, significant, and general differences, but as soon as "culture" becomes "mass culture" it becomes available to anyone. After all, the Average White Band made decent funk only a few years after "Superbad." But these observations may beg the question of appropriation, and of who benefits materially from that "culture": the Average White Band's "Pick Up the Pieces" still plays more often on rock radio stations in the United States than any of James Brown's recordings.

At any rate, I hope that chapters two and four might form a modest contribution to understanding the relationship between identity and music. In these chapters, as in the others, I was motivated by my desire to understand something about the effect of these musics on me and the many people with whom I had formed my intersubjective impressions of music over years of performing, discussing, and listening to it. Their value resides, I suspect, in how valuable or applicable these "understandings" are to readers.

Finally, I may write a thousand new prefaces, but I will not arrest the play of meaning in which these words participate, nor would I, despite appearances, choose to do so even if it were an option. Readers will continue to find what they want to here, and I am grateful to them for that.

Although I cannot thank everyone who influenced or helped make this book possible, a few specific acknowledgments must be made. Don Randel was the first to counter the "lack of encouragement" mentioned at the beginning of this preface by suggesting that a project such as this might be a viable one; and he continued to be a source of support in the years since that initial suggestion. Sarah Adams, Kofi Agawu, William W. Austin, Richard Crawford, Simon Frith, Martin Hatch, Marilyn Ivy, Anahid Kassabian, John Pemberton, Guthrie Ramsey, Penny Souster, Steven Stucky, and Peter Winkler all read sections of the book and/or discussed many of the concepts presented therein, and offered their suggestions, criticisms, and encouragement at vitally important moments. I am grateful to the International Association for the Study of Popular Music (IASPM), the national and international meetings of which provided a lively forum for the initial presentation of many of these ideas. Similarly, I would like to thank the Society for Ethnomusicology and the Society for American Music (formerly the Sonneck Society), at whose meetings I also delivered papers containing some of the ideas presented here. The students who attended the Popular Music seminar I taught while at the University of Michigan were instrumental in helping me to spin out my ideas, especially Paula Survilla. Timothy Rolls was helpful and efficient in copying the musical examples. I am thankful to Susan Cook and Dai Griffiths, who both made their unpublished work available to me. The spectrum photos were taken at the Cornell Bio-Acoustics laboratory, and I would like to thank Christopher Clark and the staff for their invaluable assistance and for indulging what undoubtedly must have seemed a peculiar project to them. I am indebted to Robert Cogan, who introduced me to the spectral analysis of music and to a wide variety of ways of approaching music outside the Western canon. I would like to thank Winslow Martin for sending several Elvis Costello interviews my way. Karel Husa, though not involved specifically with this project, helped through his encouragement in other endeavors. Finally, the support of Marion, Stanley, and Buzz Brackett, Joe Pachinko, Sabina and Bernd Lambert, and Teresa Schoendorf saw me through the task of writing and provided the emotional and intellectual sustenance that made the completion of this book possible.

In addition to those mentioned in the original preface, I would like to thank everyone who recommended that this new edition be prepared, especially Robert Walser. I also want to acknowledge two others in particular: Mary Francis, who has been a pleasure to work with and who brought the project to fruition at the University of California Press; and Lisa Barg, for her support in innumerable ways, great and small.

Binghamton, N.Y.
February 2000

CHAPTER ONE

Introduction

::

Prelude

In 1965, a recording by Gary Lewis and the Playboys, "This Diamond Ring," shot up the popularity charts shortly after its release, eventually reaching the number one position in February. At the end of 1965, *Billboard* magazine, the leading publication of the United States entertainment industry, ranked "This Diamond Ring" as the seventeenth most popular song of the year and ranked Gary Lewis the eighth most popular artist. Therefore, according to the measurements favored by the popular music industry, this was a very popular song, recorded by an artist who was very popular at the time. Exploring the phenomenon of "This Diamond Ring" – its significance and its popularity – will serve to introduce a number of issues critical to the interpretation of popular songs: the relationship of text to context, of musicians to audiences, of style to history, of artistry to commerce.

Surveying the pop styles represented in *Billboard's* "Top 100" (the most important chart for "pop" music as opposed to the "Rhythm and Blues" [R&B] and "Country" charts) in the first part of 1965 can give us some idea of the musical field against which to assess the meaning of the popularity of "This Diamond Ring." Featured in the top ten during February 1965, the month in which "This Diamond Ring" first achieved the number one position, were the "hard-rock" sounds of "British Invasion" groups such as the Beatles ("I Feel Fine") and the Kinks ("All Day and All of the Night"). The smooth soul sounds produced by the Motown record company figured prominently, with Marvin Gaye ("How Sweet It Is [To Be Loved by You]"), the Supremes ("Come See About Me"), and the Temptations ("My Girl") all represented. Other songs by R&B artists such as Shirley Ellis ("The Name Game") and Joe Tex ("Hold What You've Got") filled the upper reaches of the charts as did a song by the "blue-eyed soul" artists, the Righteous Brothers ("You've Lost That Lovin' Feeling"); also present was "Downtown" by Petula Clark, a

1

song with production values that were more closely tied to those formerly associated with Tin Pan Alley and Broadway musicals.

Of the songs mentioned in the preceding paragraph, "This Diamond Ring" resembled most closely in instrumentation and basic rhythmic approach the style of the British Invasion groups; yet aspects of the production of "This Diamond Ring" differed notably from all of the songs listed earlier. While the name "Gary Lewis and the Playboys" stood for a band, rather than for a solo singer like Petula Clark, Joe Tex, or Shirley Ellis, none of the members of the Playboys played on the recording, the instrumental portion of which was recorded entirely by studio musicians; and none of the members of the band were responsible for writing the song either. This by itself was not so unusual: of the artists listed above, only the Beatles and the Kinks were responsible for the instrumental tracks on their recordings, and only those two groups, along with Joe Tex and Shirley Ellis, wrote or co-wrote the songs they recorded. A strict division of labor was in effect for all the other recordings mentioned: the roles of singer, instrumentalist, and songwriter remained separate as they had from the inception of the popular music industry.

Put another way, there is no single "author" for these recordings. In popular songs, most listeners probably hear the lead vocalist as the source of a song's emotional content; it is the words and sounds associated with the most prominent voice in the recording that are heard to emit the signs of emotion most directly, to "speak" to the listener.[1] It is thereby easiest to conflate the song's "persona" with at least the voice, and possibly the body, media image, and biography of the lead singer. For example, only a fraction of the audience would have been interested to know that David Ruffin, lead singer of the Temptations on "My Girl," did not write the song; but that Smokey Robinson and Ronald White, who did not perform on the recording at all, in fact wrote and produced (i.e., supervised the arrangement and the recording of) it. To the majority of the audience, it was David Ruffin (insofar as he was known as an individual outside of the Temptations) exulting about "his girl," not Smokey Robinson or Ronald White.

Yet, in this respect – that is, in the construction of an author for the pop music text that conflates some combination of singing voice, body, image, and biographical details – "This Diamond Ring" is somewhat of an anomaly. Listeners may notice a strange, almost otherworldly quality to the lead vocal which they may attribute to the presumed youth of the singer, his inexperience, or some innovative double-track recording technique. However, a listener making these attributions would be only partially correct. John Morthland explains the curious genesis of this song:

Producer Snuff Garrett . . . signed Gary Lewis and the Playboys simply because he lived two doors down from Jerry Lewis in Bel Air and was intrigued by the idea of breaking a group fronted by the child of a celebrity. He moved Gary from drums to vocals, but the boy's voice made it onto "This Diamond Ring" only after it had been well reinforced by the overdubbed voice of one Ron Hicklin. Similarly, the Playboys didn't play on the song.

(Liner notes from *Superhits 1965*, Time-Life Music)

Truly, this is an example of a simulacrum that would warm Jean Baudrillard's heart: a song "recorded" by a group who doesn't play on it, who didn't write it, with a lead singer who is barely present on it.[2] One's head spins in search of the "original" in this instance of artistic production. Perhaps if we follow Roland Barthes and assert that the "Death of the Author" means that a "text's unity lies not in its origin but in its destination" leading to the "birth of the reader," then what matters in this case is whether any individual listener believed that the lead singer was Gary Lewis or Ron Hicklin.[3] Then again, the concept of "voice" and authorship in song, due to its performative nature, is a complex one, the discussion of which will have to be forestalled until later in this chapter.

Curiously enough, "This Diamond Ring" belongs to a pop music category that relies heavily on biographical details of the "artist" for its appeal. Steve Chapple and Reebee Garofalo termed this tributary of pop music "schlock-rock," a descendant of the "teenybop" music of the fifties and early sixties;[4] and in its detachment of singing voice and author, "This Diamond Ring" anticipates "bubblegum" groups such as the Archies and the Banana Splits, the recorded voices of which do not correspond to biological humans at all but instead to cartoon characters (and it also anticipates such notorious recent "fakers" as Milli Vanilli). The scene and persona described and projected by the lyrics of "This Diamond Ring" typify those of teenybop music: the image of the teenybop idol "is based on self-pity, vulnerability, and need"; he is "sad, thoughtful, pretty, and puppylike"; in the lyrics, teenybop male protagonists are "soft, romantic, easily hurt, loyal," while women emerge as "unreliable, fickle, [and] more selfish than men." Teenage magazines directed towards a female readership feature male pop stars, but make little mention of the music; instead they dwell on the star's personality, his "looks and likes."[5]

Since a tight link between the biographical details of the biological author and the actual performer heard on the recording cannot account for the appeal of "This Diamond Ring" and its resultant success, we must look elsewhere. Perhaps, as described in the preceding paragraph, it was the ability of Gary Lewis and the Playboys to fit so smoothly into the teenybop category in image and recorded material that won them their success, notwithstanding the fact that Gary Lewis' "looks and likes" did not correspond to those of the lead singer heard on "This Diamond Ring." Or perhaps elements of its musical style distinguished "This Diamond Ring" from its competitors? Musically, "This Diamond Ring" both resembles and differs from its "competition" in several respects. The song features basic "combo" instrumentation heard on many recordings of the era (electric guitar, organ, bass, drums), modal (dorian) inflections in the harmony and melody of the verse, and a basic rock beat pattern; in the chorus it features functional harmony, "closed" phrase structure (a type of phrasing associated with functional harmony and "rhyming" periodic structure), a minimum either of instrumental riffing ("open" phrase structure) or of melodic variation on the part of the lead singer, and little of the rhythmic play found in contemporaneous R&B or rock songs. Instrumentally, the verse features timpani, an instrument rarely found in R&B or rock songs, while the arrangement uses other "novelty" percussion instruments throughout the piece.[6] The transition between verse and chorus contains a modulation of a kind – C minor (dorian) to G-flat major – that is harmonically daring and rare in the popular music of the period.

"This Diamond Ring" also contains several specific references to contemporaneous popular tunes. The harmonic progression of the chorus resembles that found in many Lennon-McCartney songs: the descending bass (G-flat/F/E-flat/D-flat) is reminiscent of "Bad to Me," while the vi–iii (E-flat minor to B-flat minor) movement is found in many of the most popular Beatles songs ("Please Please Me," "I Want to Hold Your Hand," "She Loves You," "And I Love Her," to name a few). The melodic turn on "true" ("if you find someone whose heart is *true*") also resembles similar turns in many Beatles songs (e.g., "Please Please Me" – "Last night I said these words to *my* girl"; "Do You Want to Know a Secret" – "nobody knows, just we *two*") and in many other popular songs from the period. In other words, the musical style of "This Diamond Ring" skims aspects from contemporary rock songs, cobbles a "hook" together out of other hooks from successful songs, and is then produced and arranged from the aesthetic vantage point of "easy-listening" music.

As in the cover songs of R&B hits during the fifties, the musical profile of "This Diamond Ring" indicates an attempt by the music industry to produce a "rock" song according to the old Tin Pan Alley formula: a song is written by a more or less anonymous group of staff songwriters; a producer or A & R ("artists and repertoire") man assembles a group of studio musicians, hires an arranger, and organizes this around a particular singer, whose image is complemented by the song lyrics. The link to Tin Pan Alley aesthetic values was recognized by radio programmers and the music industry at large when *Billboard* included Gary Lewis and the Playboys in their rankings of the top "Easy Listening" (the category for Tin Pan Alley survivors and "middle-of-the-road" music) artists of 1965. Of the artists mentioned in the beginning of this chapter, only Petula Clark was listed in the "Easy Listening" rankings, which also included Herb Alpert and the Tijuana Brass, Robert Goulet, Frank Sinatra, and the San Remo Golden Strings.

The description of the musical features of "This Diamond Ring" has thus far stressed its "standardized" features, portraying it as little more than the product of a musical assembly line. However, "This Diamond Ring" is not without its "individualized" elements: in addition to the aforementioned modulation, it possesses a catchy hook, and features competent instrumental performances, especially that of noted LA session drummer, Hal Blaine.[7] Far from being automatons, some of the other musicians behind the scenes later became recognized as "creative" popular musicians. One of the co-songwriters, Al Kooper, went on to fame as a session musician for Bob Dylan's early electric recordings and as a member of the Blues Project, an innovative blues-rock band; and Leon Russell, keyboardist and arranger for these sessions, became known as a solo rock artist in the late sixties, and as the director for Joe Cocker's "Mad Dogs and Englishmen" tour, both musical roles ostensibly far removed from the "pop" world of "This Diamond Ring." Of course, these "rock" music worlds were unavoidably saturated with their own form of commercialism as well; however, they were more successful (and interested) in effacing the signs of commerce and substituting signs of artistry than were the perpetrators of "schlock-rock."

Despite this attempt to salvage a measure of musical value for "This Diamond Ring," the case history and synchronic comparison presented would seem to be little more than a study of how "non-musical" factors can determine the popularity of a song. And this study largely tells a story of a passive audience of consumers manipulated by the will of the music industry. If the producers of Gary Lewis and the Playboys were trying to manipulate the audience, then they did a remarkably consistent job for the remainder of 1965: although none of the subsequent releases equaled the chart success of "This Diamond Ring," "Count Me In" (number two in May), "Save Your Heart for Me" (number two in August), and "Everybody Loves a Clown" (number four in November) all performed well, a track record achieved by few teenybop (or non-teenybop) acts. Clearly, Gary Lewis fitted many of the physical (young, clean-cut but not too attractive) and sociological (white, bourgeois) requirements for his position in the pop pantheon of the time, and his hit recordings circulated widely, receiving maximum exposure to the widest possible audience.

What is interesting is how poorly the songs attributed to Gary Lewis and the Playboys have stood the test of time. Compared to another song released in 1965, "In the Midnight Hour," "This Diamond Ring" enjoyed much greater pop success at the time. However, in the years since then, "In the Midnight Hour" has become enshrined in the canon of "classic rock," recognized as a song with enduring appeal beyond the moment of its appearance, while the appeal of "This Diamond Ring" remains inextricably tied to its moment.

There are several approaches to trying to understand the fluctuations in value that occur during a text's historical reception. One way of theorizing these aesthetic judgments is by emphasizing the importance of a synchronic analysis of a series of historical moments rather than by relying on a purely diachronic approach; this emphasis helps develop an idea of convention (or "horizon of expectations") against which we may understand a specific work.[8] These cross-sectional analyses permit the understanding of categories and hierarchies of styles and genres that gain meaning in relation to one another rather than in isolation, thereby avoiding the overprivileging of "innovation" that often occurs in diachronic historical narratives about art. These analyses may also permit us to understand the aesthetic "questions to which these works pose answers." Therefore, a text continues to elicit interest if the questions to which it posed an answer continue to be asked.

We have already situated "This Diamond Ring" within the popular music field of 1965, and explored how its "meaning" derives at least partially from its similarity to and difference from contemporary styles, as well as from a connection to stylistic precursors. Using this information, we can venture that "This Diamond Ring" answered questions like the following: how can a song in the teenybop genre incorporate musical elements from the Beatles and other popular songs, orchestral effects from popular TV shows, and still remain recognizably a teenybop song? Can someone who can neither sing nor play, nor look particularly appealing in an androgynous fashion, become a teen idol? Is it still possible to create a teen idol, the heyday of which, 1955–1962, has already passed? Can the forces responsible for a popular music production – songwriters, A & R men, radio programmers, record executives, instrumentalists, singers, fan magazines – by themselves provide the impetus to make someone a star?[9] That this last question was important is pretty much conceded by Morthland's statement quoted earlier: Snuff Garrett (a leading producer of teen-oriented popular music) "was intrigued by the idea of breaking a group fronted by the child of a celebrity."

However, the aesthetic questions that "This Diamond Ring" answered have lost their relevance. Gary Lewis and the Playboys were succeeded by the Monkees (who, even more than the Playboys, benefitted from extensive television exposure; but who, unlike the Playboys, were allowed to play and sing to various extents on their recordings), and then by a plethora of teen idols such as the Partridge Family (featuring teenybop star David Cassidy), the Osmond Brothers (with teenybop idol Donny), and Bobby Sherman, all of whom provided points of identification for teenybop fans after Gary Lewis no longer could (or was no longer promoted in such a way so that he could).

Another approach to understanding the reception of "This Diamond Ring" could employ the Bakhtinian opposition of monologism/dialogism. According to Bakhtin, in a dialogic text "consciousness . . . is always found in intense relationship with another consciousness . . . Every experience, every thought of a character is internally dialogic, adorned with polemic, filled with struggle, or is on the contrary open to inspiration from outside itself." On the other hand, "Monologism, at its extreme, denies the existence outside itself of another consciousness with equal rights and equal responsibilities, another I with equal rights (*thou*) . . . Monologue is finalized and deaf to the other's response, does not expect it and does not acknowledge in it any decisive force."[10] Could it simply be that a work such as Wilson Pickett's "In the Midnight Hour" is charged with "polemic," is "open to inspiration outside itself" in a way that "This Diamond Ring" isn't? That "In the Midnight Hour" addresses an audience which still exists? "This Diamond Ring" was not produced primarily to inspire participation among its listeners; instead, it presented itself as an object to be consumed, interpellating its listeners merely as objects of consciousness, and not "another consciousness" (although it is possible that those "objects" did occasionally dance and sing along). "In the Midnight Hour" demands physical response in dance, and in its blues and gospel references summons up a social collectivity absent in the world of serialized consumption evoked by "This Diamond Ring" (although some of these socially collective "subjects" were undoubtedly happy to "consume" this recording as well). By specifically "targeting" an audience of young consumers, the production combine responsible for "This Diamond Ring" cannot acknowledge these listeners as having "rights and . . . responsibilities" equal to their own. "In the Midnight Hour" comes from a tradition of R&B music which assumed an aesthetic of participation between a performer and an audience of adult listeners, hence the more mature subject matter of the lyrics.

Yet another approach to this matter of historical reception could consider the idea of musical coding and listener "competence." Before addressing these concepts at any length, I will touch briefly on the idea of "undercoding" and "overcoding" as a way of explicating the reception history of "This Diamond Ring." In an undercoded piece, "aspects of a piece . . . are received within a general sense of 'understanding.' Pieces in this category may create their own individual codes." Examples of undercoded pieces would be avant-garde art music, and "free" jazz. On the other hand, in an overcoded piece, "every detail is covered by a network of explicit codes and subcodes. A piece in this category may be so tightly bound to socialized conventions as to be 'about' its code." Examples of overcoded pieces would include muzak and advertising jingles.[11] Twenty-nine years later, "This Diamond Ring" seems to be relatively "overcoded." Aspects of this recording such as the novelty sound effects may have sounded cute and even "novel" at the time, but now seem tightly wedded to mid-sixties situation comedy soundtracks. The harmonic and melodic hooks discussed earlier, which may have appealed at the time, again seem reminiscent only of their era, without much resonance for latter-day listeners. The teenybop lyrics, too, project an innocence and naïveté with little relevance for the modern teenybopper, who has probably been exposed to Madonna's *Erotica* despite the efforts of Tipper Gore. The lack of rhythmic and pitch inflection in the vocal part renders it ultimately predictable, a quality not contradicted by the competent but understated instrumental parts (and this would lessen its value even for a kind of "distracted listening" which may privilege physical involvement). There seem to be no competing perspectives projected by this song, nothing that prompts us to return to it again and again, no irony, satire, or self-reflection emanating from the song's persona: "who wants to buy this diamond ring?" asks the persona, who merely wants to find "someone whose heart is true." What could be simpler?

However, the preceding discussion risks glorifying and romanticizing the audience for "In the Midnight Hour" at the expense of the audience for "This Diamond Ring"; and it risks simplifying the extraordinary complexity of historical processes and their impact on aesthetic evaluation. In the end, the adaptability of cultural forms depends on an "irregular chain of historical transactions" involving countless negotiations, exchanges, and competing representations, which come into prominence or recede based on fluctuating power relations.[12] The chapters that follow explore these "irregular transactions" in more detail than has the discussion of "This Diamond Ring." For now, let us admit that we cannot fully account for why "In the Midnight Hour" is "classic rock," while "This Diamond Ring" is not.

I

Codes and competences

The previous discussion of styles, genres, aesthetics, and reception touched on several factors that influence interpretation and meaning; however, we have not really explored how musical sounds may convey meaning except through borrowings and connections to other songs, and through a brief synopsis of the content of the lyrics. The notion of the "musical code" offers a way of theorizing the connections between musical sound and such "extra-musical" factors as media image, biographical details, mood, and historical and social associations; it can explicate the connection between an individual piece and the conventions of the period that surround it, the connection between a particular piece and the general *langue* from which it derives, and permit us to speculate about the connection between the musical sounds we hear and the "human universe" implied by the lyrics.[13] The "musical code" may be explained as that aspect of musical communication that describes the relationship of a semantic system to a syntactic system, the relationship of "content" to "expression."[14] Richard Middleton has distinguished between two levels of coding, what he terms "primary" (form and syntactic relationships) and "secondary" (content and connotation) signification, both of which feed into a number of "general codes," ordered here from the most general to the relatively specific: *langue*, norms, sub-norms, dialects, styles, genres, sub-codes, idiolects, works, and performances.[15] This chapter thus far has informally discussed the following levels of "general codes" with respect to "This Diamond Ring":

a. *norms*. In this case, the mainstream conventions governing the post-1900 period of popular music;

b. *sub-norms*. The conventions associated with a particular era, in this case mid-1960s pop music – the importance and unusual quality of the modulation, the relationship of the song's hooks to other songs of the era;

c. *style*. Teenybop and Tin Pan Alley pop in the context of British rock, Motown soul, R&B;

d. *idiolect*. The style traits associated with particular performers, e.g., the Beatles, Gary Lewis;

e. *works and performances*. "This Diamond Ring" as recorded by Gary Lewis and the Playboys.

Middleton discusses three main forms of "primary signification": *sens* (links "between the verbal signifiers and the musical signifying process"), "auto-reflection" (the way in which structurally equivalent units refer to each other, including quotation, stylistic allusion, and parody), and "positional value" (the value of an element based on its syntactic position – this is the level that corresponds to the metalanguage of music analysis).[16] On this level, we have discussed structural relationships in "This Diamond Ring" using terms such as "verse" (section A) and "chorus" (section B), the positional importance of certain harmonic features (the progression of vi–iii, the modulation), and melodic events (the "turn" on "true"); the stylistic allusion of "auto-reflection" (these hooks "sound like" the Beatles); and we have employed *sens* in the use of terms such as "hook," "open and closed phrasing," and "melodic turn."

We have also touched on a number of factors in the discussion of "This Diamond Ring" that could be grouped in the category of "secondary signification," including the following:

a. *Intentional values*. These are recognized, intended connotations of specific structural or thematic effects: the finger cymbals and wind chimes in the introduction connote novelty;

b. *Positional implications*. These are connotations arising from structural position: the memorable melodic line and harmonic sequence in the chorus create the hook;

c. *Ideological choices*. These are particular, preferred meanings, selected from a range of possible interpretations: "This Diamond Ring" evokes a world of serialized consumption as opposed to the social collectivity of "In the Midnight Hour";

d. *Emotive connotations.* These refer to the agreed affective implications of musical events: teen idols singing teenybop songs are associated with vulnerability, need, self-pity, loyalty;

e. *Style connotations.* These are the associations summoned up by coding at the general level of style: teenybop pop means adolescent, middle-class, predominantly female fans, listening by themselves or in small groups;

f. *Axiological connotations.* These refer to moral or political evaluations of musical pieces, styles or genres: teenybop is a commercial sell-out/an empowering form of identity/a benign form of entertainment.[17]

It should be obvious that the "secondary" level of signification is related to, and ultimately inextricable from, the "primary" level (despite the implications of the terms "primary" and "secondary," the question of which one of the levels is the foundational one is moot). That is, categories of "secondary signification" such as "intentional values" and "positional implications" depend on knowledge of the syntactic relationships described by "primary signification." Conversely, certain aspects of "primary" signification depend on "secondary" signification: *sens* cannot exist without the discourses (and their attendant connotations) surrounding various styles and genres, without the language of musical description which arises out of specific contexts; "positional value" can rarely be perceived without an awareness of "positional implications" (although these may not be admissible or overt in certain theoretical contexts); and the aspects of quotation and stylistic allusion contained in "auto-reflection" can be either "primary" or "secondary" depending on whether the act of interpretation emphasizes either expression or content. In general, Middleton sees the difference between these types of signification as the difference "between the roles of individual effects, privileging mechanisms of connotation, and of synthesized syntactic structures, privileging primary types of significations."[18]

The idea of the "code" has been criticized for its reductionism, that is, for arbitrarily limiting the range of possible relationships between signifiers and signifieds.[19] But focusing on the purely relational aspects of every signifier to every signified without grouping them leaves us with no way of interpreting the resulting sign. Without the concept of the "code" there can be no connotation, meaning, or "communication," which throws the emphasis from meaning back to structure. And indeed, this is what Jean-Jacques Nattiez, the best-known critic of the idea of the musical code, posits as an alternative: "[We can] consider that, all in all, structuralism was not wrong in recognizing some level of material immanence in the text – a level that cannot be outlined, and that is not exclusive. This insight is worth retaining, even when pure structuralism has proven unworkable."[20] The recourse to "immanence" relegates discussion of a musical text to an ahistorical, non-cultural vacuum, a vacuum without perceiving subjects. It is true that, in some sense, codes *are* inevitably reductionist, as is any device that attempts to categorize or group utterances; but they do permit discussion of *meaning*, which forms an important part of the everyday discourse about music: "kd lang is sensuous," "Chris Isaak's guitar evokes wide-open spaces," "Springsteen means what he says," "I don't understand contemporary art music," "the Who's *Tommy* was pompous, the death of rock."

If musical meaning is conveyed through a code that is sent or produced by somebody then it also must be received or consumed by somebody. This raises the question of "competence": what is the relationship between sender and receiver, and how does this affect the interpretation of musical messages? Gino Stefani has outlined a model of musical competence which, in its hierarchies, parallels Middleton's presentation of general codes.[21] Stefani presents five levels of musical competence:

> *General Codes* (GC): basic conventions through which we perceive or construct or interpret every experience (and therefore every sound experience). This is the "anthropological" level of musical competence that everyone may exercise;
>
> *Social Practices* (SP): cultural institutions such as language, religion, industrial work, technology, sciences, etc., including musical practices (concert, ballet, opera, criticism);
>
> *Musical Techniques* (MT): theories, methods, and devices which are more or less specific and exclusive to musical practices, such as instrumental techniques, scales, composition forms, etc. It is at this level that one usually finds the definition of music as "the art of sounds";
>
> *Styles* (St): historical periods, cultural movements, authors, or groups of works: that is, the particular ways in which MT, SP, and GC are concretely realized;
>
> *Opus* (Op): single musical works or events in their concrete individuality.

Of course, different listeners will bring these levels to bear in varying ways based on their experiences. Stefani thus describes two basic competence types, which he describes as "high competence" and "popular competence." High competence focuses on pieces as autonomous works, while popular competence experiences pieces more on the levels of the General Codes (GC) and Social Practices (SP). Moreover, the degree to which a piece may be decoded depends on the range of levels available to an individual listener: a maximum "signification effect" would occur when a piece is interpreted on all levels; a relatively weak effect would occur if a General Code were interpreted without any information from the other levels, or, conversely, if a piece were interpreted purely on the Op level – as would occur if a piece were perceived solely as an autonomous work, without any social significance or connotative meaning.[22] Stefani also indicates that there may be particular regions of the GC which are of interest to those with high competence, and aspects of Op coding which are the province of those with popular competence. Thus, frequent contrast at the GC level might interest those with high competence, while specific knowledge about popular songs and performers may be the province of those with largely popular competence. Stefani's basic competence types recall the formulations of Pierre Bourdieu, with his notions of "popular" and "legitimate" aesthetics. According to Bourdieu, these aesthetic positions emphasize either function or form, and are related to the amount and type of "cultural capital" (acquired through a conjunction of class background and academic training) possessed by an individual.[23] In other words, listener "competence" in this formulation refers to the range of subject positions available to a listener dependent on that individual's history and memory.

The advantage of Stefani's model over either a purely structuralist emphasis on codes which ignores their reception or a Chomskyian notion of linguistic competence which posits a trans-cultural human "nature" into which linguistic structures are programmed, is that it introduces the notion of context. There are no ideal "addressers" or "addressees"; "context" functions not only in the Jakobsonian sense of providing a context for a specific message, but also in telling us about the larger social and cultural context, about the individual backgrounds of the senders and receivers of the message, and about the background of the message itself.[24] Furthermore, "codes" are no more static than are the types of competence that listening subjects may bring to bear on them. As discussed earlier, an "undercoded" piece may create new codes; similarly, in the act of interpretation, the way in which we "decode" a piece may change our sense of the piece we are hearing, necessitating an infinite series of new perspectives in the act of listening.

A brief example should suffice to demonstrate how these competence levels can operate in the listening process. At the GC level, we may initially perceive "This Diamond Ring" as a series of events broken up by brief pauses, followed by uninterrupted activity which still is irregular, followed by more flowing activity. On the SP level, a listener socialized by Euro-American musical practices may interpret these events heard as an "introduction," followed by a statement of an idea, then followed by a "chorus," which suggests dancing, physical movement, and singing along more strongly than the preceding material. It is here that vaguely affective qualities may become apparent: feelings of vulnerability, resoluteness, comradely advice, all parts of the "human universe" that the song inhabits, created by the words and emphasized by musical codes. At the MT level, the listener hears introduction, verse, and chorus delineated by specific rhythmic, melodic, and harmonic ideas. At the St level, correlations could be made between this song and other songs, grouped in various ways (Beatles songs, British rock, Tin Pan Alley pop music, teenybop), and even historicized (this is *mid-sixties* pop). At the Op level, there is explicit recognition of the song, "This Diamond Ring," performed by Gary Lewis and the Playboys.

II

Who is the author?

This chapter has already touched on some of the problematic aspects of "authorship" in popular song in the somewhat quirky instance of "This Diamond Ring." In some respects, that song was not anomalous: frequently there is no single origin for the popular music text; and what is perceived by the audience as the emotional focal point of the song (the lead vocalist) may or may not be responsible for other aspects of the song's production (songwriting, instrumental performance, arranging, engineering). In some cases, there may be a relatively tight link between functions: in the case of the singer-songwriter, for example, the lead singer is responsible both for writing the song and for playing an instrument around which the accompaniment is based. In this category, the song's lyrics usually fall into the "confessional" mode, appearing to reveal some aspects of the singer-songwriter's inner experience. At one level, the idea that there exists some correspondence between the biography of the singer-songwriter and his or her songs seems unquestionable. Music magazines and biographies often focus on the parallels between songs and the singer's lives: thus, Joni Mitchell's "My

Old Man" is "about" her relationship to Graham Nash; James Taylor's "Sunshine, Sunshine" is "about" his sister Kate, and his "Knocking Around the Zoo" is "about" his stay in a mental hospital – indeed, the sometimes explicitly autobiographical references invite these kinds of associations. These associations then lead to statements such as "[Joni Mitchell's] primary purpose is to create something meaningful out of random moments of pain and pleasure in her life."[25]

Yet there are distinct disadvantages to this way of conceptualizing the relationship between singer and song. Even for singer-songwriters it is questionable whether the song *only* expresses the autobiographical details of their lives. At the most basic level, if this were true it would mean that a singer-songwriter could only write or sing sad songs when sad, happy songs when happy. At another level, there exists the possibility that a song and a recording may present a range of affect that *exceeds* the composer/performer's intentions: listeners may interpret a song in a way that has little to do with what the performer "felt" when he or she recorded or wrote it. At still another level, the notion of a strict identity between lived experience and a song's meaning eliminates the effect of the song as a musical performance: the musical codes and the manner in which the song is performed may either contradict or reinforce the content in the lyrics, adding new layers of nuance by "acting out," inflecting, and contextualizing them. There is thus the possibility – even in a performance by a solo singer-songwriter in which singer, instrumentalist, arranger, and composer are one and the same person – of a *multiplicity* of authorial voices in the musical text.[26] For example, in many Bob Dylan songs in which the lyrics express rage or scorn towards someone, there are moments in which his voice conveys a sense of compassion and tenderness (e.g., the line "I didn't realize how young you were" from "One of Us Must Know [Sooner or Later]"); or, conversely, Dylan gives an ironic or humorous lilt to lyrics that could otherwise seem lustful (e.g., the title line from "I Want You"; compare this to the menacing affect produced by Elvis Costello's rendering of the same line in his "I Want You"). This does not even touch on the way in which other instrumentalists or singers may contribute "voices" to group performances, or on what happens when a singer-songwriter performs somebody else's song: when James Taylor performs "You've Got a Friend," does it mean that he actually wants to console a particular person, or that he empathizes with the desire of Carole King (the songwriter) to console somebody? The fact that Carole King sings in the background of James Taylor's recording further complicates the relationship between the authorial voices heard in the recording, and between the performers and the composer. Belief in literal correspondences could lead to a whole series of specious interpretations about the "friendship" between Carole King and James Taylor, or the possible friendships between both of them and a third party (and, indeed, this kind of speculation often fuels a certain kind of "Paul-Is-Dead" interest among members of the audience).[27]

The concept of authorship becomes more complex when we examine songs in genres other than that of the singer-songwriter. We have already touched on some of the complexities of the situation when the roles of songwriter, instrumentalist, arranger, producer, singer, and "star" are divided as in "This Diamond Ring." Group situations in which there are a multiplicity of singers, songwriters, and instrumentalists present a ready-made assortment of "voices," which individually do not maintain a strict identity between performer and authorial voice (or persona). For example, in descriptions of the Beatles' personalities, John Lennon was typically characterized as fiery and belligerent, Paul McCartney as sensitive and romantic, George Harrison as serious and spiritual. Yet John sang ballads, Paul sang hard-rock tunes, and George sang silly ditties. They sang together in different combinations, assumed different roles, and contributed additional "voices" through their instrumental parts. And, of course, there are other pop music contexts, including "This Diamond Ring," "Downtown," "My Girl," and many more, which feature different degrees of creative input between the various people responsible for a pop recording (songwriter, producer, singer, arranger, instrumentalist), and the play of "voices" that present themselves to the listener.

This idea of a multiplicity of voices within the text brings us close to Roland Barthes' idea cited earlier, that a "text's unity lies not in its origin but in its destination," an idea which questions the importance of the belief in a single, originary author. Kaja Silverman has described how a film may create a sense of multiple authorial voices through characters, plot, dialogue, and the cinematic apparatus itself; these voices can then combine to create an author "inside the text." Nonetheless, there remains the possibility that through the insistent repetition of certain ideas (in lyrics and music) and through the association of these ideas with ideas and images outside the text (interviews, biographies, etc.), the author "inside the text" may inscribe the author "outside the text" as one of the text's voices; this is the effect we observed in the case of the singer-songwriters. This suggests how we may sense that musicians are expressing "themselves" in song as *one* of the many personae they project musically.[28] In the chapters that follow, one of my concerns is to trace how different notions of authorship are shaped by performers, audiences, and others associated with the production of popular music, how these notions circulate in a variety of discourses, and how they then figure in the interpretation and resultant meaning of the songs in jazz, Tin Pan Alley pop, country, soul, and 1980s pop.

The previous discussion of "This Diamond Ring," in comparing it to "In the Midnight Hour," may have implied the aesthetic superiority of a multiplicity of voices "inside the text." This corresponds to some aspects of the work of Bakhtin who, in developing the aesthetic, moral, and political implications of his concepts of dialogism/monologism, imputes a greater value to polyphonic, "dialogic" texts that contain a multiplicity of voices as opposed to univocal, "monologic" texts. However, when applied to musical processes of production and reception, this mode of evaluation runs the risk of oversimplification. An uncritical application of this concept to discussions of popular music disregards the possibility of different listening situations having types of music most appropriate for them; specifically, it cannot account for musical practices such as dancing, listening to a walkman while roaming the city, or overhearing a neighbor's radio while cleaning the house, activities that may not permit a full appreciation of the multiplicity of voices in the popular music text, but activities which nonetheless permit the listener to engage with the music.[29] And Bakhtin's ideas, when transferred from reading to listening, imply the superiority of high competence to popular competence: for his distinctions to hold, they require an ideal listener who can discern all those voices within the text.

III

Musicology and popular music

Context to text

One of the debates that recurs most often at popular music studies conferences is the debate over the relative importance of the popular music "context" vs. the popular music "text." While proponents of each side understand that contexts consist of texts and that texts exist within a context, the lines of battle are nonetheless drawn: sociologists study contexts while musicologists study texts. There is some indication that these lines may be growing fuzzy: from the musicology side, at any rate, many have become increasingly interested over the past several years in the way in which contexts influence the perception of texts. One important aspect of context is that it establishes the codes that listeners are most likely to apply in certain listening situations. The more we know about how people listen to a piece of music, how they evaluate it, what they do with it, and the type of meanings they attribute to it, the clearer idea we can get of what is pertinent in a text.[30] In the preceding discussion of "This Diamond Ring," a rather "thin" context was presented: we examined the song within the context of the popular music field of its time, and (cursorily) in the sociological context of the assumed audience for the song. The context was developed by referring to secondary sources such as liner notes, and to an article on the differing musical preferences of young male and female pop music fans. The musical description, brief though it was, made a number of assumptions about what was musically pertinent: harmony was analyzed according to its function, melodic pitches were analyzed according to scale type, rhythm and phrasing were discussed in relation to other popular songs of the day and according to models derived from the study of Western art music; the harmonic and melodic terms used were also derived from those used to describe Western art music. The section on "secondary signification" suggested possible connotations conveyed by some of these formal features, without making explicit the process through which the connotations were established.

Ideally, analytical emphasis could arise from terminology used in the discourses which circulate around a song, style, or genre. These discourses give us a clue as to what codes are activated by the song, and to the range of possible connotations. These discourses could include ethnographic research which focused on statements of the fans themselves, gathered in face-to-face encounters; they could include written documents and interviews found in mass media publications, music industry magazines, historical documents, and "secondary literature" such as biographies. In all these cases, it is important to note who is speaking, to whom they are speaking, the context of the utterance itself (what effect is *it* trying to make), for these discourses are never disinterested: they too are constituted by texts embedded in their own contexts. This discourages an unproblematic distinction between text and context. While musical texts may retain a "relative autonomy" – music is a medium with specific properties, practices, limitations, and possibilities – they gain their meaning by circulating with other texts from other media which may include mass media publications, videos, film, industry publications, and "historical" documents.[31] Again, as in the "aesthetics of reception," one of the aims of this type of discourse analysis is to build a synchronic text of a socio-cultural moment rather than to emphasize a diachronic unfolding of autonomous works.

Contained in these discourses are statements about musical value, about what is important in a piece of music. Simon Frith has shown how the critical discourse associated with the three main musical categories into which the musical field is conventionally partitioned – art music, folk music, popular music – all produce different conventions of aesthetic value. "Art" music revolves around providing a transcendent experience; however, only those with the right training can experience the real meaning of "great" music. "Folk" music revolves around providing an authentic experience of community. "Popular" music values are created by and organized around the music industry – musical value and monetary value are therefore equated, and the sales charts become the measure of "good" pop music. Pop music can also invoke the discourses of the first two music "worlds." The problem of authenticity vs. commercialism exists across discourses as part of the shared response to music making in a capitalist society.[32] The chapters that follow explore the ways in which these "art," "folk," and "popular" music discourses are weighted in the evaluation of different pop styles and genres, and how these different styles and genres construct notions of "authenticity," that is, how they distinguish "sincere" expression from fodder for the masses.

The musicological quagmire

Yet even if we grant the possibility of context to help establish the pertinence of textual details, codes, and analytical decisions, problems still arise when we approach the "musical" text. In the event that we use terms other than those arising from the discourses associated with the context of a given song, then we will probably resort to terms drawn from musicological discourse to describe the music. And if we use musicological discourse to describe the details of a piece of music, we must recognize that the metalanguage of music analysis is not transparent, but that it is a medium that comes with its own ideological and aesthetic baggage which will affect what we can say. This is because musicological discourse, despite its seeming naturalness, is contingent on historical circumstances: it emerged in the mid nineteenth century in Europe in tandem with a whole panoply of beliefs about what the musical experience should provide, and about the relationship between performers, audiences, and composers. Audiences and scholars developed an aesthetic of distanced appreciation, and a belief in the autonomous art work and the primacy of "absolute" music (i.e., music lacking, in the words of Carl Dahlhaus, a "concept, object, and purpose"). These attitudes and beliefs were accompanied and accommodated by the context of the concert hall, a context which divorced the musical work from its previous social functions, and transformed musical performance into a sacred ritual.[33] Although these attitudes and beliefs have shifted in the last century and a half, aspects of them remain remarkably tenacious and pervasive. Their effect on the discipline of musicology was to focus attention on a small body of work (the "canon"), and to encourage a positivistic approach to musical research, an approach that was renewed vigorously in the period following World War II.

There is some validity to using musicological discourse to describe popular music: the popular music texts studied in this book emerged both from cultural contexts similar to those that spawned and subsequently nurtured musicology, and from cultural contexts with important differences as well. In the end, if we attempt to use some aspects of this discourse to analyze songs from heterogeneous cultural contexts (such as contemporary popular songs), then we must ask what guarantees the "fit" between the song, the audience, and the analytical discourse.

This is a very difficult question, and one that has been rarely asked within the context of art music analysis.[34] Music analysis has tended to focus on pieces of music as autonomous entities in order to show the relationship of the parts to the whole. The formalistic dissection of the text appears contextless, but only because the context is taken for granted; it is therefore important to reestablish the effect of contextual factors on analytical metalanguage in order to unpack the aesthetic values embedded within this metalanguage before applying it to musics outside the canon. On the other hand, it *is* true that *historical* musicology has tended to place musical works, composers, and styles in their social and cultural context. However, the majority of these writings, until very recently, have accepted the relative importance of the canon as a given and have largely foreclosed discussions of musical meaning. They have also resisted (again, until recently) exploring questions about the relationship of text to cultural context that have interested ethnomusicologists because, in the words of Joseph Kerman, "Western music is just too different from other musics, and its cultural contexts too different from other cultural contexts."[35] Yet Kerman never explains why or how this is so. That the statement could be accepted is due in large part to the persistence of the aforementioned historical circumstances in which musicology emerged, and to what Philip Tagg termed "notational centricity," an issue I will discuss in more detail later in this chapter.[36]

An awareness of the insufficiency of music analysis to tell us much of value about popular music informed some of the earliest writings on the relationship between music analysis and popular music. In 1966, Charles Keil noted the emphasis in music analysis on "syntax" and its inability to deal with "process," which he described as the "mode of understanding" in improvised musics. In improvised musics, according to Keil, the "horizontal" qualities of "pulse/meter/rhythm" take precedence over the "vertical" qualities of "harmony/melody/ embellishment" so prized in Western art music. Four years later, Andrew Chester used the terms "extensional" and "intensional" in a similar fashion to describe the aesthetic dichotomy between art music and popular music. "Extensional development . . . includes all devices that build diachronically and synchronically outwards from basic musical atoms. The complex is created by combination of the simple, which remains discrete and unchanged in the complex unity." On the other hand, "intensional development" is created by inflecting melody, timbre, rhythm, and other elements while many parameters may remain constant throughout a song. John Shepherd, along with the co-authors of *Whose Music?*, continued the critique of Western music analysis; Shepherd blamed musicology's neglect of popular music on music analysis' preference for information gathered via the "visual" mode as opposed to the "oral" mode.[37] We may note that these early discussions include some perhaps overly simplistic binary oppositions – it is difficult to find any type of music that is either purely "intensional" or "extensional", "syntactical" or "processual" – as well as a tendency toward Romantic allegory – the story of the unmediated "oral" mode supplanted by the corrupted "visual." Nevertheless, even on a sliding scale of possibilities, it is probably fair to say that music analysis tends to emphasize "syntax," "extensional development," and "visual information"; this puts a great deal of twentieth-century popular music at a disadvantage, because it often appears deficient in those areas. The recordings studied in this book range from songs with a fair degree of syntactic interest and extensional development (Bing Crosby's "I'll Be Seeing You" and Elvis Costello's "Pills and Soap"), to songs that strongly emphasize the processual mode of understanding (James Brown's "Superbad"), to songs lying somewhere in-between (Billie Holiday's "I'll Be Seeing You" and Hank Williams' "Hey Good Lookin'").

Music in culture

The early work on popular and improvised musics suggests that analyzing qualities such as "process" and "musical inflection" may be particularly fruitful, as these qualities correspond to values recognized by

performers and listeners. This returns us to the issue of the relationship
between context and text, and to the question of how we may allow our
understanding of contexts to inform our explication of texts.
Ethnomusicology is the discipline that has grappled with the issue of the
relationship between context and text in the most sustained and explicit
fashion, so we might expect to see these terms taken up and applied in
ethnomusicological analyses. Still, important differences separate the
obstacles confronting the ethnomusicologist and the popular music
researcher. In theory, ethnomusicology takes the entire range of music
made during any historical period in the world as its subject; in practice,
ethnomusicological studies tend to favor music made or originating in
non-industrialized, non-Western locales; in particular, the "art" musics of
Indonesia, Japan, and India, and the "vernacular" musics of subsaharan
Africa and Native America (the lone Westerners of the bunch). Attempts
to find relationships between social structure and musical structure
assume a stable, monolithic "culture," the characteristics of which can
then be mapped on to or derived from a musical structure or a set of
musical characteristics. Although the situation is changing – with an
increasing number of ethnomusicologically based articles, dissertations,
and books based on music from urban, industrialized contexts – the
"culture" studied is typically not one of which the researcher is a
member; and the music must be accepted by "an entire society as its
own."[38]

In terms of the relationship between musical structure and social
structure, music produced and consumed in modern, industrialized
contexts raises a host of problems not found in rural, pre-industrial
settings. When Alan Lomax applies his method for studying relations
between music and culture to Western Europe, it leads him to assert that
"in Western European culture . . . the leading singer commands and
dominates his listeners during his performance. His association with his
audience is, in sociological terms, one of exclusive authority . . . In its
role relationship the symphonic audience . . . differs from the ballad
audience only in its size."[39] A statement such as this ignores the polyglot
aspects of contemporary Western society, subsuming them into a singular
stance of domination/subordination in the act of transmission; it ignores
the way in which a participatory aesthetic may contribute to the
contemporary Western listening experience; and it ignores how various
listener subject positions informed by a variety of class-, gender-, and
culturally based attitudes may influence interpretation (as in Stefani's
model of musical competence). What is more, these "listening positions"
are not locked into place by financial status or genetic code, but can be

acquired through contact with a musical style. That a broad range of factors influences listening attitudes implies that *multiple* listening positions may be available to a single listener; this suggests the existence of a kind of double- (or multiple-) "eared" listener, a counterpart to Bakhtin's double-voiced producer of texts.

Lomax's approach represents one extreme of the ethnomusicological spectrum: the tendency to search for universal principles and general theories of music that can be applied cross-culturally. At the other end of the spectrum, we find ethnomusicological approaches that concentrate on specific "music cultures," and that base their analyses and descriptions on an "insider's approach" – that is, on using terms and theories developed by culturally informed practitioners of the music. This is somewhat closer to the approach based in discourse described earlier in this chapter, yet the particular complexities of the popular music context render a straightforward "insider's" approach problematic: in highly heterogeneous societies, meaning is more like to result from a song's similarity to and difference from other songs within the total musical field, from the codes it activates and from the subject positions and competences it makes available to listeners that permit them to identify with those codes. In this type of society, virtually anyone can be a "cultural insider" with respect to any type of music, although factors of class, ethnicity, and gender make some identifications more likely than others.

In a similar way to some of the aspects of ethnomusicological approaches, "subcultural" theories of the homologies between musical style and social identity assume a tight fit that tends to gloss over contradictions in musical tastes within the subculture, as well as to ignore how musical styles can become popular with groups outside the subculture under study. Moreover, the analyst begins from a set of already known social characteristics and then proceeds to find correspondences, producing the kind of circular logic that makes homologies possible.[40]

In the end, nothing guarantees a "fit" that all listeners of any given piece of popular music, or that all readers of this book, will find appropriate. Even the cases in which ethnomusicologists, sociologists, and cultural studies scholars base their findings on the theory and terminology of "insiders" do not produce a completely airtight match between discourses, practices, and observers: for example, John Blacking's study of Venda children's songs uses an approach based on Venda musical perception, but then goes on to make observations about the music that the Venda themselves would not make. In a sense, the "cultural insider" comes to stand in for the analyst, as the analyst selects statements that accord with his or her point of view.[41] Similarly, this book explores the "context" of the production and reception of a recording in order to establish the pertinence of musical codes. However, the analyses and interpretations for the most part go beyond those found within the discursive contexts. The form of the discussion, both in this case and in Blacking's, indicates the importance of the "audience," even for a scholarly book; that is, the scholar can never escape the influence of the social context that determines the way her or his book will be evaluated.

Metaphors for music: spatial and temporal

As mentioned earlier, in musicological analysis the written document representing the piece of music, the "score," tends to function as the main source for analysis. However, the songs under consideration here circulated primarily as recordings. Recordings tend to foreground the *temporality* of the musical text, as well as to emphasize one particular (and frequently, in some respects, simulated) performance rather than an idealized set of instructions for a performance. As a written document, a score is a spatialized representation of a piece, which, as already discussed, lends itself to an analysis of structure. Modern popular music, which circulates primarily in recorded form, seems unsuited to analytical methods that stress spatial metaphors rather than temporal ones, and that favor visual methods as opposed to aural ones. As discussed above, contemporary music analysis tends to rely on spatial metaphors such as "structure," on biological metaphors such as "organicism," or to conflate the metaphors in the notion of "organic structure."[42] It is important to remind ourselves of the historicity of these ideas. Indeed, parsing a piece into bits and then revealing the relationship of those bits to each other and to the "whole" permeates instruction in music theory and analysis. The idea of musical structure followed first the development of the idea of "structure" and then of "organic" structure in disciplines such as natural history and botany in the seventeenth and eighteenth centuries. In these disciplines, the concept of structure allowed visible forms to be transcribed into the "linear unwinding of language." For natural historians, this offered the promise of transforming their discipline into something approximating mathematics or natural science.[43] In the late eighteenth century, the idea of organic structure permitted scientists to relate phenomena to an invisible model, so that a representation of a visible object would no longer refer "back to itself," but rather to a "hidden architecture," or a "buried depth."[44] For any discussion of musical "structure" or "organicism" to take place, the temporal musical experience had first to be converted into a visual, spatial experience. The written document known as the "score" was more suited to this than the ephemerality of the live performance and it therefore gained priority in musical study. Once the score was accepted as the primary musical "object," the conversion of this now spatialized musical experience into the "linear unwinding of language" could begin. However, it is important to note that, even in the most "spatialized" experience, a residue of temporality remains: the reading of a score takes place in time, even if it does not follow the temporal continuity of the music as it would be presented in performance. And we should remember that, no matter how much we emphasize the "aural" aspects of music, once we begin to represent them visually – either in musical notation or prose – a "spatial" element unavoidably creeps in.

If we look beyond the rise of organic metaphors in the music criticism and theory of the second third of the nineteenth century we find an emphasis on the metaphor of music as an oration.[45] Music criticism in the latter part of the eighteenth century, and well into the nineteenth century, described music frequently in terms of an oration which used the art of rhetoric to communicate its effects to the listener. The organic metaphor tends to stress the structure of music, and hence to turn attention away from the impact of a piece of music on the listener towards the relationships which inhere in the work itself: pieces of music, now imbued with the "force of life," come to be seen as autonomous entities rather than as cultural artifacts embedded in a social network. This shift from rhetoric to structure suggests that eighteenth-century attitudes towards analysis and criticism, with their orientation towards the effect of a piece on the listener, may be more appropriate to analyze and describe modern popular forms than Romantic notions of music-as-art that emphasize the composer, expression, and spatial metaphors.[46]

The problem remains as to how to develop analytic methods based on rhetorical concepts. To some extent analysis – with its emphasis on individual works and their constituent parts – and rhetoric – which emphasizes conventions governing the relationships between pieces – are antithetical concepts. However, the metaphor of music as rhetoric still allows for the description of differences between orations, as well as an understanding of how individual orations follow generic conventions: treatises of the late eighteenth century stress the importance of the musical *surface* rather than seeking to explicate the hidden depths of structure (the idea of "form" as an abstract concept did not figure prominently in writings about music until the second third of the nineteenth century).[47] Typically, in these writings, the notion of a melodic line that is responsible for the musical continuity of a piece is interchangeable with the notion of form (pp. 91, 95).

The idea that the metaphor of rhetoric permits us to consider the connection between an individual piece and the conventions of genre also points out the links between eighteenth-century approaches to criticism and contemporary notions of the musical code and musical competence. If pieces are "understood" by their references to genre, then this occurs through activating codes in certain ways. And, of course, recognition of these conventions relies on different types of listener competence, a connection made by eighteenth-century theorists as well, with their discussion of the appropriateness of certain kinds of music for amateurs and connoisseurs (p. 129). "Conventions" can alert us to the levels and types of codes that signify in a given piece – in other words, to what is pertinent.

The musical analyses that follow take up the idea of musical rhetoric in a variety of ways. Throughout the book, the emphasis in the musical description tends to fall on melodic features. I chose songs with prominent vocal parts that are primarily responsible for conveying melodic interest. Another important component of some of the analyses is the emphasis on *paradigmatic* analysis.[48] This permits the comparison of small units which may repeat with slight variation. Paradigmatic analysis tends to be useful in situations in which some musical features remain invariant, because it brings into relief the elements which are varied. It may also be useful when comparing two recordings of the same song as a way of highlighting differences in the musical surface. Thus, chapter two compares two recordings of "I'll Be Seeing You," one by Bing Crosby and one by Billie Holiday, to each other and to the printed sheet music. In addition to comparing their recordings to one another, paradigmatic analysis is used to compare their approaches to variation within their respective recordings. The musical surface of the recordings of "I'll Be Seeing You" is also explored through a description and analysis of vocal tone color. Hank Williams' vocal performance in his recording of "Hey Good Lookin'" is examined through a discussion of the melodic and rhythmic inflection of his vocal line and of the variations in tone color. Of all the chapters, paradigmatic analysis features most prominently in the discussion of James Brown's "Superbad," due to the importance of repetition in that song. This analysis reveals how rhetorical and paradigmatic approaches may be compatible: in this song, rhetorical emphasis results from the discrete variation of numerous brief melodic ideas; paradigmatic analysis facilitates comparisons of the minute variations between different statements of these ideas. The analysis of Elvis Costello's "Pills and Soap" takes a "phenomenological" approach, describing the impact of the song as it passes, phrase by phrase and gesture by gesture. Although this approach does focus attention on the surface, this analysis contains more references to "structure" than the others because, as I argue in that chapter, the song's "individuality" derives at least partially from its assimilation of an aesthetic based on the Romantic notions of music-as-art.

To see or not to see: the question of transcription

This discussion of which musical metaphors are more appropriate for the analysis of popular music still leaves us with the question of how best to represent musical details. If representing an auditory artifact such as a recording by using written notation inevitably results in an emphasis on spatial metaphors, then won't any analysis that relies on music notation end up reifying the fluid, temporal process of the music being discussed? The answer is probably "yes." Yet it is difficult to move beyond vague notions of style, or to discuss musical details, without some kind of visual representation. While it is, of course, impossible to present a completely "accurate" transcription, the transcription may present observable "traces" of the musical details of the recording to the reader.[49] The approach taken here has been to transcribe the most prominent aspects of the musical surface and to comment on the melodic process, rather than to search for hidden relationships between different components of the musical texture. In addition to Western staff notation, at certain points I used an automatic transcription device, the spectrum analyzer, to "freeze" other aspects of the musical surface in order to discuss them. As all notation systems enable the representation of some features more easily than others, one always runs the risk of producing a kind of distortion when "transcribing" – that is, when using one culturally-based notation system to represent musical sounds for which the notation system was not originally intended. However, we must also note the impossibility of an unmediated, direct, and therefore non-distorted means of representing a musical performance.

Charles Seeger's distinction between "prescriptive" and "descriptive" notation remains a useful starting-point for a discussion of the pros and cons of transcription.[50] In his view, Western notation is primarily prescriptive: it consists of directions for a performance. Attempts to make Western notation describe an actual performance (or a recording of a simulated performance) involve a kind of "translation" process. When using Western notation to "describe" music for which it was not intended, we are first forced to look for elements in the music that best fit the priorities of the notation (pitch and metered rhythm), priorities that may have little to do with the aesthetic values of the music in question. Secondly, as Seeger rightly pointed out, no one can *interpret* any notation without some sort of oral (or aural) tradition; therefore, in reading a transcription of an unfamiliar form of music, the reader has no way of reconstructing it (p. 170). Western notation conveys precise information about only pitch, and, even then, only within the boundaries of the twelve-note, equal-tempered system. Duration and amplitude are displayed in relative terms and timbre, phrasing, and a whole host of minute inflections – that is, the way that music *sounds*, what Seeger called "the knowledge of 'what happens between the notes'" (p. 170) – are conveyed even less accurately by Western notation.

As discussed earlier, the "notational centricity" of Western musicology has contributed to the neglect of much of the world's music outside of a narrow canon of works. If music notation conveys information about certain elements more than others, and musicological study is based on the "score," then it follows that the music most studied is notated music in which complexity of pitch relations and form figure most prominently. This has had the effect of marginalizing not only popular and non-Western music, but musical styles in the "classical music tradition" itself that "don't look like much on the page," such as Spanish guitar music, or seventeenth-century Baroque dance music, to name a few.[51]

Ethnomusicologists have struggled with the issue of transcription; indeed, the ability to transcribe has been considered a kind of rite of passage: accusing an ethnomusicologist of making an inaccurate transcription would be tantamount to branding her or him incompetent.[52] The trouble with "accurate" transcriptions that attempt to account for all the specific details of a performance – for the way in which this music *does not* sound like Western art music – is that what they do most convincingly is show how the "notation does not look like the musical sounds it is meant to represent."[53] The transcriber outfits the transcription with an increasing density of detail in order to show how the temporal process of the piece in question contradicts the impression of stasis in the notated representation, that is, to convey all the elements either underrepresented or misrepresented by Western staff notation.

Yet the plight of the transcriber is not quite the hopeless situation that it might seem. Readers of a transcription may have access to or familiarity with the sounds of the music being transcribed and hence have acquired some of the requisite "oral tradition" to enable them to interpret the written notation. This is the assumption behind the transcriptions in this book. The occasional density of detail is meant to convey the sense that these transcriptions are in some ways fitting round pegs into square holes. They represent recorded sounds, not directions for performers to produce those sounds. Chapter two, in fact, demonstrates how recordings of a "standard" deviate from the printed sheet music.

As mentioned earlier, the analyses also employ a kind of automatic transcription, the spectrum photo. Although at one time championed as a kind of musicological cure-all, automatic transcriptions have their shortcomings as well.[54] First of all, the automatic transcription gives an impression of "scientificity"; yet, curiously, science tells us that the psychophysics of the ear creates sounds, such as combination tones and difference tones (frequencies created in the inner ear as the result of two or more pitches), that are not physically "present" outside of our heads. Thus the automatic transcription does not reflect what any human actually hears. Secondly, until sophisticated computer software became available recently, it was impossible to "check" the automatic transcription, to check the correspondence between its representations and the sounds heard in the recording. Thirdly, and most importantly, the human mind has the ability to adapt to new sounds, tuning systems, strange timbres, etc., and to make the unfamiliar familiar, to soften loud sounds, to amplify quiet sounds, to tune out "interference." Thus the "objective" measurements of the automatic transcription "give no real indication of what one experiences in any specific context."[55] Even in using the automatic transcription, the analyst must choose the examples and interpret the information. The primary advantage of the automatic transcription is that it allows us to observe musical elements that *we do not hear*, sounds that we change or distort in the act of hearing. Spectrum photos do represent timbral differences that may have cultural significance when contextualized. The danger exists in assuming that features which are observable in the photo are significant simply because they can be observed; this risks falling back on a theory of musical immanence. From the standpoint of its importance to the listener, the temptation might be to posit some sort of cross-cultural linguistic "competence," which is revealed by the presence of features in an automatic transcription.

Song analysis

Many contrasting views within the field of musicology exist on the best way to interpret the combination of words and music known as "song," almost all of these created in response to the analytical challenge of art song. One difficulty in transferring these approaches to the analysis of popular song is that they tend to rely on a strict dichotomy between the "poet" and the "composer." Thus we learn that the composer's "voice" manifests itself most directly in the accompaniment; or that a poem "retain[s] its own life . . . within the body of the music" – ideas that cannot apply in a context in which the music may well have preceded the text or have come into existence at roughly the same time.[56] Kofi Agawu has recently proposed working from "a music-to-text rather than the more familiar text-to-music approach." This approach transfers more fruitfully than previous approaches to a study of popular song; by not privileging words, it emphasizes aspects of the music/text relationship that obtain in all song. Anybody listening to song perceives music and text simultaneously; therefore Agawu's warning to "avoid a taxonomy of inputs" may be equally useful for studying either popular songs or art songs.[57] It is not as if we first hear the words, then the music, and then put the whole thing together.

Furthermore, these musical processes are communicated in a specific recording, thus eroding the sense of the "song" as an entity that can exist outside of that recording. When we analyze "I'll Be Seeing You," we are analyzing *Billie Holiday's* or *Bing Crosby's* recording of "I'll Be Seeing You," not a template of pitches and rhythms that exists uninflected by a performance.

As already intimated in the discussion of musical coding and competence, the connotations of song lyrics are affected by conventions and the genres and styles to which these conventions refer.[58] Denotation is therefore always modified by "musical processes." Middleton presents a three-pole model of different words/music relationships as found in popular music. He describes these three poles as:

(1) "affect": words as expression – tend to merge with melody; voice tends towards "song" (i.e. intoned feeling);

(2) "story": words as narrative – tend to govern rhythmic/harmonic flow; voice tends towards speech; and

(3) "gesture": words as sound – tend to be absorbed into music; voice tends towards becoming an instrument.

As discussed earlier, the context created by a wide variety of discourses as well as the relative autonomy of musical practices is crucial in establishing the conventions, style, and genres that obtain in any given popular music text. This is how we can understand the relationship between words and music heard in the recordings of "I'll Be Seeing You" as falling primarily under the category of "affect," "Superbad" as primarily "gesture," and "Hey Good Lookin'" and "Pills and Soap" as combining aspects of "story" and "affect."

IV

Postlude

The chapters that follow all take up the issues of authorship, the relationship of text to context, musical codes, and audiences. One of the arguments throughout is that there is not necessarily one way of interpreting popular music, but that different types of popular music use different types of rhetoric, call for different sorts of interpretation, refer to different arguments about words and voices, about musical complexity and familiarity, and draw upon different senses of history and tradition. However, each of the case studies approaches these issues in a slightly different fashion. Chapter two builds up its context primarily through examining music industry publications, secondarily through biographical literature. The idea of the musical code is invoked explicitly, and connotations are extrapolated from the discourses surrounding Crosby and Holiday. Chapter three explores how the idea of "country music" emerged through a confluence of forces. Hank Williams' "Hey Good Lookin'" is interpreted in light of certain "metanarratives" that have been tightly linked with country music since its emergence. Chapter four examines "African-American" music as a historical discourse based on anecdotal accounts and surviving musical practices, which are seen as implying a layer of transhistorical musical features. This provides the context for an analysis of James Brown's "Superbad." Chapter five looks at Elvis Costello's "Pills and Soap" through contemporary critical discourses about his music, his own statements about his music, discourses on modernism and postmodernism, on the aesthetics of those with "legitimate" and "popular" taste, and the conflict between sixties "countercultural" and seventies "punk" aesthetics.

In his essay, "History: Science and Fiction," Michel de Certeau writes, "While place is dogmatic, the coming back of time restores an ethics."[59] De Certeau is referring to the shift in historical writing during the seventeenth and eighteenth centuries from a period when it was affiliated with literature and the art of rhetoric to a period when it became affiliated with science. In this shift, an emphasis on the temporality of events in historical writing was replaced by a "taxonomic ordering of things," and conjunctive narratives came to compensate for social disjunction, hiding the socioeconomic conditions which enabled the production of modern historical texts. According to de Certeau, the modern historians who claim to be representing the "real" produce this effect by denouncing the false and by citing statistics produced by mechanical means such as the computer. De Certeau understands the writing of history as a conflict of authority between ethics and dogmatism. Where the former articulates an operation involving "what is and what ought to be," the latter "is authorized by a reality that it claims to represent and in the name of this reality, it imposes laws" (p. 199).

De Certeau is not trying specifically to undermine the claims of understanding made by quasi-scientific history. Instead he wants to suggest that the elements of language, rhetoric, and representation are inextricable from what he calls "the fiction of science": "Historiographical discourse is, in itself, the struggle of reason with time, but of reason which does not renounce what it is as yet incapable of comprehending, a reason which is in its fundamental workings, *ethical*" (p. 220). So, in a sense, when he writes about the "restoration of ethics," he is writing about an anticipated change in *emphasis* in historical writing; for the ethical, temporal dimension can never be fully eliminated and has never been fully absent. This emphasis can be effected by "restoring the ambiguity that characterizes relationships between object and subject or past and present," and by referring to the conditions that make a discourse possible (p. 217).

What de Certeau describes as the shift in the writing of history during the seventeenth and eighteenth centuries returns us to earlier discussions about the emergence of musicology as a discipline and about the shift in metaphors used to describe music (which, in a curious parallel to historical writing, involved de-emphasizing the importance of rhetoric). As mentioned earlier, historical musicology arose in a spirit of positivistic inquiry in the mid nineteenth century, a spirit that was renewed fervently in the decades following World War II. The historians have effaced errors from the "fables of the past," and the analysts have explicated the formal workings of individual works (although, to reiterate points made earlier, that is not *all* that they have done); neither has admitted frequently to practicing the arts of rhetoric, nor have they referred frequently to the socioeconomic conditions that have enabled them to produce their work. A canon of great works and a cadre of analytical procedures (Schenkerian theory, set theory) contribute to the impression that musicological work emanates from a fixed place rather than from a place articulated by an ever-shifting combination of personal histories, budgetary pressures, and institutional affiliations.

It is common in the debates between musicologists and sociologists involved with popular music studies for sociologists to question what musicology can contribute to our understanding of popular music. It may be fruitful to turn this question around, to ask what our understanding of popular music can contribute to musicology. And it may be, in its relentless foregrounding of its temporality, of its ephemerality, of its sociality, and of the contingency of any given song's importance (all of which undermine the emphasis on structure, on autonomy, on transcendence, on the fixity of *place*), that the study of popular music may accelerate the process, already under way, of bringing "time" back to musicology, thereby encouraging the restoration of an ethical dimension.

CHAPTER TWO

Family values in music? Billie Holiday's and Bing Crosby's "I'll Be Seeing You"

In 1944, Bing Crosby rested securely atop the entertainment industry. Multiple tie-ins with the movie studios, movie theaters, recording studios, and radio stations saturated the United States and much of the Western world with his image and voice. His activities as entertainer in the armed forces, his pleasant roles in movies, and his affable presence as radio host all made him welcome in the homes of middle America as well as in the columns of critics, who referred to him with the collegial monikers of "Der Bingle" and "The Groaner." At this time, Billie Holiday also possessed a strong and recognizable, if not as well-known, image and sound. Known as "Lady Day" or "La Holiday" to jazz connoisseurs, her voice generated a radically different response from listeners; and her image presented a contrast to Crosby's All-American "Everyman."

Both of these singers recorded renditions of the song "I'll Be Seeing You" in 1944. The public and the music industry treated these performers and their recordings very differently: in the quantity of copies bought; in the amount of radio play received; and in the degree and kind of press coverage allotted. In terms of their recorded performances, it is doubtful that any listener, then or now, would have mistaken one of these recordings for the other.

This chapter will focus on the reception and interpretation of these two recordings; this focus also raises several issues that impinge on the act of interpretation. Firstly, the conjunction of these recordings permits us to explore the impact of institutional factors on the reception of a musician's work, as well as the impact of these factors on the critical status and "popularity" of a performer. Secondly, the juxtaposition of these two very different performers provides another opportunity to explore the idea of voice: as we listen to a recording, respond to it, and interpret it, do we necessarily connect the sounds we hear to what we know of the historical personage singing them? If we do, how does this connection work, and what aspects of the biological author influence interpretation? The last section will consider the connection between the musical sounds of these recordings of "I'll Be Seeing You," the idea of the musical code, and the types and kinds of interpretations accorded Billie Holiday and Bing Crosby.

I

A tale of two (or three) recordings

"I'll Be Seeing You" was written in 1938 by Sammy Fain and Irving Kahal as part of the show *Right This Way*, and a version of it was recorded in the late thirties by the "popular chanteuse" Hildegarde. Following the re-release of Hildegarde's recording late in 1943, many versions were subsequently recorded and/or released in 1944. Bing Crosby recorded his version on February 17 with the John Scott Trotter Orchestra. He had begun featuring it on January 13, 1944 in his hour-long NBC radio variety show *Kraft Music Hall*, a show that "gave him continual exposure in millions of homes"; and he continued to include it on broadcasts until July 27, 1944.[1] This recording first appeared on the best-selling retail record charts on April 22, 1944 and ascended to the number one position on July 1, 1944, where it remained for four weeks. Bing Crosby's recording remained a total of twenty-four weeks on the best-seller charts.

Billie Holiday recorded her version on April 1, 1944, about six weeks after Crosby recorded his. It did not appear on the pop charts although her producer, Milt Gabler, described the song as a "a pretty big hit."[2] Several other recordings of the song appeared that year, including a performance sung by Frank Sinatra in his last record released with the Tommy Dorsey Orchestra (they had recorded the song in 1940). While it did not reach number one, the Sinatra/Dorsey version first appeared on the charts on May 20, 1944, rose as high as number four, and remained on the charts for a total of seventeen weeks. This information is summarized in table 2.1.

The positive public reception of Crosby's version of "I'll Be Seeing You" was not an anomaly: during the thirties and forties Crosby placed more records on the pop charts and had more number one hits than any other popular singer. Joel Whitburn (author of many books that compile *Billboard*'s popularity charts) rates him as the most popular recording artist during the period 1890–1954 on the basis of his chart success.[3] In 1944 alone, Crosby placed fourteen songs on *Billboard*'s best-selling

Table 2.1: *"I'll Be Seeing You" in 1944*

Hildegarde	Bing Crosby	Billie Holiday	Tommy Dorsey/ Frank Sinatra
Dec. 1943 – re-released			
	1/13 – *Kraft Music Hall* broadcast		
	2/17 – recorded		
		4/1 – recorded	
	4/22 – enters retail record chart		
			5/20 – enters retail record chart
	7/1 – number one on retail record chart		
			7/29 – number four on retail record chart

record charts and had six number one records; in addition to this, he produced three huge hits in collaboration with the Andrews Sisters. By comparison, Frank Sinatra, widely considered at the time to be Crosby's biggest rival as a solo singer, placed eight songs on the charts, with the highest of them ranking number four.

Although Holiday had some success on the pop charts in the late thirties, she didn't record at all for two years between June 1942 and March 1944, owing both to the strike by the American Federation of Musicians (AF of M) and to a transitional period between record companies for her. She does show up in Whitburn's list of the top one hundred artists of 1890–1954, ranked number eighty-three.

For several paragraphs now I have been invoking *Billboard*'s popularity charts, as I did at the beginning of the first chapter; this activity demands qualification, for the mere citation of these charts suggests a kind of taken-for-granted authority often wielded by putatively objective representations of reality which employ statistics. In a similar way to public opinion polls, popularity charts use statistical data to tell the public what they supposedly already think; public opinion surveys as well as popularity charts allow citizens to assume that others believe what they cannot believe themselves, thus resulting in the "continual voyeurism of the group in relation to itself."[4] By representing the popularity of music in hierarchies, categories, and divisions of style and taste, and by shrouding in mystery the factors that determine their rankings, the charts reveal themselves as profoundly ideological; in other words, musical "popularity" is as much an effect of the technocratic mechanisms of the recording industry/mass media structure as it is a barometer of a preexistent mass popularity.[5] Further compromising their claims to neutrality, the charts and articles contained in a publication such as *Billboard* also function as "free" advertising directed towards the readership of the magazine, which consists largely of record shop retailers, radio personnel, jukebox operators, and others who are trying to maximize their profits in dealing with recorded products in one form or another.[6]

The numeracy of the charts creates additional illusions of equivalence, found most prominently in the taxonomies of Joel Whitburn; in Whitburn's books we find direct comparisons of songs and musicians based on their representation in the charts even though the songs are widely separated in time, context, and sound. Even if we admit its radical contingency, employing a concept of "popularity" derived in this manner does have its uses: regardless of whether it constructs or reflects reality, "popularity" participates in the larger discursive formation of the entertainment industry at any given moment. That is, the idea of a song's "popularity" circulates among consumers and producers, thereby affecting its reception. This is borne out by comparing the reception of Crosby and Holiday, two singers with very different statuses as popular icons.

In addition to the way in which the discourse of the entertainment industry constructed a sense of their popularity, other factors contributed to Holiday's and Crosby's images in the mass media. Besides his weekly radio show and his voluminous recordings, Crosby's contract with Paramount Pictures in the 1930s guaranteed that he would make three motion pictures a year, thereby contributing to the aforementioned "saturation" of the radio and film audience. By 1944, he was as familiar to audiences as a film star as he was as a recording artist. In contrast to this, Billie Holiday made one motion picture in her career (in 1947), a film titled *New Orleans*, in which she portrays a singing maid in a supporting role alongside the supporting role of Louis Armstrong's singing, trumpet-playing butler.[7]

II

Critical discourse

From the information presented here, we might assume that Bing Crosby received greater attention of every kind than Billie Holiday in the 1940s; yet this was not the case. Since the 1940s writers have discussed the "artistic" qualities of Billie Holiday more than they have discussed the artistry of Bing Crosby and it is now much easier to find both her recordings and material written about her than it is to find either Crosby's recordings or material written about him.[8] Compared to Crosby, more of Holiday's records are reissued, more biographies are written, and few histories of jazz appear without considerable mention of her. Crosby rarely appears as more than a footnote in any jazz history; and although he is invariably mentioned in histories of pop music, references are usually to his commercial success, rarely to his artistry.

Current critical (and biographical) writing regarding Crosby and Holiday summarizes the information presented here in the terms of two sets of oppositions common to writing about popular music: the oppositions of artistry vs. commercialism, of authenticity vs. accessibility. Billie Holiday's lack of success is explained by her commitment to emotional truth, her refusal to compromise, and – by virtue of her skin color – her lack of access to the power networks that would have provided her with the same kind of distribution and exposure accorded Bing Crosby. These critical terms appeared in various guises during the 1940s: in 1943, she won *Esquire* magazine's jazz critic's poll as top vocalist; never, however, did she win the *Downbeat* readers' poll, losing to singers such as Helen O'Connell, Helen Forrest, Jo Stafford, and June Christy. Equally important, as far as public perceptions of authenticity go, are the impressions created about the artist's life in the mass media. Beginning in 1942, there were articles in the press about her personal difficulties and from 1944, articles began to appear that alluded to her drug use and increased unpredictability.[9]

This contemporaneous critical discourse merges with latter-day biographical writing. Present-day listeners may well find it difficult to separate the image of Holiday as an artist tormented by her struggles with drugs and personal relationships from the deeply felt utterances they hear in her recordings. Indeed, few references to her in even the most scholarly jazz history books are complete without reference to this aspect of her personal life.[10] What seems to be taken for granted in many discussions of Holiday's (and Crosby's and many other musicians') music is an unmediated connection between biography and musical meaning.

This demands a more detailed discussion of Holiday's and Crosby's reception in terms of both critical writing and biographical material (which to some degree overlap) in order to trace the ways in which listeners have made these connections for both singers.

Both Billie Holiday's and Bing Crosby's recordings of "I'll Be Seeing You" were reviewed in *Downbeat* magazine, a publication catering to jazz connoisseurs:

Harry [Crosby's real first name] sings these climbers ["I Love You" and "I'll Be Seeing You"], as always, with nice phrasing and perfect interpretation. John Scott, who reminds George Murphy more of the World than of Atlas and may consequently be called Globe Trotter, provides his ever satisfactory backgrounds. Both tunes, incidentally, are from the amazing *Mexican Hayride*.

(April 1, 1944, p. 8)

Billie's as fine as ever, of course, one of the few fems worth an occasional rave today. "I'll Get By" [the other side of the record] is quite similar to her rendition with Teddy Wilson years back. "Seeing You" is taken at a drag tempo, sung more effectively than I had thought possible.　　(October 15, 1944, p. 9)

Both of these reviews are quite favorable; based on references to the musical aspects of the performances alone, readers of *Downbeat* may have found it difficult to choose between them. While one has "nice phrasing" and "perfect interpretation," the other is "sung more effectively than . . . thought possible." It is the other, "non-musical" comments that reveal the different status of these singers. The review of Crosby is filled with nudges, winks, and jokes about the portliness of the bandleader and with the opinions of other members of the *Downbeat* staff, as if to draw a reassuring circle around singer, bandleader, reviewer, and reader. The use of Crosby's real name, Harry, functions as an inside joke to those "in the know." Holiday is received less congenially: she is referred to by her professional name (rather than Eleanora, her given name), and the writer of the review qualifies his praise by classifying her as "one of the few fems worth an occasional rave today." We have the impression that her artistic stature is high, but modified by and contingent upon her gender; at any rate, she certainly doesn't belong to the in-crowd which includes Crosby and the reviewer (and, by inference, the readers of *Downbeat*).

Other reviews in *Downbeat* of Crosby's recordings surrounding the release of "I'll Be Seeing You" reiterate the superlatives:

Nobody's going to top the groaner's rendition of "Poinciana," ever! This is strictly beautiful. No matter whether you like the tune or not, no matter whether you like Crosby or not, you will never hear anything of its kind done much better.　　(March 1, 1944, p. 8) (from a review of "Going My Way" and "Swinging on a Star") Bing . . . is the most consistent hit-maker of them all. Whatever he touches turns to gold, except long-legged quadrupeds! He can sing anything and make it sound good. That's just what happens here, with these two forthcoming hits from "Going My Way."   (April 15, 1944, p. 9)[11]

The reviewers seem to feel that critical commentary on the recordings themselves is superfluous: they are, after all, reviewing the "Everyman" of American popular song. Instead of criticism, the reviews function to demonstrate the easy familiarity of the reviewer with Crosby and his records, as well as to reinforce that sense of comfort between audience, singer, and writer.[12] *Downbeat's* interest in these recordings also indicates that Crosby was still considered a "jazz singer" of sorts: the same publication lists his recording of Louis Jordan's "Is You Is, or Is You Ain't" as one of the top jazz vocal recordings of the year; and he recorded with jazz- or R&B-associated recording artists such as Jordan and Louis Armstrong in 1944 as well.

No other records of Holiday's were reviewed in *Downbeat* or *Billboard* in 1944; and although a brief reference to a concert performance mentions how she "spellbinds all with her beautifully contrived singing,"[13] other references focus on her appearance. In one case, *Downbeat* published a picture of her performing; the caption below describes her as "the new, stream-lined Billie Holiday."[14] In another case, an article reflects on her possibilities for a film career:

Billie Holiday, one of the few sepia beauties to be overlooked by the film industry so far, has finally been discovered by Warner Brothers and will head for the coast in late summer to make a picture . . . Successful cinema efforts of Lena Horne and Hazel Scott probably helped WB in making up their minds about Lady Day.   ("Studios 'Find' Billie Holiday," *Downbeat*, July 1, 1944, p. 2)

In the first of these three cases, her singing is "beautiful," but "contrived." In the latter two, the focus is exclusively on her appearance: whether she is a "new, stream-lined" model (terminology more often used for automobiles than singers) or "one of the few sepia beauties," the brief articles produce her as an object to be viewed, categorized, and evaluated. Unlike those of Crosby, none of her recordings were listed among the *Downbeat* critic's top jazz vocal records of the year. In the *Downbeat* readers' poll at the end of 1944, Crosby was voted top male vocalist, while Holiday was voted fourth in the female vocalist category behind Dinah Shore, Helen Forrest, and Jo Stafford. However – and again demonstrating the aforementioned split between critical approval and public success – the following review of a Jo Stafford recording indicates the kind of respect the *Downbeat* writers felt for Holiday: "Jo has come a long way since she first hit bigtime with the Pied Pipers, but she has a long way to go before she can compare with Billie or Mildred [Bailey]" (February 1, 1944, p. 9).

Let it be said that the kind of racial and sexual objectification noted above does not stand out as particularly remarkable within the context of *Downbeat* and other entertainment magazines of that era. Their pages are filled with a kind of casual racism and sexism that appear anything but casual with the passage of fifty or so years. Illustrating this, racialist commentaries could be found sprinkled liberally throughout the pages of *Downbeat*: other prominent articles from 1944 include a front page *Downbeat* story (August 1, 1944) announcing "Racial Hatred Rears Ugly Mug in Music." Yet the "race riot" described in the article involved a conflict between African-American gangs whose only connection to music was their proximity to a nearby concert. Another lengthy article, "Jungle Music Found Near at Hand: Music As Primitive as Any African Rhythm Is That of Chiapas Indians" (January 15, 1944, p. 17), provides a transcription of a Chiapas song, titled (presumably by the magazine) "A Jungle Melody."

The representation of gender in music papers of the time differed from the representation of race only in its emphasis on the visual: *Downbeat* averaged one "cheesecake" photo of a female singer (referred to as "chirps," "thrushes," "warblers," "chicks," and "canaries") for every two pages of text. A typical caption reads: "This very attractive young lass has talents, we hear, to match her obvious charms." In another case, a photo essay from 1943 bore the headline, "Howsabout a Day in the Sun with an Enticing Band Chick?" (*Downbeat*, July 1, 1943, p. 2). An important point about these soft-core photographs of female singers is that they are all white. While African-American women could be objectified, and their appearance even mentioned with approval, it was clearly taboo to present them as desirable sex objects, a "privilege" still reserved for white women at this time. Billie Holiday, for her part, recognized that, as a female performer, she was the focus of the gaze of the male audience: "I'm supposed to go out there and look pretty and sing good and smile."[15] The contradictions between her role as a "glamorous" female singer and her status as an African-American generated enormous tension; this tension erupted in many violent incidents which were started by whites who disapproved of her fraternizing with white (especially male) patrons.[16]

A further point about the role of women in popular music during the thirties and forties is that female singers in bands were viewed as a necessary evil, an accouterment necessary for the visual pleasure of the males in the audience, but not necessarily for the aural pleasure of either audience or bands. Writers denigrated the female singers' musical abilities as routinely as they praised their visual attributes. At the same time, writers often attributed the singers' success solely to their appearance, implying that success was achieved despite their meager talents.[17]

While Holiday's next release, "Lover Man"/"That Ole Devil Called Love," received mixed critical notices,[18] the reviews for her early 1947 recording of "Good Morning Heartache"/"No Good Man" instigated a trend that continued for the rest of her life: the comparison of her recent recordings with her recordings from the period extending from 1935 to roughly 1941. Especially canonized was her work with Teddy Wilson, with whom she made the majority of her recordings between 1935 and 1938. Her singing on her post-1944 recordings is characterized as "a shade too candy-cute," "heavy and over-gingerbreaded," "over-phrased," and "pretentious" (all from 1947 reviews of "Good Morning Heartache," "No Good Man," "Solitude," and "There Is No Greater Love"). She made no recordings between February 1947 and December 1948 owing to her imprisonment for nine months on drug charges and a recording ban by the American Federation of Musicians. The critical trend that began in 1947 only intensified during the recordings recorded and/or released in 1949. A review of "Them There Eyes" compares the 1949 recording to an earlier recording of the same tune: "You might be interested in listening to the Columbia of the same tune she made in 1939. She leaned less on the band, her phrases had more force and drive" (*Downbeat*, October 6, 1950, pp. 14-15). Here are two reviews from 1949:

[review of "Porgy" and "My Man"] "Porgy" is a lovely tune, too seldom done, from the Gershwin *Porgy and Bess* score. Billie completely misses the grace and meaning of the song in her over-exaggerated phrasing and too lush pauses (only Holiday can make a pause lush). There is a limit to the distortion to which you can subject a good song for purposes of your own interpretation and this is it. It might as well be faced: what was a great singing style has lapsed into over-ornate sloppiness.   (*Downbeat*, July 1, 1949)

[review of "Baby Get Lost" and "Ain't Nobody's Business If I Do"] "Lost" is a blues sung by Billie with a big band, both of which lack finesse. "Business" will of course be interpreted by everyone in light of recent events in Billie's private life. It is, however, bad singing for Holiday.   (*Downbeat*, October 21, 1949)

Yet another new element enters the critical arsenal at this point: the association of Holiday's private life with her musical material (in the second review) is added to the relentless comparison of her current work with her earlier work (in the first review). As mentioned earlier, in 1944 and 1945 there were already veiled references in the press to her difficulties with drugs, and these references increased with her arrest in 1947. After her release from prison in 1948, interpretations of her recordings frequently incorporate details of her biography. Holiday herself believed that she had become a kind of curiosity to the audience, telling Leonard Feather in 1954, "They're not coming to hear me, they're coming to see me fall off the damn bandstand."[19] And, in a review of Holiday's 1956 Carnegie Hall Concert, Nat Hentoff wrote, "A smile often brushed Billie's lips and eyes as if, for once, she could accept the fact that there are people who *do* dig her" (*Downbeat*, December 12, 1956, p. 10).

Criticism was not necessarily monolithic about Holiday's work after 1947: Hentoff and Miles Davis, among others, were vociferous in their advocacy of her later work. Even a positive review, such as the one of her first Mercury LP (released in late 1952) which claims that her voice "remains the most compellingly warm and emotional voice . . . in jazz today," refers to her "thicker, less euphonious sound," and "the slight tightening up of her range" (*Downbeat*, January 14, 1953, p. 15). And Hentoff, while admitting that he is "injudicious" when it comes to Holiday's work, feels compelled to mention the fact that others are comparing Holiday's recordings from the fifties unfavorably with her earlier work. Hentoff does not come out and say that her vocal quality has deteriorated; rather, he emphasizes the remarkable "feeling" in her performance, the transmutation of "pain" and "joy," the change in "life-perspective" (from a review of *Music for Torching*, *Downbeat*, December 14, 1955, p. 22). Along with Hentoff, critics in the fifties increasingly employed the *topos* of "feeling" and the reflection of her life experiences in her music as a means for explaining the changes they noticed in her singing: the voice itself is "thin, cracking," it "has deepened and hardened," it has lost its "power and vitality," it "is sometimes raspy and uncontrolled," and it "quivers" in "semi-recitative style" (the idea that she is "reciting" rather than "singing" recurs regularly). This voice "reflects the effects of unhappiness," it "seem[s] sapped by too much life and too much sorrow," it "bears poignant witness to her steady deterioration" but even though the "pitch may falter," still "the vital luster in her art remained undimmed: the intense feeling, or rather range of feelings, she always communicated."[20] This debate over the merits of her later work (including not only the recordings of the fifties, but at times everything recorded after 1939) has continued in the biographical and critical writing of the last twenty years, as we shall soon see.

The critical reception accorded Bing Crosby also shifted, but in a different fashion from the shift in the reception of Holiday's work. In 1944, Crosby was widely considered a jazz singer of sorts, perhaps due to his early jazz-oriented recordings. As the forties wore on, "jazz" became less and less synonymous with "popular" music; consequently, a magazine such as *Downbeat*, which considered its primary readership to consist of jazz aficionados, paid less attention to Crosby's recordings until they instituted separate review sections for "jazz" and "pop" in 1952.[21] Even with the increased attention paid to Crosby's recordings after the establishment of these categories, the very fact that they were now classified as "pop" signalled an important change. The excitement and superlatives departed, replaced with calm appraisals of his record's marketability. Records of his released in the late forties and early fifties earned praise as "the best in some time" rather than the unrestrained effusions that greeted his recordings during the 1944-1945 period. The reaction to the reissue of "Poinciana," the earlier release of which was described in a rave review above, is indicative: "Bing, as usual, should attract his share [of attention]; he was in good crooning voice on both of these sides" (August 27, 1952, p. 10). In a review of "Nobody" (May 1955, p. 10), the writer compares Crosby's version unfavorably with Perry Como's and describes other aspects of this recording as tepid: "but though it achieves a spontaneity from its being taken from a Crosby radio show, it never quite gets off the ground." In the mind of the "jazz buff," Bing was now heard and seen more as a slickly professional, all-around entertainer. However, this was not due to an increase in his popularity: his last number one song in *Billboard* was "Now is the Hour" in 1948, his last number two "Play a Simple Melody" in 1950 (in which Crosby duetted with his son, Gary). In contrast to the fourteen songs in the charts in 1944, he placed only six in 1954 (and one of those was a reissue of "White Christmas"), none of them ranking higher than number thirteen or remaining in the charts for more than three weeks. According to these measures of popularity, his last peak years were 1944 and 1945.

III

Biographical discourse

The biographical subject as delinquent

As implied earlier, many of the topics found in the critical discourse about Holiday and Crosby occur in the biographical literature as well, although the biographical format tends to allow and encourage a greater exploration of certain issues. Billie Holiday's "autobiography" *Lady Sings the Blues* was published in 1956. It is possible to read *Lady Sings the Blues* as a long description of how the modern "justice system" creates "delinquents." "Delinquency" refers here to a special form of illegality which is "an effect of penality (and of the penality of detention)," rather than a condition that antedates the penalization of it. Understanding delinquency in this way permits us to see how this "effect" makes it possible "to differentiate, accommodate, and supervise illegalities," in Billie Holiday's life.[22]

Billie Holiday is first detained at an institution organized around normalizing techniques at the age of ten, when she is "sentenced" first briefly to a prison, then to a "Catholic institution" (an orphanage) for defending herself from rape by a "Mr. Dick."[23] The subsequent events of her life – prostitution and incarceration – prepare her to participate in the illegal, "alternative" economy of delinquency, an economy originating in the early nineteenth century through the proliferation of legal prohibitions and minor offences. This alternative economy created around prostitution, drugs, gambling, and, to some extent, entertainment, then provides a means of support for Holiday, which she prefers to the primary option available to her of domestic service. *Lady Sings the Blues* chronicles how a person born into a relatively powerless position is introduced into the world of delinquency: after the rape attempt and the experience in the girls' home, she chooses a career as a prostitute to escape the routine of domestic service and is imprisoned in short order for not "servicing" a client (pp. 24–31); as a result of this, she is sentenced first to a hospital, then to jail for four months for being a "wayward woman" with "bad character" (p. 31); the arbitrariness of this process is revealed when one notes that the judge presiding over the case was subsequently thrown off the bench for being "unfit." At all of these institutions – the girls' home, the hospital, the prison – she feels the restrictions of surveillance: she must account for her time, her whereabouts, and her actions. She then manages to create a career as an entertainer, one of the few non-menial fields open to African-Americans at the time, and incidentally, also a field that escapes the normalizing effects of the time clock, the assembly line, and (to some extent) the observation of a supervisor. Yet eventually, with her arrest for narcotics possession in 1947, she becomes the target of increased surveillance. Drug prohibition, as with other prohibitions which create "victimless crimes," is itself an essential ingredient of delinquency, as it facilitates unlimited police involvement in the delinquent milieu. She recognizes the subterranean links between the delinquent milieu and the licit economy of the nightclub when she asserts that the police would only arrest her after she had finished an engagement: "while they were trying to get a case against me they were doing the management a favor by not busting me on the premises" (p. 125). Moreover, she is prevented from working in New York nightclubs because of her felony conviction, thereby illustrating how the prison-police system in effect "brands" a delinquent as a way of keeping delinquents enmeshed in the system. Towards the end of Holiday's story, as harassment by the police increases, she reflects at length on the helplessness of delinquents in the face of the law, which is due both to the arbitrariness with which the law is applied, and to the unlimited access of the authorities to the most private aspects of the delinquent's life (pp. 148, 161–62, 181–92).

Her final encounter with the "police-prison system" – a system in which "police surveillance provides the prison with offenders, which the prison transforms into delinquents, the targets and auxiliaries of police supervisions, which regularly send back a certain number of them to prison"[24] – occurs with her struggle against hospitalization, which she avoids despite the extreme deterioration of her health. Her resistance proves well-founded when the police "bust" her for heroin (probably "planted") on her deathbed. This police operation was even understood at the time as a "tactical maneuver to impede liberalizing New York's handling of narcotics addicts" (*Downbeat*, August 20, 1959, p. 21).

The topic of the "immoral, delinquent drug addict" pervades almost every Holiday biography with its moralizing judgment, as well as quite a lot of the "aesthetic evaluation" of her work after 1948.[25] The fact of her drug addiction is probably more widely known than the sound of her recordings. Ignoring the similarity of the drug trade to other capitalist ventures, its complicity with international politics, and the fact that illegal drugs function as the ultimate commodity – an object of pure exchange value which the "dealer" purchases solely to sell at a higher price – permits the mass media/government to maintain the issue of "drugs" as a moral one and to see drug users as "others." This obscures the links between drug consumption/addiction and sanctioned forms of addictive consumption in late capitalist society.[26] As far as Billie Holiday is concerned, this attitude towards drugs encourages us to see her as an exotic "other," a suffering, tortured figure, whose art is merely a natural reflection of her experience. The movie *Lady Sings the Blues* surely contributed to this stereotype in the act of attempting to exploit it; the movie displayed little of the sensitivity to the subject contained in the book, while the book, it must be admitted, was not averse to capitalizing on the sensationalistic aspects of the story.

Before moving on, I will discuss two other topics that recur in the biographical literature on Billie Holiday: the topic of the masochistic lover and what might be called a "meta-topic," the idea of the importance of sincerity to her as a person and performer. Both of these topics probably have their root in what at least two writers have recently described as Holiday's propensity for "self-invention."[27] Although, in retrospect, biographers have detected a "pattern" of masochistic relationships dating back to her first marriage in 1941, this topic probably emerged with an interview Holiday gave to Ralph J. Gleason in 1949. After describing earlier in the article how John Levy, her partner and manager at the time, framed her for narcotics use, beat her, and exploited her financially, the interview ends with Holiday saying, "My man makes me wait on him, not him on me. I never did anything without John telling me. That's all I know."[28] The themes of failed, even masochistic, romantic love and drug addiction seem to form the major components in the "sadness" and "hard life" which so many reviewers seemed to hear in her music.

This theme also draws on a tradition of "love and trouble" in relationships between African-American men and women. The "love and trouble" topic as it emerges in blues lyrics, and in fiction by African-American women authors, describes the way in which African-American women have transformed themselves in response to violent relationships; novels such as Zora Neale Hurston's *Their Eyes Were Watching God* and Alice Walker's *The Color Purple* present this *topos* thematically and rhetorically, that is, through language that represents the growing liberation of the book's protagonist.[29] However, the "Love and Trouble" *topos* may belong to a more general set of figures that find their earliest manifestation in African-American discourse in the slave narratives: those figures described by Houston Baker, Jr. as the "economics of slavery" and "commercial deportation." From this perspective, *Lady Sings the Blues* – with its descriptions of "disrupted familial relations," and of the maintenance of "physical and psychological integrity" in the face of relentless sexual victimization – fits firmly in the lineage constituted by Harriet Brent Jacobs' *Incidents in the Life of a Slave Girl: Harriet Brent Jacobs, Written by Herself* (1861), Hurston's *Their Eyes Were Watching God* (1937), and Toni Morrison's *Beloved* (1987).[30]

A third element in the biographical topic of the masochistic lover, and perhaps the most important, is the content of the lyrics of the songs sung by Billie Holiday. While this theme is widespread in Tin Pan Alley songs of that era, after 1939 she increasingly featured songs told from a masochistic perspective. Although some of these, it must be said, were written by men, some were either written or co-written by Holiday herself, or written specifically for her. She describes in *Lady Sings the Blues* how songs like "Don't Explain" were based on real-life incidents (pp. 104–5); and songs recorded in the mid to late forties which she featured regularly in her performances, such as "Lover Man," "Deep Song," "My Man," and "Good Morning Heartache," did little to weaken the association between Billie Holiday and sad love affairs. At times the content of the recordings and her life seem to form a tight temporal link: for example, the *Downbeat* interview mentioned previously with Ralph J. Gleason appeared on July 15, 1949; "My Man," the recording of Holiday's which appeared immediately before the interview, contains the lyrics, "He isn't true, he beats me too, what can I do?"[31] Holiday implies a strong identification with "My Man" by quoting it in the concluding sentences of *Lady Sings the Blues*: "Tired? You bet. But all that I'll soon forget with my man" (p. 192). "Tain't Nobody's Business If I Do," the recording released immediately after the interview, contains the lines

> Well, I'd rather my man would hit me
> than for him to jump up and quit me
> Tain't nobody's business if I do
>
> I swear I won't call no copper
> if I'm beat up by my papa
> Tain't nobody's business if I do

It may seem difficult to square the attitude projected in these lyrics with attempts to recover Billie Holiday's work for feminism. Yet, as Michele Wallace explains, "Billie documented for all time the experience of *loss* that is so characteristic of a black woman's life . . . some of it just seeks you out and sweeps you up, and I can't deny that as a black woman."[32]

The relationship of one's lifestyle to the proficiency of the jazz musician may be as old as the saying, "if you don't live it, it won't come out of your horn." Yet surely it could have only become important to encourage other people to think that "you were living it" within a mass-mediated context once that context had created the possibility that "authenticity" could circulate as a commodified sign. Perhaps out of necessity, Billie Holiday displayed an astuteness toward the business of self-representation from an early age. This self-inventiveness was important for an extremely important practical reason: African-American women, because of a specific articulation of class, sex, and racial oppression, have had to struggle against certain negative "controlling images," specifically those of "the Mammie, the Matriarch, and Jezebel."

The "power of self-definition" is a recurrent theme in the writing of African-American women writers and activists.[33] If Holiday asserts over and over again in *Lady Sings the Blues* that she "just had it in her" (p. 176), or if Carmen McRae can say "she [Holiday] sings the way she is,"[34] then it may be due as much to Holiday's facility for self-invention as to the way she activates musical codes that signify "sincerity." *Lady Sings the Blues* dwells on the sensational and tragic, leading many to assume that Holiday's music must therefore express *only* tragedy and sadness. The assumption of a tight correspondence between her life and her music also tends to glorify her "natural" talents at the expense of the hard work and training necessary to the skill she displayed on recordings.[35]

But this assumption of a one-to-one correspondence between life experience and musical expression forces other issues to the surface as well: firstly, if Billie Holiday were simply translating her life into musical experience, it does not necessarily follow that she opposed the idea of commercial success. Even though Holiday attributed the success of a song she did not record, such as "Doggie in the Window," solely to the efforts of promotion,[36] she did strive all her life for commercial success. Anecdotal evidence suggests that after her recording of "Strange Fruit" in 1939 – during the period in which she was featured at the Café Society, an integrated nightclub in Greenwich Village — she began to develop a more theatrical way of presenting herself onstage; her recordings from this time until the end of the forties undoubtedly enhanced the sense of the "dramatic songstress" developed in her stage act. Some of this increased sense of drama is also due to the more commercial arrangements, with their predominantly slow tempi, provided for her during her contract with Decca Records between 1944 and 1949. To put it briefly, the presentation of herself as a "dramatic songstress" functioned as a commercial device, another aspect of the self-invention she had developed as a way of escaping the "controlling images" and the limited options available to her.

This discussion of *topoi* in the biographical literature of Billie Holiday is really a way of discussing the concept of authorship in popular music. As described in the introduction, the notion of multiple authorial voices in a text suggests that her recordings may contain many "voices": happy voices, sad voices, tragic voices, mocking voices, exuberant voices, sexy voices, playful voices, etc. Because of the relatively tight linkage between *topoi* in the lyrics and musical codes, and the association of these *topoi* and codes with ideas and images "outside" the songs (interviews, biographies, etc.), the author "inside the text" may inscribe the Billie Holiday portrayed "outside the text" as one of the text's voices. This suggests how we may sense that Billie Holiday is expressing "herself" in song as *one* of the many personae she projects musically.

Interlude: I'll Be Seeing You, *the movie*

In 1944, Hollywood (M-G-M) released *I'll Be Seeing You* starring Joseph Cotten and Ginger Rogers. Their characters, Zachary Morgan (a soldier) and Mary Marshall (a traveling "saleslady"), meet on a train and get off at a small town where Mary is scheduled to visit her uncle and where Zack claims to be visiting his sister, a thinly veiled pretext for staying within dating distance of Mary. Within the film's first twelve minutes we learn that they are both afflicted. Zack's problems are internal: he is suffering from a "neuro-psychiatric" disorder brought on by his experiences in World War II, fighting the "Japs." Mary's problems are external: she is a convicted felon. Both are on furlough from institutional facilities organized around hierarchical observation, he from the mental hospital, she from prison; and both have secrets they are reluctant to tell one another. Zack confesses his secret to Mary early on, and would have gladly confessed it to the rest of her family, but she stops him. She, on the other hand, keeps her secret from Zack until near the end of the film, when it is inadvertently disclosed by Mary's precocious cousin, Barbara. Mary, we learned halfway through the film (in a confession to Barbara), has been imprisoned for six years for manslaughter: an orphan, forced at an early age into the work force, she defended herself against attempted rape by a drunk employer whom she accidentally pushed out of a window. Zack, though initially disgruntled by this information, quickly forgives her and delays his readmittance to the mental hospital to meet her as she is about to reenter the gates of the women's prison; accompanying this, the strains of the title song swell, with an angelic Hollywood choir.

The predicaments of Zachary and Mary are included in what Michel Foucault has identified as the most prominent effects of what he terms "bio-power": the production of human beings as both subjects and objects "by the increasing ordering in all realms under the guise of improving the welfare of the individual and the population."[37] Zack, as "subject," must confess the truth of his psyche. At moments in the film when he is suffering an "attack," we hear a voice-over that relays his innermost thoughts, a technique which uses a sound originating outside the diegesis of the film to assert control over a threatening loss of mastery, and one which simultaneously and paradoxically conveys a sense of psychic interiority.[38] On the other hand, Mary, as "object," feels as though she "doesn't fit in anymore," even though her aunt attempts to reassure her that she isn't "branded" like prisoners were in the days of old. She finds herself in this position due to the effect of localized power relations: because she is a single female, dependent on the whims of a male boss, she is convicted of manslaughter even though the flashback (told from her point of view) reveals that she was merely defending herself. And, although not physically branded, she bears the marks of one who has fallen to the wrong side of the law: she must work vigilantly to cover up these marks, as they are always imminently in danger of disclosure. As inmates of two different "normalizing" institutions – controlled spaces in which residents must account for their time, their movements, and in which they are perpetually under surveillance – Zack and Mary both feel as though they no longer "fit" in the outside world: Zack, the subject, is helpless in the face of the truth of his psyche, which only interpretive experts (or perhaps a loyal woman) can assist him in controlling; Mary, the object, is forever in a subordinate position in power relations, forever under the observation of those more powerful than herself.

The correspondences between Mary's predicament in *I'll Be Seeing You* and Billie Holiday's autobiographical account in *Lady Sings the Blues* need not be dwelled upon. What is striking is the way in which the *topos* of delinquency arises in so many contexts with so little analysis of its function. To the painful separations induced by the arbitrary machinations of the police-prison system, the culture industry can only offer the panacea of a movie – or a song – which holds the promise of a future rendezvous. The recordings and the movie share more than a title and a release date; they share a theme of separation of uncertain duration; and they share associations of delinquency and normality in an American society that continues to believe in magical solutions that resolve all contradictions and naturalize the effects of objectification and subjectification.

The biographical subject as both Hollywood icon and tabloid headliner

In comparison to the biographies devoted to Billie Holiday, the biographical accounts of Bing Crosby present a rather different approach. Books such as Barry Ulanov's *The Incredible Crosby*, an early (1948) biography, or Crosby's 1953 autobiography, *Call Me Lucky*, paint a picture of a heroic everyman: friendly, clumsy in a normal sort of way, humble, unpretentious, hip, relaxed, casual, generous to a fault.[39] This "everyman" possesses amazing powers: he never forgets his friends; he always knows precisely how to set people at ease; *he* is never impressed by his stature and fame, even if others inevitably are; he can quiet intemperate children; he can heal the sick; he is an unerring judge of talent; he participates in philanthropic causes; he has a great, understated sense of humor, a self-deprecating wit; he is "all things to all men" (p. 206); "he not only plays Father O'Malley in *Going My Way*, he is Father O'Malley" (p. 207); he inspired all singers who followed, entering "directly in Frank [Sinatra]'s career consciousness" (p. 223); he is single-handedly responsible for turning popular records into "small works of art" (p. 85); he tirelessly champions other singers and performers, and selflessly offers sage advice; he makes films such as *Going My Way* and *The Bells of St. Mary's* that take "a firmer grip upon the problems of the world" (p. 256); he reveals his erudition in ways that are "startling" and "unrelated to situations or people" (p. 133); he's the perfect medical patient, a hunter with "amazing stamina," who "can outwalk anybody, including the cowboys who go off with him on his game hunts" (p. 259); he's a friend to children and small animals, charming them with a tune; he pays children for the privilege of dancing with *them*; his friends are combinations of saintliness and artistic greatness; any criticisms of him result from the "the anti-Roman Catholic campaign" perpetrated by "Hollywood Communists" (p. 283); he's paunchy and he takes good care of his money; he has an "astonishing ability to remain one of the people and yet to live apart" (p. 290); he gives vast sums to charity without fanfare. In other words, he's normal in every way imaginable, except for his wealth, fame, and power. But he owes his position to one factor: Luck.

We may well ask how this image, in which appearance, dress, and taste were more important than differences in material worth, is projected. According to Ulanov, publicity plays no part in the public's perception of the Crosby persona:

He wants no part of fantastic publicity stories . . . and the men who publicize his movies and radio programs and records . . . are under strict orders not to tamper with the truth, not to exaggerate the facts about Crosby, and not, especially not, to create wild stories in the time-honored tradition of press agents.   (p. 288)

Clearly, Ulanov accepts the work of Crosby's publicity agents as identical with Crosby's lived reality; but Ulanov does not deny that Crosby received a large amount of publicity, only that "it was the most desirable kind of publicity – photographs of his ranch, his horses, his children, and a few scenes taken at broadcasts and on the movie lot. But there simply were no extracurricular romances to report, no hair raising stories of any kind" (p. 110). Yet even at the time, some columnists in Hollywood noted something unusual in the press' treatment of Crosby. As columnist Florabel Muir pointed out in a 1950 *Los Angeles Mirror* column, "there has been the strangest conspiracy among even the gossip columnists to protect Bing and Dixie [Crosby's first wife] from any unfavorable stories."[40]

Writers such as Ulanov and his contemporaries assumed total identity between the image and the historical subject, Bing Crosby. Yet this tight control, this successful projection and acceptance of a non-controversial image, paradoxically created the potential for an exposé. In 1981, four years after Crosby died, *Bing Crosby: The Hollow Man* appeared. This book attempts to refute the verities contained in books such as *The Incredible Crosby* and *Call Me Lucky*. In *The Hollow Man* we learn that Crosby was opportunistic, used people, then forgot about them after they had outlived their usefulness; that his self-centeredness and coldness extended to his family, where he neglected his (first) wife and children, preferring instead to hang out with his male cronies, play golf, gamble at the race track, or put in time at his ranch; that he was irresponsible, indolent, lazy, cunning, and cold; that he was ambitious, but lacked initiative; that he deserted his saint-like first wife as she lay dying; that his stinginess extended beyond his grave, crippling his descendants financially; and that he exploited people even when he appeared to be helping them.

Two years after *The Hollow Man*, Crosby's eldest son Gary authored an autobiography, *Going My Own Way*. Devoted largely to self-analysis, this autobiography also devotes itself to debunking the myth of "The Happy Clan Named Crosby" (the title of a chapter in *Going My Own Way*.) In addition to revealing how the Crosby family weathered their father's insults, practical jokes, and militaristically strict domestic rules, *Going My Own Way* presents striking images of a family packaged as a sign that could then be incorporated into the audio flow of a radio program: Gary Crosby relates how the Crosby family's exchanging of gifts at Christmas was captured by hidden microphones for broadcast on the *Kraft Music Hall*; and how scripts for this radio show fabricated personalities for the Crosby children and then used these "personalities" as foils for their father's jokes.[41]

The existence of these contradictory narratives suggests how Bing Crosby facilitated his construction as an object: in his position as one of the first international multimedia superstars, he received heretofore unimaginable levels of publicity that traded on his wholesome image, thereby creating an image that did not rely on notions of tortured artistry to convey a sense of truth-to-self; instead, this image labored to reassure his audience of their own normalcy. Holiday, on the other hand, struggled against her objectification by attempting to project a sincere image at odds with the production process of the culture industry, an attempt that ultimately limited the extent to which she could be promoted. She, however, incorporated this sense of struggle as part of her self-created image. Therefore, subsequent biographies had no shocking details to reveal, since she had already used the notion of demystifying herself as part of her image. Crosby's more detached, deliberately "artificial" self-construction encourages the writing of multiple biographical narratives, for the sense of a managed self-image creates the possibility of revealing the hidden truth behind the image. Crosby can therefore be either the unassuming, American everyman and the heroic overcomer of humble origins, or the hidden monster under the genteel façade.

IV

Style and history

The reader may yet wonder *why* Billie Holiday and Bing Crosby received the kind of critical attention they did, as well as why they were represented by certain types and degrees of popularity. If we attempt to answer this question by using the preceding discussion of critical discourse and biography, we may be led back to the set of stark oppositions mentioned at the outset: Bing Crosby, the white male, became supremely important through the efforts of publicity agents and his own efforts to provide the public with what they wanted – in other words, he was a commercially co-opted "sell-out." On the other hand, Billie Holiday, the African-American female, triumphed over racism and personal adversity to reach the few listeners who were prepared to receive the unvarnished presentation of her soul. Yet, as we have also learned, Holiday was more than willing to "reinvent" herself when she thought it would bring her more publicity; and an important aspect of Crosby's image was the notion that he was simply "acting naturally" and being paid for it. Beyond questions of the relationship between the images of these two performers and the notions of commerce and artistry, it is important to remember that at different times both singers were lauded for revolutionizing popular singing, for changing the role of the popular singer, and for revitalizing popular music with jazz – and hence African-American – elements. Both singers modified the horizon of what constituted acceptable popular singing; both made their mark through the presentation of new mixtures of innovation (difference) and tradition (similarity). Yet the different contexts in which their styles became known and in which they circulated crucially affected the degree and kind of impact their music could have.

It may be useful at this point to recall some aspects of the "aesthetics of reception" discussed in the first chapter. When trying to assess the impact these two singers had, we can attempt to reconstruct the "questions" to which their work posed "answers." The questions that Crosby's and Holiday's work answered changed during their careers; and their recordings of "I'll Be Seeing You" were certainly responding to different questions in 1944. Holiday's recording attempts to answer questions that appear largely "musical": how can a singer incorporate the flexible phrasing and timbral nuances of a jazz soloist and at the same time project lyrics with clarity and dramatic intensity? On a sociological level, how can an African-American woman retain her dignity and display herself as a glamorous icon to an audience, when a large percentage of that audience does not view her as fully human? On the other hand, Crosby's recording seems to respond to questions more involved with "commerce": how can a performer control his or her image and project it simultaneously through film, recording, and print media while reassuring a "mainstream" public that its myths about itself are true? On a "musical" level, his recordings form a series that attempt to answer whether a solo singer can capture the imagination of the public as forcefully as a big band; and whether a male singer can convey a sense of "casualness" through singing with a relaxed technique in a low- to middle-register baritone range.

When we examine other moments in their recording careers, we find their recordings responding to rather different sets of questions. Crosby's early recordings from the late twenties through the early thirties are now the recordings most often canonized and lauded for their innovation.[42] Critics praise these recordings of Crosby primarily for his relatively sophisticated sense of swing for a popular singer, and for his ability to combine this with a relaxed type of vocal projection which exploited improvements in microphone and recording technology. These innovative aspects appear readily in a synchronic analysis of other recordings: compared with early "crooner" types such as Gene Austin, Crosby possesses a greater dynamic range and variety of timbre; and he uses the microphone to exploit a wider range of possibilities rather than using it to emphasize only the softer end of the dynamic spectrum. Compared to others, such as Ethel Waters, Helen Morgan, Fred Astaire, and Russ Columbo, Crosby introduces a greater range of rhythmic and melodic modifications to written melodies; and through these factors, as well as his "scat singing" and ornaments, he manages to convey a greater sense of spontaneity (although Columbo, considered his closest rival in the early thirties, comes close to Crosby's style).[43] This explanation does not pretend to account fully for Crosby's popularity, for there were other singers, who were perhaps as innovative, who didn't achieve his success (and I allude to some of the other factors above).

On the other hand, a diachronic analysis reveals Crosby's continuity with previous singers: his sense of swing derives from approaches based in vaudeville and the minstrel show. Biographical evidence strongly suggests that minstrel performers such as Al Jolson and Eddie Cantor were stronger influences on the young Crosby than King Oliver or Bessie Smith, although during Crosby's tenure with Paul Whiteman he was exposed to the playing of Bix Beiderbecke and Eddie Lang. The resultant "sense of swing" therefore bears traces of emotional detachment not apparent in contemporaneous approaches of singers and instrumentalists with a different relationship to swing, such as Louis Armstrong or Jack Teagarden. To combine these observations: Crosby's "relaxation" appears related both to the exploitation of technological innovations and to a certain distance from the "hot" music of the time.

Not surprisingly, the fact that much of the "jazz" influence upon Crosby arrived via the minstrel show informs much of his work: it features prominently in his role and performance in blackface as "lazy minstrel man" Dan Emmett in the 1943 movie *Dixie*; it figures in the exchange with Johnny Mercer during "Mr. Gallagher and Mr. Sheen" (in which Crosby sings "swing is really much too ancient to condemn/in the jungles they would play, in that same abandoned way"); it surfaces in the dialect during "Ac-Cent-Tchu-Ate the Positive" (recorded in 1944); it made possible his participation in a minstrel show with Al Jolson in 1947, as well as his inclusion of the numbers "I'd Rather See A Minstrel Show," "Down in Jungle Town," and "Roll Dem Bones" during the last year of broadcasting his General Electric sponsored radio show (1954). To demonstrate that African-Americans were not the sole object of minstrelsy's stereotypes, it should be observed that Crosby broadcast a rendition of "Confucius Say" in 1940; and he recorded the neo-colonialist "South America, Take It Away" in 1946 with the Andrews Sisters, a song replete with corny Latin rhythms and sung with "Latino" accents. And let us not forget the "Road" movies with Bob Hope; Barry Ulanov relates the following anecdote:

[Songwriter Jimmy Van Heusen] sat down to read the script for *The Road to Zanzibar.* He was encouraged that the story was in the [*Road to*] *Singapore* groove, that no extensive knowledge of Zanzibar, its customs, climate, or people, was called for.[44]

Throughout the thirties and early forties, both jazz and minstrel influences lessened in Crosby's recordings, and he increasingly favored a wide variety of styles, including novelty numbers, "hillbilly" tunes, sentimental ballads, medium-fast swing, western style numbers, and proto-rhythm and blues. This eclecticism resulted, at least in part, from the influence of the owner of Decca Records, Jack Kapp, who eschewed improvisation for a relentless canvassing of mainstream taste. Kapp also concentrated the bulk of his production and promotion energies on Crosby.[45] Crosby displayed his versatility at the session at which he recorded "I'll Be Seeing You," by recording the relatively hard swinging "On the Atcheson, Topeka, and the Santa Fe" (although even his swing-based songs retain a distinct 1920s sensibility).

An examination of Holiday's early recorded work raises a rather different set of questions from those raised by her recording of "I'll Be Seeing You." As far as the white, urban, middle-class audience was concerned, her early performances undoubtedly provided answers to questions that were not yet formulated. One of the main differences between her period of greatest critical acclaim, 1935 to 1938, and a recording such as "I'll Be Seeing You" (or many of the post-1939, post-"Strange Fruit" recordings) is that the earlier recordings present the vocalist more nearly as an equal partner with the instrumentalists, and that this, combined with the variety of tempi, lessens the sense of "dramatic presentation" found in the post-"Strange Fruit" recordings. However, shortcomings of the "aesthetics of reception" are revealed if we examine the milieu in which Billie Holiday received her training as a musician as well as her initial experience as a performer: we may well find that the "questions" which her work answered had indeed already been formulated and did not seem quite so extraordinary. While the Harlem audiences for which she first performed recognized the originality of her approach, they also could recognize that aspects of her style were founded in practices that were circulating among other well-known jazz performers. These audience members were not necessarily jazz "connoisseurs" such as John Hammond, who haunted uptown night spots looking for the "latest thing," but rather "regulars" at places like Basement Brownie's, Dickie Wells' Clam House, or Pod's and Jerry's Log

Cabin, all on West 133rd Street in Harlem; these venues attracted customers who were used to appraising musician's improvisations in a variety of contexts which included well-rehearsed acts as well as jam sessions.[46]

In 1939, Holiday began performing at the Café Society, a Greenwich Village nightclub which was the first New York nightclub to admit an integrated audience. Here was an audience, largely composed of white liberals, seeking more than mere "entertainment"; and such a setting undoubtedly encouraged Holiday to record a song that she had initially rejected, "Strange Fruit." Other writers have been almost unanimous both in noting the shift in style that followed this recording and in their disparaging remarks about the changes in Holiday's style after this point, generally regarding these changes as a "corruption" of a previously pristine sensibility.[47] However, many other listeners, apparently not bothered by Holiday's fall from grace, have heard an almost unbearable pathos in this recording. When we consider the historical exigencies of the recording, it becomes difficult to regard it as some kind of "sell-out." While Holiday did initially resist recording and performing the song, she became convinced of its importance; and this coincided (and was perhaps aided) by her performing the song in a context in which the audience wanted to be moved by a song with lyrics which referred to social injustice. Holiday's response to this was to increase the emphasis in her performance on the emotional resonance of the text, an element already important in her style, but one which now assumed greater importance.

V

Performance, effect, and affect

Table 2.2 presents a chart that groups songs listed in the various popularity charts found in *Billboard* during the years 1943 and 1944 into five basic categories based on style, genre, and ensemble.[48] In this period, songs in the "vocal with orchestra" (sometimes referred to as "vocal w/accompaniment") and "band with featured singer" (sometimes known as "vocal refrain") categories are the most numerous. "Vocal with orchestra" refers to songs in which the singer is the "leader" on the date, backed by a more or less anonymous orchestra, with the recording dominated by the vocal. Approximately half of the songs surveyed in this category were slow in tempo, with minimal jazz or blues elements. The lyrics were invariably about love. On some of the medium tempo songs, the instrumentation of a big band was extracted for passages of the song.

Table 2.2 *Main categories of popular music in 1943–1944*

	vocal with orchestra	band with featured singer	band instrumental	vocal with small group	novelty
leader	vocalist	bandleader	bandleader	varies	varies
relationship between vocal and instruments	vocal dominates	band instrumentals dominate	no vocal	vocal dominates	vocal dominates
tempo	predominantly slow	varies	usually uptempo	varies	usually uptempo
presence of blues-jazz elements or other "ethnic" styles	minimal	frequent jazz elements, sense of swing	frequent jazz elements, sense of swing	strong jazz and gospel, nascent R&B elements	prominent Latin rhythms, "hillbilly" sounds, "exotica"
amount of improvisation	little	significant	significant	significant	varies
subject content of lyrics	romantic	mostly romantic	no lyrics	romantic, narrative, or humorous	nonsensical or humorous
examples	Judy Garland, "The Trolley Song"	Harry James, "I'll Get By"	Duke Ellington, "Do Nothing Till You Hear from Me"	The Mills Brothers, "You Always Hurt the One You Love"	The Merry Macs, "Mairzy Doats"
	Helen Forrest, "Time Waits for No One"	Lawrence Welk, "Don't Sweetheart Me"	Stan Kenton, "Artistry in Rhythm"	The King Cole Trio, "Straighten Up and Fly Right"	Guy Lombardo, "It's Love-Love-Love"

The songs featuring "big band" instrumentation were also the songs that conveyed the strongest sense of "swing," and were most likely to include improvisational elements and pitch/rhythmic inflection. These tunes, or sections thereof, merge with the other most common type of tune during those years, the category of the "band with featured singer." These recordings were identified by the name of the bandleader, with the names of the singers listed after that of the leader. While the majority of these tunes feature jazz elements, instrumental improvisation, and a sense of swing at a variety of tempi, some of these tunes are slow ballads, feature string sections (as in Harry James' band), or are very "square" rhythmically; in other words, except for the labeling and the relative paucity of non-jazz instruments, these songs closely approximate the approach of those in the first category.

Two categories constituting a smaller percentage of songs in the hit parade are the "novelty" tune and the "band instrumental." The first of these featured either prominent Latin rhythms, hillbilly origins, nonsense lyrics, or some combination of all three. "Novelty" functioned here as a sign of the different or the exotic. The "band instrumental" was usually an uptempo, swing-oriented number, credited to a name band (sans singer).

The remaining category, "vocal with small group," occupied an intermediate level of popularity. This category contains a subgroup, the "vocal group a capella," which was an anomaly created by the AF of M strike during 1942–1943. The strike forbade "musicians" from recording; however, singers were not considered "musicians," and therefore were exempted from the ban and hence able to record. These songs were a capella arrangements which in some cases closely simulate a band arrangement. Some of the "vocal with small group" recordings come close to the sound of the a capella recordings owing to the faintness of the instrumental backing. Songs in this category by the Ink Spots and the Mills Brothers also became popular during the ban, filling the void left by the absence of the big bands and orchestras. These small group recordings during the 1943–1944 period invariably featured black groups, with musical elements either prominently derived from gospel (as in the vocal groups mentioned above), or from jazz and incipient R&B (as in the King Cole Trio or Louis Jordan).

Bing Crosby's and Billie Holiday's recordings of "I'll Be Seeing You" represent extreme examples of style categories on opposite ends of the affective spectrum. Crosby exaggerates almost all the aspects of the "vocal with orchestra" approach noted above: the tempo is extremely slow; there is no question that this is an orchestra, not a big band; and the mix and arrangement leave no doubt that this is a singer accompanied by an orchestra, not a band which happens to feature a singer. An unusual aspect is the very prominent and almost constant use of tempo rubato (although Crosby and his arranger, John Scott Trotter, used this technique in other songs of the period, such as "Too-Ra-Loo-Ra-Loo-Ra," "Where the Blue of Night," and "The Bells of St. Mary's"): the slow ballads by other singers in the "vocal with orchestra" category always convey a strong pulse even at a slow tempo. Holiday exaggerates certain features of the "vocal with small group" compared to the other examples mentioned earlier. The tempo is extremely slow throughout; the song is a *torch* song, unlike the other medium-tempo bounce tunes of King Cole and Louis Jordan; and the vocal is clearly the center of the recording, unlike the other songs of this ilk, which feature the band, or group vocals.[49]

Performance – the recordings

In his recording of "I'll Be Seeing You," Crosby delivers the lyrics straightforwardly in his "crooning" vocal style. This delivery is meant to convey a feeling of intimacy and many listeners of the time felt that it did. Crosby believed that his popularity depended on the communication of "presence,"[50] achieved technically through the technique of close-miking. Owing at least in part to his many appearances in movies, and to the orchestral scoring – which is reminiscent of movie musical scoring – this song creates the impression of someone playing a role in a film. The diction ("mornin' sun") recalls Irish ballad singing, and this may well have reminded audiences of the role of Father O'Malley that Crosby had recently played and won an Oscar for in the 1943 movie *Going My Way* (a role he reprised in 1945 in *The Bells of St. Mary's*). The effect is as if the scene has suddenly turned serious, a situation that the audience knows is only a temporary foil for the overwhelming lightheartedness of life, which is precisely the type of context that would have surrounded a song like this in a movie such as *Going My Way*. We can imagine Bing at an "old café," at a "park across the way," in almost any small town in the United States in the early 1940s.

Even though the song was not written during the war, it belongs to a type of song about generalized loss that was common and popular during World War II. This type of song differed from earlier Tin Pan Alley songs of loss and separation, in that rejection is not the cause for the separation of the characters in the song's lyrics; this allowed listeners who were separated from their families to identify with the song's sentiments. "I'll Be Seeing You" fits comfortably into this category and, indeed, Crosby was closely associated with entertaining the troops during the war; and he included many other patriotic songs, some with overt references to the war.[51] With his well-entrenched image of the "American Everyman," we can assume that many people felt consoled by his generic rendering of a soothing, uncomplicated tale of a person stranded in a small town by a loved one.

In Billie Holiday's performance we no longer hear the qualities with which Crosby's audience identified; it does not matter any more that the

song was recorded during the war: indeed, the specific details of the song
– the "park across the way," "the children's carousel," "the chestnut tree" –
all seem somewhat ludicrous in the new context. It is difficult to
determine whether our response is based on what we know about
Holiday's life, or on a socially mediated construction of affect conveyed
by certain musical gestures – in other words, the ways in which she
activates various musical codes. Holiday's performance, in contrast to the
generic reassurance provided by Crosby, vitiates the banality of much of
the song's lyrics: the clichés "every lovely summer's day" and "every thing
that's bright and gay" are withered by the sadness of Holiday's voice: we
cannot believe that this singer will experience another "lovely summer's
day"; the vocal flip on "lovely" both accentuates that word and produces
a distancing effect by emphasizing its sonic materiality. This use of
language (and the distancing effect it conveys) has been described by
Henry Louis Gates, Jr. as part of a recurring trope in African-American
discourse, a trope which he labels "Signifyin(g)."[52] In this particular form
of Signifyin(g), a parodic effect of a "dominant discourse" is produced by
means of inflection and stress (and because this is a sung text, "inflection"
and "stress" must include tone color and aspects of musical coding).
Inflection can also result in the semantic reversal of clichés used in
"Standard English."[53] In terms of the musical code, the invocation of the
jazz milieu – with its emotive and axiological connotations of an urban
landscape and sordid, delinquent activities – contradicts the small-town
Americana of the lyrics, and the elements of "torch" singing emphasize
individual suffering. At the same time, the general sense of loss conveyed
by the lyrics is retained and even intensified by Holiday's performance,
including as it does aspects of slow jazz singing that evoke the quality of
"sincere" expressivity. The parodic aspect of her performance in this
recording exemplifies the "multi-voiced" dimension of her work
discussed earlier. We will turn now to a closer examination of the
musical aspects of both Bing Crosby's and Billie Holiday's recordings.

Example 2.1 presents transcriptions of Crosby's and Holiday's
performance of the first line of the lyrics and compares them both with
each other and with the printed sheet music version. Crosby's version
deviates from the sheet music most notably in the anticipations
(indicated with arrows) by which he avoids attacking pitches squarely on
the beat. Despite slight anticipations and elongations of certain syllables,
and the rounding off of some of the stiff dotted-quarter/eighth note
rhythms ("all the old familiar places"), the same syllables occur on the
downbeats of his performance as in the printed version of the song. The
largest modification occurs on the words "familiar places" where Crosby
inserts a low C before returning to the pitch G to begin a turn around F

Example 2.1 *"I'll Be Seeing You": three versions of the first line.*
Transcriptions by David Brackett (note: the recordings of Crosby and Holiday were transposed to E-flat to permit easier comparison).

not originally in the sheet music. One aspect of rhythmic variety in this performance not conveyed through the transcription is the almost constant fluctuation of tempo which obscures the pulse and gives the vocal line a strong rubato character.

Holiday's performance of the first line demonstrates a much greater degree of rhythmic complexity and deviation from the printed version of the song. The rhythmic contrast with Crosby's recording is further exaggerated by occurring over a strong and consistent pulse. The presence of a clear pulse expands the range of possible nuances, for Holiday has the option of emphasizing or eliding the pulse, an option which does not exist for Crosby. We can observe that until the fourth measure, Holiday delays the entry of the expected syllable, so that her version "lags" behind both the printed version and Crosby's.[54] The degree of complexity within the beats is much higher in Holiday's recording, and there are no attacks on the beat until the downbeat of the last measure. As Holiday places the pitches of "familiar places" similarly

Example 2.2: *Comparison of melodic emphasis*

to Crosby while she modifies the pitches in precisely the same way as Crosby, we cannot rule out the possibility that Holiday was exposed to Crosby's recording before she made hers (he did record his first, and he had presented it numerous times on his national radio show). This raises the possibility that Holiday's recording may be an example of *musical* "Signifyin(g)," that is, a commentary both on the printed version of the song and on Crosby's recording of it. From the perspective of the audience, it is also quite possible that the audience (those in close proximity to jukeboxes in black urban areas) most likely to hear Holiday's version in 1944 probably heard it as a commentary on Crosby's version, which, in its ubiquity, few could escape.

Another primary factor in the different affective experiences produced by Crosby's and Holiday's recordings of "I'll Be Seeing You" is the difference in their treatment of dissonance. Example 2.2 compares how Holiday and Crosby treat four phrases of "I'll Be Seeing You" with the melody as notated in the sheet music. This example displays how Holiday recomposes the melodic line to emphasize pitches that clash with the underlying harmony. Although she is famous for phrasing behind the beat, at many points in this recording she phrases a segment of the melodic line so that it anticipates the placement of that segment in the sheet music notation; this results in her accentuating pitches that are not part of the underlying harmony, or which form a sophisticated harmonic alteration with the standard harmony (typically the flat fifth, ninth, thirteenth, or sharp seventh over a minor triad). On the other hand, example 2.2 shows how Crosby tends either to leave dissonant pitches quickly, or to "drift" towards a pitch which is part of the underlying harmony. The instrumental arrangements heighten this disparity in dissonance treatment: the sustained chords of Holiday's recording produce a stable background against which we can hear pitches as agreeing or disagreeing; the amorphous, quasi-contrapuntal accompaniment of Crosby's recording, with its constant fluctuations in tempo, clouds the distinction between stable and unstable pitches. Aspects of vocal timbre and production also play an important role: Crosby's constant use of a wide vibrato obscures a sense of pitch; this vibrato tends to grow wider when he sings a pitch that clashes with the underlying harmony. Holiday varies her vibrato, at times employing a near vibrato-less tone that clarifies the perception of pitch.

The spectrum photos in examples 2.3 and 2.4 corroborate these empirical observations about timbre and vibrato. The spectrum photos record all the sounding physical vibrations present in a recording. The presence or absence of higher partials sounding simultaneously with a fundamental largely determines our perceptions of a pitch's timbre or tone color (see appendix). The spatial orientation of the spectrum photos mirrors that of our hearing: lower sounds appear lower in the picture space; higher sounds appear higher. The horizontal axis of the graph represents time from left to right. To find the vocal part in these photos, look for the most prominent series of lines moving roughly parallel to one another. The lowest of these is the fundamental of the vocal line, while the parallel lines above this are the overtones for that fundamental. Example 2.3 displays the first two phrases of Crosby's and Holiday's recording. The photo of Crosby's recording reveals a peak of activity at the beginning of each phrase (on the words "I'll" and "in") and then a quick leveling off where, for the rest of these phrases, there are

Example 2.3: *Comparison of spectrum photos of the first line of "I'll Be Seeing You"*

Bing Crosby

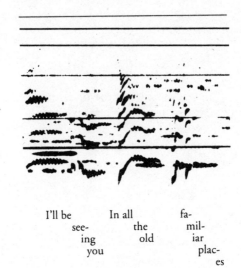

I'll be	In all	fa-
see-	the	mil-
ing	old	iar
you		plac-
		es

Brackett Figure 2.3 Top

Billie Holiday

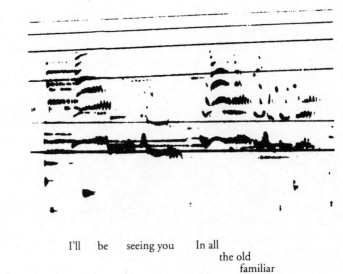

I'll   be   seeing you   In all
the old
familiar
places

Example 2.4: *Repetitions of last line of "I'll Be Seeing You"*

Bing Crosby

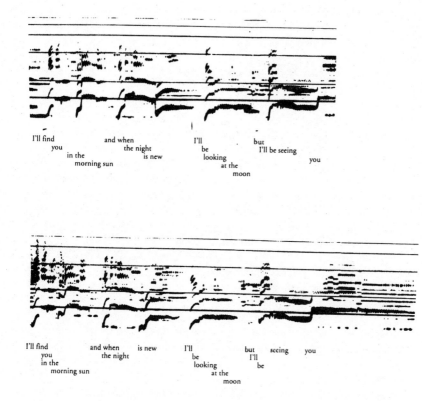

I'll find   and when   I'll   .   but
   you   the night   be   I'll be seeing
     in the   is new   looking   you
       morning sun   at the
                             moon

I'll find   and when   is new   I'll   but   seeing   you
   you   the night   be   I'll
   in the   looking   be
     morning sun   at the
                             moon

basically three harmonics present. Holiday's recording begins with a much richer overtone content on the initial word "I'll" which then drops off rapidly on "be" to one overtone. In her second phrase, the rich beginning is sustained longer than Crosby's, stretching over to the word "all," before dropping off rapidly again. The spectrum photo also reveals many differences not captured in the transcription to staff notation; this includes the great variety of vibrato and pitch-bending employed by Holiday in contrast to the almost constant wide vibrato used by Crosby. Although Crosby does occasionally "scoop" up to pitches, he usually

Example 2.4 (*cont.*)

Billie Holiday

I'll find
   you in
      the morning sun
           and when
             the night
                is new
                      I'll
                      be
                      looking
                        at the
                          moon
              but
              I'll be
                seeing you

I'll find you in
  in
    the morning sun
        and when
          the night
            is new
              I'll
              be
              looking
                at the
                moon
                    but I'll be
                          seeing you

holds the pitches after the initial attack; and he employs a far smaller number and variety of vocal inflections than Holiday.

Other passages reinforce these preliminary observations. Both Crosby and Holiday repeat the last two lines of the lyrics ("I'll find you in the morning sun; and when the night is new/I'll be looking at the moon, but I'll be seeing you"). We find much greater contrast in Holiday's repetition of these lines than in Crosby's (shown in example 2.4). The greater degree of contrast in Holiday's recording of these passages exists on many levels: the selection of pitches and durations within the phrase as a whole; as well as the number of harmonics, the various inflections of pitch (note bending, glissandi), and use of vibrato on each individual pitch.[55] The photos of these lines in Crosby's version do look different, but – except for the last pitch which is held the second time through – this is due mainly to a change in the orchestration (represented in the photo by the lines which are not moving in tandem with the

Table 2.3: *Marked levels of code.*

	Billie Holiday	Bing Crosby
sub-norms	1940s pop	1940s pop
dialects[56]	African-American	Euro-American
styles	jazz	movie-musical
genre	ballad	ballad
idiolect	knowledge of life history, image	awareness of image, life history
intentional values	tension, dissonance, spontaneous variation, lack of resolution	relaxation, resolution, planned yet casual
emotive connotations	slow jazz with sincerity, nightclub milieu, torch singing with suffering.	orchestra ballad with Hollywood, nostalgia
axiological connotations	"sordid" nightclub milieu, suffering 1940s torch singer	"wholesome" Americana of mainstream, 1940s cinema

fundamental of the vocal line). Holiday increases the overtone content during the repetition precisely at the point where she changes the melodic line to a higher register ("and when the night is new"), and at the beginning of the last line ("but I'll"), thereby creating a "richer," "warmer," "brighter" sound and heightening the sense of climax in this line.

Table 2.3 summarizes the differences discussed thus far in terms of the musical code.

What is interesting is that, even if we examine a song that both Holiday and Crosby recorded earlier in their careers, "Pennies from Heaven" (1936), we find many of the same differences observed in "I'll Be Seeing You." Again, Holiday favors a steady tempo, while Crosby chooses a rubato approach; again, Holiday takes greater liberties with the notated melody; and again, Holiday is accompanied by a small jazz group, Crosby by an orchestra (the first sixteen measures of the sheet music and of transcriptions of these two recordings are presented in example 2.5). In this recording, Crosby *does* vary the melody considerably: note his insertion of the low Ds on the words, "pennies from," his adoption of the quarter note rest in the first, third, and seventh measures, a rhythmic motive which does not arise until the ninth measure of the sheet music. Other notable aspects of this recording revealed by the transcription include the arrangement, with its perpetual use of accelerandi and ritardandi, which creates the effect of shifting meter in measures 4 and 8; the ornament (an "inverted mordent") in measure 10, and the frequent scoops up to pitches (mm. 2, 5, 11, 15, 16), both of which occur as a trademark in Crosby's work of this period. It is important to note that Crosby did not restrict his recordings to rubato ballads any more in 1936 than he did in 1944, as demonstrated by uptempo songs such as "I'm an Old Cowhand" (also from 1936).

Holiday's "Pennies from Heaven" contrasts with Crosby's (as well as her recording of "I'll Be Seeing You") in that it is performed at a medium, bouncy tempo, radiating a kind of exuberance lacking in her version of "I'll Be Seeing You" (or in other songs she recorded about the same time as "Pennies from Heaven" such as "One Never Knows Does One" – though none of her recordings from this period approach the dirge-like tempo of "I'll Be Seeing You"). On the affective level, Crosby's recording also seems "carefree" relative to his version of "I'll Be Seeing You," which is appropriate given the optimistic tone of the lyrics of "Pennies from Heaven." Holiday, as she did in "I'll Be Seeing You," exploits the presence of a clear pulse by creating a series of accents against that pulse (note again how few pitches land directly on beats), creating a sense of swing. She too includes a prominent "trill"-type ornament, featuring it more prominently in this passage than does Crosby, despite it being a trademark of his (it occurs four times in Holiday's recording, in mm. 3, 7, 10, 14; note the "rhyming" effect created by the even pairings – 3/7, 10/14 – which occur every four measures). An important difference in their use of this ornament is the placing of it in the respective recordings: Holiday's tends to occur immediately before the barline, contradicting the emphasis of the downbeat and thereby increasing the rhythmic drive and complexity. Crosby's ornament occurs here (as well as in other recordings of his) as primarily a melodic decoration and, as such, does nothing to enhance the rhythmic drive (this would be difficult to do in both of the Crosby recordings discussed here since they do not contain "rhythmic drive" in the jazz sense of the term).

Holiday in some respects modifies the melody less than Crosby: in the first line ("Ev'ry time it rains it rains/pennies from heaven") she interjects fewer new pitches into the written line. Measures 12-16 are a fine example of her propensity to *compress* a melody and, in some respects, to simplify it by reducing the number of pitches. Again, Holiday's recording emphasizes relatively dissonant pitches compared to Crosby's recording (marked by asterisks): the sharp eleventh in measures 3 and 7 ("pennies from"), the ninth in measures 13 and 14 ("Be sure that your umbrella"); many of these enhanced dissonances result from the aforementioned "compression" process.

The interpretation and analysis presented here of "I'll Be Seeing You" (and to a lesser extent "Pennies from Heaven") contains implied aesthetic values that return us to the idea of "undercoding" and "overcoding." The way in which Crosby's recording activates codes seems, at a distance of fifty years, to be relatively "overcoded": that is, aspects of this recording – the orchestral scoring, the "expressive" rubato – have turned into clichés through use in advertising and the mannerisms of countless lounge singers. This is due partly to the enormous popularity and influence of the music at the time. Paradoxically, the cultural cachet of Billie Holiday's music has risen owing to some extent to its very inaccessibility at the time of its initial dissemination, and to the way in which her style has not lent itself easily to imitation on a mass scale. Therefore, it retains those qualities of "individuality" that allow us to receive it now as "undercoded." Perhaps the absence or presence of multiple authorial voices discussed earlier also determines the perception of a recording as "under-" or "overcoded": what may have seemed clear, reassuring, and unequivocal at one time, now appears to belong *too much* to its own time, and to lack resonance in ours. And, conversely, a recording that offers competing perspectives, that may seem to mock itself, to laugh at itself, to question its own discourse, may have more to offer later generations even if it mystified the listeners of its own day. Of course, here too the idea of musical "competence" is crucial: a listener who grew up listening to Bing Crosby, and who never had much interest in jazz, Billie Holiday, or post-rock 'n' roll pop music, may revel in nostalgia upon hearing Crosby's version and feel that Holiday's version is overly mannered. A person steeped in Western art music with little enthusiasm for jazz may find the orchestral arrangement, the shifting meters, and the use of rubato in Crosby's recording intriguing, while judging the tempo and arrangement of Holiday's recording static and uninteresting. A fan of contemporary popular music with little or no exposure to popular music of the 1940s may complain that both Crosby's and Holiday's recordings are too slow, have little energy, and that they sound "old."

What I have tried to demonstrate in the discussion of the "musical code" and by the analysis of certain features of the recordings of "I'll Be Seeing You" is that the musical message can never be reduced to the mere communication of the biography of the performer. If Billie Holiday's music only communicated tragedy and sadness, it would result in a one-

Example 2.5: *"Pennies from Heaven": three versions of the first sixteen measures*
Transcriptions by David Brackett (note: the recordings of Crosby and Holiday were
transposed to C to permit easier comparison).

Example 2.5 (*cont.*)

dimensional aesthetic experience that could hardly satisfy anyone lacking an over-romantic sense of his or her own tragedy (which is not to say that her music had nothing to do with her life). And if Bing Crosby's music seems somewhat "overcoded" now at a distance of fifty years, we need not let that blind us to the artistic questions that his work answered. Questions of aesthetic value are intimately linked not only to an individual song's reception history, but as well to historical shifts in the prestige of various codes articulated by a text; and these shifts may fluctuate inversely to the initial dissemination of a recording, as an initially popular style saturates the musical soundscape, thereby eventually creating a sense of "overcoding." Furthermore, for any recording artist and recording attributed to him or her, there are a host of other factors unique to that context that must be considered: media images of the performer, and the history of the emotive and axiological connotations associated with any given style and genre, to name a few. Interpretation forms in the complex space between codes that may indicate genre, style, dialects, norms, and the "extramusical" information that circulates about performers; and this chapter has attempted to emphasize the entanglement of the motivations that we attribute to the performers with the information conveyed by the musical codes themselves.

CHAPTER THREE

When you're lookin' at Hank
(you're looking at country)

::

He took a deep drag off his Camel, squared his shoulders and started for Tootsie's. He was ready for them if they liked him and he was equally ready for them if they didn't like him. Fuck them. Who were they, anyway? They couldn't stand alone in front of a crowd, a crowd that might turn on him, you never knew, and win over that crowd, those thousands of strangers who thought they owned you anyway if they'd paid even thirty cents to get in, who demanded that you bust your nuts for them. Like you were a trained nigger. Tee-Tot had told him that once in Greenville and he hadn't really understood it until he had started working the white trash honky-tonks across the South. "They be makin' you so mad you want to take and kill 'em," Tee-Tot had told Hank when he was just a kid and Hank had laughed: Tee-Tot was a nigger. Of course white folks would tell him what to do.

Now Hank wished he could apologize to Tee-Tot. Tee-Tot had tried to tell him that race, that color had nothing to do with it: if you made your living by holding out your hand to the public, half the time the public is gonna take a pee on your hand. Hank had laughed at Tee-Tot. He laughed no more. Now he had captured the public – the number one record, he had the chart from *Billboard* in his pocket – and the Opry, the damn Grand Ole Opry *belonged* to him now, after tonight. The public had voted and he had won. It was a hollow victory. The cream of the country music ruling class had made it apparent – Hank was no fool when it came to judging people and their real messages – that he would be tolerated because of his public acceptance but that he should expect no sudden membership in the country club.   (*Your Cheatin' Heart*, pp. 80–81)

This passage, from Chet Flippo's controversial 1981 biography of Hank Williams (1923–1953), portrays a "fictionalized" account of what was arguably Williams' greatest professional triumph: the night in 1949 of his first performance on the *Grand Ole Opry*, a night on which he performed "Lovesick Blues" (the "number one record" alluded to in the passage above) a total of *seven* times – one complete rendition and six encores (an unheard of event on the *Opry*). This excerpt contains in distilled form many of the *topoi* central to the collection of recordings, images, and biographical details known as "Hank Williams": the *topos* of the white country boy who learns to sing the blues from a black man; the *topos* of a paragon of personal sincerity who could never modify his behavior to impress those who might do him a favor, a man who "was no fool when it came to judging people and their *real* messages"; the *topos* of the man, chosen by the people (essential to the country music mythos), who consequently finds it a "hollow victory" (a recurring figure in the lore of the plight of the pop culture hero); the *topos* of an intensely extroverted performer who was extraordinarily shy in his personal dealings, the theme of the "split personality"; and the *topos* of the need for "mainstream" approval, here represented by the copy of *Billboard* in his pocket, a theme which haunts country music.[1]

At the same time, these paragraphs contain some of the myth-debunking that outraged (or which Flippo may have intended to outrage) the loyal legions of Hank Williams fans.[2] This approach is exemplified by what Flippo portrays as the apparent scorn of Williams for the audience, putatively inculcated in him by the legendary "Tee-Tot" (Rufus Payne) or perhaps (as Flippo intimates elsewhere in the book) by Williams' early experiences selling peanuts and shining shoes.[3] This attitude towards the audience contradicts country music orthodoxy (as well as other biographical descriptions of Williams' attitude) which dictates that the performer remain gracious and appreciative towards the crowd and that the performer, no matter how high he or she might soar, never abandon or lose touch with the values of the audience that contributed to his or her success. Indeed, this identification with the audience can constitute one of the prime markers of that ever elusive sense of "authenticity" so important for success in the country music industry and so important to the myth of Hank Williams.

However, Flippo, in his effort to debunk the myth, can only add to it or revise it: the "debunking" above adds to other *topoi* in the Williams mythos that seek explanations of his behavior in psychoanalytical accounts of his childhood, an explanatory approach taken by other Williams biographers as well. Flippo seems to recognize his own entrapment (and he alludes to yet another of the most potent topics in the Williams myth) when he writes

The man wrote hardly any letters, read nothing but comic books, and revealed his inner self only through his songs. *Those who did know him revise his history to sweeten their own.* Plain facts and dates and cities do not explain him or his extraordinary impact on American music and particularly on whole generations in the South [my italics].[4]

Flippo argues, with this extraordinary rationalization of his approach to the biographical genre, that we are all implicated in this process of revising the Hank Williams myth, whether we know him "personally" or second- or thirdhand. In the process Flippo contributes further to the *topos* that presents Williams as someone who only "reveals his inner self through songs," a topic which recurs incessantly in the biographical literature, etching a figure of a loner who does not "confide in" others; this figure can be related to the *topos* of authenticity: he only spoke when he had something sincere to say. I will comment further on this issue later in this chapter, for it has much to do with how we listen to his music in general, how we listen to a song like "Hey Good Lookin'" (recorded in 1951) in particular, and how we understand both his importance to the history of country music and the importance of his myth to the present-day country music industry.

It is difficult to separate the myth of Hank Williams from the affect produced by his recordings; and the significance of this inseparability of myth and affect extends beyond the individual case of one performer and one song to include whatever aspects of memory and history individuals bring to the listening experience; this recalls the discussions of listener "competence" and authorship earlier in the book. To understand better the impact of this indivisibility of affect, myth, and memory/history on the "meaning" of a song such as "Hey Good Lookin'," we will return to another question asked earlier: how do voices, lyrics, and music create the effect of "authenticity" in country music and how did this effect emerge and shift historically? In addition to exploring these issues, this chapter will consider how the association of country music with the culture industry affects the production of "authentic" effects and how images of "marginality" and "resistance" may contribute to the popularity of songs and artists in country music.

I

Lyrics, metanarratives, and the great authenticity debate

Lyric analysis has often formed the starting-point for the analysis of popular songs. This may seem to be the obvious place to begin an analysis of a country song, since lyrics occupy a privileged space in the discourse of fans and critics of country music; and the forward placement of the voice in the recorded mix, the "naturalized," conversational delivery of the lyrics, and their strongly narrative character all work to focus listener attention on the voice. However, as discussed in the introduction, to analyze lyrics means not to abstract them from their context in a recorded performance; rather, it means to try to understand how lyrics and performances work to create a sense of a particular genre, a particular audience, and a particular relationship between performer and audience. And it means to try to understand how a song might be about language itself.[5] Furthermore, lyrics in country music provide a particularly graphic connection between the song as a commodity, the production and interpretation of "authenticity," and the commoditization of the very idea of "authenticity."

The lyrics of "Hey Good Lookin'" can be placed within a broader framework of "metanarratives" contained in country music, a framework described and elaborated by Aaron Fox.[6] While the latter part of this chapter will explore the historical context for the emergence of these metanarratives, we will first consider how they function in a particular song. In addition to the rationales offered above about the importance of lyrics in country songs, the lyrics and the focus on the voice are essential for communicating the "metanarratives" in a given song. The lyrics of "Hey Good Lookin'" correspond most closely with Fox's description of the "metanarrative of Desire":

The metanarrative of Desire makes people and feelings into reified objects to be bought, sold, used up and replaced. This narrative is enacted through the very practice of consuming music as a commodity, and it is explicitly and implicitly re-told in many song texts. According to this objectifying story, the old and worn out is quickly forgotten, and replaced by the shiny and brand new. The narrative subject is constituted publicly as a consumer of an endless stream of desired objects.[7]

I am not maintaining here (nor is Fox) that every country lyric narrative can be assigned securely to one or the other of these categories; many lyrics exhibit qualities of both Loss and Desire. But the power of Fox's paradigm lies in its potential as a heuristic device.

A quality of the "metanarrative of Desire" is its propensity to create a "spiral of narrative transformations and self-reproducing desires [which] is inscribed in the very act of consuming a popular musical 'product' which narratively treats desire as capable of being fulfilled through the consumption of commodities."[8] Let us see how this idea manifests itself in the lyrics of "Hey Good Lookin'" (displayed in example 3.1). The lyrics fall roughly into three modes of address which trace the formal outlines of the song. In these modes, the song's narrator addresses the song's object:

(1) through flattery and invitation in verses 1 and 2 (verses prior to the instrumental break);

(2) through promises of a future relationship in verses 3 and 4 in which he ("he" for reasons explained below) creates himself as an object (verses following the instrumental break); and

(3) through redirecting attention during the bridge (B) sections towards material goods that the narrator (now assuming agency through use of the nominative case) might offer the song's addressee.[9]

The bridge or "B" section relates most clearly to the "metanarrative of Desire," constructing a narrational subject as a consumer and conflating the subject's "love-object" with various commodity-objects: at first, the commodities become the focus of the lyrics as "the hot rod Ford," and the "two-dollar bill" supplant the object of the song's address (line 7 – "I've gotta hot rod Ford and a two-dollar bill"). The lyrics of line 9 anticipate a time when the subject and object might consume commodities (e.g., the "soda pop") and experiences (e.g., "dancin'") together. And the result of this anticipated consumption is "fun," which (it is implied) cannot be attained without rejecting a stable domestic situation in favor of the pursuit of ever-new stimulation.[10] The second bridge (lines 20–23) conflates commodity-objects and the love-object in a much more tangible sense, as the exchange value of an object (the "datebook") is stated (as "five or ten cents") and the name of the love-object literally inscribed in the commodity ("I'm writin' your name down on every page"). The experience of love is positioned as an object to be consumed as it is reified in the form of a "five or ten cent" datebook.

The narrator creates himself as an object to be consumed by announcing in verse 3 that he's "free and ready," a pun which plays on the ambiguity of "free." Of the many possible definitions of "free" the usage here comes closest to the following: (1) "not costing or charging anything"; or (2) "not united with, attached to, combined with, or mixed with something else." The pun is elaborated when the song's narrator advises the object that she should "save" all her time, thereby suggesting a conversion of a non-spatial concept ("time") into a materialized, spatial one (i.e., something that can be saved). The narrator is recommending that the song's object save her "time" in the same way one might save "money," with the goal of ultimately transferring it to him ("for me").

I will discuss one more pun that works to reify the hoped-for relationship. This pun, "cookin'" – of course, "what you got cookin'?" could simply be slang for "what are you doing?" – leads in the first verse to the image of the "recipe," thereby extending the initial pun into a

Example 3.1: *"Hey Good Lookin'" lyrics*

Verse 1 (A):	1	Say, <u>Hey</u> Good Lookin',
	2	<u>what</u> you got cookin'?
	3	How's about cookin' somethin' up with <u>me</u>?

Verse 2 (A'):	4	<u>Hey</u>, sweet baby,
	5	<u>don't</u> you think maybe,
	6	we could find us a brand new reci<u>pe</u>?

Bridge 1 (B):	7	I've gotta hot rod Ford and a two-dollar bill
	8	and I know a spot right over the hill
	9	There's soda pop and the dancin's free
	10	so if you wanna have fun come along with me

Verse 1' (A):	11	<u>Hey</u> Good Lookin',
	12	<u>what</u> you got cookin'?
	13	How's about cookin' somethin' up with <u>me</u>?

(A):		Steel Guitar Solo
(A'):		Steel Guitar Solo
(B):		Fiddle Solo
(A):		Steel Guitar Solo

Verse 3 (A):	14	I'm <u>free</u> and ready
	15	so <u>we</u> can go steady
	16	How's about savin' all your time for <u>me</u>?

Verse 4 (A'):	17	<u>No</u> more lookin'
	18	I <u>know</u> I've been tooken'
	19	How's about keepin' steady compa<u>ny</u>?

Bridge 2 (B):	20	I'm gonna throw my datebook over the fence
	21	and buy me one for five or ten cents.
	22	I'll keep it 'til it's covered with age,
	23	'cause I'm writin' your name down on every page.

Verse 1" (A):	24	Say, <u>Hey</u> Good Lookin',
	25	<u>what</u> you got cookin'?
	26	How's about cookin' somethin' up with <u>me</u>?

<u>Underlined</u> = <u>Sustained syllables</u>

metaphor that produces a visual representation of the future relationship (in the form of the "recipe," which, in the words of one Williams biographer, probably has "little to do with fat back and green beans").[11] The word "cookin'" connotes many aspects of the song's object, such as gender and expected domestic activity. The activity of "cooking" is itself a kind of reifying one, as it turns "raw" ingredients into a product that humans might consume. The "metanarrative of desire," with its consumable "love-objects" and its (in this case) "hailing" type of address which focuses on the object's physical features (particularly evident in verses 1 and 2), blurs with other discourses that construct objectified and commodified images of women. While, on the one hand, it may be true that many modern "Desire metanarratives" sung by female country singers perform a similar kind of objectification towards males, on the other hand, when we consider the *specific* scene described by the lyrics in "Hey Good Lookin'," we view a scene with a particularly strong set of gendered correspondences.

"Hey Good Lookin'" shares qualities with other songs written and recorded by Williams which express the metanarrative of Desire, such as "Honky Tonkin'," and "I'll Be a Bachelor 'Til I Die." In "Honky Tonkin'," the narrator invites a woman ("sweet mama"), who may well be someone else's wife, to go out and have some fun at the honky-tonks; paramount to their enjoyment is that she "bring along some dough." Similarly, in "Hey Good Lookin'," the narrator is attempting to lure a woman away from a domestic scene (if not from a previous marriage). Here, in a common move in the metanarrative of Desire, the "old and worn out" relationship (marriage) is replaced by a (supposedly) shiny and brand new one.[12] The activity of converting previously purchased goods (ingredients) into a meal is replaced by the activity of heightened consumption represented by drinking ("soda pop," or perhaps the kind of "soda pop" consumed in the honky-tonk) and driving cars. In the space of desire, marriages are equated with reusing old materials, new relationships with consuming ever new and glamorous goods. The narrator of "I'll Be a Bachelor 'Til I Die" similarly offers to take the desired object "honky-tonkin'," yet, as the title indicates, this offer excludes the possibility of future domestic stability.

The use of puns and clichés in "Hey Good Lookin'" introduces another prominent aspect of country lyrics: the way in which "ordinary" language is "denaturalized."[13] The exploitation of puns further heightens the sense of artifice and creates a kind of self-reflexiveness and self-consciousness that thwarts attempts to impute an unmediated sense of "authenticity" to songs. A song like "Hey Good Lookin'" may be one of the earliest country lyrics to employ the pun in this fashion; at the same time, it looks forward to recent tunes in which puns are extended to add levity to lyrics that might otherwise verge on the maudlin. Also, Williams-type self-reflexivity lacks the convoluted corniness so often found in recent songs, such as "I Just Cut Myself on a Piece of Her Broken Heart," or "Flushed from the Bathroom of Your Heart."[14] This may be why Hank Williams' recordings remain indexes of "authenticity":

they established a paradigm for language use while not calling attention to the artificial means necessary for their own production. Country recordings made in the last thirty years may be "about" the idea of "authenticity," yet the baroque self-reflexivity of the lyrics creates a "funhouse-hall-of-mirrors" effect that renders the concept of "authenticity" little but a simulacrum.

That is, on the one hand, the lyrics and their reception imply that somewhere such a thing as "true authenticity" must exist; otherwise, statements by fans such as "so-and-so really sings from the heart" (and the statement might continue "unlike so-and-so the sell-out") could not occur so frequently. On the other hand, self-reflexivity implies that there is no "outside" from which to view the "authentic," that the "authentic" is always already in play, and that "truth to one's feelings" may be recuperated at any moment for financial gain. Nothing illustrates the last part of this statement better than the combined mementoes of Hank Williams' posthumous career: the numerous recordings issued with overdubbed orchestras and choruses; the demonstration records originally made by Williams with only his own guitar accompaniment but overdubbed later with a full band, frequently including the drums that were religiously forbidden in the Nashville recordings of that era;[15] and the recordings featuring overdubbed duets with his son Hank Jr. (only three years old at the time of Hank Sr.'s death) – taken together, these products unambiguously proclaim the artificiality of the recording process through which a large share of Williams' authenticity is communicated.

As noted earlier, the performance of the lyrics in "Hey Good Lookin'," as in any text including music and words, affects their meaning. We should first note how the performance stresses certain words through duration or sonic stress (rhyming) so that they reinforce the rough formal outline noted earlier. If we follow Roman Jakobson's assertions that such "equivalence[s] in sound" and grammatical parallelisms project "semantic equivalence" promoting either "comparison for likeness' sake" or "comparison for unlikeness' sake," we produce the chart in example 3.2, which displays a kind of subliminal narrative constructed through semantic associations and Jakobson's "equivalences."[16]

These stressed words in example 3.2 reinforce the general formal outline observed earlier: in verses 1 and 2 they address the song's object through flattery and invitation; and the stressed words in verses 3 and 4 feature the narrator's attempt to persuade the object of his sincerity. The rhymed words from verses 3 and 4, "ready"/"steady," "lookin'"/"tooken'," make similar points. The word "tooken'" is especially interesting for it

Example 3.2: *Stressed words in "Hey Good Lookin'"*

Durational stress – verses 1 and 2:

Hey	= subject hails object
what	= subject requests information from object
me	= speaker repositions himself as object for listener/addressee
Hey	= subject hails object
don't	= subject requests information from object
recipe	= brings the domestic activity, the request for a relationship, and the positioning of the narrator as object together

Sonic stress – verses 1 and 2:

lookin'	= flattery of object
cookin'	= domestic activity, requesting information
me	= see above
baby	= propositioning of object
maybe	= requests consent
recipe	= see above

Durational stress – verses 3 and 4:

free	= subject states availability/exchange value
we	= subject effects a linguistic union
me	= subject again repositions himself as object
No	= promise of faithfulness
know	= expression of certainty that this is so
company	= emphasizes togetherness

directs attention to the artifice of the song's language through creation of a word to rhyme; at the same time this (invented) word serves as an emblem of the colloquial that invests the lyrics with a hint of the "authentic," meaning in this case "of the people" – namely, the southern, working class, and rural "people." While this formalist dissection of the lyrics verges on the hermeneutical, that is, on the positing of deep meaning available to the skilled interpreter but not to the "masses," the value of this exercise may lie in its underlining the relationship of "text" to the "metanarratives" elaborated earlier, and, hence, to the larger "context." The point here is that even on this micro-level, song lyrics reinforce and reproduce mechanisms of never-to-be-fulfilled desires and courtship rituals.

However, the kind of multiple resonances generated by the word "tooken'" noted above have more than merely local significance for a single case; this type of usage occurs as part of a broader rhetorical strategy across the text of "Hey Good Lookin'" as well as throughout the body of Williams' work. While presenting the words in the form of a song, investing them with this "poetic" quality, "denaturalizes" them to some extent, Williams "renaturalizes" the lyrics through two devices common to other country singers: the use of a vocal timbre close to that of a rural speaking voice; and the use of dialect, slang terms, and the tendency to drop "g"s at the ends of words.[17] The superficially unadorned character of the music and vocal delivery work to restore a sense of "naturalness" to a communication occurring in a context divorced from the everyday communications of the audience: Hank Williams, a "star," uses poetic language in a reproducible, electronic recording to express, as he put it, "the hopes and prayers and dreams of what some call the common people."[18] We must take Williams' statement at face value; there is no hint of irony or paradox here. Yet it is far too easy to halt our curiosity at this point, thereby ceding the totality of the song's meaning to the author's description of his intentions.

"Hey Good Lookin'," as an exemplar of the Desire metanarrative, belongs to a type of Williams songs featuring a "carouser" persona. He also communicated this persona in his more inspired performances, which were often described as charismatic and sexually suggestive. His biographies are sprinkled liberally with tales of his womanizing, drinking, fighting, and generally rowdy behavior. There is reason to think that audiences at the time (the late forties to the early fifties) were aware of these activities (especially the drinking) and that they regarded them as "normal" for a "good ole boy." However, songs featuring the metanarrative of Loss occur more often in Williams' output and are easier to connect to the biographical narratives than the songs of Desire. The many sad love songs led audiences of the time to believe that the songs formed a musical chronicle of his travails with his first wife Audrey (known to audiences through her performances with Williams' group, The Drifting Cowboys).[19] Here, in terms of authorship, we find a relationship between the author "inside the text" and the author "outside the text" similar to the one we observed in the discussion of Billie Holiday. As in that case, this association may form part of the basis for the "authenticity" attributed to Hank Williams, to the impression he creates that he is singing about his true feelings.

The binary grouping of song lyric types into two metanarratives divides Williams' expressive tendencies in a way that matches the practice of biographers who often explain the details of Williams' life in terms of dichotomies made popular by psychoanalysis. Most prominent in the literature is the sinner/saint dichotomy which is explained typically by the presence in Williams' early years of a strong, domineering, God-fearing mother and a weak, alcoholic father (his mother was quoted as saying "Hank's mother was always his first girl and he never forgot it").[20] Therein, or so we are to believe, lie the origins of his vacillations between alcoholic wastrel and his sermonizing persona on records, "Luke the Drifter"; as well as the origins of his vacillations in his relationships with women between violent abuse and desperate conciliation. According to Williams lore, he was a country boy who had to make it in the city; he was shy and confided in no one, yet he captivated audiences with his exuberant and sexy shows; with his band, at times, he was one of the boys, while at other times he was Herman P. Willis, a name he would assume when he wished anonymity for legal or social reasons; as "Hank Williams" he would womanize compulsively and sing "I'll Be a Bachelor 'Til I Die," and then record "Too Many Parties and Too Many Pals" as Luke the Drifter, a tale told from the point of view of a father defending his pregnant daughter to a judge; he self-destructed through drink and drugs, dying on New Year's day, 1953, yet his tombstone quotes two lines from his most famous hymn, "I Saw the Light," and features the name "Luke the Drifter" prominently in the middle.[21]

Yet despite, or because of, what might seem like a plentiful assortment of contradictions, Hank Williams has become a kind of retrospective index for "authenticity"; this is attested to by the comments of fans, musicians, and critics, not to mention the song titles addressed to him.[22] An aspect of Williams' "authentic effect" may have been the sense of community produced through live performance.[23] This probably added much to Williams' appeal and image while he was alive – he performed an average of 200 nights a year during the peak years of his popularity, and is described over and over again as a dynamic performer (when sober). This reference to performance as a forum for "authentic" communication and as a space for the experience of community upholds some of the tenets of descriptions of "traditional" or "folk" music: most prominently, that there is little or no separation between audience and performer; and it assumes that this experience of community will survive intact the transference to the mass-mediated context of pop. However, reference to Williams' charismatic stage presence does little to explain his posthumous status as an icon of personal sincerity. Even if it did, it could not remove one of the central paradoxes of the use of "authenticity" as a sign in the modern recording industry: to paraphrase Simon Frith, "[Williams'] songs suggest there is something missing in our lives, the [record company's] message is that we can fill the gap *with a [Hank Williams] record.*"[24] In other words, the individuality and populism of Williams' songs and image become available to reinforce consumption as the means for filling the gap opened by feelings of loss and desire expressed in his songs.

What did Hank Williams have to say about the issue? In a rare interview, Williams based his evaluations of country or "hillbilly" singing on the degree of "sincerity" contained in a performance; in his words

[The hillbilly singer] sings more sincere than most entertainers because the hillbilly was raised rougher than most entertainers. You got to know a lot about hard work. You got to have smelt a lot of mule manure before you can sing like a hillbilly. The people who has been raised something like the way the hillbilly has knows what he is singing about and appreciates it.[25]

The quote reveals a faith in the identity between author, affect, and audience. However, this does not explain how his music could become popular with those who had not been "raised like the hillbilly."

While it *is* true that in Hank Williams' songs a voice "inside the text" frequently coincides with the biography of the "author"; and while it is true that his songs lack the self-reflexive attitude towards "authenticity" found in modern country songs, the problematic conjunction of Hank Williams with the "authentic" effect expresses itself in other ways. Writers from his time to the present remark about the paucity of interviews and comments made about his "real" life and his songs by Williams, and about his reluctance to "confide in" others. And we can see from the interview quoted above that he felt comfortable uttering pleasant generalities in those situations. Williams, it seems, felt content to express publicly through his songs what might be considered his "private" feelings. Conversely, he appeared mystified when interviewers insisted that indeed there must be something deeper "behind" the songs themselves. While writers attribute his inarticulateness and secretive behavior to childhood traumas or to behavior exhibited by males from Williams' social/geographical location, could it be that there simply was nothing "deeper" lying behind or beneath the creation of these songs? While it may be part of our common mythology that there is always a "deeper," more "authentic" self lying behind a person's public façade, Williams' behavior does not seem to acknowledge this. The deeply personal aspect of his public "confessions" in song therefore takes on an artificial quality: he "reveals" himself only through the conventions and arrangements of the professional entertainer, a practice that threatens to stand the idea of "authenticity" as "truth-to-self" on its head.

Related to this is the issue of "resistance," and whether Williams articulated ideas both musically and lyrically that audiences found attractive because they expressed an idea of "truth" opposed to social forces of domination.[26] According to stories that propound this view, the measure of Williams' "resistance" is the degree to which he speaks the truth and throws off the yoke of repression, thereby providing an authentic discourse that resonates with the marginalized segments of his audience. While the preceding discussion has attempted to problematize the notion of unmediated "authenticity," perhaps it is still possible to account for a way in which Williams, as a mythical/musical figure, did communicate a sense of "resistance." And, rather than resulting from his liberation of the truth on behalf of the marginalized, this may well have much to do with his aforementioned aversion to "confiding in" others. If confession is "a ritual that unfolds within a power relationship," in which the interlocutor is an "authority who requires the confession," and which results in a transfer of the "agency of domination" from the one who confesses to the one who receives the confession, then it is possible that it is the degree to which Williams does not "confide in" others that marks the extent of his resistance.[27] Could it be that Hank Williams' resistance is a passive one, a resistance that blankly offers itself as the refusal to engage in a "discourse of truth," as a refusal either to overcome the intrinsic obstacles of revealing confidences or to produce the expected behavioral modifications that result from confession? He distrusted doctors almost as much as he avoided interviewers, thereby refusing to allow a record to be compiled about his body. His activities thwarted equally the compilation of a medical or psychoanalytical file, not allowing the intervention of doctors and psychiatrists to teach him the "truth" of his mind and body. But even this refusal does not constitute a "resistance" that escapes the forces of domination; instead, both his biographers and industry publicists use his behavior to teach a moral: he died because he refused the expertise of doctors, preferring to put his faith in quacks; his life thus becomes an emblem that implies we must choose between martyrdom and the compilation of a file.

Even Williams' public confessions in song owed more to the act of *listening* than to the act of *telling*: Williams acknowledged this when he told an interviewer, "I listen to people and try to understand how they feel about things. Feelings about things. That's what songs should be about."[28] This statement implies that his "sincere" confessions in song were calculated, based to some extent on what he thought people wanted to hear. However, this argument is not meant to dispute the point that

Williams' popularity and resultant deification relies heavily on the creation of authentic effects. He could not have become so meaningful to so many people if he did not convey, as few others in country music have managed to do, the impression that he is expressing his "true" feelings, simply and directly. It is only to show that authentic effects are never natural, simple, or without paradoxical implications; that the "effects" can become detached from the original stimulus and reattached to other objects in other contexts.

But this attempt to rescue a measure of a "resistant effect" for Hank Williams is based largely on his stance as a mass media icon; or, to put it another way, on what he *didn't* do or say in interviews. It is true that the quote in the previous paragraph suggests a connection between the non-confessor of the interviews and the "Hillbilly Shakespeare" who poured out heartfelt lyrics in song. While it is also true that heartfelt confession in song is a convention in the country music of the period, this does not erase the poeticizing innovations of Williams' lyrics. Some might view the mania for self-reflexivity in lyrics that Williams encouraged and that rages unabated in contemporary country music as a form of ironic commentary, which in itself "resists" the tendencies of the culture industry. The self-reflexive lyrics of much post-Williams country music comment explicitly on the inextricable links between country music and capitalism, thereby undercutting both the notion that the music transcends its status as a commodity and the notion that it is wholly determined by it. However, this very maneuver recuperates "self-reflexivity" as part of the commercial process. So, while Hank Williams' music undoubtedly created, and continues to create, powerful authentic *effects* with its audience, this and any sort of depoliticized "resistance" must always be located within the larger field of the music's status as an exchangeable commodity.

Beyond even this sense of commercial recuperation, the presence of a marginalized source of "authentic" expression has long been part of the Romantic ideology so necessary to the production and consumption of art under capitalism.[29] Fredric Jameson summarizes this aspect of authenticity:

The only authentic cultural production today has seemed to be that which can draw on the collective experience of marginal pockets of the social life of the world system: black literature and blues, British working-class rock, women's literature . . . and this production is possible only to the degree to which these forms of collective life or collective solidarity have not yet been fully penetrated by the market and by the commodity system.[30]

While this quote captures aspects of the links between marginality and authenticity, it fails to note a paradox: music (or other forms of cultural production) at the "margins" is frequently the most available for appropriation and economic exploitation precisely because it carries the greatest charge of "authenticity." Along these lines, we must mention the paradox of Williams' enormous popularity: in some respects it was the very qualities of rural "sincerity" that allowed him to appeal to an audience far beyond the immediate "community" to which he belonged. The complexity of this circulation of "authenticity" from the "margins" to the "mainstream" is underscored by the fact that his songs reached their widest audience in Tin-Pan-Alley-ified versions sung by other performers. Poignant in this context are the stories of Williams stopping to play Tony Bennett's version of "Cold, Cold Heart" on the jukebox, an act affirming the wonder he felt that his song would have reached an expanded audience in such an urbane rendition, while simultaneously expressing a sense of estrangement from his own work in the wake of its expropriation, as he is forced to "pay" to hear his own song.[31] Of course, from a different perspective, Williams was merely making an investment, paying for a golden opportunity:

Hank Williams fans loved his 1950 recording of his own song "Cold, Cold Heart," but it was Tony Bennett who really took this country classic to town in 1951. His performance earned the record 16 weeks on the Hit Parade. "It was the first time a country record was kind of citified with strings and a big Percy Faith background," says Tony of his version, "and the first time a country song went all over the world."[32]

II

Sound, performance, gender, and the honky-tonk

I have already described how we might understand Hank Williams' lyrics as a fulcrum between "early" country and "modern" country constructions of authenticity. In addition, the descriptions illustrated how interpretive strategies might be influenced by connections to the *topoi* in the Hank Williams mythos. It is unlikely that the vast majority of his audience ever considered the "lyrics" in isolation from the "music"; in fact, attempting to parse music and lyrics into separate categories for the sake of this project already removes us from the context in which the song's effects were initially felt. While the foregoing lyric analysis did not neglect the effect of the performance entirely, the focus of that analysis on the "non-performative" aspects of the lyrics – their semantic, representational, and metanarrational qualities – encouraged us to discuss certain issues. At this point, however, we might do well to remind ourselves of one of the precepts of lyric analysis mentioned earlier – namely, that lyric analysis should describe how lyrics and *performances* work to create a sense of a particular genre, a particular audience, and a particular relationship between performer and audience.

In addition to the elements discussed previously (words accented by duration, "naturalization" of the text), let us consider the following six descriptive categories:

(1) Williams' vocal timbre;
(2) rhythmic accentuation and inflection of his voice set off in relief from the implied or stated steady pulsational accents of the band, a complex that results in a lilting effect approaching that of "swing";
(3) pitch inflections of the voice;
(4) the timbre of the band;
(5) the feeling of "swing" generated by the band itself as it either reinforces the dominant accentual flow or produces accents that pull against it;
(6) the manner in which the band treats and inflects pitch within a diatonic, functional harmonic context, a treatment employing micro-tones and suggesting heterophony.

The factor mentioned most often by critics and fans as being responsible for Williams' popularity and uniqueness is his vocal timbre (or tone quality).[33] One quality of his vocal timbre – the pronounced southern accent – intersects with a quality mentioned already in connection with the pronunciation of the words: that of "naturalization." Moreover, Williams' voice is obviously "untrained," or, perhaps more accurately, it is not trained in the European bel canto tradition. However, it is "trained" in another tradition – that of southern/hillbilly/country music. This vocal technique allows him to produce a variety of vowel sounds closer to spoken vowel sounds than the bel canto technique, which tends to produce a more consistent tone color, and which neutralizes the acoustic differences of vowel sounds.[34] If we compare Williams' version of "Cold, Cold Heart" to Tony Bennett's, we notice Bennett's wider, more consistent vibrato, as well as his greater fullness and consistency of tone in all registers. Bennett, though not possessing the bel canto technique of an opera singer, does incorporate aspects of the bel canto aesthetic and technique into his style. Williams, by contrast, emphasizes the *differences* between registers: the upper range is thin and pinched, on the verge of breaking, the low register relatively rich; the differences in vowel sounds are also underscored: notice the added nasality (in "Hey Good Lookin'") of the "bright" sustained vowels "Hey" and "me" compared to the relatively dark (though still nasal) "what." Notice also how the majority of the sustained vowels are "bright," allowing Williams to exploit the twangy nasality of his voice, a timbre that forges a kind of regional and class-based solidarity.

Pierre Bourdieu has described how audiences with lower "cultural capital" tend to consume artifacts that emphasize the "functionality" of the artifacts as opposed to the "aestheticized" qualities valued by "intellectuals."[35] Even if we accept these oppositions with qualifications, we can extrapolate from them that the use of a regional accent which recalls the timbre and speech patterns of southern vernacular conversation reminds us of one of the "functions" of language – to communicate meaning – and implies a specific, localized referent, i.e., an external subject in a particular time and place.[36] On the other hand, we might say that bel canto singing evokes a style, a means of producing sound not bound to any regionally located group of subjects; and in its linguistic distortions, it effaces the semantic function of language, refocusing interest on the singing voice as an "instrument" (which is how singers of art music refer to their voices). However, we must remind ourselves that this sociological homology can only go so far, for it cannot explain the breadth of Williams' appeal beyond a specific class- or region-identified group (and it's debatable whether country music ever appealed only to the stereotypical, rural Southerner). Perhaps the issue here is not so much that some types of music are "functional" while others are not, but that different musical styles and genres evoke different *types* of functions in different ways, all of which can vary depending on the subject positions inhabited by the listener.

This description of vocal timbre, in emphasizing the regional specificity of Williams' voice, may give the distorted impression that his singing is crude and untutored; the fact is that not simply anyone could sound the way he did. Within the aesthetic boundaries in which he operated, he displayed extraordinary control and flexibility. He reintroduced yodeling in "Lovesick Blues," a technique that had largely lain dormant (excepting a few "singing cowboy"-type songs) since Jimmy Rodgers' recordings in the early 1930s;[37] his controlled use of the "tear" or vocal break was widely admired during his career; and although the range of his singing voice was not large, his sense of pitch and ability to inflect pitch micro-tonally added immensely to the expressive effects at his disposal.

Examination of the spectrum photo of verses 1 and 4 (example 3.3) reinforces earlier observations about Williams' vocal timbre. The photo of the first verse displays the aforementioned differences between the brightness of the sustained vowels in "Hey" and "me" (note the greater concentration of high spectra) and the relative darkness of "what." This bright-dark-bright pattern of sustained vowels persists in all the verses except for verse 4, in which the first sustained vowel, in "No," is also dark (example 3.3). This exception coincides with the fact that it is this verse in which Williams pledges his faithfulness, an exceptional moment with respect both to the "carouser" persona which dominates "Hey Good Lookin'" and to the metanarrative of Desire which enframes the persona.

Another important element in Williams' singing is the *rhythm* of his vocal line – the way it either emphasizes the underlying pulse of the band or strains against it. These subtle anticipations and delays contribute to an elusive sense of "swing."[38] He produces this effect in "Hey Good Lookin'" by attacking the sustained words "Hey" and "what" slightly before the pulse established by the band, leaving those words to float above their steady accents; and then by reentering the rhythmic stream with the shorter rhythmic values of "Good Lookin'" and "you got cookin'" (see example 3.4). Furthermore, the words "Lookin'" and "cookin'" are rushed slightly, propelling the song forward with greater impetus. The bridge demonstrates how Williams plays with the beat using only shorter note values, as he lands squarely on the beat for a few words only then to detach himself from it. It is precisely in this part of the song, the part in which his voice contributes most to the rhythmic drive, that he attempts to lure the "Good Lookin'" one with promises of "dancin'." Example 3.4 amply illustrates this aspect of the bridge: "hot rod" occurs on beats one and two of m. 20, while "Ford" anticipates beat three, and "two-dollar bill" syncopates the first two beats of m. 21. In m. 22, the rhythm of "I know a" duplicates the syncopation of the previous bar, the placement of the words "spot right" coincides with beats three and four, but "over the hill" rushes through the first two beats of m. 23. Measures 24 and 25 are filled with syncopations and anticipations, while mm. 26–27 play the role of the "resolver," being the only passage in the entire bridge of more than two beats ("if you wanna have fun come along with me" covers seven beats) to land more or less squarely on the beat.

The same technique of floating above the beat and then accentuating it is also presented strongly in "Lovesick Blues"; in this case, the band

Example 3.3: *Spectrum photos of "Hey Good Lookin'"*

Verse 1 (A)

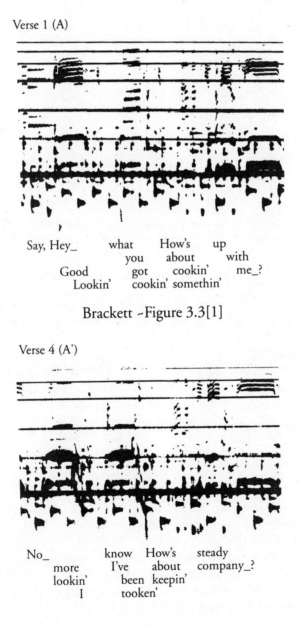

Say, Hey_   what   How's   up
      you   about   with
  Good   got   cookin'   me_?
  Lookin'   cookin' somethin'

Brackett ~Figure 3.3[1]

Verse 4 (A')

No_   know   How's   steady
   more   I've   about   company_?
   lookin'   been   keepin'
     I   tooken'

Example 3.4: *Transcription of "Hey Good Lookin'"*

Words and music by Hank Williams
Transcription by David Brackett

stops entirely, removing the underlying pulse while Williams yodels ("all I do is sit and sigh-i-i-i-i-Lord"), rupturing the linear-rhythmic continuity of the song. After the band reenters, Williams first maintains and prolongs the rhythmic tension with the heavily syncopated lines, "the last long day she said good-bye/Oh Lord, I thought I would cry"; he then realigns himself with the band's accentuations with the staccato lines, "she's got that kind of lovin'/Lord I love to hear her when she calls me";

finally, he "disrupts" the flow yet again with another a capella yodel immediately following these lines, on "[Sweet] Da-a-a-a-a-dee."

These yodeling "disruptions" in "Lovesick Blues" raise another pressing issue: that of the gender affiliation of Williams' singing persona. In addition to evoking different affective qualities – happiness, sadness, loss, playfulness, vulnerability – is there a way in which the voices "inside the text" combine to create personae with strongly gendered associations? We may note that the yodeling "disruption" in "Lovesick Blues" occurs in a register (high) and a timbre (produced by using falsetto) associated with female singing, and that it occurs in a song of Loss, that is, one that expresses the "feminine" sentiments of vulnerability and romantic loss; and that these feminized "eruptions" fracture the linearity of vocal line in terms of rhythm, pitch, and timbre ("feminine" chaos disrupting rational, "male" order?). A much more thorough study would have to be undertaken to determine whether Williams' yodeling occurs primarily in songs of Loss, although preliminary investigations seem to support this (see "Long Gone Lonesome Blues" for another example of yodeling).[39] Lest we assume too neat a correspondence here, I must add that the "honky-tonk" style in which Williams operated, and which he brought to its apex, consists almost entirely of songs expressing the metanarrative of Loss ("It Makes No Difference Now," "When My Blue Moon Turns to Gold Again," "Born to Lose," "Walkin' the Floor Over You," to name some of the best-known early examples by singers other than Williams), and that the male singers in this genre sing in many registers. The very phenomenon of the "vulnerable" male (an image circulated widely at the same time in Tin Pan Alley popular music as well), frequently perched on a bar stool in a honky-tonk, constituted one of the recurring figures of the honky-tonk style. If the expression of loss does carry with it conventional associations of femininity, then the use of those conventions by males is something of a convention itself during the period of Williams' ascendance to popularity.

"Hey Good Lookin'," on the other hand, is a song of Desire. Contrary to what other writers have asserted,[40] it's difficult to create any sort of consistent expressive homology in Williams' recordings between vocal register/timbre and masculine/feminine narratives beyond the aforementioned falsetto/yodeling connection. The highest pitches in "Hey Good Lookin'" are used for the sustained vowels in the verses and for the last line of the bridges; it is difficult to understand how maintaining that the words "Hey," "what," "me," etc. and the lines "If you wanna have fun come along with me" and "I'm writin' your name down on every page" (the last lines of the bridges) all belong to some sort of feminized persona adds to the interpretation of the song. In fact, singing in a high register in a non-falsetto, straining tone tends to be associated with spiritual/sexual power and intensity in much music derived from British-American and African-American practice (one need only listen to the timbre and tessitura of a preacher in a sanctified, African-American church service); when used by a male singer, this vocal technique can even signify *machismo*. As described in these specific musical contexts, the affect generated by a male singing in a high register is more in keeping with the macho carouser persona of "Hey Good Lookin'" than with the sensitive revelations of the singer of Loss metanarratives.

III

"A feeling called the blues"

We can appreciate some of the diachronic, historical impact of Williams' vocal style by comparing it to another singer whom Williams cited as one of his major influences: Ernest Tubb. One of Tubb's best known songs, "Walking the Floor Over You" (recorded in 1941), is recognized as one of the first "hillbilly" songs to combine honky-tonk lyric imagery with certain instrumental features (in this case, the use of an improvisational electric guitar) that Williams and others were to consolidate in the mid to late 1940s.[41] The influence of Ernest Tubb's rough hewn vocal style is also felt strongly in Williams' vocal timbre, which preserves the regional inflections of his accent and avoids the smooth crooning affected by other popular country singers of the early 1940s such as Cliff Bruner, Ted Daffan, and Tommy Duncan (of Bob Wills and the Texas Playboys). Both in "Lovesick Blues" and "Hey Good Lookin'" the higher degree of blues influence in Williams' singing compared to Tubb's in "Walking the Floor" is easily audible, even though neither of Williams' songs employs blues-type forms. Williams expresses his affinity for blues-type singing in the looseness and flexibility of his phrasing, his fondness for syncopation (factors contributing to the elusive quality of "swing" mentioned earlier), as well as in his tendency to inflect certain pitches while treating them as "melodic dissonances," creating "blue note" effects; and, perhaps most importantly, in a kind of relaxed yet intense energy that resists quantification. Both "Hey Good Lookin'" ("if you wanna have fun come *along* with me") and (especially) "Lovesick Blues" ("*I got a feeling called the* blues, *Oh Lord,* since my baby *said goodbye*") exhibit bluesy melodic inflection to a greater extent than "Walking the Floor." Williams exploits these blues effects to a higher degree than most of the other popular country singers of the 1940s, who, even when singing "blues," tend to downplay the importance of "blue notes."[42]

The subject of blues influences on Tubb and Williams raises the issue of the interrelationship during the forties between country music and R&B. While the subject of stylistic borrowings and interconnections between white and black southern musicians is far too vast to illuminate with any sort of satisfactory detail in this chapter, one of the commonplaces of country music history asserts that Williams, along with a few others such as the Delmore Brothers, injected musical elements derived from the blues and African-American music in a way that had not been as evident in country music previous to his first recordings. Moreover, Williams' group, the Drifting Cowboys, approaches rhythm and functional harmony in a manner strongly resembling that of contemporaneous African-American blues and jazz ensembles: rhythmically, with cross-accents, delays, and anticipations over a steady "metronomic" pulse either implied or stated; and harmonically, with improvised or semi-improvised polyphony verging at times on heterophony creating strong moment-to-moment dissonance over a slow harmonic rhythm. One of Williams' most extreme ventures into this heterophonic approach, "Move It On Over" (1947), is displayed in example 3.5. The obbligato fiddle part creates strong clashes with the vocal part and the bass; at the same time, none of these parts merely duplicates the pitches reiterated by the rhythm guitar part (the marvelous coordination of the phrasing between fiddle and voice also contributes strongly to the effect of this passage). The polyphonic/heterophonic texture has more in common in some respects with New Orleans jazz, or the 1930s recordings of Billie Holiday, than it does with either "Hey Good Lookin'" or a contemporaneous "jump" blues such as Louis Jordan's "Choo Choo Ch-Boogie" (1946), both of which contain only two strongly audible moving lines: the voice (or solo instrument during the breaks) and the bass (and similar textures can be found in early "hillbilly" recordings as well). However, even the spare textures of these last two numbers create the vertical dissonance that characterizes much African-American popular music.

One might conclude that this resemblance between white "hillbilly" musicians and black musicians resonates with the widespread practice of white popular musicians who drew on black popular music to reinvest their music with novel or authentic effects, resulting in a surge of popularity for those who appropriated these effects skillfully (or quickly).

This would be a hasty conclusion because, unlike the successive turns to "jazz," "swing," and "rock 'n' roll" in "mainstream popular" music, blues, rhythm and blues, and country have long shared a mutual pool of resources. Rather than "appropriation," "reconnection" might better describe the resurgence of blues influences in country music in the late 1940s. It should be mentioned, however, that these resources were not always necessarily shared between black and white musicians; one could argue that all these similarities, be they "appropriations," "expropriations," or "reconnections," are merely a covert form of blackface minstrelsy; and these arguments would have a point that hits surprisingly close to home: blackface minstrelsy survived quite openly into the 1930s in hillbilly music, with widespread public acceptance of this practice illustrated by the "Minstrelsy" column which *Billboard* continued to publish until June 10, 1939, as well as by the blackface interludes in the *Grand Ole Opry* which continued throughout the thirties.[43]

Moreover, any mention of "shared resources" between black and white musicians without a discussion of "shared" or "hoarded" rewards omits a large part of the story; and much literature on Williams and country music labors to reassure its readers of the reciprocal nature of relations between white country musicians and black musicians. If we explain the story of minstrelsy as an endless displacement of white fears/desires of miscegenation, black male potency, and a concern with the economics of slavery itself,[44] we can recognize the myriad forms this fear/desire assumes in Williams' biographies: in tales both of Williams' prowess as a blues singer and of the recognition of this prowess by black audiences; in obsessive ruminations on Williams' relationship with Rufe Payne; in the assertion that a recitation that Williams recorded as Luke the Drifter, titled "The Funeral," was responsible for his popularity with black audiences, an assertion that seems unlikely given the gross stereotypes of the black characters presented in the recitation (which depicts the funeral for a young black boy at a black church – Williams here performs a kind of auditory blackface as he conveys the sermon in the "voice" of a black preacher); in the description of a large black turnout for Williams' own funeral and of large black audiences for his performances on *The Louisiana Hayride*; in the reiterated assurance that Williams symbolically reimbursed Payne by recording "My Bucket's Got a Hole in It," a song which he learned from Payne, but which is sometimes credited to Williams, who may have received publishing royalties for it; in the "minstrelization" of the biographical texts themselves as the authors slip into black dialect to describe Williams' encounters with black musicians and audiences (e.g., the passage that begins this chapter).[45] As mentioned

Example 3.5: *"Move It On Over"*

Transcription by David Brackett

Note: voice, guitar, and bass all sound an octave lower than written.

earlier, these allusions to Williams' encounters with "blackness" form a recurring theme in the biographical literature, a theme which may mask a guilty recognition that a debt remains unpaid.

IV

The emergence of "country-western"

We have already noted some of the changes that occurred in the most widely played country recordings in the decade preceding Williams' startling burst of popularity. In addition to these changes, during the

1940s the crooning singing styles of Cliff Bruner, Ted Daffan, Tex Ritter, and Elton Britt shifted to the straining, speech-like, often nasal tones favored by Molly O'Day, Roy Acuff, Little Jimmy Dickens, not to mention Tubb and Williams. A "house" band was established at Nashville's Castle Studios around 1946, which featured the same instrumentation used by Williams on his recordings and from which musicians were drawn who accompanied him on his earliest recordings. This instrumentation had been featured in recordings of Tubb's Texas Troubadours in the early 1940s and functioned much like a small version of a Western swing band (which could include up to seventeen musicians); these groups commonly contained a fiddle, steel guitar, lead or "take-off" guitar, rhythm guitar, bass, and sometimes piano. Paralleling the shift to blues influenced styles were the increasing number of "boogie" style recordings made by groups such as the Delmore Brothers, Arthur Smith, and the Maddox Brothers and Rose. By the early fifties, honky-tonk singers such as Lefty Frizzell, Hank Thompson, and Webb Pierce all used ensembles like Williams' Drifting Cowboys and sang in "untrained" voices close in timbre to their speaking voices.

It is impossible to imagine some of the singers who achieved popularity in the early fifties – including Frizzell, Thompson, Pierce, Kitty Wells, Ray Price – without the horizon of possibilities created in part by Hank Williams. Yet, to understand the effect of his songs, it is perhaps most important to understand the differences and similarities between Williams and his contemporaries at the moment of his first recordings. Besides skillfully manipulating the honky-tonk ballad, he powerfully presented many components of country music – blues elements, boogie-type tunes, carousing and drinking songs, yodeling – that had been less prominent during the late thirties and early forties in country music's move towards broader acceptance and its resultant emphasis on crooning, Western and ersatz-cowboy songs, bands with accordions, patriotic songs, and novelty numbers. In this way, he participated in the reversal of the trend in country music towards eradicating its "wild side of life," of which there are numerous examples: Jimmy Davis, one-time singer of songs such as "She's a Hum Dum Dinger from Dingersville" (1930) and "Tom Cat and Pussy Blues" (1932), by 1940 was holding public office in Louisiana (he was elected governor in 1944, and again in 1960, this time on a segregationist platform) and crooning "You Are My Sunshine"; Roy Acuff, host of the *Grand Ole Opry* from its inception as a nationally sponsored show (1939) and an upholder of puritanical morality, at one time (1936) recorded "Doin' It the Old Fashioned Way" as a member of the "Bang Boys."[46]

Besides marking the demise of *Billboard*'s minstrelsy column and the beginning of national broadcasts of the *Grand Ole Opry*, 1939 also marked the founding of Broadcast Music Incorporated (BMI), a publishing rights organization more hospitable to "hillbilly" songwriters than the American Society of Composers and Publishers (ASCAP), previously the sole publishing rights organization for popular songwriters; and it marked the inception of a "hillbilly" section in the "Record Buyer's Guide" in *Billboard* (known at the time as *The Billboard: The World's Foremost Amusement Weekly*), the same entertainment magazine that Williams perpetually carried in his pocket ten years later. Accompanying the chart (and making its first appearance) was a disclaimer declaring the absence of any records with "double-meanings." Hank Williams seemed to accept and promulgate this in his booklet, *How to Write Folk and Western Music to Sell*: "Don't write any song which might offend a certain class of people. You should avoid especially the offending of any religious groups or races . . . *Avoid writing songs that have or could have double meanings or could be interpreted in any indecent manner*" [my italics].[47] Faithful to his own advice, the libertine of Williams' rowdiest songs seems rather tame in comparison with either Davis' early thirties recordings or the wildest rockabilly of the fifties. These tame libertines were chastened further by the solemn sermons of Luke the Drifter. The commercial struggles of the country music industry to construct itself as wholesome and All-American created tensions that were managed more effectively at some times than at others. Williams, with a copy of *Billboard* nearby at all times, with his twin personae of the carouser and Luke, appears as a particularly visible marker of this tension as well as of the upheaval in the music industry: during the period in 1949 in which "Lovesick Blues" was number one, *Billboard* changed the "folk" chart to "Country and Western" and the "Race" charts (complemented by the "Harlem Hit Parade") to "Rhythm and Blues."

The view from Billboard

Thus far we have alluded to some of the changes in image and musical style in country music's quest for acceptance by a wider audience. Yet this tells only part of the story. How did the gatekeepers of the music industry respond to country music's bid for acceptance? If we take the staff writers of *Billboard* as mouthpieces for the New York-centered music establishment of the day, we find that the "mainstream" of the music industry responded with little enthusiasm to country music. The industry's response was notable for its almost total absence. However, the few articles about "hillbilly" music in the pages of *Billboard* in 1939 reveal a fascinating dual movement: reports of "hillbilly" music's popularity come from jukebox operators in Texas, Arkansas, Danville, Illinois, Denver, and Spokane, WA throughout 1939 in a column titled "What the Records Are Doing For Me." One example:

[from Geneva, NY] We would like very much to find some ork that really plays swing. The hottest number of Shaw's is still too slow. We also think that Bing Crosby could deliver much better on the pops if the accompaniment had a little sock and less semi-classical air . . . The best locations seem to like the hillbilly numbers.[48]

Yet this popularity – despite the fact that it is not limited to the region most often associated with country music at the time (and to a lesser extent currently), the South – does not show up in the general "Record Buying Guide" section of the magazine's popularity charts. On March 25, 1939, a separate "Hillbilly Records" category starts appearing, at first irregularly, then more steadily in the last issue of every month. Stylistic uncertainty reigns in the 1939 "hillbilly" charts as Freddie Schnicklefritz Fisher, a New York polka musician with a strong novelty orientation, appears as one of the most popular "hillbilly" acts of the year, charting three songs: "Horsey, Keep Your Tail Up," "They Go Wild, Simply Wild Over Me," and the "Sugar Loaf Waltz." By 1942, the dim protests in "What the Records Are Doing For Me" would cease to appear but, in their stead, the *Billboard* staff would occasionally reserve a section of their record review column for "Western and Race" records, a brief section reviewing all the recent releases in those categories.

Billboard's dismissal of "hillbilly" music extended beyond the diverted gaze of the "popularity" charts and the gradual silencing of the dissenting voices from the provinces; the New York-centric view of *Billboard* produced front-page articles such as the following:

NEW YORK, Feb. 27. Real hillbillies rarely have good night club acts, says Meyer Horowitz, who ought to know. Jewish and Italian hillbillies usually outshine all others on showmanship, he says.

The writer of the article proceeds to list the ethnic identities of the "unreal" hillbillies as "Spanish-American," "Indian," "Italian and Irish."[49] A month later, a *Billboard* writer, Harry Knotts, confidently predicts that "King Korn will find his once mighty barnyard kingdom swept from under his royal throne of corn cobs by a mere kid who in a few years has become a sensation – a kid named SWING." However, swing won't reach quite into the deep backwoods where "King Korn . . . will continue to rule for generations to come." This is because

the backwoodsman, like the hillbilly, will never swap his fiddle, jew's-harp, banjo and harmonica for even the most terrific brand of swingaroo. He is musically isolated, so to speak, from the modern musical world. He is that quaint person whom people in the cities often confuse with the farmer when they speak of "hick" or "rube." Actually the backwoodsman is a poor renter, in a way like the Southern sharecropper. And as he is very much in the minority in the barnyard country, let's forget him.[50]

This liquidation of the "hillbilly" curiously ignored signs of popularity of the hillbilly's music. Besides the weekly reports of "What the Records Are Doing For Me," other articles suggested that "King Korn" was thriving: for instance, on April 1, 1939 *Billboard* reported that station WSM of Nashville was the top radio station "exploiter" in terms of its ability to send musicians who were associated with the station around to *fifteen* different states for publicity. The article made no mention of the musicians or their music, yet we need not wonder too long: WSM was the home of the *Grand Ole Opry*. Another article on June 24, 1939 informed readers that the "Love Life of Hillbillies Brings WLS Over Million Letters Yearly." WLS was a "hillbilly" station broadcasting out of Chicago, which featured a show, *The National Barn Dance*, the inception of which (early 1924) predated the *Opry* by a year and a half.

Billboard continued to present their charts as the most "authentic means of ascertaining the most popular tunes in the country"; and as these charts indicated, there is little doubt that Bing Crosby was the most popular recording artist in 1939 by virtually every standard (confirmed by many reports in "What the Records Are Doing for Me"). Yet the combined signs tell us that because of its orientation the New York-centered music industry literally could not *perceive* the popularity of "hillbilly" music. In 1939 the music industry was set up to produce, promote, distribute, and above all *recognize the importance of* one kind of music only – the music centered around Tin Pan Alley.

Following the war, *Billboard's* interest in country music increased, resulting in the extensive exploration of two different themes: the first of these documents the increase and spread in popularity of "hillbilly" music. Most of the articles that describe this theme deal with one or more of the following aspects of country music's popularity: the spread of interest in country music to the Northeast; the popularity of the broadcast of the *Grand Ole Opry*; and the lucrative performances of country-based entertainers.[51]

The second theme explored extensively, and perhaps the one most pertinent for the readership of *Billboard*, was the disruptive effect of the new found popularity of country music on the various facets of the music industry. Here we find concern for the increasing difficulty that representatives of record companies were having exploiting "hillbilly" performers; in early 1946 "Yankee diskers" were already bemoaning the fact that the "Situation currently is so sharply reversed the diskers can't figure out what happened to the gullible zekes." The explanation for this shift?

most diskers blame the war for part of their troubles. Claim that ridge-runners and stump-jumpers all got into the war and in the course of their G. I. travels picked up enough metropolitan savvy to hoist their market value and asking price when they returned to the farm and mountainside.[52]

The insecurity of record company executives over losing this cheap source of labor is reflected by the conclusion of an article a year later: "Whole trend prompted one major disk exec to remark painfully that 'I expect in a short time to give *The Billboard* a story on how the country bumpkins are putting things over on us'."[53]

In contrast to articles that react with astonishment to the spread of the music of the "stump-jumper," by 1946 articles began appearing in *Billboard* that expressed sentiments which have subsequently become embedded in the mythos of country music: the music is simple and easily remembered; it comes from the heart; it was written by and for the ordinary people (except for many which "have been written by commercial writers and some corrupted by the South American influence"); the songs stress ordinary emotions; the music has changed little since it was "sung by people as they pioneered the country"; the increasing popularity, like the heightened business savvy of country musicians, is due to "the migration of the country dweller to the city during the war"; another factor is "the cognizance of the trend by show business."[54] This "credo" for country music appears buried in the back of *Billboard* in a special section (which was inaugurated in July, 1944) titled "American Folk Tunes: Cowboy and Hillbilly Tunes and Tunesters"; the placement of this section, with its serious treatment of "Cowboy and Hillbilly Tunesters" contrasts with the front-page articles about "ridge-runners."

By the end of the forties, the success of "hillbilly" music was sufficient to earn an article in the *Billboard Special Disk Jockey Supplement* which listed "a series of important trends [that] have occurred during the past 18 months to establish country music as one of the major segments of the amusement industry." Besides detailing changes in the music industry designed to capitalize on the popularity of country music, this article cites as a contributing factor "the consistency of farmers' incomes, due to federal subsidies, coming at a time when revenue for other kinds of music is declining."[55] James R. (Jim) Denny, a top executive in the Nashville music scene, in a 1954 article lists four factors that contributed to the increase in country music's popularity: "the creation of the singing star, a shift in national population, the growth of radio, and a decline in the quality of the popular music that flooded the country." According to Denny, the decline in the quality of popular music led people "to look for sincerity and freshness of expression."[56]

During this period, in *Billboard* and *Downbeat* positive assessments view the upsurge in country music's popularity as resulting from its sincerity, its simplistic appeal to the common American, its rootedness in traditional music. Assessments from the standpoint of the "popular music" industry view the success as an inevitable yet deplorable development, a development which reveals the degeneration of public taste, and one which threatens their control of the market. The only moral threat to the northern, urban, white population seems to be one of musical simplicity and cultural backwardness: the surprising eruption of "lowbrow" values into an otherwise "middlebrow" milieu, prompted probably by "population shifts" and perhaps even by federal subsidies for farmers.

This describes the larger commercial milieu that welcomed Hank Williams uneasily when he signed his first recording contract in 1946. By the early 1950s, his commercial potential was widely acknowledged, but only as a songwriter. Thus his songs reached the pop audience via renditions by Tony Bennett, Jo Stafford and Frankie Laine, and Rosemary Clooney, with his nasal drawl replaced by smooth crooning, and with studio orchestras substituted for the Drifting Cowboys. The last of these cover versions, "Your Cheatin' Heart" by Joni James, was released in 1953. It would be another two years before country or R&B tunes could sneak with any regularity through the gate to the pop audience.

As we have seen, the *Billboard* chart clutched by Williams in the epigraph had only recently come into existence, and had assumed a form similar to the one it bears today during the reign of "Lovesick Blues" at the top of the charts. That is to say, the music industry's idea of "popularity" was rapidly changing, as were its ideas about "country-western music." The industry's decisions to grant country music more legitimate status coincided with the ascent of Hank Williams' popularity. Many mechanisms were synchronized to bring the man who would become "the most important person in the history of country music"[57] to a wider audience than had heretofore been available to country musicians.

In addition to those changes in musical style already mentioned, moves were made in Nashville with an eye toward broadening country music's appeal: initial concessions to Tin Pan Alley included the increasing use of the now ubiquitous AABA song form, popularized by Williams and his publisher/collaborator Fred Rose (a former Tin Pan Alley composer himself) in "Hey Good Lookin'" and many other songs.[58] In terms of musical codes, we could describe the impact of Hank Williams during this period as influencing shifts in the general levels of "dialect" (reintroduction of and emphasis on "blues" elements) and style (a synthesis of previous codes resulting in a new country paradigm). At the connotative level, the exploitation of new forms (i.e., the AABA form) created the possibility of different kinds of structural contrast ("positional implications"); and the writing and performance of the "poetic" lyrics, and the tight links between lyrics and biographical details, led to new "emotive connotations" (intensified sincerity, less inhibited sensuality, devil-may-care hedonism).

The quest to account for Hank Williams' appeal returns us to the idea of "multiple voices": even in songs of Loss, we hear Desire; in songs of Desire we hear Loss. We hear the blues, old-timey tunes, unabashed vulnerability, carousing good times, fatalism, and hope. There is a breadth of appeal as well as depth – he evokes contradictory effects simultaneously. Once again, the concept of "multiple voices" used here differs from Bakhtin's, for the monologic, "official" discourse in this context against which we hear Williams is any populist discourse that attempts to present country music as a simplistic "voice of the people." Williams *did* become a "voice of the people," but only through introducing new elements, rearranging old ones, and, in short, by setting himself apart from "the people" through the expression of a unique world view. This point only illustrates that he functioned as a star in much the same fashion as other stars function in mass culture: by becoming an object of fantasy and identification for millions of people through the projection of difference.

At least part of Hank Williams' overpowering "authentic" effect can be explained by his use of blues and gospel influences, his unusual vocal flexibility, and his ability to articulate lyrical themes with unusual forcefulness and clarity. "Hey Good Lookin'" presented its trendy slang of "hot rod Fords," "goin' steady," and "cookin'," in tropes that permitted a representation of reality that still dominates country music to the present day. This complex articulation of metanarratives combined with a new synthesis of musical elements formed a fulcrum: it brought the honky-tonk style to its apex and it pointed forward to rockabilly while simultaneously becoming a marker of "authenticity" in its lyrics, instrumentation, and musical blend for the country music that followed; at the same time, it "reconnected" country music to aspects of its tradition that had been submerged since the mid thirties. Clearly, this "authentic effect" plays a vital role in the construction of an audience which perpetuates the Hank Williams myth: an audience that emerged during the 1940s in tandem with a centralized country music industry. Hank Williams looms above other country stars and elicits these "authentic" effects most powerfully through manipulating codes that in fact have a very broad and long historical resonance. In the words of country singer Faron Young, "He was the biggest change in the business. Before he came along, they were singing songs like 'Mama's Not Dead, She Just Quit Breathing'."[59]

CHAPTER FOUR

James Brown's "Superbad"
and the double-voiced utterance

::

JB was proof that black people were different. Rhythmically and tonally blacks had to be from somewhere else. Proof that Africa was really over there for those of us who had never seen it – it was in that voice.

Thulani Davis[1]

If there is any black man who symbolizes the vast differences between black and white cultural and aesthetic values, Soul Brother No. 1 (along with Ray Charles) is that man.

David Levering Lewis[2]

During the 1960s James Brown singlehandedly demonstrated the possibilities for artistic and economic freedom that black music could provide if one constantly struggled against its limitations . . . He was driven by an enormous ambition and unrelenting ego, making him a living symbol of black self-determination . . . Motown may have been the sound of young America, but Brown was clearly the king of black America.

Nelson George[3]

As the prefatory comments indicate, members of James Brown's audience equate him with the concept of difference. This difference is usually linked to various oppositions: black to white, African to European, abnormal to normal. The recurrent and persistent manner in which these oppositions are invoked reminds us that "blackness" has operated as the figure of difference *par excellence* in the New World since the first Africans touched ground in North America. This chapter will examine the discursive space in which the concepts of "blackness" and "African-American music" have been produced; it will then suggest how these concepts function in James Brown's 1970 recording, "Superbad."[4]

I

The discursive space of black music

The following discussion will summarize some aspects of the discourses that have circulated about African-American music, including those on the status of the black community and its relationship with the white community, on musical aesthetics, on the impact of ethnicity on aesthetics, and on the impact of community on reception. These discourses are found in slave narratives, personal diaries, manuals of religious instruction, correspondence of the clergy, magazines, and scholarly articles.[5]

This introductory section is a response to two criticisms that have been leveled at writers about African-American music: firstly, that to recognize something called "African-American music" is to engage in biological essentialism; and secondly, that writers (especially white ones) construct the idea of African-American music in order to create a romantic site for notions of "authenticity."[6] While these tendencies may appear in certain writings, if we examine the wealth of documents from 1680 to the present that describe African-American music-making, these documents reveal a discursively constructed notion of "African-American music" that does not rely solely on either an essentialized or a romanticized view. We must also realize that this "discursive formation" is not a static idea either, but rather one that is consistent in some respects while undergoing constant modifications.[7]

What is interesting, in addition to the consistency of musical description, is the consistency of the attitude of the white observers towards the phenomena they are describing (and most ante-bellum accounts either report the observations of whites directly or are transcriptions made by whites of statements by blacks). Even the earliest statements reflect the consternation of those who encounter a foreign ontology, a decidedly non-European squaring of representation and the object represented, of religious ends and means.[8] This perspective persisted during the Revolutionary War with further tales of "idleness, riot, wantonness and excess" among the slaves; and, after the Revolutionary War, an army general reported that he heard his slaves sing a war song in an African language during a visit to his plantation, causing panic to ensue among the whites.[9] The following signs of difference were observed by Henry Russell, an English musician who toured the United States from 1833 to 1841:

When the minister gave out his own version of the Psalm, the choir commenced singing so rapidly that the original tune absolutely ceased to exist – in fact, the fine old psalm tune became thoroughly transformed into a kind of negro melody; and so sudden was the transformation, by accelerating the time, that, for a moment, I fancied that not only the choir but the little congregation intended to get up a dance as part of the service.[10]

Carefully inscribed boundaries begin to blur as slow tempi accelerate into rapid tempi, "fine old psalm[s]" mutate into "a kind of negro melody," singing threatens to turn into dancing, and the choir merges with the "little congregation." A sense of usurped propriety is reinforced by reports of secular music-making from the 1830s that repeat, in incredulous tones, the stories of the slaves' capacity for communal and spontaneous creation, the "peculiar" form of call and response found in the sacred realm.[11]

During the Civil War, this instantaneous sense of community emerges clearly in Thomas Higginson's account of both secular and sacred musical creation among recently freed black men ("this mysterious race of grown-up children . . . whose graces seem to come by nature"):[12]

I always wondered about these, whether they had always a conscious and definite origin in some leading mind, or whether they grew by gradual accretion, in an almost unconscious way. In this point I could get no information, though I asked many questions, until at last, one day when I was being rowed across from Beaufort to Ladies' Island, I found myself, with delight, on the actual trail of a song. One of the oarsmen, a brisk young fellow, not a soldier, on being asked for his theory of the matter, dropped out a coy confession. "Some good speriuals," he said, "are start jess out o' curiosity. I been a-raise a sing, myself, once . . ."

Then he began singing, and the men, after listening a moment, joined in the chorus, as if it were an old acquaintance, though they evidently had never heard it before. I saw how easily a new "sing" took root among them.[13]

What comes through even in this report, which is apparently sympathetic, is the by now familiar sense of transgression: transgression of the boundaries that separated the European's sense of himself or herself from the objects viewed, as the sense of communality and spontaneity threatens to undo the distance between observer and the observed; transgression of the sense of music as something presented in an orderly fashion that represents something else: the public concerts of the early nineteenth century had begun to offer the musical performance as a representation of spiritual transcendence, available as a commodity.[14] And perhaps there is an additional sense of transgression here because the form of Otherness encountered refused to conform to images held previously of the slaves by the white men. Of course, the reverse could also be true: it's difficult to know what was observed *because* it conformed to previously held images of the slaves. Higginson uses the word "evidently" in the preceding description, but that in itself does not eliminate the possibility that the singers already knew either the song being sung or another one like it.

Many of the reports focus on the ineffectual actions of religious authorities who failed to imprint efficiently the disciplinary techniques of Protestantism, which, as we have observed earlier, included singing psalms in the proper fashion. The possibilities for discipline in religious instruction were well known to missionaries:

in 1842 Charles C. Jones observed with satisfaction that one of the advantages of teaching the slaves psalms and hymns "is that they are thereby induced to lay aside the extravagant and nonsensical chants, and catches and hallelujah songs of their own composing; and when they sing, which is very often while about their business or of an evening in their houses, they will have something profitable to sing."[15]

Reverend Jones typifies the frustration felt by missionaries over the African-Americans' inability to worship in the proper fashion, with "reverence and stillness," and without "demonstrations, . . . exclamations, . . . responses, or noises, . . . nor boisterous singing."[16] These statements exemplify the manner in which practices designed to objectify the slaves' experience, to organize it into a European sense of order, encountered a foreign mode of thought; they may also reveal a conscious awareness on the part of the slaves that their failure to accede to the Master's wishes would be cloaked under the guise of their radical Otherness and would therefore be largely invisible. That the African-Americans' approach to sacred music-making did not adhere to the model presented to them is revealed by the following account, which, although published in 1919, resembles numerous ante-bellum reports:

The preacher now exhorted his flock to prayer and the people with one movement surged forward from the benches and down onto their knees, every black head deep-bowed in an abandonment of devotion. Then the preacher began in a quavering voice a long supplication. Here and there came an uncontrolable cough . . . and now and again an ejaculation, warm with entreaty, "O Lord!" or a muttered "Amen, Amen" – all against the background of the praying, endless praying.

Minutes passed, long minutes of strange intensity. The mutterings, the ejaculations, grew louder, more dramatic, till suddenly I felt the creative thrill dart through the people like an electric vibration, that same half-audible hum arose – emotion was gathering atmospherically as clouds gather – and then, up from the depths of some "sinner's" remorse and imploring came a pitiful little plea, a real Negro "moan," sobbed in musical cadence. From somewhere in that bowed gathering another voice improvised a response: the plea sounded again, louder this time and more impassioned; then other voices joined in the answer, shaping it into a musical phrase; and so, before our ears, as one might say, from this molten metal of music a new song was smithied out, composed then and there by no one in particular and by everyone in general.[17]

While the repeated "ejaculations" of this passage, "the creative thrill" that "dart[s] through the people," may lead us to ponder whether the proximity of this musical description to other well-known stereotypes in the discursive formation of blackness is accidental, this proximity need only emphasize the sense of Otherness pervading even the most sympathetic reports of the era. This sense of Otherness manifests itself as well in the curious and somewhat contradictory mixture of condescension ("a pitiful little plea") and of attributions of naturalness to the musical process under observation ("emotion was gathering atmospherically as clouds gather").

Although many of the musical qualities and religious practices which so dismayed the religious authorities at the time are now ascribed to the retention of Africanisms, observers at the time such as the Reverend Robert Mallard blamed the impiety of the slaves on their imperfect imitation of the "Masters": "What better, indeed, could we expect of those who only imitate (somewhat exaggerating it, of course) the conduct of some of their masters, who should know better?"[18] It could not have helped that one of the ostensible fundamental processes of the slaves' religious procedures – catharsis through spirit possession – presented an ethos both horrific and compelling to white observers, who were at times reduced to hysteria and shame at having been so affected by "the energy of a people of simple and literal faith and strong and inflammable emotions."[19] Again, this horror seems to have been engendered by the apparent refusal of the slaves to conform to a European sense of order. The frustration here of the white observers seems to revolve around "objects" who do not seem to recognize themselves as either objects or subjects and who, furthermore, persist in practices such as "spirit possession," designed to dissolve subject/object boundaries.

Among many reports of unusual musicality within the slave community, especially notable is the attention paid to their voices and superior "natural" equipment. Informants range from Thomas Jefferson (*Notes on the State of Virginia* [1782]) to numerous plantation owners, to *Dwight's Journal of Music* (1856). Reports of the slaves' playful mockery abound, frequently interpreted by white folk of the time as ineptitude – apparently, these people did not recognize that the slaves' coded epithets were often directed towards them.[20] Accounts of the religious revivals and camp meetings during the first half of the nineteenth century attest to the unique and strong mode of singing employed by blacks compared to whites, regularly recognized as a special, musical talent; again, the tone of the reports makes clear the degree of investment that the reporters had in the idea of "natural talent." Similar comparisons were made (of white and black singing ability) as early as the mid eighteenth century by a minister who preached to a congregation of blacks and whites:

I cannot but observe, that the *Negroes*, above all the Human Species that ever I knew, have an Ear for Musick and a kind of extatic Delight in *Psalmody* . . . Sundry of them have lodged all night in my kitchen; and, sometimes, when I have awakened about two or three a-clock in the morning, a torrent of sacred harmony poured in my chamber."[21]

Observers recognized musical traits – conceptual and material – with remarkable consistency: the emphasis on group participation, on dance, bodily movement and expression; and on improvisation and antiphony. While these traits undoubtedly existed in contemporary European musical practice, these reports, by both black and white observers, were produced within a discourse that emphasized "difference." One strategy for creating and reinforcing that gap was to emphasize the African-Americans' origins. In 1845, James Fenimore Cooper described the celebration of Pinkster Day, a holiday of Dutch origin:

Nine tenths of the blacks of the city [New York], and of the whole country within thirty or forty miles, indeed, were collected in thousands in those fields, beating banjos [and African drums], singing African songs [accompanied by dancing]. The features that distinguish a Pinkster frolic from the usual scenes at fairs . . . however, were of African origin. It is true, there are not now [1845], nor were there then [1757], many blacks among us of African birth; but the traditions and usages of their original country were so far preserved as to produce a marked difference between the festival, and one of European origin.[22]

The discourse on "difference" could obviously embrace topics such as ancestry, physical attributes, customs and rituals, and sense of community. Interesting, as well, is the way in which synchronic "difference" emerges from ostensible efforts to create a discourse of diachronic "sameness": certain figures – stereotypes, if you will – crop up with regularity in the reports of abolitionists, philanthropic ministers, and musicologists vouching for the impact of spirituals.

Who were these observers and what were the contexts for their observations? They included white slave-owners who attested to the slaves' cheerful spirits and love of singing; Frederick Douglass, who, having experienced life under the gaze of the slave-owners, attested to the slave-owners encouraging the slaves to sing and then subsequently portraying falsely the slaves' joy in doing so; Thomas W. Higginson, a white officer in the Union Army, who led a black regiment of freedmen, an abolitionist who claimed that the black race possessed talent, though undoubtedly "of a different kind and type" from white folks; Mary Boykin Chestnut, a southern white woman who "happened" to appear in the slaves' place of worship on her plantation, subsequently to observe and chronicle ("It was a little too exciting for me"); European men and women like Fredrika Bremer, who were curious about the people of African descent, often marvelling at the slaves' musical abilities; or Elizabeth Kilham, a white southern schoolteacher writing a series of picturesque articles for *Putnam's Magazine* after the Civil War.[23]

Over and over again, we find hysteria in the blurred space where the boundaries between observer and object threaten to dissolve in the face of a "way of life" that does not present itself as an exhibit of some previously extant structure, of some anterior "reality" beyond itself. The practices of the African-Americans did not order themselves up so as to allow a gaze that could create a sense of the "real" in the space between representation and "reality."[24] Instead of simulated religious ecstasy – the "reality" of which could only lie beyond the religious service, or be described in the Scriptures, mediated by the minister in a sermon – the white observers beheld a service that did not "present" itself as distant from a "real" spiritual experience. This is not to say that African-Americans were somehow closer to nature than white Americans; it is merely to say that what the white observers beheld did not present itself in a way that they could comprehend as ordered.

There is also a danger here in viewing slave life as a form of depoliticized "resistance": whether it be through an apparent lack of a subject/object split in slave ontology or through practices such as parody or irony, by taking this view we may forget to recognize that whatever space for resistance existed, existed as one of the effects of a larger disciplinary technology. The economy of the southern United States played an important role in the developing textile industry and this industry, in turn, relied on the cheap labor of Others, be they (East) Indians, Egyptians, or African-Americans, all non-Europeans who came to be objectified during the nineteenth century.[25]   The resistance of African-Americans therefore occurred in a space in which it functioned as part of a larger apparatus and remained invisible for the most part (except for actual physical revolts) to European observers. At the same time, and as part of the same mechanism, it is important to recognize that the simultaneous differential in power relations, the persistent segregation and discrimination, and the African-American deployment of covert tactics designed to salvage a sense of self-mastery, family history, and traditional cultural practices, preserved a sense in which African-American difference could persist, retain positive connotations, and remain largely unrecognized by Euro-Americans.[26]

African-American music as a musicological subject

Attempts in the twentieth century to describe African-American music did so first in the context of the African-retention-vs.-European-acculturation controversy and in terms of style traits.[27] Arguing for the African retention hypothesis, Richard Alan Waterman identified the following traits in African-American music: metronome sense, dominance of percussion, polymeter, off-beat phrasing, and overlapping call-and-response patterns.[28] Even in these early studies the artificiality of the dichotomy between the "musical" and the "conceptual" becomes apparent, as Waterman noted the lack of a division between the sacred and the secular as an important component in African-American musical life.[29] Beginning in the 1960s – with Charles Keil's "appropriation-revitalization process" – and continuing through the 1970s – with Olly Wilson's "shared conceptual approach" between West African and African-American music – we can see the shift from the earlier emphasis on style traits to a concern with attitudes towards music-making. Keil proposed, in his appropriation-revitalization process, that each form of African-American pop music becomes "more African in its essentials" in response to the previous style's "appropriation" into Euro-American pop music.[30] Wilson sought to modify this by emphasizing that it is not simply that African-American music is becoming "more African in its essentials" – which in Keil's formulation implied that Africanisms in African-American music are a static body of practices that will eventually be depleted – but rather, that the manifestation of African qualities in African-American music is potentially infinite, as are the forms this manifestation may take.[31] Wilson attempted to bring the trait of polymeter under the rubric of the "conceptual approach": "if one assumes that the essence of the multi-meter practice is the clashing of rhythmic accents or the creation of cross-rhythms (and not the manner in which this is produced), then the incidence of multi-meter in Afro-American music is large."[32]   Writers who accept Wilson's premise of a shared conceptual approach locate the following topics that such an approach might include: emphasis on communal, participatory music-making; delivery style, sound quality, and mechanics of delivery; and the above-mentioned conflation of the secular and sacred.[33]   Gospel music in particular is presented as a "reservoir of cultural resources that contributed to the development of black popular music."[34]   The notion of a "conceptual approach" – perhaps because it eludes quantification and hence certain normative notions of legitimacy – is useful in that it allows for a range of analytic descriptions that do not attempt to reify the fluidity of the concept "African-American music."

In the 1980s, scholars working in African-American literature developed theories drawing on black vernacular rhetorical figures. Houston Baker, Jr., in his *Blues, Ideology, and Afro-American Literature: A Vernacular Theory* (1984), organized his theory around a "blues matrix," while Henry Louis Gates, Jr., in *The Signifying Monkey: A Theory of African-American Literary Criticism* (1988), designated the term "Signifyin(g)" as the black "trope of tropes."   Samuel A. Floyd, Jr. has recently proposed a theory derived from the literary work of Gates and Baker and from the historical work of Sterling Stuckey, a theory which seeks to ground analysis of black music in the musical practices of the black vernacular.[35]   Floyd, drawing upon Stuckey, asserts that these practices were present in protean form in the ring shout. In the ring, the participants circle about counterclockwise in a shuffling motion, usually accompanied by a spiritual and a steady percussive rhythm generated by hand-claps or foot-pats.[36]   Floyd describes the musical elements of the spiritual which developed within the ring shout:

These included elements of the calls, cries, and hollers; call-and-response devices; additive rhythms and polyrhythms; heterophony, pendular thirds, blue notes, bent notes, and elisions; hums, moans, grunts, vocables, and other rhythmic-oral declamations, interjections, and punctuations; off-beat melodic phrasings and parallel intervals and chords; constant repetition of rhythmic and melodic figures and phrases (from which riffs and vamps would be derived); timbral distortions of various kinds; musical individuality within collectivity; game-rivalry; hand-clapping, foot-patting, and approximations thereof; and the metronomic foundational pulse that underlies all Afro-American music.[37]

Besides noting that elements of this description resemble the quantitative and qualitative aspects observed by Waterman and Wilson, it is also important to note that Floyd emphasizes the absolute interconnection of physical movement, dancing, and music-making.

Floyd contends that the "musical practices of Stuckey's ring can provide the means for discourse on the musical performances of which they came to be a part" (pp. 270–71). Just as Gates' Signifyin(g) contains within it many forms of black vernacular speech, so does the ring shout contain the musical figures of the black vernacular. Furthermore, according to Floyd, "genres also Signify on other genres" (and we have already glimpsed how this can work in Billie Holiday's recording of "I'll Be Seeing You"), a practice which helps explain the relationship of African-American musical practice to European musical forms. Different types of musical Signifyin(g), derived from the shout, include the following:

(1) when an instrument performs a kind of sonic mimesis as in the instrumental "response" in a blues;

(2) cutting contests;

(3) use of vernacular in concert music; and

(4) the presence of "swing," which occurs "when sound-events Signify on the time-line, against the flow of its pulse, making the pulse itself lilt freely . . . the effectiveness of the Signifyin(g) tropes of black music can be measured in part by the extent to which they create and contribute to [a feeling of swing]" (pp. 271–73).

Floyd proposes the term "Call-Response" as the African-American musical "trope of tropes" analogous to Gates' literary concept of Signifyin(g). Floyd's Call-Response is not the same thing as "call and response"; rather, it is a term meant "to convey the dialogical, conversational character of black music" (p. 277). It contains within it the musical practices found within the ring. Its primary value as an analytical concept is that it functions as a source pool of black vernacular musical practices and seeks to relate those practices to a wide range of music associated with African-Americans.

One of the qualities adumbrated above, repetition, is elevated to a position of ontological importance as a distinctive marker of "black" and "European" cultural difference by James A. Snead.[38] He begins with Hegel's nineteenth-century comparison of African and European culture: Hegel disparages "the African" for not being goal-oriented enough because he or she lives "in the moment." Snead claims that black culture accepted the inevitability of repetition as a form of beauty while, during the nineteenth century in particular, European culture attempted to cover up repetitive cycles (as in nature) and present repetitive occurrences as accumulations. Snead uses the term "cut" to describe what he considers to be the truest expression in music of black culture's acceptance of repetition:

The "cut" overtly insists on the repetitive nature of the music, by abruptly skipping it back to another beginning which we have already heard. Moreover, the greater the insistence on the pure beauty and value of repetition, the greater the awareness must also be that repetition takes place not on a level of musical development or progression, but on the purest tonal and timbric level.[39]

Repetition and the "cut" are what make improvisation possible, since the improviser relies on recurrence on several levels: the beat, the ostinato, the harmonic sequence. "Progress in the sense of 'avoidance of repetition' would at once sabotage such an effort."[40]

Indeed, one can find the "cut" inscribed within *all* black vernacular forms, from the ring to rap. A quick survey of representative forms will confirm this: the blues, with its three phrase, twelve-bar, AAB phrase-cycle; "Rhythm" changes (the harmonic progression based on Gershwin's "I Got Rhythm") in jazz, and especially in bebop, the AABA, thirty-two-bar form of which at extremely fast tempi begins to assume a similar experiential cast as the AAB form of the blues, with one phrase added (that is, it becomes a four-phrase, thirty-two-bar form); the ostinato vamp at the end of gospel songs and most soul songs, which allows for vocal/instrumental improvisations of increasing intensity causing a corresponding shift in the music to a higher energy level; the short ostinatos of funk which allow for the same kind of improvisational intensity, now dispersed across the entire song; and the samples of rap, which create their "cuts" on two levels: the ostinatos formed from the samples and the intertextual repetition of previously recorded and circulated material.[41]

Since repetition exists within European art music, traditional music, and nineteenth-century popular music, how may we distinguish between the types of repetition identified with African-American music and those identified with European music? Richard Middleton distinguishes between what he calls "musematic" (or "epic-lyric") and "discursive" (or "narrative-lyric") structures of repetition. Although overlapping to some degree, musematic repetition is marked by the riff or ostinato and is more typical of African-American forms. On the other hand, discursive repetition is characterized by repetition of contrasting phrases, "narrative" harmonic sequences, a teleological orientation, and is more typical of European popular and traditional forms.[42] For an example of the way the former can be superimposed upon the latter, we may think of the arrangement of blues changes, "rhythm" changes, or other thirty-two-bar Tin Pan Alley compositions in a large band format: musematic repetition in the form of riffs of various lengths (cymbal patterns, call-and-response horn parts, rhythmic punctuations) creates a sense of the "cut" within the larger discursive repetition of the harmonic pattern.

The preceding discussion of historical and musicological discourses on black music demonstrates that there are some widely shared ideas about what constitutes "African-American music," some of which have circulated for over 300 years. These ideas have been used as a means of domination – when they functioned as stereotypes and emphasized the "non-human" or "primitive" qualities of African-Americans – or alternatively as a source of identification, communal strength, and solidarity. The positive and negative uses of the idea of "black music" have been available to members of many racial and ethnic groups; this tempers charges of essentialism (i.e., the idea that "black music" is music made by black people), although some subject positions are more likely to be available to members of some groups than others. As for the charges of romanticism, simply admitting that a concept such as "black music" exists need not mean that the music is any more or less "authentic" than any other kind of music. With our sense of the values and elements associated with black music, let us turn to a recording by James Brown, one of the performers most tightly linked to the idea of black music in the sixties and seventies.

II

Signifyin(g) – words and performance

Example 4.1: Lyrics of "Superbad"

Introduction:	1	Watch me, watch me
	2	I got it, watch me, I got it, yay
A1:	3	I got something that makes me want to shout
	4	I got something that tells me what it's all about.
	5	Huh! I got soul and I'm Superbad
	6	I got soul and I'm Superbad.
A2:	7	Now I got a mood that tells me what to do
	8	Sometimes it feels, Hah!
	9	Now I got a mood that tells me what to do
	10	Sometimes I feel so nice, I want to try myself [a few?].
	11	I got soul and I'm Superbad, Huh!

A3:   12   I love, I love to do my thing, ah
       13   And I, and I don't need no one else.
       14   Sometimes I feel so nice, good God!
       15   I jump back, I wanna kiss myself
       16   I got soul – huh! – And I'm superbad
       17   Hey!   Said I'm superbad – Bridge, come on!

B1:   18   Up and down, and round and round
       19   Up and down, all around.
       20   Right on people, let it all hang out
       21   If you don't brothers and sisters
       22   Then you won't know, what it's all about
       23   Give me, give me, etc.

A4:   24   (sax solo) Unh! Come on!
       25   I got that something that makes me want to shout
       26   I got that thing, tells me what it's all about.
       27   I got soul, and I'm superbad.
       28   I got the move, that tells me what to do
       29   Sometimes I feel so nice, said I wanna [try myself a few].
       30   I, I, etc.
       31   I got soul, and I'm superbad. Bridge! With me!

B2:   32   Up and down and all around.
       33   Right on people, let it all hang out,
       34   If you don't brothers and sisters
       35   then you won't know, what it's all about.
       36   Give me, give me, etc.

A5:   37   (sax solo) Unh, come on, come on, Robert, etc.

B3:   38   Good God! Up and down and all around.
       39   Right on people, ayy; let it all hang out.
       40   If you don't brothers and sisters
       41   then you won't know what it's all about.
       42   Said give me, give me, etc.
       43   Right on people, let it all hang out,
       44   Don't know, what it's all about.
       45   I'm Superbad, I'm Superbad.
       46   Early in the morning, about noon,
       47   right on brother, make it soon.
       48   In the evening, I get my groove,
       49   got the soul, got to move.
       50   I've got it, I've got it!
       51   Said I'm superbad.
       52   Do your thing Robert (sax solo) Superbad.
       53   Fellas, I need some power, [yeah], soul power.
       54   Gimme, gimme, etc.[43]

A quick glance at the lyrics (example 4.1) introduces us to a discursive universe far removed from the poetry of Western art song, the urbane witticisms and sentimentality of Tin Pan Alley, and the folksy, anecdotal narrative of country-western music. The linguistic content in "Superbad" raises the issue of differences in the role and use of language, specifically in rhetorical styles and performances, between "Black English" and "Standard English."

Let us first begin by examining ways in which socio-linguists have attempted to define African-American linguistic practice with respect to Euro-American practice. Socio-linguist Roger D. Abrahams describes it in the following fashion:

Blacks differ from other American groups in the varieties of speech they employ and in the ways they use these varieties in carrying out the ritual (predictable) dimension of their personal interactions. Or, to put it in Hymes' terms for speech community, they "share rules for the conduct and interpretation of speech, and rules for the interpretation of at least one linguistic variety."

We recognize, then, this sense of community in Black speaking in a great many ways – not least of which is the kind and intensity of talk about talk which one encounters in conversations and the special in-group names given by the speakers to ways of talking . . . There is thus a ground-level recognition of speaking differences among Blacks that gives the idea of a distinct speaking community a sense of analytic reality.[44]

Abrahams appeals here to a notion of the community's recognition of itself as a distinct community, manifested in speech styles and the "kind and intensity of talk about talk." In light of the discussion at the beginning of the chapter, Abrahams could well have included the European's recognition of a distinct community as a constituent feature of the idea of the African-American speech community. That is, the idea of an "African-American community" is not a static, essentialized concept, but rather one that is constituted discursively (and of course, in a fluid manner, physically) both by those who belong to it and those who don't. Abrahams proceeds to list a series of binary style traits in an attempt to distinguish between what he terms Standard English (SE) and Black English (BE). He summarizes these linguistic differences as follows: emphasis on the *sound* of the words (BE) rather than on their meaning (SE); speech as a performance or a game (BE) rather than an act of information giving (SE); patterns of expression without clear distinctions between performer and audience (BE) as against patterns of expression with clear distinctions between performer and audience (SE);

conversations which are consciously stylized (BE) as against conversations which are unplanned, spontaneous (SE); performance as a process (BE) rather than performance as a thing (SE).[45] While this description taken at face value risks essentializing linguistic differences along racial boundaries – differences that could not be rigidly maintained upon close scrutiny of actual linguistic practices in "white" and "black" communities – the traits listed by Abrahams do resonate with tropes of difference such as Gates' Signifyin(g), Baker's Blues Matrix, and, in music, Floyd's Call-Response. The pertinence of these tropes to the study of African-American music lies in their ability to function as part of a potential "associative" homology between African-American social values and music; in other words, "the network of connective meanings built up within black culture over generations,"[46] which produce subject positions that will be more accessible to African-Americans than to members of other groups.

Henry Louis Gates, Jr.'s theory of Signifyin(g) relies as well on a dualistic notion of BE and SE similar to Abrahams'. Since a good deal of the analysis in this chapter is based on Gates' theory (as well as on Floyd's Call-Response, which in turn depends heavily on Gates), a brief explanation is in order. Gates identifies the term "Signifyin(g)" as the black rhetorical "trope of tropes," a term which subsumes the many varieties of black rhetorical strategies – that is, African-American linguistic difference as it manifests itself in speech, and in oral and written narratives. Gates describes the difference between the black linguistic sign "Signification" (which he denotes in upper case) and the standard English sign "signification" (which he denotes with lower case) as the difference between paradigmatic and syntagmatic relations.[47] The emphasis on paradigmatic relations means that speakers (or writers) "draw on . . . figurative substitutions" that "tend to be humorous, or function to name a person or a situation in a telling manner" (p. 49).

The text of "Superbad" embodies the difference between these uses of the term "Signification" as well as between Black English and Standard English (as described by Abrahams): in "Superbad" we find an extreme emphasis on the materiality of the signifier, an almost complete lack of emphasis on narrative and on syntagmatic or chain-like continuity. So much of what others have described as free association and non sequiturs results from this emphasis on sound.[48]

Another highly important aspect of Signification that figures prominently in the text of "Superbad" is what Gates terms "intertextuality."[49] This type of intertextuality stresses the creative use in oral narration of "formulaic phrases" rather than the creation of novel content. The emphasis, then, in these narratives – including "toasts," casual conversations, preaching, and other forms of public speaking – is on reusing and recombining stock phrases in an original way from one context to another rather than on creating phrases that are strikingly original in themselves. Similarly, evaluations of performers depend not so much upon the ability of the narrator "to dream up new characters or events" but rather "to group together two lines that end in words that . . . bear a phonetic similarity to each other" (pp. 60–61). This concept of intertextuality provides a key to understanding the text of "Superbad." Beginning with the title word, "Superbad," formulaic phrases of BE slang permeate the song: "what it's all about," "I got soul," "I love to do my thing," "jump back," "Right on people," "let it all hang out," "brothers and sisters," and "I need some soul power." The importance of the ability to end lines with two words that sound alike is certainly evident; at times this seems to influence strongly certain lines of the text. The first two verses, comprising lines 3–6 and 7–10, have an a-a-b-b rhyme scheme; this changes to an a-b-c-b pattern in the third verse, lines 12–15, presumably to increase the emphasis on the striking phrase, "I jump back, I wanna kiss myself," in line 15.[50] This parallels a tendency that Gates has detected in the "Signifying Monkey" poems in which "disturbances in the rhyming schemes often occur to include a particularly vivid or startling combination of signifiers" (p. 61).

Another factor contributing to the proliferation of meanings is the importance of *delivery*; that is, the manner of delivery profoundly affects the semantic content. Nowhere is this more apparent than in the title itself, particularly the "bad" part of it. This exemplifies what Gates has observed as one of the primary qualities of black discourse, what he terms (after Bakhtin) the "double-voiced" utterance: the manner in which a word can partake simultaneously of both black and white discursive worlds (pp. 50–51).[51] These semantic shifts occur primarily through changing inflection. The semantic reversal of the term "bad" may also be due to the glorification of the outlaw or badman in the black community, perhaps because the badman/hustler figure refuses to be defined by white discourse.[52] In general, Gates sees this disruption of "the signifier . . . displacing its signified" as "an intentional act of will" most notably present in the term "Signification" itself (p. 51). In this context, the act of titling a song "Superbad" appears as a celebration of black difference, as a refusal to be defined by white attitudes.

Another striking aspect of the text is the hyberbolic glorification of self. This too is a familiar strategy in African-American rhetoric. Roger D. Abrahams, in his study of African-American urban folklore, termed this identification of the narrator with the hero of the narrative, the "Intrusive I."[53] Brown indulges this rhetorical device to the extreme in "Superbad," except for in the bridge (sections **B1**, **B2**, **B3**; lines 18–22, 32–35, 38–44), in which he addresses the audience. The narrator instructs the audience/band members with his first words to "watch" him, and continues to proclaim repeatedly that he has "soul" and that he's "Superbad." All the lines except the aforementioned lines in the bridge continue this strategy, which perhaps reaches its apex in lines 14 and 15 (already referred to in a different context): "Sometimes I feel so nice, good God!/I jump back, I wanna kiss myself." More evidence of the "Intrusive I" can be found in line 30, which consists of only the pronoun (we could even say vowel sound) "I," and lines 23, 36, 42, and 54, which consist of the phrase "give me" (or "gimme") repeated up to twenty-four times (line 42). Besides creating an identification between narrator and hero, this performance implies a second identification: that of James Brown with the narrator/hero. In the words of Nelson George, Brown possessed an "unrelenting ego, making him a living symbol of black self-determination . . . Brown was clearly the king of black America." Unlike the toasts analyzed by Abrahams, "Superbad" contains no hint of narrative; there is really no hero with whom the narrator can identify except for Brown himself. Statements such as the quotation by Nelson George at the beginning of the chapter indicate that this interpretation would probably have occurred to a large part of Brown's 1970 audience as well. The implications of this in terms of authorship are clear: more so than in the cases of Billie Holiday or Hank Williams, "Superbad"'s textual voices emphasize their identity with "James Brown."

Performance/environment

Two qualities mentioned by both Gates and Abrahams in their attempts to differentiate Black English from Standard English are its emphasis on speech as performance rather than on speech as an act of information giving, and the tendency of speech acts to weaken the distinction between performer and audience. These two linguistic notions – of speech as performance and of the loss of distinction between audience and performer – have far-reaching implications for the analysis of "Superbad." Before exploring these implications directly, I would like to raise another issue that bears on the interpretation of "Superbad."

One Marxist critique of mass entertainment maintains that, in a capitalist society, a work of art masks its ideology by effacing the means of its production; in other words, hiding the means of production serves to "naturalize" the text. The Brechtian notion of "distanciation" argues that conscious reference to the means and contingent conditions of producing art will expose the ideology behind it. In other words, calling the audience's attention to the discrepancy between a representation and the "real" object represented should expose the artificiality of a society based on a notion of reality that depends on representation.[54] "Superbad"'s relationship to "distanciation" is a curious one: on the one hand, this particular recording effaces the signs of its own production, overdubbing audience sound to simulate a live recording.[55] This contrasts with the way studio recordings typically efface the signs of their production by seeking to minimize the effect of human *performance*: individual mistakes can be re-recorded, weak voices bolstered, "thin" accompaniments "sweetened" by additional instruments. "Superbad," though effacing signs of its original studio production, emphasizes the recording as a performance: Brown instructs his "audience" to "watch" him; he exhorts the members of his band by name and engages in a call and response with them at the end of the song. Brown's vocals and the sax solos appear improvised: rather than presenting a safe, sanitized product, "Superbad" calls attention to its rough edges; it attempts to eliminate the distance between the original "performance" and the representation of that performance in the recording, rather than to exaggerate the sense of distance. While the effects of representation in "Superbad" possibly engender a sense of distance from the "mainstream" pop audience, they serve as an invitation for involvement with another – and Brown's principal – audience.[56] The crowd noise positions the listener at a live performance; the words "Watch me, watch me" invite the audience to scrutinize the performer; the identification of parts of the song (as when Brown calls out "bridge" in lines 17 and 31) gives an effect of immediacy, as though the course of the song were being decided spontaneously; this identification also directs attention toward the artifice of the song's structure. Although some of these qualities may intersect with those advocated by Brecht, Brown confuses the whole idea of aesthetic distance because of the ambiguous role of the opposition "spontaneity/artifice" in this text, and because of the differing demands of audiences within the African-American community, in which performer/audience interaction assumes a level of importance in a way that Brecht undoubtedly did not take into account. The importance of this interactive element coincides to some degree with Bourdieu's theory of working-class rejection of the aestheticizing tendencies of high art, that "pleasure purified of pleasure."[57]

There exists another level of relationship between "Superbad" and the African-American community: the manner in which the song, musically and lyrically, evokes the late 1960s movement known as "Black Nationalism." In the late sixties, Brown became known as "Soul Brother No. 1," due to his influence in the black community and the release of such "message" songs as "Papa's Got a Brand New Bag," "Don't Be a Drop Out," "Say It Loud – I'm Black and I'm Proud," and "Soul Power." Brown agreed to televise his Boston concert the evening after Martin Luther King, Jr.'s assassination on April 4, 1968, a decision that helped avert race riots in that city.[58] Many of the lyrics index slogans popular in the sixties "black power" movement: "right on, brother," "let it all hang out," "brothers and sisters," and, particularly evident in the closing call-and-response section – "I need some power – soul power." The manner of saxophone playing in the solo sections evokes styles of jazz players such as John Coltrane, Pharoah Sanders, and Albert Ayler, all players identified to some extent with the Black Nationalism movement.[59]

Before leaving this discussion of the performative aspects of James Brown's recording we must not fail to consider Brown's dancing, a duly celebrated aspect of his performances. Indeed, a viewing of a canonical concert film such as his performance in the TAMI show reveals the absolute centrality of his dance movements to the audience's reaction.[60] The audience in the TAMI show (a largely white, teenage audience, hardly the sort of audience Brown would have encountered at, say, the Apollo theater, and an audience probably less schooled in responding to his performance) responds perhaps more consistently to his flamboyant dance moves than to his musicianship. To some extent this is begging the point, for the two are not strictly separable. Clearly, his ability to communicate skillfully with his body movements constitutes a vital part of the overall impact of his performance. Brown's body presents, in a particularly intense form, the kind of reaction his music seeks to provoke from the audience. Brown becomes the site onto which the audience can project the desire to dance inculcated by the music.

Another crucial aspect of Brown's performance styles (live and recorded) from the audience's perspective is how Brown repeats and revises – that is, *Signifies* – on the black vernacular: his dancing, in its evocation of previous dance styles and in his revision of those styles, Signifies on the black dance tradition (both sacred and secular); his interaction with the audience, the "individuality within collectivity" mentioned by Floyd earlier, Signifies on black preaching styles and religious services; the lyrics themselves Signify upon the toasting and preaching traditions; the saxophone playing in "Superbad" Signifies on "free jazz"; and the sax playing, in conjunction with the phrases of vernacular associated with black power, Signifies on Black Nationalism.

III

Musical Signifyin(g)

Intertextuality and fragmentation

Towards the end of his chapter "Figures of Signification" in the *The Signifying Monkey*, Gates discusses the Count Basie composition "Signify" as a musical embodiment of Signifyin(g), that is, as a piece "structured around the idea of formal revision and implication."[61] Gates finds a parallel between African-American literature and music in what he calls the "trope of revision." The Basie composition "Signify" exemplifies this "trope of revision" by alluding to previous styles of piano playing in African-American music. By doing this, "Basie has created a composition characterized by pastiche. He has recapitulated the very tradition out of which he grew and from which he descended."[62] Many of James Brown's songs contain this sort of recapitulation, but Brown accomplishes this by referring both to other people's as well as to his own previous recordings, thus conflating the idea of Signifyin(g)/pastiche with the idea of the "Intrusive I." An example of this can be found in the introduction to "Lost Someone" from his famous recording *Live at the Apollo*, in which he recites a list of his previous recordings: "I'll Go Crazy," "Think," "Bewildered," "You've Got the Power," "I Don't Mind." In later recordings, such as "There Was a Time" and "Mother Popcorn," he recites a series of previous dance records – "The Mashed Potato," "The Jerk," "The Camel Walk," "The Boogaloo" – recorded or performed by himself or other black artists. Self-referentiality, in Brown's unique manifestation of the "Intrusive I," continues in such lines (from "There Was a Time") as "Sometimes I laugh, sometimes I clown/But you can bet, you haven't seen nothin' yet/till you see me do The James Brown."[63] This playful, ambiguous, substitutive, self-referential line gains another level of intertextuality when it occurs in "Cold Sweat" as well.

This kind of cross-referencing, itself a form of Signifyin(g), occurs frequently within African-American popular styles. Wilson Pickett's 1966 recording "Land of 1000 Dances" and Sly and the Family Stone's 1970 "Thank You (Falettinme Be Mice Elf Agin)" represent only two particularly notable examples of this practice from roughly the same period. "Land of 1000 Dances" references previous dance records by other artists and is itself a revision of previous recordings of the song, while "Thank You" recapitulates previous songs by Sly and the Family Stone. The title "Thank You (Falettinme Be Mice Elf Agin)," with its perverse spelling, is yet another form of Signifyin(g), this time upon "Standard English," a Signifyin(g) move which underlines the arbitrary relationship between signifier and signified on two different levels: the sonic and the visual.[64]

There are two main ways in which Brown enacts the "Signifyin(g)" practice of repetition and difference in musical terms in "Superbad." The first case may be termed an intertextual (following Gates' usage for rhetorical figures) referentiality: Brown, in the course of a performance, invokes other musical referents – in the form of songs, gestures, modes of performance, dances – which refer to other musical texts. In terms of musical codes, this takes place on the "primary" level of "auto-reflection." At the same time, this quotation technique evokes a community of listeners who can recognize the self-references. On the other hand, the previously mentioned allusions to Black Nationalism in the lyrics and saxophone solo are two of the ways Brown "Signifies" or comments on other texts in "Superbad" that may be understood as forms of "secondary signification": here we find connotations at the level of style.

The second form of Signifyin(g) that plays an important role in creating variety in this song is the repetition with variation of small musical figures: bits of text, a syllable, or a type of scream; basing an analysis on this form of Signifyin(g) has affinities with the method of paradigmatic analysis mentioned in the introduction. Example 4.2 displays five figures, lettered *a* through *e*. These figures create a "Signifyin(g)" commentary when they are repeated and varied in parallel parts of sections: for instance, figure *b* (which contains the words "I got soul") tends to occur towards the latter part of the A section of the piece, shown in lines 6, 11, and 16 in example 4.1. Another kind of Signifyin(g) occurs when a figure becomes detached from its initial place in the formal structure, thereby *revising* the meaning of the figure in the larger context of the song. Figure *d*, which consists of rhythmic manipulation of the word "gimme," exemplifies this procedure: it appears first towards the end of the **B1** section (the names and numbers of sections are shown in example 4.1), it appears a second time in a similar position toward the end of the second B section, but its third appearance occurs during the long sax solo in the **A5** section. Figure *d4* appears in the third B section closely parallel to its position in sections **B1** and **B2**; however, it is varied by being extended for twenty measures.

Example 4.2. *"Superbad": melodic figures a-e*
Transcriptions by David Brackett.

Figure *a*

Example 4.2 (*cont.*)

Figure *b*

Figure *c*

Example 4.2 (*cont.*)

Figure *c* (*cont.*)

Example 4.2 (*cont.*)

Figure *d*

Example 4.2 (*cont.*)

Figure *d* (*cont.*)

Figure *e*

Yet another important manner in which a performer can comment on an aspect of his or her performance is what Gates describes (again regarding the Basie composition "Signify") as "playing the upbeat into the downbeat of a chorus, implying their formal relationship by merging the two structures together to create an ellipsis of the downbeat" so that the performer is "free to 'comment' on the first beat of the chorus" with "the musical phrase . . . begin[ning] before the downbeat of the chorus and end[ing] after the downbeat."[65] At the level of coding, this refers to both "positional values" (the value of an element based on its syntactic position) and "positional implications" (connotations arising from structural position). Gates' idea of the downbeat/upbeat ellipsis was anticipated by Olly Wilson, who argued (referring specifically to the introduction of "Superbad") that these anticipations create an emphasis on the downbeat. The work of these authors suggests that the upbeat to the beginning of another repetition is a musical space of the utmost importance, the space for fills and melodic/rhythmic flourishes of all kinds. Almost all of the figures in example 4.2 tend to anticipate the downbeat. In many of the cases, the examples presented here confirm that interpretation, especially when the figures act as an explicit anacrusis to a downbeat as in figures *b* and *c* (and in the introduction which Wilson analyzed).[66] Many other cases exhibit a sense of play with the expectations of an emphasis on beat one. Figure *d* is a fine example: at times it fulfills the anacrusis function as in its last repetitions during *d1*; at other times it leaves the first beat completely empty; at still other times, as in *d4*, the figure is reshuffled in a complex manner which creates a sense of rhythmic disorientation. "These elastic phrases," writes Gates, "stretch the form rather than articulate the form. Because the form is self-evident to the musician, both he and his well-trained audience are playing and listening with expectation. Signifyin(g) disappoints these expectations; caesuras, or breaks, achieve the same function. This form of disappointment creates a dialogue between what the listener expects and what the artist plays."[67] However, the texted figures *b*, *c*, *d* tend to emphasize the downbeat so that these become the expected norm against which repetitions that do not follow this norm can be felt as exceptions. Other utterances that might be considered marginal from a Eurocentric viewpoint, including a variety of grunts and groans, also occur on the latter part of beat four: the "hunh"s, transcribed in figure *b4* and in figure *d3*, are examples of this phenomenon.

The issue of "marginal" musical elements in analysis underscores the fact that these Signifyin(g) relationships came to my attention when I concentrated on phenomena that I had originally assumed to be "marginal": the various "extemporaneous" exhortations that occur during the sax "solos" (a part of the piece in which musical interest frequently shifts from the vocalist to the instrumentalist); the vast variety of grunts and groans; and the other fragmented phrases illustrated in example 4.2. These aspects of the song, blind spots from the viewpoint of art music analysis, correspond readily to traits mentioned in Floyd's Call-Response trope: the repetition of fragments with discrete variations that alternately create expectations and thwart them; the self-referentiality and the self-conscious allusions to the act of performance; and the breakdown of the distance between performers and audience through the introduction of the group and then through the group's verbal interaction. Musically, as well, these passages provide clear examples of musical Signifyin(g): the fragmentation and variation of various figures, complex rhythmic elision of the downbeat, and intertextual references to Black Nationalism.

The screams that constitute figures *a* and *e* deserve further comment, for close analysis of them also contradicts commonplace assumptions. Rather than being gestures without pitch, more or less extemporaneously added to enhance the musical flow, these figures evidence specific characteristics with regard both to pitch and to their formal placement. Specifically, figure *a* focuses on the pitch D, while figure *e* focuses on the pitch E. Figures *a* and *e* tend to occur in tandem at the end of the B sections. At the very end of the song, the last two statements of figure *a* occur at the end of section **B3** and frame within them the final statements of both figure *d* and figure *e*. This illustrates how figures can be recombined to create "new" musical ideas, similar to the way in which the stock phrases of the "toast" are reused and recombined.

Figures *b* and *c* are both striking in their consistency: figure *b* emphasizes pitch A while figure *c* encircles pitch D. While figure *b* tends to retain its place in the larger formal structure, figure *c* is elaborated much more freely, not only in terms of its content from statement to statement but also in terms of its placement. Since this figure contains the title of the song, it's not surprising that Brown uses a fragment of it as a basis for extensive vocal play.

The process of incremental repetition and variation in melodic figures and gestures shares many characteristics with those that we observed in the song's linguistic processes. The important characteristics in the melodic parameter reside neither in the creation of new melodic lines as the song proceeds nor in the totality of its dramatic form; rather, interest lies in the complex reshuffling – with subtle variation in pitch and rhythm – of small fragments that are used first to create, then to disrupt listener expectations. Many elements, marginal from the standpoint of European common practice, belong to Floyd's Call-Response trope and play a crucial role both in the sharp characterization of the melodic figures, and in their subsequent transformation.

Timbre

Let us open the discussion of timbre in "Superbad" with a quote from Olly Wilson that both comments on the connection between James

Brown's music and West African music, and provides a response to some of the previous citations in this chapter regarding texture in Brown's music:

The following features common to both [West African and Afro-American music] may be briefly noted. There tends to be an intensification of the stratification of the musical lines by means of emphasizing the independence of timbre (color) for each voice. Just as the different tonal colors of various size drums are clearly differentiated from each other and from the gongs, rattles, hand clapping, and voices in West African music so we find that the typical violin, banjo, bones, and tambourine of the eighteenth century or the clarinet, trumpet, trombone, guitar, bass, and drum set of early twentieth-century Afro-American music maintain this independence of voices by means of timbral differentiation. The sound ideal of the West African sphere of influence is a heterogeneous one.

Another common characteristic is the high density of musical events within a relatively short musical space. There tends to be a profusion of musical activities going on simultaneously, as if an attempt is being made to fill up every available area of musical space.[68]

Everywhere in "Superbad," as we might expect from its inclusion in Wilson's article, we find contrasting, heterogeneous features superimposed on one another in a "high density of musical events." I will suggest how, in a few instances, these highly differentiated timbres are produced, turning later to a discussion of the texture in terms of its polymetric patterns.

This "high density of musical events" creates a correspondingly dense spectrum photo, rendering use of photos as an aid in visualizing sonic processes in "Superbad" rather impractical. This consistent density also corresponds to the largely non-teleological aesthetic at work in this song. We can, however, discuss a few of the heterogeneous strands of the song, in particular, the remarkable sonic quality of the tenor saxophone and the similarity between it and Brown's vocal timbre. This resemblance between saxophone and voice is particularly striking when we consider certain specific vocal gestures such as the screeching falsetto "reeee" of figure *e*. The saxophone emphasizes a limited range of its sonic possibilities by concentrating on its uppermost register – the *altissimo* register, the saxophone's aural equivalent to the male falsetto singing voice – which exceeds its customary range. These two extraordinary sounds are linked at crucial points in the song such as the transition between section **B2** (featuring the falsetto of figure *e*) and section **A5** (featuring the saxophone solo).

Careful examination of the melodic figures also reveals that the tessitura of the voice plays an important role in the formation of Brown's vocal timbre, described as "one of the harshest in rhythm and blues."[69] Brown takes care to choose the key of a song so that it places his voice in the uppermost portion of his range. In his songs, one rarely finds instances of pitches lower than G below middle C, the pitch which forms the lower vocal boundary of "Superbad." In fact, songs that center around the pitch D are exceedingly common in Brown's output; a far from exhaustive list of songs with a tonal center of D includes such stylistic antecedents of "Superbad" as "Cold Sweat," "There Was a Time," and "Mother Popcorn," to take only songs released as singles during the 1967-1970 period. Brown exploits this consistency of tessitura by recycling many vocal figures at identical pitch levels from song to song, thereby implementing another variant of the first form of "intertextuality" mentioned earlier. "There Was a Time" provides a case in point: the line, "there was a [dance, day, time]," is virtually identical in contour and pitch level to figure *b* (containing the words "I've got soul"; see example 4.2) in "Superbad."[70] Other passages in "Superbad" closely resemble the pitch content of figure *b*, among them the phrase "I've got something" that begins line 3 and the phrase "all around" that occurs many times in section B. That Brown emphasizes the words "I've got soul" by using this familiar "bluesy" melodic gesture is entirely in keeping with the song's celebration of African-American cultural practices. A later demonstration of Brown's awareness of the sonic advantageousness of the key of D can be found in the song "Doing It to Death" (1973); although the song begins in F, Brown requests that the band change keys to D about two-thirds of the way through, exclaiming "in order for me to get down, it's got to be in D." After Brown repeats his request several times, the band complies and switches keys from F to D![71]

Signifyin(g) on the time-line

Rhythm as a separate field of inquiry in Western music did not develop until the nineteenth century. Until then, treatises had regarded rhythm largely as a function of pitch.[72] Partly as a result of this, rhythmic analysis has not developed to nearly the same extent as the analysis of pitch; when it does occur, it tends to contain many of the same epistemological biases as pitch analysis: the analyst searches for resemblances between small units; after locating these, the way in which they create a sense of "unity" or "coherence" is revealed; then attention shifts to the way the small units recombine "organically" to create larger structures with many "architectonic levels."[73] Needless to say, these studies are based on spatialized observations derived from a score rather than a performance. Little work has been attempted on popular music; however, rhythmic studies are a bit more common in ethnomusicological literature, especially on West African music.

We may begin our consideration of rhythm by recalling Floyd's comment that "swing" is communicated by the way in which sound-events Signify on the time-line (i.e., a recurring pattern of beats based on the "metronome sense"). Olly Wilson, in his discussion of polymetric patterns in "Superbad," finds three different rhythmic patterns in the texture displayed in texture *v* in example 4.3:

(1) the accents of the horns and drums imply an alternating meter of 3 + 3 + 2;

(2) the bass, through heavy accents, implies a four-beat pattern beginning on beat two;

(3) the melodic goal of the bass, low D, creates a counter stress of a four-beat pattern beginning on beat one.[74]

This last pattern is reinforced by the entrance of the guitar after eight measures (texture *w* in example 4.3), which begins its eight-beat pattern of 6 + 2 on beat one. The guitar part frequently features a slight anticipation of beat one, forming an upbeat-downbeat ellipsis similar to that noted previously in many of the vocal figures.

Although texture *y* (which dominates section B) shares many features with textures *v*, *w*, and *x*, it reorganizes them significantly. Following Wilson, we could analyze texture *y* in the following way:

(1) the horns and drums now play an eight-beat pattern which begins on beat two;

(2) the guitar plays a sixteen-beat pattern which features constant sixteenth notes broken off abruptly on the thirteenth beat; this accents the first beat of every fourth measure;

(3) the bass and bass drum produce a pattern that divides the first two beats into a pattern of 3 + 3 + 2 *sixteenth* notes, thereby producing a rhythmic diminution of the characteristic pattern of the horns and drums in texture *v*;

(4) the bass pattern for the whole measure divides the eighth notes into 3 + 3 + 4 (an eighth tied over to another eighth) + 6 (further subdivided into 3 + 3 when the bass plays sixteenth note fills);

(5) meanwhile the drums, in the second four beats of their pattern, engage in some extremely complex cross accents. Beginning on the second accented beat, the ride cymbal divides the twelve remaining sixteenth beats of the measure into a pattern of $3 + 3 + (2 + 2) + 2$.

The third texture, texture z, provides a rhythmic antithesis to the preceding textures: it consists solely of eight evenly accented eighth notes, producing the only texture in the piece that consists essentially of rhythmic homophony. Texture z is also anomalous in other respects: it lasts for only one measure each time it occurs, compared to the extended durations of the other textures; and it is the only texture to occur with a "dominant" harmony.

We might say that Wilson answered the question implied earlier (how do the sound-events of "Superbad" Signify on the time-line?) by emphasizing the transmutation of West African polymetric practice in the music of James Brown.[75] Another way of conceptualizing the effect produced by the song is to emphasize how the different accentual patterns create a complex, compelling "groove" by Signifyin(g) on the time-line of eighth-note pulses, "making the pulse itself lilt freely," which results in "swing," that elusive quality regarded by Floyd as the *sine qua non* of Signifyin(g) and the Call-Response trope.[76] The web of accents is enhanced by the slight anticipations and delays within the patterns (e.g., where exactly does the second accent of the horn's "dunht, dunht" in texture v fall?). Snead's idea of the "cut" comes into play here in a nearly unmediated form: the matrix of one- and two-measure ostinati reminds us of Snead's claim that "the greater the insistence on the pure beauty and value of repetition, the greater the awareness must also be that repetition takes place not on a level of musical development or progression, but on the purest tonal and timbric level."[77] Figure $d4$ from example 4.2, in the context of texture y in which it occurs, illustrates the way in which "sound-events" (generated by the voice in this case) can Signify against a time-line (already made complex by ostinati which are themselves Signifyin[g] on the time-line) creating an extreme, almost vertiginous sense of "swing." In example 4.4, which shows the rhythmic groupings in figure $d4$, Brown's voice briefly implies in the first measure yet another stratum in the polymetric matrix by accenting beats one and four, recalling the snare drum pattern in texture v. Brown contradicts this pattern in the next measure by accenting beats two and four (the only other time in which these beats are explicitly accented in "Superbad" occurs during the sax solo in section **A5** when the guitar plays the figure shown in texture u in example 4.3). The rest of this example displays

Example 4.3: *"Superbad": rhythmic textures*

Texture *v*

Texture *w* (texture *v* with guitar added)

Example 4.3 (*cont.*)

Texture *x*

Texture *u* (texture *x* during sax solos)

Example 4.3 (*cont.*)

Texture *y*

Texture *z*

Example 4.4: *Figure d4 – rhythmic groupings*

very complex rhythmic groupings, some of which fall into various combinations of three and two eighth notes beginning at different points on the time-line; these create a further sense of disorientation, obscuring the relationship between the voice and the underlying pulse.

Both the rhythmic analysis presented here and the analysis presented by Wilson in his "Significance" article imply that the presence of polymeter may be responsible for the kinetic quality of the music. Wilson's article implies as well that this is the source of the similarity between West African and African-American music. One of the major insights of Wilson's work is that he points out connections between West African polymetric practice and rhythms played by a single instrumentalist in African-American music which are not obvious. However, there is a risk that Wilson's idea might be misinterpreted, reducing it to a positivistic formula such as "multi-meter=groove." Discerning why some bands "groove" more than others is a complex affair. Besides studying further the already mentioned phenomenon of anticipations and delays within a groove, we need to understand better how performers communicate a sense of rhythmic freedom and play while at the same time communicating a strong sense of pulse; and how members of the ensemble primarily responsible for communicating the music's metronomic sense create a unified, yet relaxed, sense of pulse. An often unrecognized aspect of groove is the role played by the voice or lead instrument; the discussion of example 4.4 and the analysis of anticipations and delays in the vocal part hint at the importance of the lead vocal in the creation of vital drive. While there is much work to be done on how specific grooves are created, we must not forget the all-important factor of social "competence": a groove exists because musicians know how to create one and audiences know how to respond to one. Something can only be recognized as a groove by a listener who has internalized the rhythmic syntax of a given musical idiom. This assertion contains a degree of tautology, but scientific analysis of the rhythmic components of a given groove would be meaningless if the analyst (or the analyst's "informants") could not distinguish between a "good" groove and a "bad" one.

Harmonic stasis or harmonic Signifyin(g)?

Let us turn to Robert Palmer's description of the changes in Brown's music *circa* 1964:

Brown would sing a semi-improvised, *loosely* organized melody that *wandered* while the band riffed rhythmically on a single chord, the horns tersely punctuating Brown's declamatory phrases. With no chord changes and precious little melodic variety to sustain listener interest, *rhythm became everything*. Brown and his musicians and arrangers began to treat every instrument and voice in the group as if each were a drum [italics added].[78]

Later in the same article, Palmer accuses critics who would dismiss Brown as monotonous of applying irrelevant criteria. I will argue that Palmer's own description repeats this critical move but in a much more subtle guise. Close inspection reveals very few songs with "no chord changes"; it also reveals songs that possess a great deal of "melodic variety" if the concept of "melody" is based on subtle nuances and variations of melodic figures rather than on the European ideal of a sustained (preferably legato) melodic line. Much has been written about the absence of harmonic motion in James Brown's music. Although harmonically static ostinati occurred in his music from 1964

Example 4.5: *Harmonic proportions in "Superbad"*

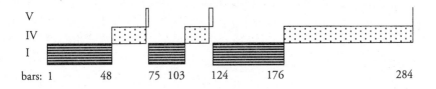

on, complete songs consisting of long ostinati only began appearing in
1967 with songs such as "Cold Sweat," "There Was a Time," and
"Mother Popcorn"; however, most of these songs *do* feature harmonic
shifts and more than one ostinato, thereby avoiding complete harmonic
stasis.[79] Songs heralded as innovative for their concentration on rhythm
in the 1964–1965 period, such as "Out of Sight," "Papa's Got a Brand
New Bag," and "I Got You (I Feel Good)," are actually based on
I–IV–I–V–IV–I blues progressions. "Superbad," despite long passages
in which the bass ostinato focuses on a single pitch, does contain
harmonic movement – indeed, harmonic movement that may be
understood as an extended I–IV–V harmonic progression. Example
4.5 displays the relative amount of time spent in each harmonic area.
This use of the I–IV–V progression results in a Signifyin(g)
commentary on the use of this progression in Western music, an
instance of a "double-voiced utterance" in yet another parameter. In
Western art music, the IV (subdominant) harmony usually serves as an
intermediate step between the structurally more important I (tonic)
and V (dominant) harmonies; instead, in "Superbad," harmonic weight
shifts toward the subdominant, while the tonic is emphasized
somewhat less and only brief allusions are made to the dominant. The
concluding section lasts 108 measures and centers around the
subdominant pitch, G. This has the effect of eclipsing D – the putative
tonic – as the tonal focus. The final shift to the dominant on A for the
concluding beat of the song comes as an abrupt jolt and effectively
proscribes a sense of tonal closure. Thus the most common harmonic
progression in the common practice period of Western art music is
present in "Superbad" but is presented in an almost unrecognizable
form. This places the harmonic context of the song in a position
similar to the linguistic context: it belongs to, while it simultaneously
comments upon, the langue and "norms" of Western music of the past
250 years.

Example 4.6: *"Superbad": modes*

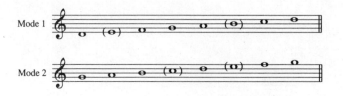

A few more words are in order here concerning the relationship of melody to harmony in "Superbad." If we are to take previous statements regarding James Brown's post-1964 music seriously, then we might be inclined to believe that this music is without melody, differing from "African drumming" only by virtue of its instrumentation. But even the difference in instrumentation, according to these accounts, has little effect on the melodic aspects of the music since every "instrument and voice in the group" is "treat[ed] as a drum."[80]

However, from the previous description of melodic figures in "Superbad" we can see that Brown's vocal sounds are *specifically* singing sounds; that is, they do concentrate on definite pitches which do, in fact, generate their own kind of melody. The many glissandi, though of a type not common in European bel canto singing, nonetheless create the effect of *sung* (as opposed to spoken) vocal sound. Even what might be considered marginal vocal phenomena – grunts, groans, screams – focus on distinct pitches. Figures *a*, *b*, and *d* reveal this focus in the following ways (see example 4.2 for transcriptions of the figures):

(1) figure *a*, in its first seven manifestations, focuses on pitch D;

(2) figures *b1*, *b2*, and *b4* focus on pitches F and A with pitch G as a passing tone, while figure *b3* focuses on pitches D and A and figure *b5* focuses on pitches D and F;

(3) figure *d*, in most of its occurrences, emphasizes pitches D and F with pitch C included as a neighbor tone. As discussed above, there are many variants of this figure; these variants emphasize pitches B, E, G, and A.

The melodic content of all these figures taken together is indeed, as others have remarked, modal. Example 4.6, mode 1 summarizes the pitch content of these figures which could be described as the dorian mode with an emphasis on the minor (or blues) pentatonic.

How do harmonic shifts affect the modal content of the figures? Figures *d1* and *d2*, though occurring over a "subdominant" harmony, still

Example 4.7: *Bass line emphasizing pitch G*

retain the pitch content of mode 1. The horn line shown in example 4.3, texture *y* – an ostinato present in most of the B sections – also retains the D pentatonic quality of the A section through the top voice's 5-4-3-1 descent. A modal shift occurs in the great extension of the "subdominant" harmony during the **B3** section. The elaboration of figure *d*, in figure *d4*, illustrates this shift in pitch emphasis:

(1) initially, pitch B is emphasized;

(2) beginning in the third measure of *d4*, pitches G-D are emphasized by a passage in which this fifth is chromatically filled. The bass answers imitatively, as shown in example 4.7, in such a way so as to confirm emphasis on pitch G;

(3) the remainder of figure *d4* continues to focus on a mode centering on pitch G.

The pitch content of this mode is summarized in mode 2, example 4.6. Later in section **B3**, with the reentry of the horn line of texture *y*, example 4.3, emphasis shifts back to mode 1.

The third passage with differing modal content accompanies figure *e*. Figures *e1* and *e2* occur over a "dominant"-type harmony; therefore, scale degree 2 becomes the fifth of the underlying harmony. This "dominant" harmony does not contain a raised leading tone, reinforcing the modal flavor of the passages centered on D and existing more as a subset of mode 1 than as an independent mode.

Another important point is the pitch content of the saxophone solo. The remarkable tonal quality of the saxophone is due to its playing rapid flurries of pitches that resemble glissandi in an extremely high register. However, the saxophone does emphasize some pitches more than others. In the solo of **A4**, the saxophone exploits pitches in mode 1, but they are the "marginal" pitches of the mode, pitches E and B, scale degrees 2 and 6. Pitch E is carried over from the screech of figure *e* which immediately precedes, and in some cases overlaps, the solo. Also, an emphasis on these pitches can be seen in statements *2, 4, 9*, and *10* of figure *c*.

While not denying the importance of rhythm in "Superbad," we must not let rhythm overshadow the very real expressive importance of pitch. That the pitch information is contained in short phrases, screams, and

glissandi should not blind us to the presence of discrete pitches and to
the far from haphazard manipulation of pitch in this song. The extent to
which the melodic aspects of the music escape notice or are denigrated
may be related to the extent to which they Signify; that is, the melodic
content of the song frustrates standard definitions of melody to the
degree that it emanates from Floyd's Call-Response trope and that it
incorporates elements from the ring.

Proportional Signifyin(g)

As rhythmic analysis has had a relatively brief and undistinguished
history, so has the musicological analysis of proportion been relatively
neglected. However, the analysis of proportion has a somewhat curious
history, including as it does the conscious use of (at times convoluted)
proportional schemes by European composers.[81] The musicological
approach to proportional analysis can be described as a process with two
stages. In stage number one, an analyst demonstrates a rigorous system
of proportions contained in the score. By counting notated beats and
measures, the analyst purports to show that the composer consciously or
unconsciously structured the piece using a consistent set of proportions.
These proportions may be simple arithmetic ones, complex geometrical
ones; they may be based on magic squares, superstitious personal
numerical systems (as in the case of Berg), or the "Golden Section" (or
"Golden Mean"). The second stage bases itself on those aspects of the
proportional systems discovered in the first stage that claim natural
origins, such as the magic square or the Golden Section (hereafter
referred to as "GS"). The demonstration of these systems may be used
implicitly to legitimate the composers and their works, a strategy that
varies depending on the circumstances surrounding the work's creation.
When biographical information confirms conscious use of a proportional
system by a composer, the composition can be praised for its unity, rigor,
and the "freedom" attained despite the use of such an inhibiting system.
Whether conscious or not, confirmed by biography or not, analysts will
usually invoke the GS to imply that the value of the composition lies in
the connection between its "deep" structure and natural phenomena. If
no biographical information confirms the conscious deployment of an
involved proportional scheme, then this provides all the more evidence to
bolster claims that the beauty of the work springs from its structural
similarity to the patterns of rings in sea shells, the patterns of branches
and leaves on trees, and the reproductive rates of rabbits (the proportions

or ratios of which can all be related to the GS); the following statement encapsulates this perspective: "[The] GS is a natural principle, like the harmonic series, whose physical existence antedates mankind."[82] One aspect of this is the conversion of the perceptual mode from a temporal to a spatial one, a move which we encountered in the discussion of analytical metaphors in chapter one.

As is usually the case with analytical techniques used in conjunction with the European tradition, why the reader/listener should feel that the presence of GS proportions (or another proportional system) is important is rarely explained. The analyses frequently imply something like the following: since the GS is found "objectively" in "natural" structures, pieces that structurally incorporate the GS (in the durations present in the score) are "closer" to nature; i.e., the presence of the GS explains why the durational proportions in a piece of music feel "right." Conveniently, it is usually overlooked or left unexplained that a piece could incorporate GS proportions in its score and not feel right (and, undoubtedly, many non-masterworks rely on these proportions just as heavily as the masterworks; that a mathematically precise proportional scheme cannot account for a work's greatness is borne out by the great number of "masterworks" that do not contain such a scheme).

Given a background tradition that relies so heavily on the notion of the transcendent, autonomous *objet d'art*, how shall we approach the subject of form and proportion in "Superbad"? Let us first examine "Superbad" on the level of the phrase. The term "phrase" is used loosely here: at various times, "phrase" denotes an antecedent/consequent complex, a shorter portion of text delimited by a textural change, or verbal fragments grouped together by type, e.g., as in sections **A5** and **B3** where Brown repeats some fragments for as many as 20 measures. The common thread uniting these methods is a concern for how textural/linguistic factors segment the musical surface. Table 4.1 reveals the following features:

(1) 4-measure phrases establish themselves as something of a norm in the first two A sections, a norm which is disrupted by a 6-measure phrase at the beginning of section **A3**; this phrase is "balanced" by a concluding phrase of 2 measures;

(2) irregular phrases occur in section **B1** on the words "If you don't brothers and sisters, then you won't know, what it's all about" (6 measures); and with the fragment "Give me" (7 measures, figure *d1*, example 4.2);

Table 4.1: *Phrase lengths in "Superbad"*

First line of text (by phrase)	number of measures	harmony and texture[83]
(Intro)	8	I (*v*)
A1		
I got something	4	I (*w*)
I got soul and I'm Superbad	4	I (*w*)
I got soul and I'm Superbad	4	I (*x*)
A2		
Now I got a mood	4	I (*w*)
I got a mood	4	I (*w*)
I got soul and I'm Superbad	4	I (*x*)
A3		
I love to do my thing	6	I (*w*)
Sometimes I feel so nice	4	I (*w*)
I got soul and I'm Superbad	4	I (*w*)
I said I'm Superbad	2	I (*x*)
B1		
Up and down, and round and round	4	IV (*y*)
Up and down, all around	4	IV (*y*)
Right on people, let it all hang out	4	IV (*y*)
If you don't brothers and sisters . . .	6	IV (*y*)
Give me . . .	7	IV (*y*)
Ayyyy	1	IV (*y*)
Reeee	1	V (*z*)
A4		
(sax solo)	8	I (*u*)
I got that something	4	I (*w*)
I got soul, and I'm Superbad	4	I (*w*)
I got the move	4	I (*w*)
I, I, I, I, I	4	I (*w*)
I got soul	4	I (*x*)
B2		
Up and down	4	IV (*y*)
Right on people	4	IV (*y*)
If you don't brothers	6	IV (*y*)
Give me, give me . . .	5	IV (*y*)
Reeee	1	IV (*y*)
(instrumental)	1	V (*z*)
A5		
(sax solo)		
Come on Robert	8	I (*u*)

Table 4.1 (*cont.*)

First line of text (by phrase)	number of measures	harmony and texture[83]
Give me	8	I (*u*)
Said I'm Superbad	16	I (*u*)
come on, He's Superbad	8	I (*u*)
Got it! He's Superbad	8	I (*u*)
Griggs! He's Superbad	4	I (*u*)
B3		
Good God! Up and down and all around	6	IV (*y*)
Right on people, let it all hang out	4	IV (*y*)
If you don't brothers and sisters	6	IV (*y*)
Give me, give me . . .	20	IV (*y*)
Superbad	6	IV (*y*)
I don't miss nothin', I never had	4	IV (*y*)
I'm Super, Superbad	4	IV (*y*)
Right on people, let it all hang out	4	IV (*y*)
I'm Superbad, yay, yay, hay	10	IV (*y*)
Early in the mornin', about noon	4	IV (*y*)
In the evening, I get my groove	4	IV (*y*)
I've got it	4	IV (*y*)
Said I'm Superbad	6	IV (*y*)
Do your thing Robert (sax solo), Superbad	7	IV (*y*)
Fellas [yeah], I need some power	7	IV (*y*)
Give me, Give me	5	IV (*y*)
Ayy, yay, Reeee, gimme, Ayyy	7	IV (*y*)
(instrumental)	1 beat	V (*z*)

(3) section **B2** features a similar irregularity: rather than repeating **B1** literally, Brown eliminates one of the 4-measure phrases and shortens the "gimme" segment to 5 measures (also shown in figure *d2*);

(4) section **B3**, by far the longest section in the song (108 measures), features the most irregular segmentation of phrases. Notable are the extensions of the first phrase, "Up and down" to 6 measures, the elaborate extension on "gimme" to almost 20 measures (figure *d4*), and the highly irregular phrase lengths of 7, 7, 5, and 7 measures occurring towards the end of the section, deriving largely from the highly flexible declamation of text "fragments."

The irregularities on the surface level have their ramifications on the sectional level. Except for sections **A1** and **A2**, no two sections are the same length. The total number of measures in all the A sections are multiples of 4. The **B1** (27 measures) and **B2** (21 measures) sections, on the other hand, owing principally to the irregular length of figure *d*

Table 4.2: *Duration of sections in "Superbad"*

Section	Crowd noise	Intro	A1	A2	A3	B1	A4	B2	A5	B3
Measures		8	12	12	16	27	28	21	52	108
Total			20	32	48	75	103	124	176	284
Time	5"	15"	23"	23"	31"	51"	54"	41"	1'39"	3'28"
Total		20"	43"	1'06"	1'37"	2'28"	3'22"	4'03"	5'42"	9'10"

("gimme"), are an odd number of measures long. This might seem no more than a rather mechanical account of an irregularity attributable to the music's "semi-improvised" quality; after all, who would expect music that was not thoroughly arranged to have phrases and sections of even length?[84] The questions arising from this are: how were the lengths of the sections determined? And, are the differing lengths of the sections random or methodical?

Without interviewing people present at the recording we cannot know to what extent "Superbad" is improvised or arranged (and even interviews would not guarantee the "truth"). Although many passages may seem relatively improvisatory, we must exercise caution in equating "improvisatory" with "haphazard." Perusing the lengths of the sections in table 4.2 reveals a far from haphazard arrangement: with the exception of sections A1 and A2 – which are equal – and section B2 – which is slightly shorter than the two preceding sections – all the sections are progressively longer. Moreover, they share a strikingly similar proportional relationship with one another, a proportional relationship that bears a strong resemblance to the GS. The most striking property of the GS proportional scheme is that the relationship of the smaller part to the larger part is equivalent to the ratio of the larger part to the whole; this is expressed in the numerical ratio of 0.618 to 1. The line displaying "total measures" in table 4.2 most clearly demonstrates this property of "Superbad." The total number of measures after the introduction and section A1 is 20, of which section A1 comprises 12. The ratio of 12 to 20 is 0.6. The total after A2 is 32 measures and the larger part (20 measures) has a ratio of 0.625 to the whole (32 measures). Example 4.8 displays the rest of these relationships in a proportional chart.

Perhaps the most striking GS division occurs at the largest formal juncture between section B3 and the rest of the piece. The ratio of B3 (108 measures) to the rest of the piece (176 measures) is 0.61. Furthermore, one of the most obviously "arranged" aspects of the performance, the beginning of a long build-up after 42 measures of B3, stands in the same ratio (0.61) to the rest of section B3 (66 measures).

Example 4.8: *Proportional chart of sections in "Superbad"*

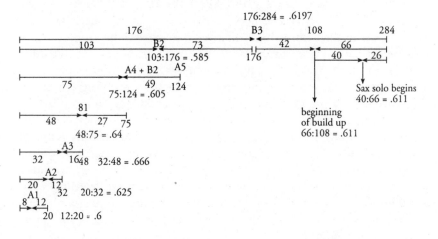

While my purpose in invoking such a proportional scheme in the context of "Superbad" has not been to ensure its inclusion in a canon of late sixties-early seventies soul music or to prove that it is just as great as the first movement of Bartók's *Music for Strings, Percussion, and Celeste,* Bach's Chaconne in D minor for violin, or Debussy's "Jardin sous la pluie" (all pieces analyzed previously with respect to their GS proportions), my use of this proportional scheme suggests that it does have some sort of explanatory power. Again, if we are to discuss the *effect* of these formal properties, we need to make a move from the "expression plane" to the "content plane." This throws us onto the level of "primary signification," specifically the aspect of "positional values." That is, the sections acquire meaning through their internal relationships to one another. These proportions may provide simultaneously a sense of similarity (a constant set of relationships between sections), and a sense of difference (the lengths are all different) – a simultaneous sense of variety and repetition. This has very much to do with how pieces can Signify upon themselves on the formal level, constantly revising sections even as they are repeated.[85] The idea of Signifyin(g) connects the idea of proportional relationships in this case to the larger "interpretive frame" we have been using on other parameters.[86]

It seems fairly certain that James Brown did not mathematically calculate the proportions of "Superbad" (although this does not rule out the possibility that they were worked out consciously in some way). We do not know why the **B** section is 21 measures long one time and 27 measures long the next, or why the final section is 108 measures long.[87]

To some extent, this might make claims for the "naturalness" of this music's proportions more viable than the implied claims for the "naturalness" of art music composers who often do calculate the proportions of their music mathematically; moreover, the proportions of "Superbad" are virtual (the analysis here is of an unvarying, recorded performance), they occur in real time, whereas the proportions of a piece of art music may not be realized in performance owing to tempo fluctuations. While the "spontaneity," "looseness," or "improvisatory" quality of James Brown's music is usually emphasized in critical accounts, the precision with which the piece conveys a simultaneous sense of repetition and difference might lead us to problematize these terms. Similarly, the presence of a set of proportions used to legitimate art music in "Superbad" could motivate us to question the very "legitimacy" of invoking the figure of "naturalness" as a criterion for legitimation in the analysis of art music. Furthermore, the problematic aspects in this mode of analysis can point out the implied hierarchies so often invoked in the almost incidental exegesis accompanying the analyses; these hierarchies are often expressed in doublets: composer/improviser, planned/ spontaneous. In the study of Western music over the last two centuries, "improvised" can all too easily assume a dismissive cast in proximity to "composed." That proportional analysis in "Superbad" reveals the uncertain status of descriptions that emphasize only its "spontaneity" should lead us to greater circumspection regarding how we deploy these terms.

In light of the introductory paragraph of this section, the evidence presented here could be used to make several contradictory claims for "Superbad": one could assert that James Brown is a constructive genius, communicating the sense of improvisation within a unified structure that contains within it both consistency and diversity. Or one could assert that this proves the "naturalness" of James Brown's music: it flows out of him like leaves grow out of a tree. While the second claim may be closer to the kinds of myths reproduced in much writing about James Brown and about black music in general, the first claim does not clash entirely with the kinds of values and myths advanced about Brown by Brown: over and over again, interviews with Brown and former colleagues stress his dedication to hard work (the "hardest-working man in show business") and his diligent and regimented rehearsal routine. We may never know for sure whether the proportions of "Superbad" were planned meticulously or improvised on the spot. The value of this analysis may well rest more in its ability to upset easy assumptions about this music than in its ability to provide a verifiable answer.

James Brown remains an enigmatic figure shrouded in controversy; in the late eighties his legal difficulties made him a frequent subject of caricature and derision. This is symptomatic of the manner in which the threat of a man whose music once formed a vigorous challenge to the aesthetic of "mainstream" pop can be marginalized within the discourse of the mainstream media.[88] Brown affirms a system of alternative values both in lyrics – through the explicit references to black power slogans, African-American street language and values – and in music – through the explicit invocations of specific African-American practices and a perhaps unconscious reference to West African music. His music exemplifies what Charles Keil termed the "appropriation-revitalization" process: the manner in which each form of African-American pop music has become "more African in its essentials" in response to the previous style's "appropriation" into Euro-American pop music.[89] In fact, Brown's post-1965 music is central to many of the stylistic shifts in African-American music since then. "Funk" music, as Brown's post-1965 music is usually labeled, became widely influential in the late sixties, first through Sly Stone's importation of funk elements into his hybrid of "psychedelic" music, and later through its wider dissemination in the music of such seventies bands as the Ohio Players, Kool and the Gang, KC and the Sunshine Band, and Funkadelic. Disco, in the late seventies, simplified many of the rhythmic complexities of funk but still retained an obvious debt to Brown, as he was only too happy to point out in his 1979 release, "The Original Disco Man." Rap represents the latest manifestation of the appropriation-revitalization process, bringing "material that was exclusively the province of the black oral tradition and race-record tradition" into the cultural mainstream.[90] Moreover, rap owes multiple debts to James Brown, primarily in its use of ostinati; rap further elevates the ostinato to a position of importance through the use of "sampling," whereby fragments of previous recordings overlap or are superimposed on to the basic rhythm track, or are even used as the basis for the rhythm track. This forms an obvious instance of the Signifyin(g) practice identified by Gates as "intertextuality," as many pre-recorded snippets are combined heterogeneously. These samples often form an even further primary link with Brown's music in that the samples for many rap songs are frequently taken from Brown's late sixties-early seventies recordings.

Olly Wilson's statement – that "Africanness consists of the way of doing something, not simply something that is done" – and Henry Louis Gates, Jr.'s observation – that "the black tradition emphasizes refiguration, or repetition and difference, or troping, underscoring the foregrounding of the chain of signifiers, rather than the mimetic representation of a novel content" – echo what many other writers have observed: Brown's lyrics matter not so much for what he says as for how he says it; his music matters not so much for the pitches it uses as for how those pitches are inflected.[91] This is most certainly not to say that pitch and the semantic content of the lyrics are unimportant; to say this would be merely to reinforce the critical discourse which this analysis sought to problematize. The preceding analysis, similar to the phenomena analyzed here, has had a dual focus: that the notion of the "center" and the "margins" can never be taken for granted when analyzing texts not created in the same tradition as the critical terminology used to describe them; and that connections exist between the musical processes and the linguistic processes within this text. Building on the work of Wilson, Gates, and Floyd, I have attempted to explicate further the process by which Brown varies small musical figures through repetition and recombination, and through variation of pitch, rhythm, and timbre.

A few words of methodological caution are in order at this point. In discovering connections between linguistic, cultural, and musical processes, one runs the danger of finding overly pat homologies. And "the difficulty with using such homologies is not that they cannot be produced. It is that they can always be produced."[92] What is important here is not the homologies that have been produced; it is that social/cultural differences noted in other domains – linguistics, literature – might influence a music analysis so as to suggest a relationship between the musical object and the evaluative discourses used by people who produce and consume the music.

The more I analyzed and thought about James Brown's music, particularly "Superbad," the more I found that I could not avoid discussing the "critical difference" between African-American and Euro-American music and culture – that this text compelled me to confront this issue. If soul is, in Charles Keil's words, "the ability to communicate something of the [African-American] experience," we must interpret a line like "I've got soul and I'm Superbad" as the singer's affirmation of that experience. Both in what it expresses and in how it expresses it, "Superbad" results in a musical and lyrical celebration of that very "experiential" difference.

CHAPTER FIVE

Writing, music, dancing, and architecture in Elvis Costello's "Pills and Soap"

In an interview published in *Musician* magazine in October 1983, Elvis Costello responded to a question with an oft-quoted retort: "writing about music is like dancing about architecture – it's a really stupid thing to want to do."[1] It is important to consider the implications of this statement – which could be interpreted as a dismissal of the entire project of this book – in order to understand the context in which a musician such as Elvis Costello could come to public prominence and find a niche in the music industry.

On one level, the quote appears to comment on the untranslatability of one art form to another: according to this notion, music and architecture possess an irreducible essence that other media cannot express. Presumably, one should play music as a way of expressing oneself about music, make blueprints as a commentary about architecture, and write about writing.[2] We can moderate the bluntness of Costello's remark in several ways, first by noting how he contradicts himself: by consenting to the interview, he is contributing to the discourse about himself and his music; consequently, his spoken words will appear in print, that is, as *writing about music*. We can also take the particular context of the remark more fully into account: Costello is responding to a question about the music press harassing him, he projects an amiable persona in the interview, and he discusses and even *analyzes* his own work extensively throughout the interview. Nevertheless, he reinforces the point of the above-mentioned quotation by preceding it with the statement, "Framing all the great music out there only drags down its immediacy. The songs are lyrics, not speeches, and they're tunes, not paintings."

Even if we can dismiss aspects of Costello's statement by questioning whether any form of communication is completely separable from all others, and by asserting that architectural concepts may play a role in

other art forms (and they certainly play a major role in structuralist
analyses of art), we can still not allay the impression that Costello is
implying that "writing about music" is somehow particularly distasteful:
while nobody actually "dances about architecture," people *do* write about
music. "To write about" something is to analyze it, to adopt a distanced
approach, to observe rather than to participate. Costello may not be
claiming that "music" (or architecture) is irreducible to another medium,
so much as that *analyzing* an art form is antithetical to producing art.
This invokes a rather common anti-intellectual stance adopted by both
artists and lay people: art is spontaneous; it results from inspiration;
knowing too much about it or thinking about it too much will interrupt
the flow of inspiration and disturb the cultivated innocence that it needs
to flourish. A host of deeply ingrained oppositions support this attitude:
nature/culture, body/mind, feeling/thinking.

Eleven years later, Costello himself gives the lie to this rigid separation
of technique and inspiration (as he did even at the time by his elaborate
replies to questions about his work); when reflecting about the idea that
learning musical technique "would corrupt . . . his innate gifts," he
comments:

It doesn't change you in the way that people expect it to, which is that you're
then gonna go, "Oh, I can't do that now, oh, that's a falling third," that you're
gonna suddenly be inhibited . . . it allows me to communicate with people what
will work best if I give them the music in that form.[3]

While this statement does not necessarily grant *carte blanche* to
musicological analysis, it reveals that he does not subscribe to the notion
that technique is antithetical to creativity or "inspiration." Technique, in
Costello's description here, allows a composer to communicate a wider
range of ideas to a wider range of musicians.

However, in the same 1994 article, the writer asserts that Costello "has
forged an entity out of his musicological expertise." Again, this does not
mean that Costello has produced a scholarly monograph; rather it refers
to the studious manner in which he pilfers an eclectic range of music as
source material for his own compositions. At the same time this sort of
attitude toward transforming one's art reflects an orderly, analytical bent
far removed from the "primitive savage" model of inspiration so popular
in mass media descriptions of creativity in popular music (or, for that
matter, popular belief about style changes in a group such as the Beatles).
Articles and interviews tend to play up the musical illiteracy (the fact that
they don't "read" music) of pop musicians, marvelling at how they
manage to create what they do without "technique."[4]

Yet this recent portrait of Costello still leaves us with a gap between his 1994 reflections on the artistic process and his statement of 1983 which appears to advocate a Romantic notion of unmediated artistic spontaneity. The tension between calculation and spontaneity characterizes the music produced by Costello and others who occupy a somewhat marginal place in the popular music industry. On one level, this tension is part of the industry itself: recordings must present themselves as different enough to attract attention for their uniqueness; at the same time, they need to remain similar enough to provide a sense of familiarity. Pop musicians are in a similar bind: they must continue to attract a sizable enough audience to make the record company a profit so that the record company will permit them to continue to release recordings; at the same time, if the musicians don't wish to see themselves as existing solely to please the public, they may try to create an aura of artistic "growth," which risks making their music less "accessible" and hence less popular. Among fans and musicians alike, this takes root in the modernist idea "if it's popular it must be bad."[5] That this sense of the "marginal" is maintained by both the artists in question and the industry is a subject that I will explore at greater length later in this chapter.

I

The "popular aesthetic"

Costello's recent admission of interest in technique and the solution of formal problems seems to lead us far away from a typical characterization of the "popular aesthetic" – that is, an attitude towards art that privileges functional use over contemplation of form.[6] Pierre Bourdieu stresses the conjunction of class background and academic training in the formation of "taste," and points out that it is those with the greatest capacity for the appreciation of "legitimate" art works who can extend this "pure gaze" (i.e., attention to formal features rather than to context or function) to objects not usually classified as "legitimate." Bourdieu assumes that a consumer with high cultural capital will begin to acquire the "pure gaze" in connection with "legitimate" works of art and then extend this mode of perception to less "legitimate" works.

However, the mere existence both of a pop musician with a "musicological" approach to the acquisition of technique and the study of style, and of an audience who values these qualities, may signal a breakdown between the "legitimate" and the "popular." Since the mid-sixties, a sizable segment of the pop music audience with a high level of cultural capital has existed that may have never applied the pure gaze to classical music. This does not necessarily contradict an aspect of Bourdieu's argument, which states that cultural capital is acquired through early exposure to, and familiarity with, high cultural artifacts and not necessarily through active engagement with these materials or through the educational system. Nonetheless, it is important to note that during the period in the mid- to late sixties in which Bourdieu conducted his ethnographic research, mass media and music industry discourses associated pop music largely with the working class, rarely with intellectuals; up until this time, these discourses had circulated a notion of popular music as disposable teen product, not as timeless art. It is possible that since Bourdieu conducted his research, a shift in the discourse of "legitimate" and "popular" art has accompanied the increasingly frequent detachment of the pure gaze from the necessity to privilege "legitimate" art works; and that, as part of this shift, the ability to bestow aesthetic distance on any object has begun to mark those with cultural capital more than the willingness either to gaze upon legitimate art objects or to be familiar with them. The formation of a new audience has led to the possibility that popular music, once disposable, could be appreciated as art. By the time Costello made his first recording in 1977, he could take this possibility for granted, as could those who purchased his records.

Intellectual pop music

Arguably, a new mode of listening to pop music arose in the 1960s. No longer simply "product" for working-class and/or teen audiences, certain types of pop metamorphosed into music that could, under the right conditions, produce something of "timeless value." This intellectual approach to listening to pop music is not identical with the approach adopted by the fans of "art-rock" or "progressive rock," although these approaches overlap with each other. In some rock forms, it is the "rawness" or spontaneity that is cherished, qualities antithetical to "progressive rock" with its highly elaborated formal structures. This aesthetic transformation occurred in tandem in the US and Great Britain, although in different milieus. In the US, these changes were signaled by the growth of a specifically college-oriented, "bohemian" audience for commercialized folk music, an audience that in the fifties would have probably preferred jazz, classical music, or some form of non-Western (such as Indian) music. Folk songs were meaningful, either because they represented the "pure" traditions of the "people," or because they were newly composed songs with either poetic or politically relevant, topical lyrics. The audience for this music also often included enthusiasts for African-American blues artists. Eventually, these unblemished, yet intellectual, strains found their way into popular music in a multitude of hyphenated styles, including the "folk-rock" of Dylan and the Byrds; the "blues-rock" of the Butterfield Blues Band, the Blues Project, and others; the "underground-rock" of the Velvet Underground; and the "psychedelic-rock" of San Francisco bands such as the Grateful Dead and the Jefferson Airplane.

In Great Britain, this intellectualization of pop music took a somewhat different path. Frith and Horne describe the scene in Great Britain as the coming together of two worlds:

the obsessive record collectors and earnest "students" of the blues on the one hand, and youthful pleasure-seekers on the other . . . it was in these settings that the new generation of art school musicians, who straddled both worlds, developed an ideology of music-making that kept both groups of fans in play together.[7]

The art school in Britain played a central role in these transformations in British pop, either through the dissemination of art school theories by musicians who attended art school (including John Lennon, Keith Richard, Pete Townshend, and Ray Davies, to name a few of the most influential mid-sixties British pop musicians), or through the musicians influenced by the attitudes of those art school-trained musicians. Because the *attitude* toward music-making in the British scene inevitably influenced Elvis Costello more directly than that of the North American scene, it is important for the rest of this discussion to summarize the primary effects of art schools on the development of British pop, effects which can be traced from the late fifties to the present.

In the British art school curriculum, the interplay of aesthetic and commercial judgment manifests itself in a concern with image, as a means of differentiating the *artist* from the mass of commercialized schlock, as a means of eliding personal taste with mass taste.[8] Art school fosters a Romantic image of the artist as a rebel at the margins (and, in fact, practitioners of "fine art" do indeed remain marginal), resisting the mediocrity of the practical; yet art students turn "the critical edge marginality allows . . . into a sales technique, a source of celebrity" (p. 30). With the idea of the Romantic artist celebrating the margins comes the idea of "authentic" artistic production opposed to commercialism.[9] This idea also comes laden with a set of Romantic images that glorify the working class and non-white racial groups. Rather than in the US, where "authentic" musical populism asserts its ties with the rural and the dispossessed, "authenticity" in British pop relies on establishing a sense of difference from the routine of commercial pop "along the axes of passion, commerce and complexity" (p. 148). The emphasis on image allows pop stars to be marketed despite their claims of anticommercialism. The problem persists of how to create a relationship with an audience without "selling out," how to maintain individuality without seeming to partake of the usual sorts of sales pitch (p. 171). "Cult audiences" can sustain a belief in the individuality and non-commercial aspects of a pop musician by seeming to make "a properly 'artistic' (or non-commercial) assessment of their work" (p. 175).

Although it may seem too easy to find aspects of the British art school approach to managing the tension between "authenticity" and marketing in Costello's approach to his career, it is difficult to think of any North American parallel to his combination of artifice and sincerity. Critics frequently compared him to Bruce Springsteen early in his career, but, with the distance of a decade and a half, Costello and Springsteen resemble each other faintly if at all in sound, lyrics, or image (although the instrumentation and style of both occasionally relies on Dylan's mid-sixties sound).[10] From the outset, Costello used artifice to create a distinctive image: adopting the most hallowed first name in the history of rock music and combining this with the visual image of Buddy Holly-turned-geek, the cover of Costello's first record attracted attention without having to produce a sound. Since then, he has employed the "rebel-at-the-margins" image as a sales technique in a wide variety of ways that bear closer scrutiny.

Costello himself has described how he struck a stance in his lyrics that was neither the hard-rock macho image nor the "sensitive" image of the singer-songwriter.[11] Other writers have described the personae of his early songs such as "Miracle Man," "Mystery Dance," and "(The Angels Wanna Wear My) Red Shoes" as a collection of losers and wimps; however, examining these songs in the context of his later work reveals continuity between these personae and a more complex persona projected throughout his work – one that simultaneously expresses sympathy with losers, a willingness to admit his own faults, and an inability to take himself too seriously.[12] He presents a persona full of contradictions: at various points in his career, he's been an ambitious, aggressive, stylish, charismatic rock star stricken by anger, frustrations, insecurity, and self-doubt. This stance is unusual and difficult enough to market so that its very contradictoriness places him at the margins.

II

Style and aesthetics

Costello, punk, and classic rock

Paradoxically, it is this sense of unmarketability that contributes to Costello's sense of difference and makes it possible to market him. When we add a sense of historical specificity to this situation it clarifies how this particular "rebel-at-the-margins" attitude could take the form that it did. He first received mass media attention in 1977, the year of his initial commercial record release, and the year in which punk began receiving widespread publicity. For a brief instant, it seemed as if "deliberately troublesome behavior" could at the same time be "blatantly commercial."[13] Costello, at times described in the press as a punk, was more often grouped with the "new wave" movement – an umbrella term that included punk musicians along with other artists (such as the Talking Heads) who seemed to be reacting to the grandiosity, pomposity, overblown images, stadium shows, and slickness of older rock superstars in the mid-seventies. Importantly, Costello had participated in another, early-seventies, English music scene: "pub-rock," a style with clearer connections to authentic, "roots" music such as R&B, country, and sixties beat, styles that didn't inform punk rock in any obvious way. New wave shared with punk a self-consciousness that attempted to

exploit hype while challenging it on its own ground, both through its consistent attack on the values of the music industry and by exposing to its audience how that industry worked. However, this self-consciousness proved extremely difficult to sustain for those post-punk bands of the late seventies who were left to carry the torch.[14]

The connections between punk and new wave discussed thus far center on image. Costello's lyrics have attracted much attention and might seem to be the obvious place to continue the discussion of his relationship to punk; however, as discussed previously in this book, focusing on song lyrics in isolation removes them from the musical context in which they acquire much of their affective charge. And while it is true that the lyrics of Costello's songs create a complex persona, the way in which he delivers these lyrics adds both to the sense of his difference and "marginality," and to his complex stance towards punk. First, the vocal delivery: while increasingly recognized as a melodicist, Costello's vocal timbre, most notably on the uptempo, harder rock numbers on his early albums, did not yet display the timbral and melodic variety he would develop from *Trust* (1981) onwards (notable exceptions on the first two albums include the ballads "Alison" and "Little Triggers"); his voice approaches a punk-like monotone even while singing melodies that more closely approximate art music and "popular" European melodic conventions than any melodies in songs by the Sex Pistols or the Clash. Some of his songs do approach the simplified melodic profile of punk, such as "Pump It Up," which foreswears even the limited melodic motion of other "hard-rock" songs from this period such as "Miracle Man" or "I'm Not Angry." Yet even the monotone, melodically static vocal of "Pump It Up," while sharing a "declamatory" or "motorial" vocal style with much of punk, differentiates itself from punk in its sound (compared with Johnny Rotten's either non-sung or deliberately off-pitch vocals, Costello sings on a definite, "correct" pitch), and in its quality of homage to previous pop models: it references earlier one-note chanted vocals that form a line from Chuck Berry's "Too Much Monkey Business" to Bob Dylan's "Subterranean Homesick Blues" to John Lennon's (co-credited to Paul McCartney) "Come Together."[15] This sort of historical referencing is alien to punk, although punk bands such as the Sex Pistols did quote previous rock tunes (the Who's "Baba O'Riley" in "Pretty Vacant," Jonathan Richman's "Road Runner" in "EMI") in order to highlight the *incongruity* of punk to earlier pop styles.[16]

Instrumentally, as well, Costello's songs blend "classic rock" style with punk; this became especially noticeable after his adoption of the Attractions as a backing band: compare the studio version of "Miracle Man" recorded with Clover on *My Aim Is True* to the live recording of the same song with the Attractions taken from *Stiffs Live*. The Attractions feature both a driving attack with accents on every eighth note – a rhythmic approach closely associated with early punk – and a kind of melodic-harmonic nimbleness that can be traced to the virtuosity valued in art music, sixties rock music, and a wide range of music throughout the world, but rarely found in the self-consciously "artless" presentation of punk (however, despite the hype, punk *does* rely on notions of competent musicianship). The instrumental sound, particularly Steve Nieve's Farfisa organ, is reminiscent of mid-sixties groups such as ? and the Mysterians (a kind of proto-punk garage band, famous for "96 Tears") and the Sir Douglas Quintet (who had a hit in 1965 with "She's About a Mover"). In the area of performance practice as well, Costello distances himself from the punk aesthetic: Costello's brand of spontaneity draws more on the conventions of R&B, country music, jazz, and early rock 'n' roll than it did on punk avant-gardist notions of performance art. Costello's performance style has shifted: his early performances tended to stick close to the recorded versions of his songs while speeding up the tempi and playing more aggressively, a style approximating what Frith and Horne term "mainstream" punk as opposed to "avant-garde" punk; since at least 1982, a looser, more improvisational approach informed by jazz and R&B has been evident in his performances.[17]   In this way too, Costello's music established its difference in relation both to the blatant commercialism of pop and mid-seventies hard rock, and to the pop situationist-based "marginalized" commercialism of punk; he thereby established his own precarious, *individualized* stretch of commercial turf.   And this difference, it turns out, relies on notions of Romantic creativity and authorship which share more with late-sixties notions of pop music artistry than with the opportunistic artlessness of punk.[18]

Discussing the way in which "Pump It Up" refers to other musical styles raises another important issue in Costello's musical approach, and one which marks it as a manifestation of its historical moment.   In a 1994 interview, Costello described the instrumental approach of the Attractions to different songs as a kind of "sampling": that is, they consciously adopt the instrumental style appropriate to the style of the song in question much as a digital sampler records sounds and reproduces them.[19]   While, indeed, other pop musicians have changed "styles" even within a single album (the Beatles in their post-*Rubber Soul* albums come to mind as perhaps the earliest and best-known example of this with their music hall, European classical, and Indian influences), the innovation here is that Costello consciously plunders other pop styles. Yet his recordings remain recognizably his, primarily because of his voice, but also through certain melodic turns and idiosyncrasies in the lyrics.   In the songs in which the Attractions accompany him, their adaptations of previous instrumental approaches remain recognizably theirs through the imprint of *their* idiosyncratic approaches to their instruments (and this relies on notions of individualized creativity and virtuosity as well). Costello has occasionally approximated the sound of the Attractions using other musicians (e.g., "Coal Train Robberies" from *Spike*) without, however, managing to duplicate it.   At other times, Costello has literally sampled *himself*:   "Chewing Gum" from *Spike* samples the phrase "what they mean" from the earlier "Mystery Dance."[20]

This conscious mimesis of other pop styles would seem to threaten the stability of Costello's authorial voice, a voice which I described earlier as relying on certain Romantic notions of individuality; these notions in turn rely on a sense of stability in order to produce a recognizable, "individual" author from one appearance to the next.   Again, the historical moment in which Costello appeared carried with it specific notions of authorship that could acknowledge an individual in a series of works with a style that might have seemed inconsistent or unstable only a brief period of time earlier. In aesthetic terms, the issue may be explored by examining the concepts of "parody" and "pastiche." According to Fredric Jameson, pastiche is

the imitation of a peculiar or unique style, the wearing of a stylistic mask, speech in a dead language: but it is a neutral practice of such mimicry, without parody's ulterior motive, without the satirical impulse, without laughter, without that still latent feeling that there exists something *normal* compared to which what is being imitated is rather comic.[21]

Parody, on the other hand, contains the "satirical impulse" as well as the sense that a norm still exists against which a gesture may be understood as parody. An example of relatively straightforward parody in popular music is Simon and Garfunkel's "A Simple Desultory Phillipic." This song, released in 1966, clearly announces itself as a parody of Bob Dylan's "folk-rock" style, which had become widely known in 1965 through the huge popularity of Dylan's "Like a Rolling Stone." Simon's voice approximates the speech-like inflection of Dylan's; this contrasts with Simon's usual pretty, "folk-"type singing timbre. The words, in their ostentatious, beat-(poetry-)type rhymes suggest an exaggerated Dylan lyric as opposed to the non-modernist, "poetic" narrative of Simon's own lyrics. The music closely resembles Dylan's "From a Buick Six" from *Highway 61 Revisited* (the album containing "Like a Rolling Stone") in instrumentation, groove, and chord changes. Assuming an overlap of audience between Dylan and Simon and Garfunkel, Simon could have expected his audience to recognize the parodic intention of "A Simple Desultory Phillipic." In other words, parody assumes a relative stability of codes, while pastiche does not.

Let us return to "Pump It Up": it is difficult to hear it as parody, primarily because, despite its wealth of predecessors, it does not explicitly invoke *any* of them in the way that Simon's "Phillipic" does. It does not form an explicit homage either; rather, it is "the wearing of a stylistic mask" as suits the occasion. A listener with a detailed knowledge of rock 'n' roll history may recognize the reference, but it is not important that the listener make the connection in order to appreciate the song, a connection essential to the understanding of "A Simple Desultory Phillipic." At the same time, the recording of "Pump It Up" evokes its own feeling of passion and sincerity, both by drawing on the intensity of the chanted vocal "tradition" and by conveying energy through the high-pitched vocal tessitura (compared to "Subterranean Homesick Blues" or "Too Much Monkey Business") and the supercharged instrumental backing (which derives in part from the performance practice of punk).

As mentioned earlier, Costello's eclecticism is extreme; the sense that previous pop history exists as a source pool for him runs through his work: Motown and soul music for "Sneaky Feelings," the entire *Get Happy* album, and "Everyday I Write the Book"; country music for "Stranger in the House," "Radio Sweetheart," "Different Finger," the entire *Almost Blue* album, and much of *King of America*; Dylan, the Beatles, the Stones, the Who, the Kinks, Van Morrison, the Band, reggae, funk, R&B, jazz balladry, British Isles traditional music, commercial folk music – all these styles and more can be found throughout Costello's work, often within the same song. This eclecticism has been even more pronounced in his post-1984 work without the Attractions, which often features musicians who can provide a specific sound for the style and genre of the song at hand.

The absence of a belief in stylistic progress also separates Costello from eclectic progenitors such as the Beatles.[22] The work of the Beatles up to 1968 (including *Sergeant Pepper's Lonely Hearts Club Band* and *Magical Mystery Tour*) encouraged a belief in artistic growth and development (a belief challenged by *The Beatles* [the "White Album"], with *its* eclectic rummaging through pop styles). Their music steadily grew more "complex" harmonically, formally, and instrumentally, a kind of "development" which attracted musicologists to their work because it seemed to reinforce taken-for-granted connections between music analysis and musical value. The Beatles' music gradually assimilated a broader range of sources: classical music, music hall ballads, Indian music, electronic *musique concrète*, and surrealist poetry. Although Costello has explored sources recently that he did not explore in his earlier work (most notably classical music), his work began from a basis in stylistic pluralism. The Beatles may have evidenced a wide range of sources in their early cover material (fifties R&B, rockabilly, the Brill Building, Motown) but their early compositions display a stylistic *synthesis* not readily apparent in Costello's work in any phase. This disappearance of a teleological style model renders more plausible what could otherwise seem like a move "backwards" – going from the classically influenced *The Juliet Letters* (1993) to the Attractions-backed, rock pastiche of *Brutal Youth* (1994).

In Costello's music, the "flattening of history" and the failure of the belief in progress merge with another aspect of "Postmodernism and Consumer Society" discussed by Jameson: the eradication of the distinction between "high" and "low" culture. Costello's failure to "progress" in the aesthetic terms of Western European art music, when he follows the string quartet-accompanied song cycle of *The Juliet Letters* with the rock combo-accompanied and non-cyclical assortment of songs of *Brutal Youth*, becomes more understandable if we infer that to Costello, art music is merely more source material, not an elevated musical practice that, once ascended to, may never be left. The very fact that he could produce the albums in the order he did implies that he does not value "art music" over "rock," nor does he view producing art music as an advance from producing rock music.[23] At the same time, if the distinction between "high" and "low" has truly been eradicated, then there is no need to avoid classical music because of the snobbish associations with "high" culture that tend to alienate those who identify with "rebellious youth at the margins." What I am trying to emphasize here is that the manner in which Costello appropriates art music, when seen in the context of his output to date, avoids the claims to seriousness that dogged the practitioners of "progressive rock," and even to some extent the Beatles (and Motown's Holland-Dozier-Holland), in the sixties and early seventies. At the same time, this particular appropriation of classical music does not negate the different types of discourse that govern aesthetic judgments in art music and pop music, nor does it negate the different types of prestige associated with these musics.[24]

Costello and the sixties rock aesthetic

Examination of the response to Costello's early work in a publication such as *Rolling Stone* reveals how Costello's ambivalent relationship to sixties aesthetic values was received by listeners and critics with a particularly strong investment in those values. Greil Marcus greeted Costello's first album, *My Aim Is True*, by effusing that "much of Costello's album does not refer back to classic rock: it is classic rock." At least part of this appreciation rested on recognizing the difference between Costello and punk acts: "he has the musical sophistication, which is to say access to the musical credibility . . . that . . . at the moment, the Sex Pistols don't."[25] That is, in terms of musicianship and aesthetics, Costello had a more obvious affinity with sixties pop than the Sex Pistols. Yet despite this affinity, aspects of Costello's recordings perplexed reviewers; writing five months later, Ken Tucker, in an otherwise glowing review, noted that "Elvis Costello works in mysterious ways, his motives known to few."[26] Another year later, in a review of

Armed Forces, Janet Maslin summarized some of Costello's qualities that evoked both admiration and perplexity:

He writes short, blunt compositions that don't pretend to be artful, though they are, and don't demand to be taken seriously, even though they're more stunning and substantial than anything rock has produced in a good long while. He doubles back on himself at every turn, and you're forced to take it or leave it . . . Costello draws so heavily on the recent rock past that his reliance upon it amounts to a kind of cheapening, a repudiation. But that's only one more in a long line of quicksilver contradictions.[27]

The search for the "real" Costello beneath the façade continued in Mikal Gilmore's review of a Costello concert from the same period. His songs "create the illusion of disclosure while masking the artists' true passions and disillusions." Yet Gilmore is relieved when he can come "away from an Elvis Costello concert with the feeling that something, after all, had been revealed."[28] Here we see how Costello's performance elicits the desire for an unproblematic revealing of the inner self and then thwarts it. The unease in these reviews seems to stem from Costello's simultaneous rapprochement with and repudiation of "classic rock," from a penchant for self-reflexivity that questions his emotions even as he exposes them.

These reviews come from a period when Costello's work found its largest audience. As with the punks, however, the difficulties in presenting oneself as a commodity while simultaneously exposing the process of commoditization limited the duration of Costello's "mainstream" appeal. The audience he is left with now is the "highbrow," intellectual pop fan, the discerning listener who enjoys decoding the word games, the self-references, the historical allusions; the listener who appreciates the formal subtleties, the stylistic range, the presentation of the individualized persona of an inexhaustibly creative artist; the fan who responds to the way in which the instruments, vocals, and lyrics signify virtuosity and spontaneity, again based on codes learned from "authentic" pop styles (R&B, country, sixties British rock, folk-rock), jazz, and art music. This fan is Bourdieu's possessor of high cultural capital who has extended the pure gaze to non-legitimate objects, the fan of sixties rock who wants something new. These fans constitute Costello's cult.[29]

Thus far, we have examined how Billie Holiday, Hank Williams, and James Brown create (or, in the case of Bing Crosby, fail to create) authentic effects; in the case of Holiday and Williams, this occurs through the identification of the "author outside the text" – details known through biography, interviews, etc. – with one of the personae projected by the "author inside the text" – that is, one of the voices we hear in the recordings. Although James Brown's use of the "Intrusive I" creates a strong identification between textual voice and author, the conventions of artistic truth differ somewhat in his case and rely on invoking the codes of communal participation, hard work, and, ultimately, African-American preaching. Costello achieves his authentic effect in a way similar to that of Holiday and Williams, but it derives in his case specifically from a conflation of British and American sixties rock ideology with the self-consciousness of post-punk detachment. The ideology of sixties rock has to do with the uninhibited revealing of the self through the performance codes of spontaneity and passion: here, it is the raw display of "desires and feelings" that is important, not representing or pleasing an audience, the typical strategies of folk and pop performers respectively.[30] However, in this style of performance, the sincere display of passion is precisely what pleases the audience. Costello evokes this ideology more consistently in his post-1981 performance style (by contrast, early concert reviews stress his anger, arrogance, unwillingness to connect with the audience) and the majority of his recordings since 1986.

However, despite important links to sixties pop values, contradictions abound in Costello's songs in this elision of private and public selves, unlike the self-important "artistry" of many of the sixties post-beatniks. In his first three albums, the clipped, staccato vocal delivery and the occasional glittering, highly polished instrumental sound (particularly on *Armed Forces*) convey a sense of musical detachment, while the songs constantly refer to sixties pop styles and even specific songs ("Party Girl" on *Armed Forces* quotes the guitar riff from the Beatles' "The End" from *Abbey Road*), evoking sincerity through homage, but from a distance. The increasing use of a pastiche of non-pop forms in recent albums at times (folk, country, and blues in *King of America*) creates a greater sense of "roots" immediacy, but at other times (classical music in *The Juliet Letters*, and in parts of *Spike* and *Mighty Like a Rose*) creates a greater sense of distance from the members of his audience who have difficulty detaching themselves from high/low dichotomies focused on the opposition of art music to pop music. He restricts listener identification with the lyrics of his songs by inhabiting them with multiple personae and multiple subject positions, sometimes within a single song, confusing the sense of "who" is speaking. This strategy could derive either from the punk contempt for "meaningful" lyrics, or from the "artistic" evasion of realistic narrative of the Beat poets. What's more, Costello often writes lyrics from the perspective of an *observer*, thereby throwing into question the relationship between author and text.[31] Put another way, he makes the relationship between author and text more oblique to the extent that he makes it more difficult to hear the lyrics as a direct outpouring of his feelings.

III

Interpretation and (post)modern pop

Given all the aesthetic "contradictions" in Costello's recordings, what is an appropriate interpretative and/or analytical approach for any given Costello song? Difficulties still tend to arise when attempting to move from contextual issues to the interpretation of a specific text. Issues that may seem relatively clear when dealing with semiotic systems which are more obviously representational, such as media images and lyrics, may be more difficult to detect in musical syntax. To take an example, as discussed earlier Costello combines two different aspects of art school ideology in his music-making: the individualized artist adopted from sixties pop music practitioners, and the self-reflexive ideology of punk. The individualized artist (in Costello's work) needs connoisseurs to appreciate his work; the punk seeks to distance himself from commerce and side with "the people" as a paradoxical means of differentiating himself from commercial music so that he too can find a market of connoisseurs. While some of the techniques used by Costello to create a distanced effect were discussed earlier, how does the sense of individual artistry manifest itself in the "musical" aspects of his recordings? One way to distinguish the individual from the collective in musical terms is to employ forms that do not rely on strict, strophic repetition. Many of Costello's songs feature verses that differ slightly in length from verse to verse or that vary some other feature significantly: multiple bridges and codas are inserted or appended, creating very few cases of songs with a regular strophic form. This tends to infuse the circular, "mythic" quality of songs consisting largely of discursive repetition (repetition as it occurs in strophic song or ballad forms) with elements of the developmental, narrative, and teleological forms characteristic of post-Enlightenment art music in which every event plays a singular structural role.[32] This move from formal analysis to interpretation involves explicating both a "primary" level of signification such as "positional values," and the interconnection of this level with "secondary" levels such as "positional implications," "emotive connotations," and "rhetorical connotations" (these are associations arising from correspondences with rhetorical forms and styles).

"Pills and Soap," the song which I will examine most closely in this chapter, was chosen partly because it provides a good example of Costello's tendency towards through-composed, teleological forms in the relatively early part of his recording career (the song was recorded in 1983). I also chose "Pills and Soap" because the conditions of its production and reception exemplify many of the paradoxes between art and commerce, political integrity and financial practicality, in which Costello finds himself imbedded. Finally, in its approach to music, "Pills and Soap" is an important precursor of Costello's later explicit interest in the hierarchically organized structures of Western art music. Before interpreting the song at greater length, let's examine some of the particular contextual factors surrounding "Pills and Soap."

"Pills and Soap," or, a case study of an "oppositional" pop song

Costello released "Pills and Soap" in May 1983, shortly before the UK general election, under the pseudonym "the Imposter" owing to legal and contractual complications which prevented him from releasing a song under his own name at the time. The lyrics, according to Costello (as reported by Costello biographer Mick St. Michael), were "inspired by television news footage of a funeral in Northern Ireland," and sought to describe the "manipulation of the 'human animal, in all its many ways . . . particularly misplaced sentiment, including patriotism'."[33] Reportedly, Costello linked the song to the election, vowing to withdraw the song on Election Day. His political views assumed a more overt, public form in several interviews given around this time:

it's actually morally wrong to vote for the Tories . . . it's an insensitive government, it doesn't have any compassion for people who are not self-made business people. They have no feeling for people who haven't got any money or a job. They're quite prepared to *damn* large portions of the population to miserable lives.[34]

"Pills and Soap" turned out to be his biggest hit single since "Oliver's Army" in 1979, and Costello subsequently failed to withdraw the song on Election Day. According to St. Michael, "the episode was to many an unexpected climbdown by one of pop's most principled personalities – a feeling intensified when a near-identical 'remodelled version' was included on [an] album" (p. 94). This notion of an "unexpected climbdown" returns us to many of the contradictions raised by the attempt to produce through the culture industry an "oppositional" or "resistant" message that critiques capitalism, imperialism, and disciplinary society. Costello needs to sell recordings in order to maintain his career as a professional entertainer; the record company needs to sell recordings in order to remain in business. If critiques of mass media sell recordings, then this enables Costello and the record company to produce more recordings. Yet writers such as St. Michael and the staff of *Rolling Stone* continue to dream of a popular music that can proceed oblivious to the needs of commerce. It is only really partially possible to maintain the appearance of invulnerability to commerce on the local level; and, indeed, it is the trajectory of bands from the local to the national/international level that creates one of the most common narratives based on the opposition of authenticity vs. selling out.

Analysis of "Pills and Soap"

Example 5.1 displays a transcription into staff notation of "Pills and Soap." What does an analysis of the harmonic and motivic content of the first seventeen measures (the introduction and section A) tell us?

(1) That the underlying harmony is fundamentally static: there is no sense of harmonic progression, only a pedal tone on C, which is briefly displaced by G-flat;

(2) that the vocal line is similarly static: a single melodic idea – containing the pitches E-flat-D natural-C natural – pervades the section, is subsequently transposed to G-flat-F natural-E-flat, and is then restated at the initial level;

(3) that the transposition of the melodic idea in conjunction with the tritone movement in the bass (C to G-flat) creates a temporary sense of an octatonic pitch collection (see example 5.2).[35]

This formalist account tells us little about the affect produced by the passage in question, but it does help explain its "syntactical" meaning. A musically trained listener may sense the tonal stasis, and the fact that some non-standard mode, such as the octatonic collection, may have sounded briefly. A musically non-literate listener may attribute a vague kind of "creepy" effect to the whole proceeding. To explain this we must rely on the processes of "secondary signification," such as "emotive connotations" or "style connotations," in which a kind of pastiche or quotation technique is employed. The reversed timbre at the beginning connotes a kind of otherworldliness (an effect taken from movies and

Example 5.1: *Transcription of "Pills and Soap"*

Words and Music by Elvis Costello
Transcription by David Brackett

Example 5.1 (*cont.*)

Example 5.1 (*cont.*)

Example 5.1 (*cont.*)

Example 5.1 (*cont.*)

Example 5.1 (*cont.*)

Example 5.1 (*cont.*)

Example 5.1 (*cont.*)

musique concrète which may date back to mid twentieth-century modernism?); this "reversed" timbre, the deadpan, slightly flat vocal delivery, and the tritone/octatonic quality all evoke a feeling of terror, horror, evil, which we can trace back through the use of such gestures in horror films, and back even further to the use of the tritone and octatonic scale to depict evil in operas and ballets from the turn of the century (e.g., Stravinsky's *The Firebird*).[36] The relentless mechanical quality of the synthesized hand claps and the harsh piano accents further contributes to the grim atmosphere (suggesting a gangland confrontation in a back alley, "Cool" from *West Side Story*?).[37]

This account of the first seventeen measures contends that the music reinforces the meaning of the lyrics, which on the whole convey an ominous effect. A line-by-line analysis of text and music provides information on how these syntactical processes operate on a more detailed level:

They talked to the sister, the father and the mother

This line occupies eight beats, during which the three-note melodic idea is stated and repeated. Verbs and nouns are stressed on beats one and three: "talked," "sister," "father," "mother," with the predominant emphasis on nouns – hence, the impression created is one of a static tableau of objects rather than of a sense of action. The stasis of the melodic idea, the repetition of the ostinato in the bass, the mechanical

Example 5.2: *Octatonic pitch collection in "Pills and Soap"*

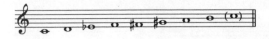

hand claps, and the lack of resonance in the voice all reinforce the
monotony of this recitation of the list of family members. The spectrum
photo (example 5.3) displays the lack of overtones and the resulting
"dryness" of the voice in this section of the song. Note that above the
fundamental of the vocal line, there is usually one line (overtone) moving
in parallel, at times two overtones (above "tears"), and at other times no
overtones ("sister").

with a microphone in one hand and a cheque book in the other

As in the first line, this line occupies eight beats and repeats the same
melodic idea. Again, three of the four accented words are nouns –
"microphone," "cheque book," "other" – with the same resultant
emphasis. The piano accents in mm. 7 and 9 create a sonic link between
"father" and "cheque book," while the rhyming of the endings of the
antecedent-consequent phrase formed by these two lines links "mother"
and "other" (a comment on patriarchal stereotypes and attitudes?). The
obsessive musical repetition creates a sense of lifelessness, ominousness,
foreboding, meaninglessness. Here, the *internal* musical relationships
(the fact of repetition) result in an effect of "primary signification"; the
lyrics and our knowledge of Costello provide the "interpretive frame"
which in turn suggests the "content" of the syntactical process.

and the camera noses into the tears on her face

Again, this line brings no new musical information; and again, accents
stress important objects in the line: "camera," "tears," "face." Previous
sensations intensify as the repetition continues relentlessly, exemplifying
how the effect of musical stasis can produce a kind of change.

the tears on her face, the tears on her face

While continuing to employ a variant of the primary melodic idea, the
twofold repetition of the last phrase of the previous line creates an
unprecedented emphasis on two words: "tears" and "face." The slight
change in the melodic motive – pitch D on beat three is replaced by
pitch C – "rounds off" the first eight measures by eliminating the small
amount of melodic motion provided by the tension of the "appoggiatura"

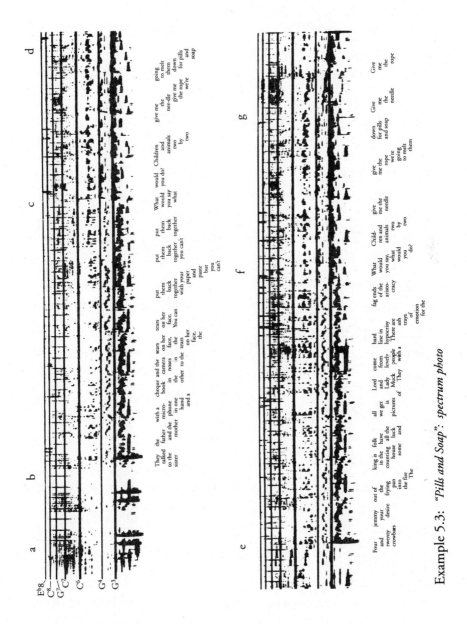

Example 5.3: *"Pills and Soap": spectrum photo*

h

i

j

k

l

m

n

o

The sugar coated pill is getting bitterer still
you think your country needs you but you
know it will never
pack up your bag so
stolen hand-bag your troubles in a
Don't dilly dilly boys
rally round the flag
Give us our daily bread
Indi-vidual slices daily in
some-thing in the daily rag to
cancel any crisis
What would you say what
would you do?
Children and animals two by two
give me the needle
give me the rope we're
going to melt them down for
pills and soap

Give me the needle
give me the rope

We're going to melt them down

for pills and soap

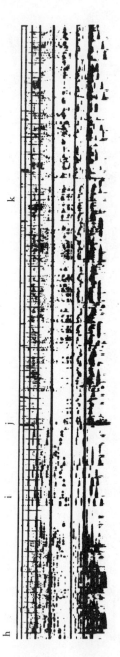

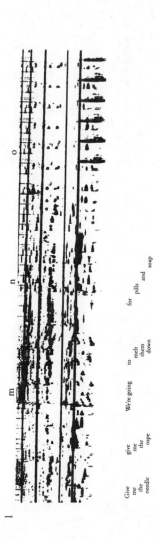

Example 5.3 (cont.)

created by the D against the C minor triad played by the piano. Of course, the emphasis on this line of the text focuses attention on the tragic aspects of the scene described by the narrator.[38] The spectrum photo reveals a sonic emphasis on the word "tears" as it activates two overtones in the most sustained fashion so far.

You can put them back together with your paper and paste

Measure 14 continues with a variant of the primary melodic idea, which is now recontextualized by the change of the bass to G-flat; this creates dissonances between the melody and the bass where none existed previously despite the fact that the pitches of the melody have not changed. Does this increase in tension cast doubt on the ability of the ambiguous "you" to put the almost equally ambiguous "them" back together? That is, does the fact that the melody and bass are not "together" themselves undercut the possibility of "putting them back together"? (This may be a good example of "dancing about architecture": does this notion of musical "togetherness" rely on analytical preconceptions rather than on aural experience? Do the melody and bass *sound* "untogether" at this point in any absolute sense? Or is the change in affect due to the G-flat in the bass and the linear tritone relationship?) The leap of the voice to the pitch G-flat on the word "paper" creates a momentary coordination of melody and bass, subsequently destroyed by the pitch D on "paste."

but you can't put them back together, you can't put them back together

As in mm. 12–13, this line repeats a previously heard phrase with an important difference: it contradicts the meaning of the previous line. The text/music relationship is particularly implicative at this moment, for while the previous line claimed that "you" "can put them back together" while the melody and bass were *not together*, this line synchronizes melody and bass while stating that "you can't put them back together" (previous caveats about musical "togetherness" still apply). The repetition of these lines and the music/text coordination emphasize the priority of the negative form of the statement. The rhythmic anticipations begun in m. 15 with "paste" continue with "together" in mm. 16–17, and serve to propel the song forward. This "anticipation" effect is enhanced in mm. 16–17 by the chordal accents on beat one and the second half of beat two, while the change in harmonic rhythm to two chords per measure anticipates the harmonic motion of the B section and leads into it by way of the bass (i.e., the pitch movement from C to G leads to F).

By contrast, the affect of the music in the B section (mm. 18–27; see example 5.1) for the most part *contradicts* the overall tenor of the lyrics (which intensify the feeling of doom in the first section and imply suicide as a "solution"). While the voice continues its static reiteration of its melodic idea – now transposed to A-flat-G natural-F natural – the bass becomes more active, anchoring a flowing harmonic succession consisting of four chords. This bass line reinforces the centricity of F through its outlining the interval of a perfect fifth, F natural-C natural; in retrospect, the insistence in the A section of the bass on pitch C makes that section function as a long "upbeat" for the B section. The lack of a raised leading tone in the B section creates a strong Dorian, modal flavor, and the raised fourth-scale degree in the bass recalls the emphasis of that scale degree in the A section. The strongest aural precedent for this sort of tonal effect is probably certain jazz-oriented passages associated with "cool" jazz, perhaps more the 1950s TV version of that music (or perhaps, again, a "jazzy" musical such as *West Side Story*) than the music actually created by leading musicians associated with the style. This "coolness" in the face of the impending doom of the lyrics and of the preceding tone of the A section may indicate a cynical acceptance of the inevitability of catastrophe. Here, the contradiction between music and lyrics may indicate a calm acceptance of suicide as a solution.

Again, a line-by-line analysis of this section amplifies these observations and reveals some moments in which the music reinforces as well as contradicts the sense of the lyrics.

What would you say, what would you do?

The song's persona turns here from the "neutral" observation of the first section to the active posing of a question. The increased musical activity finds sympathy with the accented action words: "say," "would," "do." The transposition of the melodic idea to a higher pitch level increases the energy, as does the added resonance of the voice on the brighter vowel in "say" (note the dense band of overtones above this word in example 5.3). The rhythmic anticipation begun at the end of the last section continues here on the second half of the second beat in m. 19 on "do," coordinated again with accents in the piano.

Children and animals two by two

This line repeats almost literally the music from the preceding line while stressing objects such as "children," "animals," "two" – a treatment of the text recalling that in the first section. The semantic sense of the text does not clearly function as an answer to the question posed in the preceding line.

Give me the needle, give me the rope

Again, the transposed version of the basic melodic idea repeats, now accenting the words "give," "needle," and "rope." The spectrum photo (example 5.3) reveals that "needle" activates higher partials even more than "say" did in the first line of this section. The parallelism of these bright vowels in the first and third lines is strengthened by the overall grammatical parallelism of the two lines, suggesting that it is this line, not the second, which answers the question posed in the first line of the section.[39]

we're going to melt them down for pills and soap

If the previous line referred back to the question of mm. 18–19, then the "them" of this line probably refers to the "children and animals" of m. 20 for similar reasons of grammatical parallelism. The title "Pills and Soap" is duly emphasized by the fourth repetition of the melodic idea at this pitch level.

The beginning of the C section transposes the bass and initial pitch of the melodic idea up a perfect fourth with respect to the beginning of the B section, duplicating the relationship between the A and B sections. However, unlike the transposition at the beginning of the B section, the B-flat that begins the C section in the bass does not establish a new tonal center, but is quickly heard retroactively as the subdominant (IV) of F. The descending bass movement in mm. 28–29 (the first two measures of this section) is then followed by a repetition of the progression which dominates the B section (mm. 30–31), further emphasizing pitch F as the tonal center. The exploration of a higher vocal tessitura is not the only factor involved in creating the sense of "progress" as the music moves from one section to the next. The details of the spectrum photos in example 5.4 show the way in which increasingly bright vowel sounds accompany the steady rise in pitch. The repetition of "needle" in the C section generates the most intense spectral activity thus far; this reinforces the stress that "needle" receives both as a registral high point and as the most strongly accented melodic dissonance thus far in the piece (the pitch C-flat which resolves to B-flat). The first repetition of a complete line of the lyrics ("give me the needle, give me the rope") also contributes to the emphasis in this section. This repetition heightens the sense that the "needle" (self-destruction through drugs?) and the "rope" (self-destruction through suicide?) are the solution of choice to at least one of the song's personae (the one addressed by the question of the B section – "What would you say, what would you do?")

Example 5.4: *"Pills and Soap": correlation of tessitura and timbral brightness*

Section A

tears　　　on　her　face

tears
on her
face

Section B

give me the nee — dle

give me
the
nee-dle

Section C

give me　the　nee - dle

give
me
the
needle

The continuation of the C section, with its emphasis on pitch C in the bass in both the interlude (mm. 32–35) and the coda (mm. 42–45), acts as a "dominant upbeat" to a cadence on F at the end of those sections, a process reminiscent of the way in which section A functioned in relation to section B. In a procedure consistent with the rest of the song, linear motions do not lead to this "cadence" in a common-practice fashion in the interlude/coda: the bass voice consists of an ostinato framed by C and G while the upper voice consists of interlocking minor thirds, E-flat-C, D-flat-B-flat; this produces a sense of "linear counterpoint" with little sense of vertical harmony compared to the other sections of the piece (a vertical sense of harmony is particularly strong in the B section, mm. 28–31). In terms of "connotative" meaning, this type of linear counterpoint recalls practices derived from modernist art music; the ponderous synthesizer sounds create a mechanical effect, perhaps implying that the heavily automated technological aspects of modern life are part of the dehumanization described in the lyrics. Also important are the striking, organum-like passages of parallel fifths and octaves (mm. 38–39), with their connotations of ecclesiastical austerity and foreboding – affective qualities in keeping with the overall mood of the song. That this passage follows the despair expressed by the text/music of the C section suggests the obliteration of the song's persona in a cold, nightmarish, mechanized holocaust.

The strophic treatment of the A section casts an affective slant on the second and third verses similar to that of the first verse. Every time this section returns – with its almost expressionless, droning vocal, narrow range, dark vowel sounds, ostinato bass, and piano accents – its relentless, ominous character increases. After the cataclysmic interlude following the first statement of the C section material, the return of the A section for the third verse ("The sugar coated pill is getting bitterer still") appears almost as a eulogy. An interesting point is that the lines that appear in verses 2 and 3 in the place analogous to mm. 14–15 in verse 1 (which contained the text "You can put them back together with your paper and paste"), where the melody "separates" from the bass as the bass moves to G-flat, also imply a kind of separation which is then resolved by the following line: verse 2 – "They come from lovely people with a hard line in hypocrisy" – emphasizes the separation between the inner and outer selves of the ruling class, presented with the sarcastic modifier "lovely"; the next line – "There are ashtrays of emotion for the fag ends of the aristocracy" – suggests that these hypocritical emotions have nonetheless found a socially sanctioned receptacle. The equivalent line in verse 3 – "Give us our daily bread in individual slices" – conveys a sense of alienation in its emphasis on individuality (do whole loaves, then, emphasize social collectivity?), while the following line – "and something in the daily rag to cancel any crisis" – shows how the media pacify any sense of dissatisfaction through their interminable presentation of hystericized events: this is the "re-solution" to the sense of alienation engendered by life in the (post)modern, post-industrial age.

I should clarify here that the point in these hermeneutic ruminations is not to imply that there is one semantic interpretation possible for the signifying union of music and text: in some cases, it is easier to demonstrate conventional, referential associations, as in the horror film, cool jazz pastiche/quotations noted earlier; in other cases, such as the "mechanical" quality of the interlude just mentioned, the value may lie *in intimating the performer/composer's attitudes to the sentiments expressed in the lyrics.* In these cases, the "interpretation" may seem more arbitrary than in those cases in which references with long historical associations can be demonstrated.

Can we extract further conclusions from a consideration of the more abstract features of the song's tonal relationships that could contribute to a "poetics of song"?[40] As discussed earlier, the tonal motion of the B section, C section, interlude, and coda furnishes what sense of tonal closure exists in the song. The text in these sections features the posing of questions by (one of) the song's narrator(s), and the resultant bleak replies. Does this imply that the description presented by the text in the A section (which is harmonically static and functions as a "dominant upbeat" to the B section) rests outside the main action of the song and, correspondingly, that it is less important to the narrator's world view than thoughts of self-destruction and annihilation? Or that the question and answer of the B section is relatively bounded in relation to the descriptive passages of the A section, which, because they do not contain a sense of closure, are fated to continue indefinitely (reinforced by the fade-out at the end of the recording)?

Rhythm and gesture

Example 5.5 displays a "gestural" chart.[41] This reinforces observations made earlier about vocal register and harmonic motion, and adds to it the component of "groove." The levels of the vocal and chords in section A display what I referred to earlier as the static effect of this section. The level of the groove shows a combination of two accentual patterns – a steady accent on the "backbeat," beats two and four, and a pattern dividing the measure into 3 + 3 + 2 eighth notes – that produces a kind

Example 5.5: *"Pills and Soap": gestural chart*

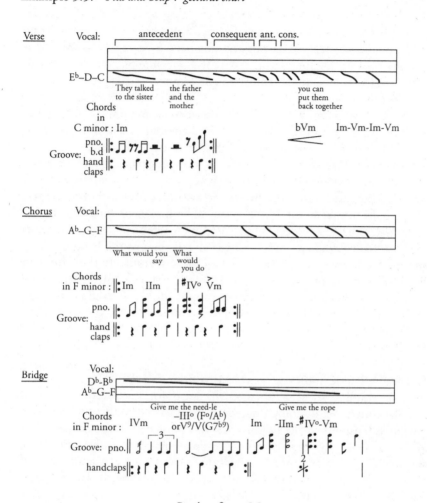

Brackett figure 5.5

of polymetric effect. The tension between these patterns, felt most prominently in the anticipation of the third beat, is felt as a kind of physical jerk or twitch against the relentlessly mechanical hand claps. The vocal often reinforces this sense of anticipation, either by attacking the accent between beats two and three simultaneously with the hand claps, or by a more subtle rhythmic inflection slightly ahead of the beat.

The gestural chart for section B reveals the continuing stasis of the vocal line, albeit in a higher register; and a more rapid harmonic rhythm with a quality of tension and release resulting from the I–V motion in the bass and the increased busyness of the groove. Now the accent between beats two and three is played by a piano chord, and frequently doubled by the vocal. The physical analogue here can be described as walking forward resolutely (the new mobility of the piano part), with an occasionally exaggerated, truncated, or stumbling step (the accented anticipation).

The C section presents the most contrast so far in terms of gesture and its corresponding somatic response. The antecedent vocal phrase once again ascends to a new register, but the consequent phrase returns to the register of the B section. The harmonic movement up to IV and back to I, while not producing the relaxation typical of harmonic movement towards the subdominant, produces a kind of tension and release different from that heard in the verse. The dissonant diminished triad accentuates the word "needle" and implies a temporary glance towards the dominant (an altered II?). The groove maintains the hand clapping backbeat, but now adds to this a feeling of "suspended rhythm" through the introduction of sustained durations (half-note) and quarter-note triplets. This heightens the dramatic impact of this climactic reiteration of the line "give me the needle, give me the rope."

Lyrics

Until now I have consciously avoided considering the lyrics in isolation because this has so often formed the basis for the interpretation of popular songs. Yet in doing this, the analysis of "Pills and Soap" has thus far ignored aspects of the lyrics which *do* contribute to the overall effect of the song. The lyrics reveal an approach as self-consciously "arty" as the music. They do not convey a straightforward narrative, nor do they fall into one of the many pop music genres, such as the love ballad, the let's-party-and-dance number, or the story or fantasy narrative song. They express neither loss nor desire in any overt way. They do fall loosely into what might be termed the "social criticism" genre, but, in contrast to "protest" songs, these lyrics only criticize through allusion; specifically, they criticize the way the mass media and corporations incite desire in the masses ("four and twenty crowbars jemmy your desire"). As in much poetry, the images function paradigmatically; that is, certain characters or figures recur in various guises, accumulating meaning through a dense web of associations, rather than through a syntagmatic, narrative chain. Example 5.6 shows some of these relationships, which I have grouped under the headings of "them" and "us": "them" includes both personages

Example 5.6:   *"Pills and Soap": analysis of lyrics*

Lyrics	The mass media/technocracy: "them"	"us"
Verse 1: They talked to the sister, the father and the mother	They	sister, father, mother
with a microphone in one hand and a cheque book in the other	microphone, cheque book	
and the camera noses into the tears on her face.	camera	<u>her</u> face
You can put them back together with your paper and paste, but you can't put them back together.		together you, them
Refrain: What would you say, what would you do?		you
Children and animals two by two,		children and animals
give me the needle give me the rope,		me
we're going to melt them down for pills and soap.	we're	them
Verse 2: Four and twenty crowbars jemmy your desire,		your
out of the frying pan into the fire,		
the king is in the counting house, some folk have all the luck,	king some folk	
and all we get are pictures of Lord and Lady Muck.	Lord and Lady Muck	we
They come from lovely people with a hard line in hypocrisy,	They lovely people	
there are ashtrays of emotion for the fag ends of the aristocracy.	aristocracy	
Verse 3: The sugar coated pill is getting bitterer still		
you think your country needs you but you know it never will,	your country	you
so pack up your troubles in a stolen handbag,		your troubles
don't dilly dally boys, rally round the flag.	the flag	
Give us our daily bread in individual slices,		us individual slices
and something in the daily rag to cancel any crisis.	daily rag	

Example 5.7: Topoi *in the text of "Pills and Soap"*

Biblical allusions	Nursery rhymes (clichés)
Children and animals two by two	You can't put them back together (Humpty Dumpty)
Give us our daily bread	four and twenty "crow" bars
	The king is in the counting house
	out of the frying pan, into the fire
	pack up your troubles

such as the king, Lord and Lady Muck, the aristocracy, and lovely people, as well as objects such as the microphone, the camera, the cheque book, the flag, and the daily rag; while "us" includes the sister, father, mother, children, and animals. Certain pronouns, such as "you" and "they," accentuate their potential as "shifters," indicating fluctuating subject positions between the various verses and refrains, heightening the sense of confusion and creating an almost hallucinatory or dream-like quality.[42] For example, the pronoun "we" in "*we're* going to melt them down for pills and soap" and "all *we* get are pictures of Lord and Lady Muck" clearly implies two different groups of people. The prominence of these shifters also contributes to an aspect of Costello's lyrics mentioned earlier: the way in which he creates a sense of multiple narrators or authorial voices. Yet the paradigmatic associations do end up creating a consistent critique of the mass media, and one which is amplified in numerous other Costello songs: "Blame It on Cain," "Clubland," "Watch Your Step," "Worthless Thing," "Tramp the Dirt Down," "Satellite."

Example 5.7 presents two other important *topoi* in the text of "Pills and Soap." These *topoi*, containing biblical allusions and nursery rhymes, heighten the effect of ironic distance, as lines connoting the innocence of childhood are used to convey brutal aspects of modern life.

Timbre

We have thus far used information from spectrum photos to add to our sense of how the music of "Pills and Soap" reveals something of Costello's attitude towards the text. An overview of the photo (example 5.3) corroborates earlier statements about the teleological nature of the song. The timbral transformations in "Pills and Soap" both correspond to and expand upon the formal divisions implied by the arrangement of the lyrics into stanzas and refrains. The spectrum photo in example 5.3

displays some of these transformations: the gradual accumulation of acute spectral elements during the first two verses between letters *a* and *h* leading up to the intense opposition during the instrumental interlude at letter *h*; the repetition of this building process between letters *j* and *n* climaxing with the final statement of the line – "We're going to melt them down for pills and soap"; and the final contrast between high and low registers at letter o during the fade-out.

This type of play with registral opposition is much more typical of pieces of Western art music than it is of almost any other form of music in the world, be it popular, "traditional," or non-Western "art" music. Examination of the photos in Robert Cogan's *New Images of Musical Sound* reveals a greater similarity between the spectrum photo of "Pills and Soap" and the photos of a Gregorian chant, a Beethoven piano sonata, the "Confutatis" from Mozart's *Requiem*, Debussy's "Nuages," and Varèse's *Hyperprism*, than between "Pills and Soap" and the Tibetan Tantric chant or Balinese Shadow-play music. For that matter, the photo of "Pills and Soap" more closely resembles these pieces of art music than it does the photo for "Hey Good Lookin'," the photo of which may reveal timbral contrast on a local level without that contrast contributing to a larger sense of teleological form.

IV

A question of influence

"Pills and Soap," while an extreme example of certain tendencies of Costello's songwriting at the time it was recorded, is in other ways clearly connected with lyrical and musical tendencies in his work. Musically, the use of stylistic pastiche and a complex combination of strophic and through-composed song forms recalls predilections in other works. Moreover, the vocal style, through the use of rhythmic anticipation and delay, and through the use of stressed non-harmonic tones that resolve downwards (as in "They talked to the *Mo*ther"), incorporates what has been termed "snaking the voice": the way in which country musicians (and practitioners of most African-American styles) "ornament" melodies using stressed non-harmonic tones.[43] Costello may have acquired this musical habit from several sources: from his well-publicized devotion to country music; from a jazz singer such as Billie Holiday (who often substitutes scale degree $\hat{2}$ for scale degree $\hat{1}$ at cadences, a favorite Costello device); from Bob Dylan, whose timbre and manner of phrasing and ornamentation Costello's closely resembles at times; and from soul singers in general, and from Smokey Robinson in particular. Both Robinson and Costello (and to some extent Dylan) frequently portamento (or slide) down a perfect fourth either beginning or ending on a non-harmonic tone: hear Robinson sing "I'm *crying*" from "Ooh, Baby, Baby," and compare with Costello singing "When you don't call *up*" from "Little Triggers." Both singers frequently slide from the second scale degree down to the first, creating a dissonance over the tonic triad: listen to Robinson singing "smile" in the second line of the chorus of "Tracks of My Tears" ("if my *smile* looks out of place") and compare it with Costello singing "My aim is *true*" from "Alison," or "I know what I've *done*" from the first two verses of "Accidents Will Happen." Even when not "snaking the voice" in this fashion, Costello frequently ends a phrase by landing on a non-harmonic tone.[44] "Pills and Soap" is somewhat anomalous in this respect, in that it uses the devices of portamento and of ending phrases on non-harmonic tones very little; the clearest example is the final "We're going to melt them down," in which Costello sustains the pitch G on the word "down" against F in the bass (see example 5.1, mm. 45–47).

"Pills and Soap" also recapitulates many *topoi* that appear in Costello's lyrics, principally those of the pernicious influence of the mass media and the oppressive effect of centralized power. These *topoi* offer a critique of capitalism and disciplinary society that refers to the way in which fear and desire are attached to capitalist enterprises; this is prominent in "Pills and Soap" and in songs such as "Night Rally." Songs such as "The Beat" and "Strict Time" link these ideas to the idea of *musical* discipline through puns (the most obvious source of Costello's noted use of puns, inverted clichés, and extended metaphors can be found in Robinson and country music). This idea of musical discipline is also linked to fear and desire, with their negative and positive qualities, as the relentless rock pulse is presented both as imprisoning (as described by the words) and liberating (the music encourages physical movement). The fact that "Pills and Soap" takes "politics" as its subject rather than personal relationships does not mean that a stark gap separates Costello's songs about the "personal" and the "political"; rather, Costello's lyrics remind us that "the personal is the political." Greil Marcus wrote in 1979 in a review of *Armed Forces* that Costello's lyrics "merge . . . our political shadows with our private affairs." This "suggests a secret, shared longing for a real police state: a vengeful, guilty authoritarianism that, in the emotional fascism [the original title of *Armed Forces*] of everyday life, we are already acting out."[45]

In terms of authorial "presence," the use by Declan MacManus (Costello's "real" name) of the "Imposter" moniker in the initial release of "Pills and Soap" recalls and anticipates his use of such names as Napoleon Dynamite, Howard Coward, the Emotional Toothpaste, the Little Hands of Concrete, the Beloved Entertainer, and "Elvis Costello"; this calls into question typical pop assumptions that link the singer's/songwriter's biography (who is "Elvis Costello"?) and the content of song lyrics, as do the lyrics themselves with their ever-shifting point of view. His use of stylistic pastiche thwarts Romantic notions of authorship, while, contradictorily, sly in-jokes and certain types of stylistic references (most prominently to the Beatles) create a sense of authorial continuity.[46] Lastly, the apparent contradictions between his political intentions in the distribution of "Pills and Soap" and what he actually did (threatening to withdraw it and then not withdrawing it) recall all the debates about art and commerce that have raged since music became involved with capitalism; but they particularly recall the arguments that swirled around the punk avant-garde and other kinds of protest singers.

Roland Barthes, at the height of his infatuation with structuralism in 1966, quoted a sentence from Edgar Allen Poe's *The Murders in the Rue Morgue*: "It will be found in fact that the ingenious are always fanciful and the truly imaginative never otherwise than analytic." In other words, while "fancy" – in Barthes' formulation the quality responsible for "statements of detail" – may be indispensable to the creation of art, "*imagination* is mastery of a code."[47] That is, without mastery of a code, creative work is not possible. But the very fact that narrative is "coded" means that it lends the appearance of the natural to the artificial, thereby rendering form invisible in a novel or a pop song. While much of the enjoyment of Costello's music is undoubtedly visceral, we can assume that a large portion of his audience, as well as Costello himself, delights in his imaginative manipulation of codes, in the way in which he calls attention to formal artifice. It is true that lyrics are not speeches, and that tunes are not paintings: they all rely on different codes in order not to call attention to their particular forms of contrivance. Thus we continue dancing about architecture while passionately decrying artifice, forgetting that there is nothing natural about contemporary popular music, and that we even enjoy the manipulation of form (without necessarily verbalizing that that is what we enjoy).

Granted that, few listeners (and certainly not Costello himself) would feel the need to "translate" even a formally complex pop song from the realm of "music knowledge" about music to "speech knowledge" about music (although this separation assumes that some aspect of knowledge exists anterior to language). The point here is not whether the approach taken here is appropriate for "high" or "low" cultural artifacts, for members of Costello's audience, or for Costello himself; the point is that this approach is directed toward the audience for this book, rather than to some ideal fan of the song. As stated earlier, the legitimate gaze can be turned toward any object; and this is emerging as the primary determinant of high culture, rather than an essence that resides in the object itself.[48]

In aesthetic terms, Elvis Costello flirts with, and distances himself from, the signs of high culture, emphasizing that those signs are in play. This stance is ideally suited to encouraging the audience's perception of him as a "cult" figure. Maintenance of cult status requires him to negotiate the tricky business of remaining in the popular music business while not achieving or maintaining mass popularity. This position *vis-à-vis* the music industry motivates the complicated self-reflexivity of his songs, which struggle to express a critical stance towards the technocratic music business even while admitting obliquely to being trapped within the system itself. Aesthetically as well, his songs blend an arty, "highbrow" concern with certain types of complexity and teleological form with moves that simultaneously mock those forms. In a sense, Costello's deviousness results from the fact that he is trapped: he must remain popular enough to ensure that the record company receives some return on its investment, while at the same time he must remain "different enough" to maintain the effect of "expressing himself" regardless of the restraints of the culture industry.

Elvis Costello provides art music for an audience that looks to popular music for formal sophistication, that wants new music with the signs of passion and complexity that they associate with pop music of the sixties without the sixties' naïveté and optimism. It's an audience that wants to believe that artifacts can still pass through the culture industry that criticize the industry without compromising themselves. They want a musician who can synthesize the sincerity and musicianship of sixties pop with the anger and self-criticism of punk. They want someone who can evade the objectifying processes of disciplinary society through the endlessly creative subjectification of the self. And in "Elvis Costello" the audience finds someone whom they can believe wants those things too.

Afterword: the citizens of Simpleton

■■
■■

Never been near a university
Never took a paper or a learned degree

Thus begins XTC's 1989 recording, "The Mayor of Simpleton." The "human universe" of these lyrics returns us to the Romantic anti-intellectual stance expressed by Elvis Costello in the last chapter. The song also serves as a vehicle for discussing issues raised by the preceding case studies, in particular, that of the tension between academic discourse and the constitution of the popular song as an object of study.

Yet while the music of "The Mayor of Simpleton" – with its driving rhythm track and occasionally rasping vocals – may convey the signs of uncalculated emotion to those who are sympathetic towards this particular blend of pop and rock, the song is also obviously a very sophisticated piece of music (and although the songwriter, Andy Partridge, never did take "a paper or a learned degree," he did attend art school, and his motives for doing so would have fitted easily into Frith and Horne's *Art into Pop*).[1] "The Mayor of Simpleton" contrasts a tonally "static" section, featuring a two-chord riff with a bass line roaming freely over the mode implied by the chords, with a chorus featuring a functional chord progression and a wide-ranging melody. The bridge contains a complex chord progression and carefully arranged, intricate vocal harmony reminiscent of the Beatles at their most baroque.

At the same time, the song is *fun*: the self-deprecation of the words meshes and contrasts with the obvious intelligence of the music. The songwriter, the band, and the "voice inside the text," clearly do have brains, but seem to be saying that they feel intelligence is unimportant. Or are they saying that they don't want their audience to think that they think it is important to them? Perhaps the song is a gentle mockery of those who place a premium on braininess? Or perhaps the song recognizes the essential fallibility and "simplicity" of even the most "intelligent" person, and the virtue of not taking one's own "intelligence" too seriously: if these observations have any validity, then we can interpret the song as saying that we would all do well to consider ourselves "citizens of Simpleton."

These lyrics, despite their contradictions, confront us with the fact that, even among the brainiest pop musicians,[2] it is clearly undesirable to display one's analytical tendencies. On the other hand, in contrast to pop musicians and fans, academic discourse advocates a distanced, analytical attitude towards its objects of study. Yet the analysis and interpretation of popular music lie outside the discourse of musicology as well. The resistance to analysis in both of these contexts rests on different arguments that nonetheless overlap: musicologists often refuse to acknowledge that the aesthetic value they find in art music is relative; therefore, to take music that is so closely tied to commerce seriously may seem laughable – this argument rests on the myth that art music is free from commerce, rather than recognizing the fact that it is linked with commerce in ways that differ from pop music. Fans' resistance rests on a related argument that works in a different way. Here "naturalness" is opposed to "calculation." "Calculation" in this context means either openly attempting to gain commercial success or creating music methodically or intellectually. In both cases, the overt association with commerce taints the musical product.

It's not as if popular music has been off-limits for all academics. Beginning in the early fifties, sociologists recognized the importance of popular music; they undoubtedly found it difficult to ignore the type of music that was listened to and consumed by the most people.[3] Sociologists tended to study the "function" of this music in people's lives, and to discuss its content in terms of the lyrics or image of the performer. But the "forbiddingly special" character of music prevented excursions into the areas of musical syntax and of the relationship between expression and content. Because of this barrier to discussing specifics, sociological studies have had difficulty establishing why one kind of music and not another is used in a particular context in a particular way, and *how* one kind of music produces one effect while a different kind of music produces another.

The difficulties encountered by sociologists would have seemed to be the cue for musicologists to enter the picture, but instead, the very "commonness" of popular music evoked a reaction against it. Furthermore, for reasons discussed in the introduction, the descriptive and analytical techniques at the disposal of musicologists made it seem as if there were nothing to describe in much popular music. Songs with little or no harmonic or melodic motion could seem devoid of musical content because the analytical techniques, oriented around pitch measured in a certain way, revealed little contrast or distinctiveness in those parameters. Therefore, musicologists could easily justify their continued focus on the music for which their analytical metalanguage was devised in the first place.

At the same time, musicologists seldom studied the social and political *content* of art music. The point here (and I return to the closing argument of the introduction) is that the musicological study of popular music, precisely because it is so clearly imbricated with function that it makes claims for autonomy and transcendence incongruous (not that it can't produce "transcendent" moments), forces issues to the surface that can be easily ignored when studying the "masterworks." Popular music reminds us that all music arises in a social context, that all music from the Romantic era onward struggled with the contradictions of artistic production in a capitalist economic system, and, most importantly, that we remember a piece of music and return to it again and again because it *means* something, because it has the power to change our lives.

This underscores the importance of moving from the "expression" plane to the "content" plane. In a sense, this is a move from analysis – the discussion of how parts relate to one another – to interpretation – what is the effect and meaning of these "parts" or, for that matter, the "whole." The point is not so much simply to interpret something as to understand why we interpret a given song in the manner that we do. At the same time, I cannot claim to have made all my interpretive decisions explicit: why is the music of "The Mayor of Simpleton" "fun," and what makes the music "obviously intelligent"? The passages in this book in which I have made the process more explicit should at least establish that it is possible to understand both how we form our interpretations, and how it is that we are more likely to make some interpretations than others.

I am well aware that the subjects of this chapter and the last were recordings made by "cult" groups: musicians with much critical acclaim, but little popular success. The attention lavished here risks reiterating the idea that anything that is "really good" will never be widely popular. The fact that I have virtually ignored what are arguably the two most popular types of popular music in the eighties and nineties – rap and heavy metal – could reinforce the popular belief that art is ineluctably opposed to commerce. But, as discussed in the introduction, value can never inhere in an aesthetic object; we must always take into consideration the listening context, function, and individual "competence" – that is, the memory and history – of the listener. And we must take into account as best we can "the irregular chain of historical transactions" that influence how we evaluate music in the present. "This Diamond Ring" may well produce authentic effects for those who purchased or listened attentively to the recording (and it undoubtedly evokes a range of responses for those who hear it on "oldies" radio stations or on a "Time-Life" collection of hits). The critical attention and degree of popularity accorded Bing Crosby and Billie Holiday fluctuated widely from the 1930s to the present, with the two factors in a constantly changing relationship. And neither Hank Williams nor James Brown could be considered cult figures even though they represent portions of the musical field away from the "mainstream."

One possibility raised by a study such as this is that, in the course of subjecting popular songs to scholarly analysis, the songs will become "aestheticized," effacing those contextual factors that differentiated popular music from art music in the first place. But, as discussed in the last chapter, it may well be that the "artistic autonomy," or reliance on "function and context" of different types of music depends as much on the attitude of the perceiver as on anything inherent in the musical object itself. As stated earlier, it is not so much that popular music is "functional" while art music is "autonomous," as that different types of music have different functions, even if one possible function is to propagate the belief in the "autonomy" of music. In the end it may be difficult to maintain distinctions between "functional" and "autonomous" music; and it may well be that our evaluations and interpretations arise more from our familiarity with specific musical histories, musical *topoi*, and genealogies of genres than they do from whether a type of music falls into one term or the other of a binary pair.

Appendix

A

Reading the spectrum photos

The spectrum photos present a pitch-time graph in which pitch lies along the vertical axis, time along the horizontal. The rate of the film was 2 centimeters per second. The horizontal lines in the graph are placed at 200 hz. (G3; pitch register terminology is explained below in this appendix), 400 hz. (G4) or 500 hz. (C5), 1000 hz. (C6), 2000 hz. (C7), 3000 hz. (G7), 4000 hz. (C8), and 5000 hz. (E-flat 8). The pictures were taken in three stages: a photo was first made covering a range of 40-500 hz., then a second photo was taken covering a range of 80-1000 hz., and finally a third photo was taken covering a range of 500-5000 hz. The scale is logarithmic.

The physical process of taking the photos was as follows: recorded sounds were played into a real-time spectrum analyzer, then sent to a display tube where the picture was taken of them. The range of the display could be adjusted as well as the intensity or amount of detail that it was possible to observe. The photos were taken on a model SD 301C-C Real Time Analyzer made by the Spectral Dynamics Corporation.

Note: "Hey Good Lookin'" contains a marker line at 500 hz. (C5) while "Pills and Soap" contains a marker line at 400 hz. (G4).

B

Registral terminology

Occasionally, throughout this book, I have referred to pitches lying in a particular register. Example 1 displays where these registers lie in relation to the tempered Western scale (middle C is "C4").

Example 1: *Pitch registers*

Register 1   Register 2   Register 3   Register 4   Register 5   Register 6   Register 7

Notes

1. Introduction

1 See Simon Frith, *Sound Effects* (New York: Pantheon Books, 1981), 34–38; and *idem*, "Why Do Songs Have Words ," in *Music for Pleasure: Essays in the Sociology of Pop* (New York: Routledge, 1988), 120.

2 For Baudrillard's exposition of his notion of the "simulacrum," see Jean Baudrillard, *Simulacra and Simulations*, trans. Paul Foss, Paul Patton and Philip Beitchman (New York: Sémiotext[e], 1983). I refer here specifically to what Baudrillard terms a third-order simulacrum, that is, a copy of an object for which there exists no original.

3 Roland Barthes, "The Death of the Author," in *Image-Music-Text*, trans. Stephen Heath (New York: Noonday Press, 1977), 148.

4 Steve Chapple and Reebee Garofalo, *Rock 'n' Roll Is Here to Pay* (Chicago: Nelson-Hall Inc., 1977), 246–48.

5 Simon Frith and Angela McRobbie, "Rock and Sexuality," in *On Record: Rock, Pop, and the Written Word*, ed. Simon Frith and Andrew Goodwin (New York: Pantheon Books, 1990), 375, 378–79. Originally published in *Screen Education* 29 (1978).

6 A note on pop orchestration: timpani and other auxiliary percussion instruments (besides drum kit) feature in numerous other 1965 hits. For example, recordings using Phil Spector's "wall-of-sound" such as the Righteous Brothers' "You've Lost That Lovin' Feeling" employ a range of dense orchestral effects; a song such as Little Anthony's "Hurts So Bad" uses timpani and effects such as violins playing in artificial harmonics. The difference between these songs and "This Diamond Ring" lies in the way the latter song's instrumentation signifies "novelty," an effect which I suspect could be corroborated by studying the sound track of contemporaneous TV shows such as *I Dream of Jeannie and Bewitched*.

7 The usage here (and intentional blurring) of the opposition "standardized/individualized" refers to Theodor Adorno's usage in his scathing attack on popular music, "On Popular Music" (with the assistance of

205

George Simpson), in *Studies in Philosophy and Social Science*, vol. 9 (New York: Institute of Social Research, 1941), 17–48 (reprinted in Frith and Goodwin, ed., *On Record*). However, Adorno would never concede that a piece of popular music was "individualized," and he therefore used the term "psuedo-individualized."

8 This approach is derived from the "aesthetics of reception" developed by Hans Robert Jauss. For an introduction to this approach, see Jauss, "Literary History as a Challenge to Literary Theory," in *Towards an Aesthetic of Reception*, trans. Timothy Bahti (Minneapolis: University of Minnesota Press, 1982), 3–46. Objections have been made that this approach relies on a static, essentialized notion of a decontextualized "audience" or "reader." For overviews and criticisms of Jauss and the Konstanz school, see the following: Paul de Man, "Introduction" to Jauss' *Towards an Aesthetic of Reception*, vii–xix; and Terry Eagleton, *Literary Theory: An Introduction* (Minneapolis: University of Minneapolis Press, 1983), 78–85.

9 Greg Shaw comments on the "machinery" for producing teen idols: "a good-looking teenager could be spotted on the street (as was Fabian, according to legend), cut a record, and, aided by a few bribed DJs, within a few weeks have a hit on the national charts – no uncertainties, no risks" ("The Teen Idols," in *The Rolling Stone Illustrated History of Rock and Roll*, ed. Jim Miller [New York: Random House, 1980], 97).

10 Mikhail Bakhtin, *Problems of Dostoevsky's Poetics*, ed. and trans. by Caryl Emerson (Minneapolis: University of Minnesota Press, 1984), 32, 292–93.

11 Richard Middleton, *Studying Popular Music* (Milton Keynes: Open University Press, 1990), 173; and see Umberto Eco, *A Theory of Semiotics* (Bloomington: Indiana University Press, 1976), 129–39.

12 The phrase "irregular chain of historical transactions" and this conception of historical processes comes from Stephen Greenblatt, *Shakespearean Negotiations: The Circulation of Social Energy in Renaissance England* (Berkeley: University of California Press, 1988), 7.

13 This phrase is David Laing's, quoted in Middleton, *Studying Popular Music*, 228.

14 Leonard Meyer made this distinction between the different aspects of the musical code as early as 1956 using the terms "absolutist" and "referentialist"; recent writers have substituted "syntactic" and "inherent" for "absolutist," and "delineated" and "analogue" for "referentialist." See Leonard Meyer, *Emotion and Meaning in Music* (Chicago: University of Chicago Press, 1956), 1; Lucy Green, *Music on Deaf Ears* (Manchester: Manchester University Press, 1988), 12–31; and Allan Moore, *Rock, The Primary Text: Developing a Musicology of Rock* (Buckingham: Open University Press, 1993), 28–29.

15 This discussion of musical coding is adapted from Richard Middleton, *Studying Popular Music*, 172–246 (for a fuller description of general codes, see 174). The most extensive discussion of the "code" in terms of communication theory is Umberto Eco's *A Theory of Semiotics*, 38–150. For an application of

the concepts of "primary" and "secondary" signification to the Classic style, see Kofi Agawu, *Playing with Signs: A Semiotic Interpretation of Classic Music* (Princeton: Princeton University Press, 1991).

16 Middleton, *Studying Popular Music*, 220–22.

17 These terms and their description come from Middleton, *Studying Popular Music*, 232. Other types of secondary signification listed by Middleton include "links with other semiotic systems" ("visual, kinetic, verbal, even olfactory associations: 'funky' soul; 'steamy' swamp-rock"), and "rhetorical connotations" ("associations arising from correspondences with rhetorical forms . . . and styles"). The most extensive exploration of connotation in a single piece of popular music is Philip Tagg's *KOJAK, 50 Seconds of Television Music: Toward the Analysis of Affect in Popular Music* (Göteborg: Studies from the Department of Musicology, 1979). Tagg tests the pertinence of his observations through elaborate methods of "intersubjective" and "interobjective" comparison.

18 Middleton, *Studying Popular Music*, 237.

19 This criticism is made by Jean-Jacques Nattiez, *Music and Discourse: Toward a Semiology of Music*, trans. Carolyn Abbate (Princeton: Princeton University Press, 1990), 16–28.

20 Nattiez, *Music and Discourse*, 28.

21 Gino Stefani, "A Theory of Musical Competence," *Semiotica* 66:1–3 (1987), 7–22.

22 Middleton, *Studying Popular Music*, 175.

23 Pierre Bourdieu, *Distinction: A Social Critique of the Judgement of Taste*, trans. Richard Nice (Cambridge, MA: Harvard University Press, 1984), 1–96. See chapter five for a more in-depth discussion of Bourdieu's ideas and their application to the study of popular music.

24 This refers to the model of communication proposed by Roman Jakobson, in which an "addresser" sends a "message" to an "addressee"; to be operative the message requires a "context," a "contact," and a "code" ("Linguistics and Poetics," *in Language in Literature*, ed. Krystyna Pomorska and Stephen Rudy [Cambridge, MA: Harvard University Press, 1987], 66).

25 Timothy Crouse, review of Joni Mitchell's *Blue*, *Rolling Stone*, August 5, 1971; reprinted in *The Rolling Stone Record Review Volume II* (New York: Pocket Books, 1974), 471–74. The reviews of the singer-songwriters collected in this volume and in *The Rolling Stone Record Review Volume I* (New York: Pocket Books, 1971) exemplify the tendency to make autobiographical connections.

26 Within the musicological literature, Edward T. Cone has posited the notion of a composer's "voice" within the text, but one, however, that largely relies on a unitary relationship between the "composer" and the "voice" heard in the piece of music (*The Composer's Voice* [Berkeley: University of California Press, 1974]). Carolyn Abbate has formulated a rather different conception of "voices" in classical music (a conception closer to one used in this book),

one in which voices "manifest themselves . . . as different kinds or modes of music that inhabit a single work" (*Unsung Voices: Opera and Musical Narrative in the Nineteenth Century* [Princeton: Princeton University Press, 1991], 10).

27 This refers to the controversy surrounding the "clues" alluding to Paul McCartney's death allegedly contained in several Beatles' songs and other pieces of memorabilia (including album covers) during the period 1967–1969.

28 See Kaja Silverman's discussion in *The Acoustic Mirror: The Female Voice in Psychoanalysis and Cinema* (Bloomington: Indiana University Press, 1988), 189–218. Silverman draws heavily on the ideas of Roland Barthes contained in his essay "The Death of the Author" and his book *The Pleasure of the Text*, trans. Richard Miller (New York: Hill and Wang, 1975).

29 Bakhtin discusses these ideas extensively in *Problems of Dostoevsky's Poetics* and *The Dialogic Imagination: Four Essays*, ed. Michael Holquist, trans. Caryl Emerson and Michael Holquist (Austin: University of Texas Press, 1981). For more on the importance of context in value judgments about popular music, see the discussion on "subjectivity and value" in Middleton, *Studying Popular Music*, 249–58.

30 Cf. Middleton, *Studying Popular Music*, 240–41.

31 For a discussion of "The 'Relative Autonomy' of Music History," see Carl Dahlhaus, *Foundations of Music History*, trans. J. B. Robinson (Cambridge: Cambridge University Press, 1983), 108–29.

32 Simon Frith, "What Is Good Music?," *Canadian Music Review* 10 (1990), 99–100.

33 See Carl Dahlhaus, *The Idea of Absolute Music*, trans. Roger Lustig (Chicago: University of Chicago Press, 1989), 7; *Esthetics of Music*, trans. William W. Austin (Cambridge: Cambridge University Press, 1982); and Lawrence W. Levine, *Highbrow/Lowbrow: The Emergence of Cultural Hierarchy in America* (Cambridge, MA: Harvard University Press, 1988), 83–168, for an account of the transformation of the "classical" concert in the nineteenth century. For examinations of the effect of disinterested contemplation on listening practices, see Rose Rosengard Subotnik, "Toward a Deconstruction of Structural Listening," in *Explorations in Music, the Arts, and Ideas: Essays in Honor of Leonard B. Meyer*, ed. Eugene Narmour and Ruth A. Solie (New York: Pendragon Press, 1988), 87–122; and Nicholas Cook, *Music, Imagination, and Culture* (Oxford: Oxford University Press, 1990). And for a collection of essays that explores the effect of canon formation on contemporary musicology, see Katherine Bergeron and Philip Bohlman, eds., *Disciplining Music: Musicology and Its Canons* (Chicago: University of Chicago Press, 1992).

34 However, for examples of a few of the recent works that do theorize this question explicitly (in addition to works already cited in this chapter), see Lawrence Kramer, *Music as Cultural Practice, 1800–1900* (Berkeley:

University of California Press, 1991); Susan McClary, *Feminine Endings: Music, Gender, and Sexuality* (Minneapolis: University of Minnesota Press, 1991); Rose Rosengard Subotnik, *Developing Variations: Style and Ideology in Western Music* (Minneapolis: University of Minnesota Press, 1991). For a work that anticipates much of the current concern with contextual issues, see William W. Austin, *"Susanna," "Jeanie," and "The Old Folks at Home": The Songs of Stephen C. Foster from His Time to Ours*, second edition (Urbana: University of Illinois Press, 1987 [1975]).

35 Joseph Kerman, *Contemplating Music: Challenges to Musicology* (Cambridge, MA: Harvard University Press, 1985), 174.

36 Tagg, *KOJAK*, 28.

37 Charles Keil, "Motion and Feeling through Music," *The Journal of Aesthetics and Art Criticism*, 24 (Spring 1966), 337–49; Andrew Chester, "Second Thoughts on a Rock Aesthetic: The Band," *New Left Review* 62 (1970), 78–79 (reprinted in Frith and Goodwin, eds., *On Record*); John Shepherd, Phil Virden, Graham Vulliamy, Trevor Wishart, *Whose Music? A Sociology of Musical Languages* (London: Latimer, 1977) – see especially, chapter one (by John Shepherd), "Media, Social Process and Music," 7–45; and Shepherd's later article, "A Theoretical Model for the Sociomusicological Analysis of Popular Musics," in *Popular Music 2: Theory and Method*, ed. David Horn and Richard Middleton (Cambridge: Cambridge University Press, 1982), 145–78.

38 Bruno Nettl, *The Study of Ethnomusicology: Twenty-nine Issues and Concepts* (Urbana: University of Illinois Press, 1983), 7, 9, 136. Charles Seeger criticized (in 1964) ethnomusicology's emphasis on the "purity or authenticity" of "static traditions" as opposed to music that exhibited outside influences or "changing traditions," labeling this "ethnocentrism in reverse" ("The Musicological Juncture: Music as Value," in *Studies in Musicology 1935–1975* [Berkeley: University of California Press, 1977], 51–52). Mantle Hood raises the issue of the ethnomusicologist's attitude towards popular music indirectly, as he discusses "beatle music" in the "Introduction" of *The Ethnomusicologist* (New York: McGraw-Hill, Inc., 1971). He concludes that "to understand the conditions and motivations responsible for the attitudes . . . towards this kind of music," we need "the help of the psychologist, sociologist, psychiatrist, physiologist, the medical profession, the brain research institute, experts in commercial marketing, and a host of others" (17). While his point is well taken, Hood makes it clear that he does not intend to undertake this study. For anthropological approaches to the study of popular music, see Ruth Finnegan, *The Hidden Musicians: Music-Making in an English Town* (Cambridge: Cambridge University Press, 1989), and Sara Cohen, *Rock Culture in Liverpool: Popular Music in the Making* (Oxford: Oxford University Press, 1991).

39 Alan Lomax, "Song Structure and Social Structure," *Ethnology* 1:4 (October 1962), 440. To be fair, Lomax's "cantometrics" method has since been

extensively critiqued within the field of ethnomusicology itself, e.g., Steven Feld, "Sound Structure as Social Structure," *Ethnomusicology* 28:3 (September 1984), 383–410 (and see the rest of this issue of *Ethnomusicology* for a debate on this issue). Kofi Agawu offers a trenchant critique of social structure/musical structure homologies in "Representing African Music," *Critical Inquiry* 18 (Winter 1992), 264–66.

40 Probably the best-known examples of the subculturist approach to the study of popular music are Dick Hebdige, *Subculture: The Meaning of Style* (London: Methuen, 1979); and Paul Willis, *Profane Culture* (London: Routledge and Kegan Paul, 1978). For critiques of this approach, see Angela McRobbie, "Settling Accounts with Subcultures: A Feminist Critique," in Frith and Goodwin, eds., *On Record,* 66–80; and Gary Clarke, "Defending Ski-Jumpers: A Critique of Theories of Youth Subcultures," in *On Record,* 81–96.

41 John Blacking, *Venda Children's Songs: A Study in Ethnomusicological Analysis* (Johannesburg: Witwatersrand University Press, 1967). Nettl discusses this work of Blacking's in *The Study of Ethnomusicology,* 98.

42 For more on the use of organic metaphors in music analysis, see Ruth Solie, "The Living Work: Organicism and Musical Analysis," *19th-Century Music* 4 (1980), 147–56; and Janet Levy, "Covert and Casual Values in Recent Writings about Music," *Journal of Musicology* 6:1 (Winter 1987), 3–27.

43 Michel Foucault, *The Order of Things: An Archaeology of the Human Sciences* (New York: Vintage Books, 1973), 134–36. The quest for objective status has haunted both the historical and theoretical branches of the discipline of musicology through the twin emphases on positivism and formalism. For a critical historical overview, see Kerman, *Contemplating Music.*

44 Foucault, *The Order of Things,* 229.

45 The following discussion is based in large part on the argument put forward by Mark Evan Bonds in *Wordless Rhetoric: Musical Form and the Metaphor of the Oration* (Cambridge, MA: Harvard University Press, 1991).

46 Simon Frith also argues for the appropriateness of a rhetorical approach to popular music analysis in "Adam Smith and Music," *New Formations* 18 (Winter 1992), 77–78.

47 Bonds, *Wordless Rhetoric,* 1–2. All subsequent citations in this chapter will be noted by page numbers in parentheses.

48 For an introduction to paradigmatic analysis, see Nicholas Ruwet, "Methods of Analysis in Musicology," *Music Analysis* 6 (1987), 11–36; and for a good summary of paradigmatic approaches, see Middleton, *Studying Popular Music,* 183–89.

49 For similar caveats regarding the use of transcription in the analysis of popular music, see Tagg, *KOJAK,* 31; and Peter Winkler, "Randy Newman's Americana," *Popular Music* 7:1 (January 1988), 11

50 Charles Seeger, "Prescriptive and Descriptive Music Writing," in *Studies in Musicology 1935–1975*. All subsequent citations in this chapter are noted by page numbers in parentheses.

51 See Hugo Cole, *Sounds and Signs: Aspects of Musical Notation* (Oxford: Oxford University Press, 1974), 12; Don M. Randel, "Canons in the Musicological Toolbox," in *Disciplining Music*, ed. Katherine Bergeron and Philip Bohlman, 10–22; Middleton, *Studying Popular Music*, 104–6.

52 See Nettl, *The Study of Ethnomusicology*, 74. See both Nettl (*The Study of Ethnomusicology*, 67) and Hood (*The Ethnomusicologist*, 50–55) for their descriptions of their "initiations" into ethnomusicology through a rite of transcription.

53 Hood, *The Ethnomusicologist*, 85–86.

54 Seeger was the most prominent proponent of the automatic transcription (see "Prescriptive and Descriptive Music Writing"); he was followed in this respect by Hood (*The Ethnomusicologist*, 94–101). The best critique of automatic transcription is Nazir Jairazbhoy, "The 'Objective' and Subjective View in Music Transcription," *Ethnomusicology* 21:2 (May 1977), 263–73.

55 Jairazbhoy, "The 'Objective' and Subjective View," 268.

56 Quotations are from Edward T. Cone, *The Composer's Voice*, 12; and Lawrence Kramer, *Music and Poetry: The Nineteenth Century and After* (Berkeley: University of California Press, 1984), 127. In a later section of *The Composer's Voice* (40–45), Cone ruminates on different relationships between composers and song, briefly considering "the poet-composer" and relationship of words and music in popular song.

57 Kofi Agawu, "Theory and Practice in the Analysis of the Nineteenth-Century *Lied*," *Music Analysis* 11:1 (March 1992), 25.

58 Frith, "Why Do Songs Have Words," 120; Middleton, *Studying Popular Music*, 228–31.

59 Michel de Certeau, "History: Science and Fiction," in *Heterologies*, trans. Brian Massumi (Minneapolis: University of Minnesota Press, 1986), 220–21. All subsequent citations in this chapter are noted by page numbers in parentheses.

2. Family values in music? Billie Holiday's and Bing Crosby's "I'll Be Seeing You"

1 This quote is from the liner notes from *The Time-Life Bing Crosby* (1985) by Charles K. Wolfe. Information about recording and broadcast dates was obtained from Timothy A. Morgereth, *Bing Crosby: A Discography, Radio Program List, and Filmography* (Jefferson, NC and London: McFarland and Co., 1987).

2 Milt Gabler interview in the liner notes for *Billie Holiday: The Complete Decca Recordings* (MCA GRD2–601, 1991).

3 Joel Whitburn, *Joel Whitburn's Pop Memories, 1890–1954: The History of American Popular Music* (Menomonee Falls, WI: Record Research, 1986). The other chart figures in this paragraph are also taken from *Pop Memories*. Further samples of Whitburn's research may be found in *Top 40 Albums, USA Top 1000 Singles, Top Rhythm and Blues Singles 1942–1988*, and many more.

4 This phrase is Jean Baudrillard's and may be found in "The Masses: The Implosion of the Social in the Media," in *Jean Baudrillard: Selected Writings*, ed. Mark Poster (Stanford: Stanford University Press, 1988), 210. For more on the circular reasoning of the public opinion poll, see Michel de Certeau, *The Practice of Everyday Life*, trans. Steven Rendall (Berkeley: University of California Press, 1984), 188–89.

5 This discussion of the pop charts is a summary of the discussion in the beginning of my article, "The Politics and Practice of 'Crossover' in American Popular Music, 1963–65," *The Musical Quarterly* 78:4 (Winter 1994), 775–78. See Martin Parker, "Reading the Charts – Making Sense with the Hit Parade," *Popular Music* 10:2 (May 1991), 205–19, for a more in-depth look at the mystique of charts. Parker emphasizes the tautological nature of the charts: the charts are supposedly based partially on radio airplay while radio playlists rely on the charts (208). Parker also examines many of the myths reproduced by the charts, with the most telling one being perhaps the myth of democratic "free" choice by the consumer. This tends to "conceal the extent to which the agenda of consumer choices is set in the first place by an oligopoly of transnational entertainment corporations based on a logic of profit" (211). For more on the uses of statistics to confer legitimacy on media events, see Ian Hacking, "Biopower and the Avalanche of Printed Numbers," *Humanities in Society* 5:3 & 4 (1982), 279–95.

6 These are the groups specified in a January 9, 1961 *Billboard* editorial, "The 'New' Billboard" (3).

7 Although she detested the movie and her role in it, Holiday told Leonard Feather that "I'll be playing a maid, but at least she's really a cute maid" (John Chilton, *Billie's Blues: Billie Holiday's Story, 1933–1959* [New York: Day Books, 1978], 107). The portions of *New Orleans* featuring Holiday jarringly juxtapose scenes of her singing confidently with a band with scenes of her as a servant (replete with "Yes ma'am" and "No ma'am").

8 For instance, the Fall 1993 *Schwann Catalog* of available recordings lists thirty-five titles for Crosby and fifty-seven titles for Holiday.

9 See, for example, "Stream-lined Billie Holiday Now at Downbeat," *Downbeat*, November 15, 1944, 2; and "Billie Holiday Is Worrying Her Associates," *Downbeat*, July 15, 1945, 1.

10 For examples, see James Lincoln Collier, *The Making of Jazz: A Comprehensive History* (New York: Dell Publishing, 1978), 303–12; Frank Tirro, *Jazz: A History*, second edition (New York: W. W. Norton and Co., 1993), 249–51; Grover Sales, *Jazz: America's Classical Music* (New York: Prentice Hall, 1984), 20–21; Gunther Schuller, *The Swing Era: The*

Development of Jazz, 1930–1945 (New York: Oxford University Press, 1989), 544–47.

11 The *Billboard* reviews of these songs reiterate the superlatives.

12 On Crosby's reassuring function, see Will Friedwald, *Jazz Singing: America's Great Voices from Bessie Smith to Bebop and Beyond* (New York: Charles Scribner's Sons, 1990), 44, 312; Gary Giddins, *Riding on a Blue Note: Jazz and American Pop* (New York: Oxford University Press, 1981), 19 (Giddins refers to Crosby as "a national security blanket"); Henry Pleasants, *The Great American Popular Singers* (New York: Simon and Schuster, 1974), 128, 142.

13 "Wartime Dollars Boom Music on Swing Alley," *Downbeat*, March 15, 1944, 3.

14 *Downbeat*, November 15, 1944, 2. Chilton terms this description "courteous," and interprets it as a reference to her drug use (*Billie's Blues*, 95).

15 Billie Holiday, *Lady Sings the Blues* (with William Dufty) (New York: Penguin Books, 1984 [1956]), 170. For more on the historical discourse of the differential status of African-American and white women, see Evelyn Brooks Higginbotham, "African-American Women's History and the Metalanguage of Race," *Signs*, 17:2 (1992), 251–74. Particularly interesting in light of Holiday's nickname, "Lady Day," is Higginbotham's discussion of how black women were denied the status of "ladies" (261). The struggle over the accentuation of the sign "Lady Day" is the focus of Susan Cook's important article, "When Lady Day Sings . . . Race, Gender and Performance Politics."

16 See Holiday, *Lady Sings the Blues*, 94–96.

17 For an example of this attitude, see "Vocalistic Headaches: Femme Singers May Give a Band Sex-Appeal, but That's Not All," *Billboard*, November 25, 1939, 4, 61. For a summary and analysis of articles from the late thirties and early forties that take this approach, see Susan Cook's "When Lady Day Sings."

18 *Downbeat*'s review was hostile, stating that "La Holiday alone can be commended here. The material is sad, and the orchestra far less than exciting" (April 1, 1945, 9). By way of contrast, *Billboard*'s review waxed enthusiastic: "never lacking in sophistication in her song delivery, Miss Billie gets a smart musical setting from Toots Camarata to frame her pash pipes" (March 17, 1945, p. 17).

19 "Requiescat in Pace," *Downbeat*, August 20, 1959, 21. For more on this topic, see the following: Maya Angelou's recollections of her meeting with Holiday in *The Heart of a Woman* (New York: Bantam Books, 1982), 6–16; Chilton, *Billie's Blues*, 122–23; "A Great Lady" (interview with Barry Ulanov), *Metronome*, October 1948 (quoted in Chilton, *Billie's Blues*, 123); Holiday, *Lady Sings the Blues*, 154; Schuller, *Swing Era*, 546.

20 These quotes are taken from the following reviews published in *Downbeat* (authors given when provided in original): *Ella Fitzgerald and Billie Holiday at Newport*, February 6, 1958, 24; Martin Williams, review of *Lady in Satin*, August 7, 1958, 24; *Songs for Distingue Lovers*, March 19, 1959, 38; *Stay with*

Me, September 17, 1959, 30; Don DeMichael, review of *All or Nothing at All*, December 24, 1959, 46.

21 For more on the increasing separation of pop and jazz in the mid-forties, see Charles Hamm, *Yesterdays: Popular Song in America* (New York: W. W. Norton, 1979), 385–87; and Schuller, *Swing Era*, 747, 844–49.

22 This discussion of "illegalities and delinquency" is adapted from the discussion in Foucault's *Discipline and Punish: The Birth of the Prison*, trans. Alan Sheridan (New York: Vintage Books, 1977), 271–92. Foucault uses the term "penality" to describe the state of being penalized.

23 Holiday, *Lady Sings the Blues*, 16–18. All subsequent citations will be marked by page numbers within parentheses. In addition to orphanages, other examples of "institutions organized around normalizing techniques" include prisons, hospitals, boarding schools.

24 Foucault, *Discipline and Punish*, 282.

25 This *topos* figures prominently in Chilton's *Billie's Blues*; John White, *Billie Holiday: Her Life and Times* (New York: Universe Books, 1987); and James Burnett, *Billie Holiday* (New York: Hippocrene Books, 1984).

26 For further explanation of these issues, see Susan Willis, *A Primer for Daily Life* (New York: Routledge, 1991), 146–57.

27 See Robert O'Meally, *Lady Day: The Many Faces of Billie Holiday* (New York: Little, Brown and Company, Arcade Publishing, 1991); and Cook, "When Lady Day Sings."

28 *Downbeat*, July 15, 1949, 3.

29 I owe the linkage of these two books to the discussion in Henry Louis Gates, Jr.'s *The Signifying Monkey: A Theory of African-American Literary Criticism* (New York: Oxford University Press, 1988), 239–58; he views Walker's book as "Signifyin(g)" on or troping Hurston's. Patricia Hill Collins also discusses the *topos* of self-transformation in *Black Feminist Thought: Knowledge, Consciousness, and the Politics of Empowerment* (New York: Routledge, 1991), 183–89.

30 See Houston Baker, Jr., *Blues, Ideology, and Afro-American Literature: A Vernacular Theory* (Chicago: University of Chicago Press, 1984), 22–63 (especially 50–60).

31 Holiday omits this line in her 1937 recording of "My Man." John Moore credits "My Man" with being one of the earliest "torch songs." This is significant because Holiday's image and repertory was evidently influenced by the torch singers of the twenties and thirties. See John Moore, "The Hieroglyphics of Love: the Torch Singers and Interpretation," *Popular Music* 8:1 (January 1989), 31–58 (especially 32).

32 Michele Wallace quoted in John White, *Billie Holiday*, 118–19.

33 See Collins, *Black Feminist Thought*, 67–115. On self-invention, see Susan Cook, "When Lady Day Sings," and Robert O'Meally, *Lady Day*.

34 Nat Hentoff and Nat Shapiro, *Hear Me Talkin' to Ya* (New York: Rinehart and Company, 1955), 199.

35 See Albert Murray's statement on the preparation necessary for the "spontaneity" of the Holiday/Wilson recording sessions, and Robert O'Meally's comment on this in O'Meally's *Lady Day*, 109–12.

36 Holiday, *Lady Sings the Blues*, 175.

37 Hubert L. Dreyfus and Paul Rabinow, *Michel Foucault: Beyond Structuralism and Hermeneutics*, second edition (Chicago: University of Chicago Press, 1983), xxvi. Foucault's most detailed discussions of the genealogy of the modern object and subject are, respectively, *Discipline and Punish* and *The History of Sexuality, Volume One: An Introduction* (New York: Vintage Books, 1979).

38 This formulation of the implications of the "voice-over" is derived from the lengthy discussion in Kaja Silverman, *The Acoustic Mirror*, 1–100.

39 All references and citations in this passage are from Barry Ulanov, *The Incredible Crosby* (New York: Whittlesey House, 1948), and are hereafter marked by page numbers in parentheses. Crosby's autobiography (as told to Pete Martin), *Call Me Lucky* (New York: Da Capo Press, 1953), reiterates many of these ideas in a milder form, and one which reeks less of hagiography.

40 This quote is taken from Donald Shepherd and Robert F. Slatzer, *Bing Crosby: The Hollow Man* (New York: Pinnacle Books, 1981), 254.

41 Detailed in Gary Crosby and Ross Firestone, *Going My Own Way* (Garden City, NY: Doubleday and Co., 1983), 45–67.

42 See for instance, Will Friedwald, *Jazz Singing*, 30–37; Gary Giddins, *Riding on a Blue Note*, 14–21; and Henry Pleasants, *The Great American Popular Singers*, 127–42.

43 Sample recordings of the all the above-named artists may be found in *The Smithsonian Collection of American Popular Song*. Waters' style varied over time, and occasionally featured more overt jazz influences than Crosby.

44 Ulanov, *The Incredible Crosby*, 174. See *The Incredible Crosby*, 185–86 and Giddins, *Riding on a Blue Note*, 17, for references to Jolson's influence, what Giddins calls the "mammified" moment.

45 For Kapp's influence on Crosby, see Friedwald, *Jazz Singing*, 37–39; Giddins, *Riding on a Blue Note*, 18 (Giddins calls it the "Jack Kapp treatment"); Ulanov, *The Incredible Crosby*, 116–17. Kapp is also responsible for some of the changes in musical contexts for Billie Holiday during the period in which she recorded for Decca (late 1944–1950).

46 O'Meally gives a good account of this milieu (*Lady Day*, 26–30).

47 An oft-quoted remark of John Hammond's summarizes this view: "she had neither the wisdom nor the strength to make the most of her opportunities . . . The more conscious she became of her style, the more mannered she became, and I suppose that artistically the worst thing that ever happened to her was the overwhelming success of her singing the Lewis Allen poem, 'Strange Fruit,' which amassed a host of fans with the intelligentsia and the left" (from the liner notes of *Billie Holiday: The Golden Years* [Columbia Records,

1962]). Several writers, including O'Meally, Friedwald, and Martin Williams (*The Jazz Tradition* [Oxford: Oxford University Press, 1983]) disagree strongly with this judgment against Holiday's post-1939 work.

48 The categories used here correspond loosely to those used by *Downbeat* to classify recordings: "Hot Jazz," "Swing," "Vocal," "Dance," and "Novelty."

49 One of the versions of "I'll Be Seeing You" not discussed extensively here, the version by Tommy Dorsey featuring Frank Sinatra, does fit comfortably into one of the generic categories delineated above, the "band with featured vocalist" category. In fact, it is so much one of its kind that Charles Hamm discusses this recording to demonstrate the constancy of the big band with singer format between the years 1936 and 1944 (*Yesterdays*, 385). For more on torch singing, see John Moore, "The Torch Singers and Interpretation."

50 Charles Wolfe, liner notes to *The Time-Life Bing Crosby*.

51 A quick perusal of Crosby's radio playlist during the period in which he was performing "I'll Be Seeing You" provides plentiful examples: "What Do You Do in the Infantry?," "One Sweet Letter from You," "G.I. Jive," "This Is the Army, Mr. Jones," "There'll Be a Hot Time in the Town of Berlin," "The Bombardier Song," "Bless Them All," "Something to Remember You By," etc. Barry Kernfield in *The New Grove Dictionary of Jazz*, vol. 1, in the section on jazz and film, mentions "I'll Be Seeing You," as one of the songs frequently performed in swing arrangements in films made during the war to foster patriotic sentiments among US citizens and to boost "the morale of men in the services by reassuring them that everything at home – the way of life they were fighting to preserve – was just as they remembered it" (378). Kernfield also mentions "Don't Sit under the Apple Tree (with Anyone Else but Me)," and "When Johnny Comes Marching Home."

52 Henry Louis Gates, Jr., *The Signifying Monkey: A Theory of African-American Literary Criticism* (New York: Oxford University Press, 1988), 60–61. I discuss Gates' theories and their application to the analysis of African-American music extensively in chapter four.

53 See Gates, *The Signifying Monkey*, 44–51; Abrahams, *Talking Black* (Rowley, MA: Newbury House, 1976), 21. Gates connects the "parodic" aspects of Signifyin(g) with Bakhtin's notion of "dialogic" or double-voiced discourse.

54 She is famous for phrasing behind the beat. On Holiday's complexity in rhythm, phrasing, and ornamentation see Gunther Schuller, *Swing Era*, 530, 532, 537, 538, 540; and see Chilton, *Billie's Blues*, 89–91, for Johnny Guarnieri's and Joe Springer's (both pianists who accompanied Holiday) anecdotes about Holiday's tendency to delay her entrances and sing behind the beat.

55 Schuller lingers on the extraordinary aspects of Holiday's timbre and use of vibrato as well (*Swing Era*, 537–38, 545, 547).

56 The categories "African-American" and "Euro-American" run the risk of essentializing racial difference along the lines of musical style. In this case,

these terms refer to discursively constructed associations between race and style. These matters are discussed in greater detail in chapter four.

3. When you're lookin' at Hank (you're looking at country)

1 Other "splits" in Hank Williams' personality in the biographical literature include the sinner/saint and the macho man/mother-dominated divisions. These *topoi* were culled from the following biographies: Roger Williams, *Sing a Sad Song: The Life of Hank Williams*, second edition (Urbana: University of Illinois Press, 1981); Chet Flippo, *Your Cheatin' Heart: A Biography of Hank Williams* (Garden City, NY: Doubleday & Co., 1981); George William Koon, *Hank Williams: A Bio-Bibliography* (Westport, CT: Greenwood Press, 1983).

2 Commentaries on *Your Cheatin' Heart* may be found in Koon, *Hank Williams*, 102–4; Bill C. Malone, *Country Music USA*, revised edition (Austin: University of Texas Press, 1985), 477; and Simon Frith, "Rock Biography," in *Popular Music 3: Producers and Markets*, ed. Richard Middleton and David Horn (Cambridge: Cambridge University Press, 1983), 276. We could describe the difference between Flippo and biographers such as R. Williams and Koon in the following manner: Flippo does not "mediate between alternative modes of language use" or "alternative tropological strategies" (Hayden White's terms; see his *Tropics of Discourse: Essays in Cultural Criticism* [Baltimore: The Johns Hopkins University Press, 1978], 129); instead, he maintains a narrative voice closer to that which we associate with fictional discourse. Flippo, unlike Williams' other biographers, does not confine his narrative to documented events that can be placed in a specific time and place; his approach tends to draw attention to the *constructed* nature of his story which, as even Koon is forced to admit, may be strangely appropriate for depicting a musician who contributed mightily to a form of music with a remarkable self-consciousness towards language. For more on historians' attempts to distance themselves from fiction, see the article by Michel de Certeau discussed at the end of chapter one, "History: Science and Fiction," 202.

3 Williams' voice as created by Flippo in the opening passage is a case in point, with its liberal use of "nigger" and its subsequent depiction of Williams' urge to "apologize," which then functions as a kind of compensating device. As for information on Rufus (Rufe) Payne, the biographical material on Hank Williams agrees that he was an African-American street singer who performed in Greenville, Alabama during the 1930s and who taught Williams songs and performing techniques.

4 Flippo, *Your Cheatin' Heart*, 240.

5 This formulation derives from Simon Frith's discussion in "Why Do Songs Have Words?," 120–21.

6 Aaron Fox, "The Jukebox of History: Narratives of Loss and Desire in the Discourse of Country Music," *Popular Music* 11:1 (January 1992), 53–72.

7 Ibid., 54. Fox summarizes the "metanarrative of loss" in the following passage: "The metanarrative of Loss resists this equation of subjective fulfillment with the consumption of objects and inverts the terms of the metanarrative of Desire" (54). He later contrasts the "metanarratives of Loss and Desire": "Where the narratives of fulfilled desire convert *feelings* into goods and services, the narrative of Loss converts *objects* into signs of intense feeling, or even into subjects" (62).

8 Ibid., 60.

9 This formal description is indebted to observations made by Paula Survilla.

10 And as Adorno and Horkheimer recognized, the association of "amusement" with the consumption of commodities is fundamental to the functioning of the culture industry (*Dialectic of Enlightenment*, trans. John Cumming [New York: Continuum, 1991], 135–44). Jean Baudrillard echoes and expands this in his discussion of the "fun-system" ("Consumer Society," in *Jean Baudrillard: Selected Writings*, ed. Mark Poster [Stanford: Stanford University Press, 1988], 48–49). In Baudrillard's formulation, the conjoining of "fun" and consumption turns "fun" into a *duty* rather than a privilege, the task now being to convert from a society based on production to a society based on consumption.

11 Koon, *Hank Williams*, 79.

12 Fox, "The Jukebox of History," 54–55.

13 Fox also discusses the denaturalization of "ordinary" language (ibid., 54–55).

14 Both titles are mentioned in Koon, *Hank Williams*, 76.

15 Williams' last recording session in September 1952 did include drums, most audibly on "Kawliga"; in that case, the Native American "tom-tom" effect was featured prominently, undoubtedly for programmatic reasons.

16 Roman Jakobson, "Linguistics and Poetics," 83, 106; and "Poetry of Grammar and Grammar of Poetry," in *Language in Literature*, ed. Krystyna Pomorska and Stephen Rudy (Cambridge MA: Harvard University Press, 1987), 135. Jakobson meant "equivalence in sound" to refer to words that rhyme; I have extended "equivalence in sound" here to include "durational equivalence" as part of "sonic equivalence." I am again indebted to Paula Survilla for her observations about the relationship between sonic and semantic qualities in "Hey Good Lookin'."

17 This is also noted by Richard Leppert and George Lipsitz ("Everybody's Lonesome for Somebody: Age, the Body and Experience in the Music of Hank Williams," *Popular Music* 9:3 [October 1990], 271). Fox discusses the idea of "naturalization-denaturalization-renaturalization" as well ("The Jukebox of History," 54–56).

18 Quoted in Roger Williams, *Sing a Sad Song*, 107.

19 See Roger Williams, *Sing a Sad Song*, 198–200, for information on the audience's awareness of and attitude towards Williams' drinking; and see

Koon, *Hank Williams*, 41, for information on the audience's awareness of Williams' relationship with Audrey Williams.

20 Koon, *Hank Williams*, 57.

21 Ibid., 81–82. Williams recorded several recitations with religious or moralizing themes under the pseudonym "Luke the Drifter." D. K. Wilgus sees these oppositions as flowing from the history of country music itself, and Hank Williams as summarizing the oppositions in the "polarization of the urban hillbilly," which included the diverse strands of "country" and "western" (formerly the domain of the singing cowboy) music ("Country-Western Music and the Urban Hillbilly," *Journal of American Folklore* 83 [April–June 1970], 151–72).

22 Song titles include "Hank Williams You Wrote My Life," "The Life of Hank Williams," "The Death of Hank Williams," "That Heaven Bound Train," "Hank, It Will Never Be the Same Without You," "Hank Williams Meets Jimmie Rodgers," "Tribute to Hank Williams," "Hank and Lefty Raised My Country Soul," "Hank Williams Will Live Forever," "Are You Sure Hank Done It This Way," Hank Jr.'s "Family Tradition," "The Ride," "Hank Williams Sings the Blues No More," "In Memory of Hank Williams," "Thanks Hank," "Hank's Home Town," "Good Old Boys Like Me" (the good old boys are Hank and Tennessee Williams), "If You Don't Like Hank Williams," "Why Ain't I Half as Good as Old Hank (Since I'm Feeling All Dead Anyway)?," "The Last Letter" (Mississippi disc jockey Jimmy Swan's reading of a letter to Williams by M-G-M boss Frank Walker), Charley Pride's album, "There's a Little Bit of Hank in Me." Another kind of tribute occurred in January, 1954 when *Country Song Roundup* published the lyrics to a song Williams allegedly left behind: "My Cold, Cold Heart Is Melted Now" (described in Nick Tosches, *Country: Living Legends and Dying Metaphors in America's Biggest Music* [New York: Charles Scribner's Sons, 1985], 233).

23 Frith elaborates on the connections between "authenticity," live performance, and community in *Sound Effects*, 73. This connection is also reminiscent of certain Marxist arguments about non-alienated labor, use value, and preservation of the spectacle and "aura"; for the classic formulation of these issues, see Walter Benjamin, "The Work of Art in the Age of Mechanical Reproduction," in *Illuminations*, ed. Hannah Arendt, trans. Harry Zohn (New York: Schocken Books, 1969), 217–52. For a discussion of how aesthetics may be linked to the creation of authentic effects, see Frith's "Towards an Aesthetic of Popular Music," in *Music and Society: The Politics of Composition, Performance and Reception*, ed. Richard Leppert and Susan McClary (Cambridge: Cambridge University Press, 1987), 133–50.

24 Frith, "The Real Thing – Bruce Springsteen," in *Music for Pleasure: Essays in the Sociology of Pop* (New York: Routledge, 1988), 99.

25 Rufus Jarman, "Country Music Goes to Town," *Nation's Business* 41:2 (February 1953), 51. "Hillbilly" was the original music industry label (dating

from 1925) for the category of commercial music that became known as "Country and Western" (*Billboard* changed the name of their popularity chart in 1949). Williams would also use the terms "folk music" and "folk singer" interchangeably with "hillbilly" and "country." The term "hillbilly" can carry a particularly charged cluster of connotations; for a discussion of the terms "hillbilly" and "hillbilly music," see Archie Green, "Hillbilly Music: Source and Symbol," *Journal of American Folklore* 78 (July-September 1965), 204–28.

26 See, for example, Richard Leppert and George Lipsitz, "Everybody's Lonesome for Somebody"; and Kent Blaser, "'Pictures from Life's Other Side': Hank Williams, Country Music, and Popular Culture in America," *The South Atlantic Quarterly* 84:1 (Winter 1985), 12–26.

27 I am drawing upon and quoting from Michel Foucault's discussion of the effects of confession in *The History of Sexuality, Volume One: An Introduction*, 56–63.

28 Roger Williams, liner notes from *The Time-Life Country and Western Classics: Hank Williams*, 2. A similar quote appears in R. Williams' *Sing a Sad Song*: "If you're gonna sing, sing 'em something they can understand" (32). Koon maintains that Williams adopted a similar attitude toward interviews: "He simply did not talk much to the press; and when he did, he told them only what he thought they expected to hear" (*Hank Williams*, 88).

29 This is the focus of Jon Stratton's, "Capitalism and Romantic Ideology in the Record Business," in *Popular Music 3: Producers and Markets*, ed. Richard Middleton and David Horn (Cambridge: Cambridge University Press, 1983), 143–56. Fox recognizes the phenomenon in the conclusion of "The Jukebox of History," 64, 69.

30 Fredric Jameson, "Reification and Utopia in Mass Culture," *Social Text* 1 (Winter 1979), 140.

31 Koon recounts this story (*Hank Williams*, 73). In the movie *The Last Picture Show* (1971) – which takes place in rural Texas during the early fifties – nothing could better indict the character of Jacy (Cybill Shepherd), or display her shallowness, than the fact that she listens to Bennett's "Cold, Cold Heart" in her bourgeois bedroom. Meanwhile Sonny (Timothy Bottoms), the movie's paragon of sincerity and opposing pole to Jacy, listens to "Hey Good Lookin'" in his pickup truck. Later in the movie, Sonny's fall from grace is signalled by Jacy's "seduction" of him to the strains of Bennett's "Blue Velvet."

32 Liner notes from *Time-Life Legendary Singers: Tony Bennett*.

33 According to Montgomery journalist Allen Rankin, writing in 1953 shortly after Williams' death, "he had a voice that went through you like electricity, sent shivers up your spine, and made the hair rise on the back of your neck with the thrill. With a voice like that he could make you laugh or cry" (quoted in R. Williams, *Sing a Sad Song*, 141).

34 See Robert Cogan, *New Images of Musical Sound* (Cambridge, MA: Harvard University Press, 1984), 38, for a description of the difference between bel

canto singing and the voice of Billie Holiday. Despite the differences in timbre between Holiday and Williams, many of Cogan's points remain relevant here.

35 Pierre Bourdieu, *Distinction: A Social Critique of the Judgement of Taste*. Bourdieu's oppositions derive from Kant's distinction (in *The Critique of Judgement*) between "that which pleases and that which gratifies." For a critique of the essentializing tendencies in Bourdieu's work, see Michel de Certeau, *The Practice of Everyday Life*, 50–60.

36 Cf. Joli Jensen's discussion of the greater regional specificity of "honky-tonk" style country music as opposed to the diffused effect of the "countrypolitan" Nashville Sound ("Genre and Recalcitrance," *Tracking* 1:1 [Spring 1988], 37).

37 See Tosches for a fuller description of the history of yodeling in country music (*Country*, 109–14).

38 For one of the best socio-musicological descriptions of "swing" in African-American music, see Samuel A. Floyd, Jr., "Ring Shout! Literary Studies, Historical Studies, and Black Music Inquiry," *Black Music Research Journal* 11:2 (Fall 1991), 265–88. This article is discussed extensively in chapter four.

39 The overall association of Williams with metanarratives of Loss is difficult to deny: band members referred to him as "Lovesick," and he often referred to himself as the "Lovesick Blues Boy." Extrapolating from a classification scheme constructed by Kent Blaser, roughly four-fifths of Williams' "fifty most important songs" contain metanarratives of Loss ("'Pictures from Life's Other Side," 23).

40 See Leppert and Lipsitz, "Everybody's Lonesome for Somebody," 270–71.

41 And in a canonical collection such as the *Smithsonian Collection of Classic Country* (SCCC), it is one of the songs in the ten years preceding "Hey Good Lookin'" that most closely resembles it, although the connection may sound somewhat distant.

42 Peter Van der Merwe also notes the following factors which "all blues tunes" have "in common": syncopation and the "blues mode," which consists not only of the usual taxonomy of flattened or neutral scale degrees but, more importantly, in the distinctive manner in which these "blue notes" are treated, a treatment Van der Merwe calls "melodic dissonance" (*Origins of the Popular Style: The Antecedents of Twentieth-Century Popular Music* [Oxford: Oxford University Press, 1989], 118–20).

43 The "Minstrelsy" column appeared in *Billboard* between columns for "Magic," "Endurance Shows," and a regular feature titled "The Final Curtain." On the shared resources of "black" and "white" rural musics, see Tony Russell, *Blacks, Whites and Blues* (New York: Stein and Day Publishers, 1970). For a good discussion of blues influences and minstrelsy in early country music, see Tosches, *Country*, 162–66. For an examination of the relationship between minstrelsy and the early popular music industry (and in

particular the work of Stephen Foster), see William W. Austin, *"Susanna," "Jeanie," and the "Old Folks at Home."*

44 This is the thesis of Eric Lott as detailed in "Love and Theft: The Racial Unconscious of Blackface Minstrelsy," *Representations* 39 (Summer 1992), 23–50.

45 See R. Williams, *Sing a Sad Song*, 23–24, 28–29, 74–75, 168, 232; Charlie Gillett, *The Sound of the City: The Rise of Rock and Roll*, revised and expanded edition (New York: Pantheon Books, 1983), 8; Koon, *Hank Williams*, 10–11, 28, 54; Flippo, *Your Cheatin' Heart*, 22–26, 30, 50, 70, 133, 209; and Leppert and Lipsitz, "Everybody's Lonesome for Somebody," 269–70.

46 Tosches details this shift away from direct blues influences (*Country*, 121–45). Tosches also indicates that raunchy lyrics in hillbilly songs may also share a kind of "dual citizenship," as he finds condemnations of "all kinds of lascivious songs, filthy ballads, scurvy rhimes" in British ballads in the Puritan Philip Stubbes' *Anatomie of Abuses*, published in 1583 (*Country*, 130).

47 Quoted in R. Williams, *Sing a Sad Song*, 113.

48 *Billboard*, June 24, 1939, 132.

49 "West Virginia Hills Are in the Bronx, Says Barn Barnum," *Billboard*, March 4, 1939, 3, 8 (also cited in Tosches, *Country*, 157). This article also features a reference to Freddie Fisher and his Schnicklefritz Band, frequent stars at Horowitz's club. In defense of this article, fans of Kinky Friedman, the "Texas Jewboy," might argue that the article's claims have never ceased to be true.

50 "Modern Dancing in the Barnyard," *Billboard*, April 8, 1939, 18.

51 "Strongly Rated" in "American Folk Tunes," *Billboard*, August 2, 1947, 114; "Hillbilly Bash in Carnegie Perks Stem Interest," *Billboard*, September 27, 1947, 3, 21, 34; Hal Webman, "Gold in Them Hillbills! Folk Grosses Give Bookers New ($) Look," *Billboard*, December 27, 1947, 3, 18; "Hillbilly Center (54th St., NY) Not in Hills, But All Is Rosie," *Billboard*, December 31, 1949, 14. Two other articles may have been prompted by little more than delight with the fact that "hillbilly" rhymes with "Philly" as in "Flowers That Bloom in Spring Return Hillbillies to Philly," *Billboard*, May 25, 1940, 6; and "Down in Philly, They Go Silly for Hillbilly – But Rilly, Silly," *Billboard*, July 5, 1947, 22.

52 "Today's Platter Pilgrimages Show Folk Fellahs Plenty Hep," *Billboard*, February 16, 1946, 20.

53 "Hillbillies Are Hepping to Dollar Sign, Dotted Line and Biz of 'Yours Is Mine'," *Billboard*, January 18, 1947, 31.

54 "People's Music" in "American Folk Tunes: Cowboy and Hillbilly Tunes and Tunesters," *Billboard*, August 17, 1946, 120.

55 "Rustic Rhythm Reaps $$ Reward," *Billboard Special Disk Jockey Supplement*, October 22, 1949, 97.

56 James R. Denny, "Why the Upsurge in Country Music?" *Downbeat*, June 30, 1954, 66.

57 "The 100 Most Important People in the History of Country Music," *Life Collector's Edition: The Roots of Country Music*, September 1, 1994.

58 Tosches, *Country Music*, 152; and for more on Williams, Rose, and the movement of country towards Tin Pan Alley and on the increasing acceptance by Tin Pan Alley of country, see James Manheim, "B-side Sentimentalizer: 'Tennessee Waltz' in the History of Popular Music," *The Musical Quarterly* 76:3 (Fall 1992), 337–54.

59 Liner notes from *The Time-Life Country and Western Classics: Hank Williams*, 2.

4. James Brown's "Superbad" and the double-voiced utterance

1 Quoted in Guralnick, *Sweet Soul Music: Rhythm and Blues and the Southern Dream of Freedom* (New York: Harper and Row, 1986), 242–43. Guralnick identifies Davis as a *Village Voice* reporter and the context given is "writing of growing up . . . black and female." Davis is the author of *Playing the Changes, 1959: A Novel*, and the librettist of *X: The Life and Times of Malcolm X*.

2 Quoted in Guralnick, *Sweet Soul Music*, 240. Guralnick describes Lewis as a "young black historian" writing "in 1968." Lewis is the author of *King: A Biography*, *When Harlem Was in Vogue*, and co-author of *Harlem Renaissance: Art of Black America*.

3 Nelson George, *The Death of Rhythm and Blues* (New York: E. P. Dutton, 1988), 98–99.

4 The only previous study of "Superbad" of which I am aware is Olly Wilson's examination of the polyrhythmic structure and its relationship to West African rhythmic procedure, "The Significance of the Relationship Between Afro-American Music and West African Music," *The Black Perspective in Music* 2 (Spring 1974), 3–22.

5 This discussion of statements on African-American music is indebted to the following: Eileen Southern, ed., *Readings in Black American Music* (New York: W. W. Norton and Co., 1971); Dena J. Epstein, *Sinful Tunes and Spirituals: Black Folk Music to the Civil War* (Urbana: University of Illinois Press, 1977); Lawrence W. Levine, *Black Culture and Black Consciousness: Afro-American Folk Thought from Slavery to Freedom* (Oxford: Oxford University Press, 1977); Portia K. Maultsby, "Africanisms in African-American Music," in *Africanisms in American Culture*, ed. Joseph E. Holloway (Bloomington: Indiana University Press, 1990), 185–210.

6 This criticism is presented most forcefully by Philip Tagg in his "Open Letter: Black Music, Afro-American Music, and European Music," *Popular Music* 8:3 (October 1989), 285–298.

7 See note 5 for a listing of source material. The use of Foucault's notion of the "discursive formation" is also employed by Houston Baker to produce an anti-essentialist conception of African-American difference. Baker outlines his use of Foucaultian archaeology in *Blues, Ideology, and Afro-American*

Literature (17–19), and invokes it specifically to dismantle scientistic claims about the impossibility of "race" based on biological evidence in "Caliban's Triple Play," in *"Race," Writing and Difference*, ed. Henry Louis Gates, Jr. (Chicago: University of Chicago Press, 1986), 384–86.

8 Morgan Godwyn, *Negro's and Indians Advocate, Suing for Their Admission into the Church: or, A Persuasive to the Instructing and Baptizing of the Negro's* [sic] *and Indians in Our Plantations* . . . (London: Printed by F. D., 1680), 33; quoted in Epstein, *Sinful Tunes and Spirituals*, 28.

9 [Alexander Hewatt], *An Historical Account of the Rise and Progress of the Colonies of South Carolina and Georgia* . . . (London: Printed for A. Donaldson, 1779), 100, 103; and William Moulton, a statement from 1782, collected by the Society for the Preservation of Spirituals, *Carolina Low-Country* (New York, 1931). Both of these are quoted in Epstein, *Sinful Tunes and Spirituals*, 41.

10 Henry Russell, *Cheer! Boys, Cheer!: Memories of Men and Music* (London: John Macqueen, Hastings House, 1895), 85.

11 See James Hungerford, "Music on the Plantation," from observations made in 1832, originally published in 1859. Excerpts reprinted in Southern, *Readings in Black American Music*, 71–81. See also [J.] Kinnard, Jr., "Who Are Our National Poets?," *Knickerbocker Magazine* 26 (October 1845), 338.

12 Thomas W. Higginson, *Army Life in a Black Regiment* (Boston: Fields, Osgood, 1870); excerpts reprinted in Southern, *Readings in Black American Music*, 165–66.

13 Ibid., 189–90.

14 For the phenomenon of "representation" in European music during the nineteenth century, see Attali, *Noise: The Political Economy of Music*, trans. Brian Massumi (Minneapolis: University of Minnesota Press, 1985), 46–86. For the development of a "reality effect" based on the separation of a representation and the object represented, see Martin Heidegger, "The Age of the World Picture," in *The Question Concerning Technology and Other Essays*, trans. William Lovitt (New York: Harper and Row, 1977), 115–54; for the effect of this phenomenon in nineteenth-century Europe, see Walter Benjamin, "Paris, Capital of the Nineteenth Century," in *Reflections: Essays, Aphorisms, Autobiographical Writings*, ed. Peter Demetz (New York: Harcourt, Brace, Jovanovich, 1978), 146–62.

15 *Religious Instruction of the Negroes in the United States* (Savannah: T. Purse, 1842), quoted in Levine, *Black Culture*, 18.

16 Charles Colcock Jones, *Suggestions on the Religious Instruction of the Negroes in the Southern States* . . . (Philadelphia: Presbyterian Board of Publication, [n.d.]), quoted in Epstein, *Sinful Tunes and Spirituals*, 201.

17 Natalie Curtis Burlin, "Negro Music at Birth," *Musical Quarterly* 5 (1919), 88. An even more vivid account is offered by Clifton Furness from 1926, "Communal Music among Arabians and Negros," *Musical Quarterly* 16

(1930), 46–51. For a summary of these and other ante- and post-bellum accounts, see Levine, *Black Culture*, 25–30.

18 Letter from Rev. R. Q. Mallard to Mrs. Mary S. Mallard, Chattanooga, May 18, [1859], quoted in Epstein, *Sinful Tunes and Spirituals*, 205.

19 John Mason Brown, "Songs of the Slaves," *Lippincott's Magazine* 5 (1868), 618. For more on spirit possession in African-American religious services, see Morton Marks, "Uncovering Ritual Structures in Afro-American Music," in *Religious Movements in Contemporary America*, ed. Irving I. Zaretsky and Mark P. Leone (Princeton: Princeton University Press, 1974), 60–134; and for a study of trance in the African diaspora, see Gilbert Rouget, *Music and Trance: A Theory of the Relations Between Music and Possession* (Chicago: University of Chicago Press, 1985).

20 Levine, *Black Culture*, 17.

21 Letters of Rev. Samuel Davies, dated June 28, 1751 and March 2, 1756, quoted in Epstein, *Sinful Tunes and Spirituals*, 104. See also the previous quote by Thomas W. Higginson.

22 J[ames] Fenimore Cooper, *Satanstoe*, I (London: S. & L. Bentley, Wilson, and Fley, 1845), 122–23; quoted in Maultsby, "Africanisms in African-American Music," 196.

23 See Frederick Douglass, "From *My Bondage and My Freedom* [1855]," in Southern , *Readings in Black American Music*, 84; Fredrika Bremer, "From *Homes of the New World* [1853]," in ibid., 103–16; Mary Boykin Chestnut, *A Diary from Dixie*, ed. Ben Ames Williams (Boston: Houghton Mifflin, *c.* 1949), 148 – her diary entries are from the early 1860s; Elizabeth Kilham, "Sketches in Color: Fourth," *Putnam's Magazine* 5 (March 1870), 308–9. Dena Epstein notes the greater interest of white women in the slaves' lives and a corresponding prevalence of statements by women in ante-bellum accounts about black music (*Sinful Tunes and Spirituals*, xiv).

24 See Heidegger, "The Age of the World Picture," especially 132–34.

25 See Timothy Mitchell, *Colonising Egypt* (Berkeley: University of California Press, 1991), 15. The idea of disciplinary technology draws heavily (both in Mitchell's case and in mine) on Michel Foucault's *Discipline and Punish*.

26 Michel de Certeau has written extensively about the importance and validity of such "tactics" (his term), and how they, in their very invisibility, remain unquantifiable (*The Practice of Everyday Life*, 29–42 and *passim*). One could also make a case for the persistence of what Foucault has termed "popular illegalities" in the African-American community (*Discipline and Punish*, 82–89; and see note 52 below).

27 This debate over origins polarized around the figures of Melville J. Herskovits, whose *Myth of the Negro Past* (1941) argued for the retention of Africanisms in the diaspora, and E. Franklin Frazier, whose *The Negro Church in America* (1963) argued that Africanisms had been effaced from African-American culture during slavery. Nineteenth- and early twentieth-century assumptions that spirituals and other forms of African-American music

contained African influence were dismissed as spurious by writers such as
Newman White (*American Negro Folk Songs*, [1928]) and George Pullen
Jackson (*White and Negro Spirituals*, [1943]), who claimed that black music
originated in European music. See Levine's "A Question of Origins" (*Black
Culture*, 19–30) and Joseph E. Holloway's "Introduction," in *Africanisms in
American Culture*, ed. Holloway (Bloomington: Indiana University Press,
1990), ix–xxi, for summaries of this debate.

28 These traits are listed in Waterman, "African Influence on the Music of the
Americas," in *Mother Wit from the Laughing Barrel: Readings in the
Interpretation of Afro-American Folklore*, ed. Alan Dundes (Jackson:
University Press of Mississippi, 1990), 81–94 (originally published in 1952).
For a technical description of the effect of African and African-American
rhythmic inflections as elaborations of the "metronome sense," see
Waterman, "'Hot' Rhythm in Negro Music," *Journal of the American
Musicological Society* 1 (1948), 24–37. The use of style traits for determining
the relationship between African and African-American music has been
criticized sharply by Tagg in his "Open Letter."

29 Waterman, "African Influence," 90.

30 Charles Keil, *Urban Blues* (Chicago: Chicago University Press, 1966), 43.

31 Wilson, "The Significance," 20.

32 Ibid., 7.

33 Maultsby, "Africanisms in African-American Music," 188.

34 Ibid., 202.

35 Samuel A. Floyd, Jr., "Ring Shout!"; Sterling Stuckey, *Slave Culture:
Nationalist Theory and the Foundations of Black America* (New York: Oxford
University Press, 1987).

36 "Ring Shout," 266. For more on the centrality of the ring shout in the ante-
and post-bellum African-American community, see Stuckey, *Slave Culture*,
3–97. For an earlier description of the ring shout, see Robert Winslow
Gordon, "Negro 'Shouts' from Georgia," in *Mother Wit from the Laughing
Barrel*, 445–51.

37 Floyd, "Ring Shout," 267–68. All citations are hereafter marked by page
numbers in parentheses.

38 Snead, "Repetition as a Figure of Black Culture," in *Black Literature and
Literary Theory*, ed. Henry Louis Gates, Jr. (London: Routledge, 1984),
59–80. For a different explanation of the pleasurable effects of repetition in
African-American music, see Richard Middleton's psychoanalytic account,
framed by the Barthesian notions of *jouissance* and *plaisir* in *Studying Popular
Music*, 269–92. See Barthes, "The Grain of the Voice," in *Image-Music-Text*,
179– 89, and *The Pleasure of the Text* for his distinction between *plaisir* and
jouissance.

39 Snead, "Repetition as a Figure," 69. Here Snead is drawing heavily on John
Chernoff's *African Rhythm and African Sensibility: Aesthetics and Social Action
in African Musical Idioms* (Chicago: University of Chicago Press, 1979).

40 Snead, "Repetition as a Figure," 68.

41 Much of my formulation of repetition in African-American music is indebted to Guthrie Ramsey.

42 Middleton, *Studying Popular Music*, 269–70.

43 Words and music by James Brown. "Superbad" was recorded on June 30, 1970 and released in a shorter version without the crowd noise as a single in October 1970.

44 Abrahams, *Talking Black*, 36.

45 Ibid., 8–9.

46 Middleton, *Studying Popular Music*, 153.

47 Gates, *The Signifying Monkey*, 46–48. All citations are hereafter marked by page numbers in parentheses.

48 Guralnick makes the following observation. "by the time that '(When You Touch Me) I Can't Stand Myself' and 'There Was a Time' came out as a double-sided hit in the winter of '67–'68, lyrics had reduced themselves to free association, melody has virtually disappeared" (*Sweet Soul Music*, 242). Cliff White adds: "I like his style . . . enjoying the inevitable non-sequiturs once he's made the initial point" (liner notes to *James Brown, the Second CD of JB*).

49 Gates' usage of the term "intertextuality" differs from Julia Kristeva's, which is perhaps the more commonly used one in literary criticism. Kristeva uses the term to denote a "passage from one sign system to another," a process she also refers to as "transposition" (*Revolution in Poetic Language*, trans. Margaret Waller [New York: Columbia University Press, 1984], 59–60).

50 This line must have also seemed striking to Iain Chambers, who precedes his discussion of developments in African-American music in the late 1960s with this line (*Urban Rhythms: Pop Music and Popular Culture* [New York: St. Martin's Press, 1985], 142).

51 The dual meaning of "Signification" is another striking example of this phenomenon. Abrahams adds: "Perhaps the most dynamic and most inverse of all the performance-centered word categories are those slang terms with high affect in Standard English parlance, used in senses which are sometimes diametrically opposed to their accustomed meanings . . . The meaning of the utterance, 'Man, you bad,' depends almost entirely on the inflection of the voice" (*Talking Black*, 21). For Mikhail Bakhtin's notion of the "double-voiced (or dialogic) utterance," see his "Discourse Typology in Prose," included in *Problems of Dostoevsky's Poetics*, 185–203.

52 A great quantity of literature exists on the heroic figure of the "badman" in African-American discourse. Abrahams identifies the figure of the "badman" as one of the two primary categories of heroes in the toasts, the other being the "trickster," which is exemplified by the namesake of the "Signifying Monkey" toast (*Deep Down in the Jungle: Negro Narrative Folklore from the Streets of Philadelphia*, second edition, [Chicago: Aldine Publishing, 1970], 62). For an account of how the "badman" archetype might be manifested in

the personae of recent African-American musicians and their music, see Greil Marcus' portrait of Sly Stone (*Mystery Train: Images of America in Rock 'n' Roll Music*, revised edition [New York: E. P. Dutton, 1982], 75–111). Charles Keil cautions against attaching negative value judgments to these archetypes: "If we are ever to understand what urban Negro culture is all about, we had best view entertainers and hustlers as culture heroes – integral parts of the whole – rather than as deviants or shadow figures" (*Urban Blues*, 20). Lawrence Levine presents a thorough overview of the discourse of the badman as African-American hero in *Black Culture*, 407–40.

53 Abrahams expands upon the concept of the "Intrusive I": "Throughout the narratives we are conscious of a close relationship between the hero of the tale and the person doing the narrating. In most cases, especially in the toasts, the point of view is strictly first person, allowing the complete identification of narrator and hero" (*Deep Down in the Jungle*, 58–59).

54 For a summary and critique of Brecht's writings on distanciation see Stephen Heath, "Lessons from Brecht," *Screen* 15 (1974), 103–28. For a sympathetic and concise explication, see Walter Benjamin, "What Is Epic Theater?," in Arendt (ed.), *Illuminations*, 147–54.

55 The information on "Superbad" derives from the lengthy discography found in Brown's autobiography, *The Godfather of Soul* (with Bruce Tucker) (New York: Macmillan, 1986), 269–326. The discography in *Godfather of Soul* notes that the crowd noise on this particular recording, released on the album *Superbad*, was added after the initial studio recording. This was obviously an important effect for Brown and his recording company, and one they employed on numerous recordings beginning in 1964. This may well have been a response to the extraordinary success of his 1962 recording, *Live at the Apollo*, released in 1963, a recording cited by virtually every account of James Brown and 1960s soul music as enormously influential. See Peter Guralnick's reverential account (*Sweet Soul Music*, 233–38), and Brown's recollection (*Godfather of Soul*, 133–44).

56 Benjamin argues that one of the goals of epic theater is to increase participation of the audience through the reduction of mechanical props ("What Is Epic Theater?," 152). The apparent contradictions of this application may again revolve around the idea of dual focus: Brown works within codes that are conventional for part of his audience and at the same time distancing for another part of the audience.

57 Bourdieu, *Distinction*, 6. See also his discussion of "The Popular 'Aesthetic,'" ibid., 32–34.

58 George, *The Death of Rhythm and Blues*, 102–3.

59 Frank Kofsky goes to considerable lengths to demonstrate the presence of social content in jazz, specifically linking the black avant-garde jazz musicians of the late 1960s with the Black Nationalist movement of that period (*Black Nationalism and the Revolution in Jazz* [New York: Pathfinder Press, 1970]). For more on the historical formations of social content in African-American

music, see LeRoi Jones, *Blues People: The Negro Experience in White America and the Music That Developed from It* (New York: William Morrow, 1963).

60 The TAMI (Teenage Awards Music International) show was filmed for TV in November 1964 and broadcast in 1965. It featured a cross-section of popular acts of the day including Brown, the Rolling Stones, Chuck Berry, the Supremes, and many others. Brown's account can be found in *Godfather of Soul,* 152–53. For an analysis of what the TAMI show implied about changes in audiences and the music industry, see George, *The Death of Rhythm and Blues,* 92.

61 Gates, *The Signifying Monkey,* 123.

62 Ibid., 124.

63 This could be either a sly commentary on his own construction of the "James Brown" persona or an idea for a fanciful (albeit somewhat modest) name for a new dance.

64 Sly Signifies yet again on and with this text in "Thank You for Talkin' to Me Africa," a later "version" of the song which Signifies on the optimistic tone of the first with a tone of (to use Greil Marcus' words) "folly, failure, betrayal, and disintegration . . . [this is] the confession of a man . . . trapped . . . by the flimsiness of the rewards a white society has offered him" (*Mystery Train,* 84). For a discussion of previous versions of "Land of 1000 Dances" see George Lipsitz, *Time Passages: Collective Memory and American Popular Culture* (Minneapolis: University of Minnesota Press, 1990), 145–46.

65 Gates, *The Signifying Monkey,* 123.

66 Wilson, "The Significance," 12.

67 Gates, *The Signifying Monkey,* 123.

68 Wilson, "The Significance," 15–16. Wilson proposes a link between James Brown's music and the music of West Africa in order to explain the popularity of his music there. John Chernoff also comments on Brown's popularity in West Africa and speculates on the musical connections (*African Rhythm and African Sensibility,* 55, 73–74, 115). Chernoff also adds a different view on the subject of density in West African (and, by extension, James Brown's) music: "The music is perhaps best considered as an arrangement of gaps where one may add a rhythm, rather than as a dense pattern of sound" (ibid., 113–14).

69 Palmer, "James Brown," in *The Rolling Stone Illustrated History of Rock and Roll,* ed. Jim Miller (New York: Random House, 1980), 139.

70 These figures also derive from a common pool of vocal gestures found in blues and gospel music. See Jeff Todd Titon, *Early Downhome Blues: A Musical and Cultural Analysis* (Urbana: University of Illinois Press, 1977), 157–69.

71 "Doing It to Death" (the title is another instance of the humorous paradigmatic substitutions typical of Signifyin[g]) was originally released and credited to Brown's backing band, "Fred Wesley and the JBs." Despite this, there can be little doubt as to the identity of the lead vocalist. The

alliteration of the title provides a further connection to Brown's preference for "D-ness."

72 Maury Yeston, *The Stratification of Musical Rhythm* (New Haven: Yale University Press, 1976), 19. In a sense, this separation of parameters, which dates from the nineteenth century, remains an illusion, as pitch impinges on the perception of rhythm, timbre impinges on the perception of pitch, etc. Indeed, the analysis of pitch in this chapter has been to a large extent an analysis of rhythm and accent; conversely, the rhythmic analysis cannot help but be influenced by way the way in which pitches are emphasized.

73 Grosvenor W. Cooper and Leonard B. Meyer, *The Rhythmic Structure of Music* (Chicago: University of Chicago Press, 1960), 2.

74 Wilson, "The Significance," 13.

75 Chernoff finds the polymetric effect to be stronger in James Brown's music than in other Western popular music of the early seventies (*African Rhythm and African Sensibility*, 115).

76 Floyd, "Ring Shout," 273, and see the discussion earlier in this chapter. For another perspective on the creation of swing, see Charles Keil's discussion of what he terms "vital drive" in "Motion and Feeling through Music."

77 Snead, "Repetition as a Figure," 69. Snead also recognizes Brown as a "brilliant American practitioner of the 'cut'."

78 Palmer, "James Brown," 140.

79 Chernoff comments on the importance of timing in these harmonic shifts and how this aspect of his music is especially appreciated by West African musicians (*African Rhythm and African Sensibility*, 115).

80 Robert Palmer, "James Brown," 140. The phrase "African drumming" is extracted from a passage in the same article by Robert Palmer: "But attacking [Brown] for being repetitive is like attacking Africans for being overly fond of drumming" (141).

81 See the chapter, "Duration and Proportion," from Jonathan Kramer's *The Time of Music: New Meanings, New Temporalities, New Listening Strategies* (New York: Schirmer Books, 1988), 286–321 (and elsewhere throughout the book), in which he discusses the application of various proportional analytical strategies and evaluates the flaws and benefits resulting from such analyses. For studies of proportional systems in specific composers, see Roy Howat, *Debussy in Proportion: A Musical Analysis* (Cambridge: Cambridge University Press, 1983); Ernö Lendvai, *Béla Bartók: An Analysis of His Music* (London: Kahn and Averill, 1971); George Perle, *The Operas of Alban Berg: Volume Two/Lulu* (Berkeley: University of California Press, 1985).

82 Roy Howat, *Debussy in Proportion*, 9.

83 All chord functions are marked with upper case Roman numerals; the chord quality of these functions in "Superbad"" is ambiguous, containing both major and minor thirds, although the "I" harmony tends to favor the minor third while the "IV" harmony favors the major third.

84 It is worth noting here that many African-American improvisatory group forms such as blues and jazz (swing and bop in particular) feature sections highly *regular* in length. Following Richard Middleton, we might say that "Superbad" features literal repetition on the musematic level but does not repeat literally on the discursive level.

85 Again, it is striking that it is precisely this aspect (the timing of sections relative to one another) that Chernoff found was particularly admired by the West African musicians with whom he worked (*African Rhythm and African Sensibility*, 115).

86 See Middleton, *Studying Popular Music*, 222, for a discussion of how the "interpretive frame" enables structural relationships to become "meaningful."

87 Although we cannot ignore the presence of the verbal cue, "bridge," which precedes the bridge. It is interesting to note that Brown calls "bridge" twice before the last bridge, with the band shifting only after the second statement. Does this mean the shift was prearranged and that the verbal "cue" has the same spontaneous status as the "crowd noise"?

88 The squelching of the positive aspects of Brown's message can be viewed as part of what Fredric Jameson has identified as the "disappearance of a sense of history" in the moment of postmodernity ("Postmodernism and Consumer Society," in *The Anti-Aesthetic: Essays on Postmodern Culture*, ed. Hal Foster [Port Townsend: Bay Press, 1983], 125).

89 Keil, *Urban Blues*, 43.

90 Henry Louis Gates, Jr. quoted in Jon Pareles, "Rap: Slick, Violent, Nasty and, Maybe, Hopeful," *New York Times*, Sunday, June 17, 1990, sec. 4.

91 Wilson, "The Significance," 20; Gates, *The Signifying Monkey*, 79.

92 Don M. Randel, "Crossing Over with Rubén Blades," *Journal of the American Musicological Society* 44 (1991), 320; cf. Middleton, *Studying Popular Music*, 150.

5. Writing, music, dancing, and architecture in Elvis Costello's "Pills and Soap"

1 Timothy White, "Elvis Costello: A Man Out of Time Beats the Clock," *Musician*, October 1983, 52. Costello repeats his disparaging remarks about critics and analysis in subsequent interviews; see Christian Logan Wright, "The Man Who Would Be King?," *Spin*, May 1989, 46; and David Wild, "Elvis Costello: The Rolling Stone Interview," *Rolling Stone*, June 1, 1989, 66.

2 Among musicologists, Charles Seeger has grappled in the most sustained fashion with the idea of the impossibility of "translating" what he calls the "music knowledge" of music into the "speech knowledge" of music; see his *Studies in Musicology*, 16–44.

3 Quoted in Jeffrey Stock, "Elvis Citing," *Pulse*, April 1994, 50. Costello analyzes his creative process in light of changes in his musical style in Mark Rowland, "Strange Bedfellows," *Musician*, March 1991, 48, 52.

4 For an exception to this pop myth, see Robert Walser's study of heavy metal musicians which demonstrates the importance of "legitimate" technique in metal ("Eruptions: Heavy Metal Appropriations of Classical Virtuosity," *Popular Music* 11:3 [October 1992], 263–308). Costello has often emphasized his musical illiteracy in interviews, as has Bruce Thomas, the bassist for the Attractions, Costello's band from 1977–1984 and intermittently since then (Dan Forte, "Bruce Thomas Pumps It up with Elvis Costello," *Guitar Player*, March 1987).

5 This is discussed in Simon Frith, "The Good, the Bad, and the Indifferent: Defending Popular Culture from the Populists," *diacritics* 21:4 (Winter 1991), 102–3, 109–10.

6 This notion of the "popular aesthetic" and the various formulations of "taste" espoused in this paragraph derive from Pierre Bourdieu, *Distinction*, 1–96.

7 Simon Frith and Howard Horne, *Art into Pop* (London: Methuen, 1987), 88.

8 Frith and Horne, *Art into Pop*, 18–19. The following discussion summarizes the argument advanced in *Art into Pop*. All citations are hereafter marked by page numbers in the text.

9 Although, as discussed extensively throughout this book, the opposition of "authenticity" vs. "commercialism" is linked inextricably to the production of art in capitalist society, and therefore does not derive solely from art school ideology.

10 In an early interview, Allan Jones (the interviewer) relates that "the prospect of [Costello's] being compared to Springsteen . . . fills Elvis with anguish and dread." Costello's comments on the subject could generously be described as vituperative ("The Elvis [Costello, That Is] Interview," *Melody Maker*, June 25, 1977).

11 Bill Flanagan, "The Last Elvis Costello Interview," *Musician*, March 1986. Interestingly, a review from 1979 compared him to that paragon of sensitivity, Jackson Browne: "Like Browne, Costello sings of intimate matters impersonally. Both artists' songs seem to be subterfuge: communiqués that create the illusion of disclosure while masking the artists' true passions and disillusions" (Mikal Gilmore, "Two Sides of Elvis Costello" [review of February 14 and 16, 1979 concerts], *Rolling Stone*, April 5, 1979).

12 Costello himself refers to his early image as that of a loser in "The Last Elvis Costello Interview," *Musician*, March 1986. Also see David Gouldstone, *Elvis Costello, God's Comic: A Critical Companion to His Lyrics and Music* (New York: St. Martin's Press, 1989), 9–24, for an interpretation of the early Costello persona as a loser. In a review of *My Aim Is True*, Allan Jones commented on Costello's focus on "the emotional violence that attends the disintegration of love affairs, and with the frustrations and occasional humiliations of early adolescent love and sexual encounters" ("Deep Soul

from Elvis," *Melody Maker*, July 23, 1977).

13 Frith and Horne, *Art into Pop*, 132.

14 Mary Harron, "McRock: Pop as a Commodity," in *Facing the Music*, ed. Simon Frith (New York: Pantheon Books, 1988), 205. Unwittingly commenting on the contradictory aspects of "new wave," a *Rolling Stone* article on the "Heatwave" concert (which took place August 23, 1980) discusses the possible demise of new wave (the concert included Nick Lowe, Rockpile, the Rumour, the Pretenders, the B-52s, Talking Heads, Elvis Costello): "Heatwave symbolized new wave's death; by making the music acceptable to so many people, and by making it the centerpiece of what was partially intended as a moneymaking venture, the movement's original ideals and beliefs were compromised once and for all" (James Henke, "Heatwave: Did New Wave Sell Out?," *Rolling Stone*, October 16, 1980).

15 Dave Laing distinguishes between the "declamatory" mode ("rooted in mainstream soul music, the 'shouting' style of R&B singing") and the "confidential" mode (associated with "the lyric ballad"). These modes of singing tend to "be aligned with specific genres of music, different lyric subject-matter and contrasting 'modes of address' in the lyric." He finds "the confidential stance" to be very rare in punk rock (*One Chord Wonders* [Milton Keynes: Open University Press, 1985], 57). See Stefani, "Melody: A Popular Perspective," *Popular Music* 6 (January 1987): 21–35, for a provisional socio-musicological description of European "popular" melody and for distinctions between what he terms "spoken melody," "motorial melody," "expressive melody," "descriptive melody," and "musical melody."

16 For more on the "outlandish" effect of this humor, see Paul Nelson's review, "The Sex Pistols Drop the Big One," *Rolling Stone*, February 23, 1978.

17 For the differences between "mainstream" and "avant-garde" punk, see *Art into Pop*, 134; and Laing, *One Chord Wonders*, 103.

18 Although these notions share many features; Harron argues for continuity between the punks and the hippies ("McRock," 204–5). For a discussion about the commercial savvy of punk Svengali Malcolm McLaren, see Frith and Horne, *Art into Pop*, 130–38.

19 Jeffrey Stock, "Elvis Citing," *Pulse*, April 1994.

20 I owe this and many of the other observations in this chapter about Costello and late-seventies pop music to Buzz Brackett.

21 Jameson, "Postmodernism and Consumer Society," 114. Allan Moore describes Costello's music as "pastiche" and "parody" without distinguishing between the terms. He does, however, convincingly trace stylistic precedents for several Costello songs (*Rock, The Primary Text*, 176–79).

22 Jameson also cites the "disappearance of history" as one of the qualities of postmodernism, a quality which includes the loss of faith in progress ("Postmodernism and Consumer Society," 125). Costello disparages the use of the term "evolution" to characterize changes in his songwriting in Timothy

White, "Elvis Costello: A Man Out of Time Beats the Clock," *Musician*, October 1983, 47.

23 Costello recently espoused a similar view: "You don't have to renounce rock 'n' roll, like it's a religion, to take up more serious art music. It's all serious, and it's all as much fun as you want to make it" (Brett Milano, "Elvis Costello: A Brutal Youth," *CD Review*, March 1994).

24 On the different types of values judgments and discourses in pop, folk, and art musics, see Frith, "What Is Good Music?" and the discussion in chapter one of this book. And on the particular prestige associated with the string quartet (the instrumental medium for *The Juliet Letters*), see Carl Dahlhaus, *The Idea of Absolute Music*, 15–17.

25 Greil Marcus, "Don't Tread on Me" (review of *My Aim Is True*), *Rolling Stone*, December 1, 1977. This review is reprinted along with several other pieces on Costello in Greil Marcus, *Ranters and Crowd Pleasers: Punk in Pop Music, 1977–92* (New York: Anchor Books, 1993).

26 Ken Tucker, review of *Stiffs Live*, *Rolling Stone*, May 4, 1978.

27 Janet Maslin, "Elvis Costello in Love and War" (review of *Armed Forces*), *Rolling Stone*, March 23, 1979.

28 Mikal Gilmore, "Two Sides of Elvis Costello" (review of February 14 and 16, 1979 concerts), *Rolling Stone*, April 5, 1979.

29 See Tad Friend, "The Case for Middlebrow," *The New Republic*, March 3, 1992, for a comparative assessment of Costello as a "highbrow" pop musician (for the sake of comparison, Friend lists Deee-lite as "highlowbrow," Madonna as "middlebrow," and Metallica as "lowbrow"). A recent article claimed that "it is now clear that his diversity, which can frustrate the best-laid marketing strategies, has also contributed to sustaining his audience's long-term interest" (Jeffrey Stock, "Elvis Citing," *Pulse*, April 1994). Maslin recognizes in her 1979 review of *Armed Forces* how Costello "works hard to make himself more than marginally accessible" and how he "serves as a feisty and furiously talented middleman, halfway between rock's smoothest sellouts and the angriest fringes of its New Wave" ("Elvis Costello in Love and War," *Rolling Stone*, March 23, 1979). And Costello himself reflects on how his perception of the (limited) size of his audience affected his music in Timothy White, "Elvis Costello: A Man Out of Time Beats the Clock," *Musician*, October 1983.

30 Frith, "Rock and the Politics of Memory," in *The Sixties Without Apology* (special double issue of *Social Text* 3:2 & 4:1 [Spring-Summer 1984]), 64; for a fuller account of how folk notions of authenticity entered pop discourses, see Frith, "'The Magic That Can Set You Free': The Ideology of Folk and the Myth of the Rock Community," in *Popular Music 1: Folk or Popular? Distinctions, Influences, Continuities*, ed. David Horn and Richard Middleton (Cambridge: Cambridge University Press, 1981), 159–68.

31 For Costello's awareness of the shifting subject positions in his songs, see Jeffrey Stock, "Elvis Citing," *Pulse*, April 1994; and the video *Elvis*

Costello/The Brodsky Quartet: The Juliet Letters (A Hummingbird Production for BBC Television, 1993). See Dave Laing, *One Chord Wonders*, 66–68, for a discussion of the use of multiple subject positions in punk. Dai Griffiths has also noted Costello's penchant for concocting third-person narratives ("'Sleep of the Just': Analytical Notes Between Context and Text," unpublished manuscript).

32 This terminology is adapted from the discussion of song types in Middleton, *Studying Popular Music*, 216.

33 Mick St. Michael, *Elvis Costello: An Illustrated Biography* (Omnibus Press: London, 1986), 93. Subsequent citations are hereafter marked by page numbers in parentheses. While "Pills and Soap" has attracted attention in every review of *Punch the Clock* and in every book about Costello, the only other article devoted to it of which I am aware is Greil Marcus' "In the Fascist Bathroom," *Artforum*, January 1984 (reprinted in *Ranters and Crowd Pleasers*). For another study of a Costello song that considers the impact of musical processes on interpretation, see Dai Griffiths, "'Sleep of the Just.'"

34 Timothy White, "Elvis Costello: A Man Out of Time Beats the Clock," *Musician*, October 1983.

35 Arthur Berger coined the term "octatonic pitch collection" to refer to a scale of alternating whole steps and half steps ("Problems of Pitch Organization in Stravinsky," *Perspectives of New Music* 2 [1963], 11–42).

36 For the historical uses and referential associations of the octatonic scale, see Richard Taruskin, "Chernomor to Kashchei: Harmonic Sorcery; or Stravinsky's 'Angle'," *Journal of the American Musicological Society* 38:1 (Spring 1985), 72–142.

37 Greil Marcus describes the hand claps as "a hipster snapping his fingers in front of a firing squad" ("In the Fascist Bathroom").

38 Regarding this phrase, Christopher Connelly claimed in a review of *Punch the Clock* that "the repetition of that one phrase packs a bigger emotional oomph than many of his tangled, tortured lyrics. In a single image, Costello captures both the crassness of the press – and, more significantly, the agony of a sorrow-filled parent. The impact is stunning" ("Elvis Costello: Too Much Yakety-yak," *Rolling Stone*, September 1, 1983).

39 This type of structural analysis of texts, similar to the one employed in the analysis of "Hey Good Lookin'," draws on the work of Roman Jakobson; see his "Linguistics and Poetics," 83 and "Poetry of Grammar and Grammar of Poetry," 135. This type of "New Critic" approach is probably foreign to the temporal experience of hearing the song (although it may be incorporated into a "rehearing" of it).

40 This term is Agawu's ("Theory and Practice," 24).

41 This gestural chart follows the charts presented by Middleton in "Popular Music and Musicology: Bridging the Gap," *Popular Music* 12:2 (May 1993), 177–90.

42 See Emile Benveniste, *Problems in General Linguistics*, trans. Mary Elizabeth Meek (Coral Gables: University of Miami Press, 1971) 197–201, for a discussion of the contextually dependent nature of the third person pronoun. Alan Durant discusses shifters in the context of rock music in *Conditions of Music* (Albany: State University of New York Press, 1984), 201–11. For more on the paradigmatic analysis of narrative, see Roland Barthes, "Introduction to the Structural Analysis of Narratives," and *S/Z*, trans. Richard Miller (New York: Noonday Press, 1974).

43 See Sammie Ann Wicks, "A Belated Salute to the 'Old Way' of 'Snaking' the Voice on its (*ca*) 345th Birthday," *Popular Music* 8:1 (January 1989), 59–96.

44 Costello recognized this when he admitted (while evidently in an analytical frame of mind) that he "love[s] tunes that get outside of the chords and have this interfering note in it" (Jeffrey Stock, "Elvis Citing," *Pulse*, April 1994).

45 "Doom Squad," *New West*, February 12, 1979; reprinted in *Ranters and Crowd Pleasers*, 37.

46 By "sly in-jokes" I refer to a process such as the following: the album *Almost Blue* did not contain the song "Almost Blue," which appeared on the next album, *Imperial Bedroom*, which, however, did not contain the song "Imperial Bedroom"; instead, the song "Imperial Bedroom" appeared as the B-side of the single "Man out of Time." Another example of this kind of practice begins with the song "Jack of All Parades" on *King of America* (1986) which includes a reference to "the crimes of Paris" which is the title of a song on the next album, *Blood and Chocolate* (1986). In turn, "The Crimes of Paris" contains a line – "you better leave that kitten alone" – which alludes to the title of a song that Costello was performing in concert in the late eighties (Little Willie John's "Leave My Kitten Alone") but which he has yet to release on a commercial recording.

47 Barthes, "Introduction to the Structural Analysis of Narratives," 123.

48 This point is made by Simon Frith in "The Good, the Bad, and the Indifferent."

6. Afterword: the citizens of Simpleton

1 This is described in Chris Twomey, *XTC: Chalkhills and Children, The Definitive Biography* (London: Omnibus Press, 1992), 18.

2 Jon Pareles referred to XTC's music in a 1980 review as "Brain Pan Alley"; see "XTC: This is pop? (Brain Pan Alley)" (review of *Drums and Wires*), *Rolling Stone*, March 6, 1980, 67.

3 For an early, classic study, see David Riesman, "Listening to Popular Music," *American Quarterly* (Summer 1950); reprinted in *On Record*, ed. Frith and Goodwin, 5–13.

Bibliography

Abbate, Carolyn. *Unsung Voices: Opera and Musical Narrative in the Nineteenth Century*. Princeton: Princeton University Press, 1991.

Abrahams, Roger D. *Deep Down in the Jungle: Negro Narrative Folklore from the Streets of Philadelphia*. Second edition. Chicago: Aldine Publishing, 1970.

Talking Black. Rowley, MA: Newbury House, 1976.

Adorno, T. W. "On Popular Music" (with the assistance of George Simpson), in *Studies in Philosophy and Social Science*, vol. 9, 17–48. New York: Institute of Social Research, 1941. Reprinted in *On Record: Rock, Pop, and the Written Word*, edited by Simon Frith and Andrew Goodwin, 301–14.

and Max Horkheimer. *Dialectic of Enlightenment*. Translated by John Cumming. New York: Continuum, 1991.

Agawu, Kofi. *Playing with Signs: A Semiotic Interpretation of Classic Music*. Princeton: Princeton University Press, 1991.

"Representing African Music," *Critical Inquiry* 18 (Winter 1992), 245–66.

"Theory and Practice in the Analysis of the Nineteenth-Century *Lied*," *Music Analysis* 11:1 (March 1992), 3–36.

Angelou, Maya. *The Heart of a Woman*. New York: Bantam Books, 1982.

Attali, Jacques. *Noise: The Political Economy of Music*. Translated by Brian Massumi. Minneapolis: University of Minnesota Press, 1985.

Austin, William W. *"Susanna," "Jeanie," and "The Old Folks at Home": The Songs of Stephen C. Foster from His Time to Ours*. Second edition. Urbana: University of Illinois Press, 1987 [1975].

Baker, Houston, Jr. *Blues, Ideology, and Afro-American Literature: A Vernacular Theory*. Chicago: University of Chicago Press, 1984.

"Caliban's Triple Play," in *"Race," Writing and Difference*, edited by Henry Louis Gates, Jr., 381–95. Chicago: University of Chicago Press, 1986.

Bakhtin, Mikhail. *The Dialogic Imagination: Four Essays*. Edited by Michael Holquist. Translated by Caryl Emerson and Michael Holquist. Austin: University of Texas Press, 1981.

Problems of Dostoevsky's Poetics. Edited and translated by Caryl Emerson. Minneapolis: University of Minnesota Press, 1984.

Barthes, Roland. *S/Z*. Translated by Richard Miller. New York: Noonday Press, 1974.

The Pleasure of the Text. Translated by Richard Miller. New York: Hill and Wang, 1975.

"The Death of the Author," in *Image-Music-Text,* translated by Stephen Heath, 142–48. New York: Noonday Press, 1977.

"The Grain of the Voice," in *Image-Music-Text,* translated by Stephen Heath, 179–89. New York: Noonday Press, 1977.

"Introduction to the Structural Analysis of Narratives," in *Image-Music-Text,* translated by Stephen Heath, 79–124. New York: Noonday Press, 1977.

Baudrillard, Jean. *Simulacra and Simulations.* Translated by Paul Foss, Paul Patton, and Philip Beitchman. New York: Sémiotext(e), 1983.

"Consumer Society," in *Jean Baudrillard: Selected Writings,* edited by Mark Poster, 29–56. Stanford: Stanford University Press, 1988.

"The Masses: The Implosion of the Social in the Media," in *Jean Baudrillard: Selected Writings,* edited by Mark Poster, 207–19. Stanford: Stanford University Press, 1988.

Benjamin, Walter. "What Is Epic Theater?," in *Illuminations,* edited by Hannah Arendt, translated by Harry Zohn, 147–54. New York: Schocken Books, 1969.

"The Work of Art in the Age of Mechanical Reproduction," in *Illuminations,* edited by Hannah Arendt, translated by Harry Zohn, 217–52. New York: Schocken Books, 1969.

"Paris, Capital of the Nineteenth Century," in *Reflections: Essays, Aphorisms, Autobiographical Writings,* edited by Peter Demetz, 146–62. New York: Harcourt, Brace, Jovanovich, 1978.

Benveniste, Emile. *Problems in General Linguistics.* Translated by Mary Elizabeth Meek. Coral Gables: University of Miami Press, 1971.

Berger, Arthur. "Problems of Pitch Organization in Stravinsky," *Perspectives of New Music* 2 (1963), 11–42.

Bergeron, Katherine, and Philip Bohlman, ed. *Disciplining Music: Musicology and Its Canons.* Chicago: University of Chicago Press, 1992.

Blacking, John. *Venda Children's Songs: A Study in Ethnomusicological Analysis.* Johannesburg: Witwatersrand University Press, 1967.

Blaser, Kent. "'Pictures from Life's Other Side': Hank Williams, Country Music, and Popular Culture in America," *The South Atlantic Quarterly* 84:1 (Winter 1985), 12–26.

Bonds, Mark Evan. *Wordless Rhetoric: Musical Form and the Metaphor of the Oration.* Cambridge, MA: Harvard University Press, 1991.

Bourdieu, Pierre. *Distinction: A Social Critique of the Judgement of Taste.* Translated by Richard Nice. Cambridge MA: Harvard University Press, 1984.

Brackett, David. "The Politics and Practice of 'Crossover' in American Popular Music, 1963–65," *The Musical Quarterly* 78:4 (Winter 1994), 774–97.

Brown, James. *The Godfather of Soul* (with Bruce Tucker). New York: Macmillan, 1986.

Brown, John Mason. "Songs of the Slaves," *Lippincott's Magazine* 5 (1868), 618.

Burlin, Natalie Curtis. "Negro Music at Birth," *The Musical Quarterly* 5 (1919), 86–89.

Burnett, James. *Billie Holiday.* New York: Hippocrene Books, 1984.

Chambers, Iain. *Urban Rhythms: Pop Music and Popular Culture.* New York: St. Martin's Press, 1985.

Chapple, Steve, and Reebee Garofalo. *Rock 'n' Roll Is Here to Pay.* Chicago: Nelson-Hall Inc., 1977.

Chernoff, John Miller. *African Rhythm and African Sensibility: Aesthetics and Social Action in African Musical Idioms.* Chicago: University of Chicago Press, 1979.

Chester, Andrew. "Second Thoughts on a Rock Aesthetic: The Band," *New Left Review* 62 (1970), 75–82.

Chestnut, Mary Boykin. *A Diary from Dixie.* Edited by Ben Ames Williams. Boston: Houghton Mifflin, c. 1949.

Chilton, John. *Billie's Blues: Billie Holiday's Story, 1933–1959.* New York: Day Books, 1978.

Clarke, Gary. "Defending Ski-Jumpers: A Critique of Theories of Youth Subcultures," in *On Record: Rock, Pop, and the Written Word,* edited by Simon Frith and Andrew Goodwin, 81–96. New York: Pantheon Books, 1990.

Cogan, Robert. *New Images of Musical Sound.* Cambridge, MA: Harvard University Press, 1984.

Cohen, Sara. *Rock Culture in Liverpool: Popular Music in the Making.* Oxford: Oxford University Press, 1991.

Cole, Hugo. *Sounds and Signs: Aspects of Musical Notation.* Oxford: Oxford University Press, 1974.

Collier, James Lincoln. *The Making of Jazz: A Comprehensive History.* New York: Dell Publishing, 1978.

Collins, Patricia Hill. *Black Feminist Thought: Knowledge, Consciousness, and the Politics of Empowerment.* New York: Routledge, 1991.

Cone, Edward T. *The Composer's Voice.* Berkeley: University of California Press, 1974.

Cook, Nicholas. *Music, Imagination, and Culture.* Oxford: Oxford University Press, 1990.

Cook, Susan. "When Lady Day Sings . . . Race, Gender and Performance Politics." Unpublished manuscript.

Cooper, Grosvenor W., and Leonard B. Meyer. *The Rhythmic Structure of Music.* Chicago: University of Chicago Press, 1960.

Crosby, Bing (as told to Pete Martin). *Call Me Lucky.* New York: Da Capo Press, 1953.

Crosby, Gary, and Ross Firestone. *Going My Own Way.* Garden City, NY: Doubleday & Co., 1983.

Dahlhaus, Carl. *Esthetics of Music.* Translated by William W. Austin. Cambridge: Cambridge University Press, 1982.

    Foundations of Music History. Translated by J. B. Robinson. Cambridge: Cambridge University Press, 1983.

    The Idea of Absolute Music. Translated by Roger Lustig. Chicago: University of Chicago Press, 1989

de Certeau, Michel. *The Practice of Everyday Life.* Translated by Steven Rendall. Berkeley: University of California Press, 1984.

    "History: Science and Fiction," in *Heterologies.* Translated by Brian Massumi, 199–221. Minneapolis: University of Minnesota Press, 1986.

de Man, Paul. "Introduction" to Jauss' *Towards an Aesthetic of Reception.* Minneapolis: University of Minnesota Press, 1982.

Dreyfus, Hubert L., and Paul Rabinow. *Michel Foucault: Beyond Structuralism and Hermeneutics.* Second edition. Chicago: University of Chicago Press, 1983.

Durant, Alan. *Conditions of Music.* Albany: SUNY Press, 1984.

Eagleton, Terry. *Literary Theory: An Introduction.* Minneapolis: University of Minnesota Press, 1983.

Eco, Umberto. *A Theory of Semiotics.* Bloomington: Indiana University Press, 1976.

Epstein, Dena J. *Sinful Tunes and Spirituals: Black Folk Music to the Civil War.* Urbana: University of Illinois Press, 1977.

Feld, Steven. "Sound Structure as Social Structure," *Ethnomusicology* 28:3 (September 1984), 383–410.

Finnegan, Ruth. *The Hidden Musicians: Music-Making in an English Town.* Cambridge: Cambridge University Press, 1989.

Flippo, Chet. *Your Cheatin' Heart: A Biography of Hank Williams.* Garden City, NY: Doubleday & Co., 1981.

Floyd, Samuel A., Jr. "Ring Shout! Literary Studies, Historical Studies, and Black Music Inquiry," *Black Music Research Journal* 11:2 (Fall 1991), 265–88.

Foucault, Michel. *The Order of Things: An Archaeology of the Human Sciences.* New York: Vintage Books, 1973.

    Discipline and Punish: The Birth of the Prison. Translated by Alan Sheridan. New York: Vintage Books, 1977.

    The History of Sexuality, Volume One: An Introduction. New York: Vintage Books, 1979.

Fox, Aaron. "The Jukebox of History: Narratives of Loss and Desire in the Discourse of Country Music," *Popular Music* 11:1 (January 1992), 53–72.

Friedwald, Will. *Jazz Singing: America's Great Voices from Bessie Smith to Bebop and Beyond.* New York: Charles Scribner's Sons, 1990.

Frith, Simon. "'The Magic That Can Set You Free': The Ideology of Folk and the Myth of the Rock Community," in *Popular Music 1: Folk or Popular?*

Distinctions, Influences, Continuities, edited by David Horn and Richard Middleton, 159–68. Cambridge: Cambridge University Press, 1981.

Sound Effects. New York: Pantheon Books, 1981.

"Rock Biography," in *Popular Music 3: Producers and Markets*, edited by Richard Middleton and David Horn, 271–77. Cambridge: Cambridge University Press, 1983.

"Rock and the Politics of Memory," in *The Sixties Without Apology*, a double issue of *Social Text* 3:2 & 4:1 (Spring–Summer 1984), 59–69.

"Towards an Aesthetic of Popular Music," in *Music and Society: The Politics of Composition, Performance and Reception*, edited by Richard Leppert and Susan McClary, 133–50. Cambridge: Cambridge University Press, 1987.

"Why Do Songs Have Words?," in *Music for Pleasure: Essays in the Sociology of Pop*. New York: Routledge, 1988.

"The Real Thing – Bruce Springsteen," in *Music for Pleasure: Essays in the Sociology of Pop*. New York: Routledge, 1988.

"What is Good Music?," *Canadian Music Review* 10 (1990), 92–102.

"The Good, the Bad, and the Indifferent: Defending Popular Culture from the Populists," *diacritics* 21:4 (Winter 1991), 102–115.

"Adam Smith and Music," *New Formations* 18 (Winter 1992), 67–83.

and Andrew Goodwin, ed. *On Record: Rock, Pop, and the Written Word*. New York: Pantheon Books, 1990.

and Howard Horne. *Art into Pop*. London: Methuen, 1987.

and Angela McRobbie. "Rock and Sexuality," in *On Record: Rock, Pop, and the Written Word*, edited by Simon Frith and Andrew Goodwin, 371–89. New York: Pantheon Books, 1990. Originally published in *Screen Education* 29 (1978).

Furness, Clifton. "Communal Music among Arabians and Negros," *Musical Quarterly* 16 (1930), 38–51.

Gates, Henry Louis, Jr. *The Signifying Monkey: A Theory of African-American Literary Criticism*. New York: Oxford University Press, 1988.

George, Nelson. *The Death of Rhythm and Blues*. New York: E. P. Dutton, 1988.

Giddins, Gary. *Riding on a Blue Note: Jazz and American Pop*. New York: Oxford University Press, 1981.

Gillett, Charlie. *The Sound of the City: The Rise of Rock and Roll*. Revised and expanded edition. New York: Pantheon Books, 1983.

Gordon, Robert Winslow. "Negro 'Shouts' from Georgia," in *Mother Wit from the Laughing Barrel: Readings in the Interpretation of Afro-American Folklore*, edited by Alan Dundes, 445–51. Jackson: University Press of Mississippi, 1990. Originally published in 1927.

Gouldstone, David. *Elvis Costello, God's Comic: A Critical Companion to His Lyrics and Music*. New York: St. Martin's Press, 1989.

Green, Archie. "Hillbilly Music: Source and Symbol," *Journal of American Folklore* 78 (July–September 1965), 204–28.

Green, Lucy. *Music on Deaf Ears.* Manchester: Manchester University Press, 1988.

Greenblatt, Stephen. *Shakespearean Negotiations: The Circulation of Social Energy in Renaissance England.* Berkeley: University of California Press, 1988.

Griffiths, Dai. "'Sleep of the Just': Analytical Notes Between Context and Text." Unpublished manuscript.

Guralnick, Peter. *Sweet Soul Music: Rhythm and Blues and the Southern Dream of Freedom.* New York: Harper and Row, 1986.

Hacking, Ian. "Biopower and the Avalanche of Printed Numbers," *Humanities in Society* 5:3 & 4 (1982), 279–95.

Hamm, Charles. *Yesterdays: Popular Song in America.* New York: W. W. Norton, 1979.

Harron, Mary. "McRock: Pop as a Commodity," in *Facing the Music,* edited by Simon Frith, 173–220. New York: Pantheon Books, 1988.

Heath, Stephen. "Lessons from Brecht," *Screen* 15 (1974), 103–28.

Hebdige, Dick. *Subculture: The Meaning of Style.* London: Methuen, 1979.

Heidegger, Martin. "The Age of the World Picture," in *The Question Concerning Technology and Other Essays,* translated by William Lovitt, 115–54. New York: Harper and Row, 1977.

Hentoff, Nat and Nat Shapiro. *Hear Me Talkin' to Ya.* New York: Rinehart and Company, 1955.

Higginbotham, Evelyn Brooks. "African-American Women's History and the Metalanguage of Race," *Signs* 17:2 (1992), 251–74.

Holiday, Billie. *Lady Sings the Blues* (with William Dufty). New York: Penguin Books, 1984 [1956].

Holloway, Joseph E. "Introduction," in *Africanisms in American Culture,* edited by Joseph E. Holloway, ix–xxi. Bloomington: Indiana University Press, 1990.

Hood, Mantle. *The Ethnomusicologist.* New York: McGraw-Hill, Inc., 1971.

Howat, Roy. *Debussy in Proportion: A Musical Analysis.* Cambridge: Cambridge University Press, 1983.

Jairazbhoy, Nazir. "The 'Objective' and Subjective View in Music Transcription," *Ethnomusicology* 21:2 (May 1977), 263–73.

Jakobson, Roman. "Linguistics and Poetics," in *Language in Literature,* edited by Krystyna Pomorska and Stephen Rudy, 62–94. Cambridge, MA: Harvard University Press, 1987.

"Poetry of Grammar and Grammar of Poetry," in *Language in Literature,* edited by Krystyna Pomorska and Stephen Rudy, 121–44. Cambridge, MA: Harvard University Press, 1987.

Jameson, Fredric. "Reification and Utopia in Mass Culture," *Social Text* 1 (Winter 1979), 130–48.

"Postmodernism and Consumer Society," in *The Anti-Aesthetic: Essays on Postmodern Culture*, edited by Hal Foster, 111–25. Port Townsend: Bay Press, 1983.

Jarman, Rufus. "Country Music Goes to Town," *Nation's Business* 41 (February 1953).

Jauss, Hans Robert. *Towards an Aesthetic of Reception*. Translated by Timothy Bahti. Minneapolis: University of Minnesota Press, 1982.

Jensen, Joli. "Genre and Recalcitrance: Country Music's Move Uptown," *Tracking* 1:1 (Spring 1988): 30–41.

Jones, LeRoi. *Blues People: The Negro Experience in White America and the Music That Developed from It.* New York: William Morrow, 1963.

Keil, Charles. "Motion and Feeling through Music," *The Journal of Aesthetics and Art Criticism* 24 (Spring 1966), 337–49.

Urban Blues. Chicago: Chicago University Press, 1966.

Kerman, Joseph. *Contemplating Music: Challenges to Musicology.* Cambridge, MA: Harvard University Press, 1985.

Kernfield, Barry, ed. *The New Grove Dictionary of Jazz.* 2 vols. London: Macmillan Press, 1988.

Kilham, Elizabeth. "Sketches in Color: Fourth," *Putnam's Magazine* 5 (March 1870), 304–11.

Kinnard, [J.], Jr. "Who Are Our National Poets?," *Knickerbocker Magazine* 26 (October 1845), 331–41.

Kofsky, Frank. *Black Nationalism and the Revolution in Jazz.* New York: Pathfinder Press, 1970.

Koon, George William. *Hank Williams: A Bio-Bibliography.* Westport, CT: Greenwood Press, 1983.

Kramer, Jonathan. *The Time of Music: New Meanings, New Temporalities, New Listening Strategies.* New York: Schirmer Books, 1988.

Kramer, Lawrence. *Music and Poetry: The Nineteenth Century and After.* Berkeley: University of California Press, 1984.

Music as Cultural Practice, 1800–1900. Berkeley: University of California Press, 1991.

Kristeva, Julie. *Revolution in Poetic Language.* Translated by Margaret Waller. New York: Columbia University Press, 1984.

Laing, Dave. *One Chord Wonders.* Milton Keynes: Open University Press, 1985.

Lendvai, Ernö. *Béla Bartók: An Analysis of His Music.* London: Kahn and Averill, 1971.

Leppert, Richard and George Lipsitz. "Everybody's Lonesome for Somebody: Age, the Body and Experience in the Music of Hank Williams," *Popular Music* 9:3 (October 1990), 259–74.

Levine, Lawrence. *Black Culture and Black Consciousness: Afro-American Folk Thought from Slavery to Freedom.* Oxford: Oxford University Press, 1977.

Highbrow/Lowbrow: The Emergence of Cultural Hierarchy in America. Cambridge, MA: Harvard University Press, 1988.

Levy, Janet. "Covert and Casual Values in Recent Writings about Music," *Journal of Musicology* 6:1 (Winter 1987), 3–27.

Lipsitz, George. *Time Passages: Collective Memory and American Popular Culture.* Minneapolis: University of Minnesota Press, 1990.

Lomax, Alan. "Song Structure and Social Structure," *Ethnology* 1:4 (October 1962), 425–51.

Lott, Eric. "Love and Theft: The Racial Unconscious of Blackface Minstrelsy," *Representations* 39 (Summer 1992), 23–50.

Malone, Bill C. *Country Music U.S.A.* Revised edition. Austin: University of Texas Press, 1985.

Manheim, James M. "B-side Sentimentalizer: 'Tennessee Waltz' in the History of Popular Music," *The Musical Quarterly* 76:3 (Fall 1992), 37–56.

Marcus, Greil. *Mystery Train: Images of America in Rock 'n' Roll Music.* Revised edition. New York: E. P. Dutton, 1982.

Ranters and Crowd Pleasers: Punk in Pop Music, 1977–92. New York: Anchor Books, 1993.

Marks, Morton. "Uncovering Ritual Structures in Afro-American Music," in *Religious Movements in Contemporary America,* edited by Irving I. Zaretsky and Mark P. Leone, 60–134. Princeton: Princeton University Press, 1974.

Maultsby, Portia. "Africanisms in African-American Music." In *Africanisms in American Culture,* edited by Joseph E. Holloway, 185–210. Bloomington: Indiana University Press, 1990.

McClary, Susan. *Feminine Endings: Music, Gender, and Sexuality.* Minneapolis: University of Minnesota Press, 1991.

McRobbie, Angela. "Settling Accounts with Subcultures: A Feminist Critique," in *On Record: Rock, Pop, and the Written Word,* edited by Simon Frith and Andrew Goodwin, 66–80. New York: Pantheon Books, 1990.

Meyer, Leonard B. *Emotion and Meaning in Music.* Chicago: University of Chicago Press, 1956.

Middleton, Richard. *Studying Popular Music.* Milton Keynes: Open University Press, 1990.

"Popular Music and Musicology: Bridging the Gap," *Popular Music* 12:2 (May 1993), 177–90.

Miller, Jim, ed. *The Rolling Stone Illustrated History of Rock and Roll.* New York: Random House, 1980.

Mitchell, Timothy. *Colonising Egypt.* Berkeley: University of California Press, 1991.

Moore, Allan. *Rock, The Primary Text: Developing a Musicology of Rock.* Buckingham: Open University Press, 1993.

Moore, John. "The Hieroglyphics of Love: The Torch Singers and Interpretation," *Popular Music* 8:1 (January 1989), 31–58.

Morgereth, Timothy A. *Bing Crosby: A Discography, Radio Program List, and Filmography*. Jefferson, NC and London: McFarland and Co., 1987.

Nattiez, Jean-Jacques. *Music and Discourse: Toward a Semiology of Music*. Translated by Carolyn Abbate. Princeton: Princeton University Press, 1990.

Nettl, Bruno. *The Study of Ethnomusicology: Twenty-nine Issues and Concepts*. Urbana: University of Illinois Press, 1983.

Nketia, J. H. Kwabena. "African Roots of Music in the Americas: An African View," in *Report of the 12th Congress, London, International Musicological Society* (1981), 82–88.

O'Meally, Robert. *Lady Day: The Many Faces of Billie Holiday*. New York: Little, Brown and Company, Arcade Publishing, 1991.

Palmer, Robert. "James Brown," in *The Rolling Stone Illustrated History of Rock and Roll*, edited by Jim Miller, 136–42. New York: Random House, 1980.

Parker, Martin. "Reading the Charts—Making Sense with the Hit Parade," *Popular Music* 10:2 (1991), 205–19.

Perle, George. *The Operas of Alban Berg: Volume Two/Lulu*. Berkeley: University of California Press, 1985.

Pleasants, Henry. *The Great American Popular Singers*. New York: Simon and Schuster, 1974.

Randel, Don Michael. "Crossing Over with Rubén Blades," *Journal of the American Musicological Society* 44 (1991), 301–23.

"Canons in the Musicological Toolbox," in *Disciplining Music*, edited by Katherine Bergeron and Philip Bohlman, 10–22. Chicago: University of Chicago Press, 1992.

Riesman, David. "Listening to Popular Music," *American Quarterly* (Summer 1950); reprinted in *On Record: Rock, Pop, and the Written Word*, edited by Simon Frith and Andrew Goodwin, 5–13. New York: Pantheon Books, 1990.

Rouget, Gilbert. *Music and Trance: A Theory of the Relations Between Music and Possession*. Chicago: University of Chicago Press, 1985.

Russell, Henry. *Cheer! Boys, Cheer!: Memories of Men and Music*. London: John Macqueen, Hastings House, 1895.

Russell, Tony. *Blacks, Whites, and Blues*. New York: Stein and Day Publishers, 1970.

Ruwet, Nicholas. "Methods of Analysis in Musicology," *Music Analysis* 6 (1987), 11–36.

St. Michael, Mick. *Elvis Costello: An Illustrated Biography*. London: Omnibus Press, 1986.

Sales, Grover. *Jazz: America's Classical Music*. New York: Prentice Hall, 1984.

Schuller, Gunther. *The Swing Era: The Development of Jazz, 1930–1945*. New York and Oxford: Oxford University Press, 1989.

Seeger, Charles. *Studies in Musicology 1935–1975*. Berkeley: University of California Press, 1977.

"The Musicological Juncture: Music as Value," in *Studies in Musicology 1935–1975*. Berkeley: University of California Press, 1977.

"Prescriptive and Descriptive Music Writing," in *Studies in Musicology 1935–1975*. Berkeley: University of California Press, 1977.

Shaw, Greg. "The Teen Idols," in *The Rolling Stone Illustrated History of Rock and Roll*, edited by Jim Miller, 96–100. New York: Random House, 1980.

Shepherd, Donald, and Robert F. Slatzer. *Bing Crosby: The Hollow Man*. New York: Pinnacle Books, 1981.

Shepherd, John. "A Theoretical Model for the Sociomusicological Analysis of Popular Musics," in *Popular Music 2: Theory and Method*, edited by David Horn and Richard Middleton, 145–78. Cambridge: Cambridge University Press, 1982.

Shepherd, John, Phil Virden, Graham Vulliamy, Trevor Wishart. *Whose Music? A Sociology of Musical Languages*. London: Latimer, 1977.

Silverman, Kaja. *The Acoustic Mirror: The Female Voice in Psychoanalysis and Cinema*. Bloomington: Indiana University Press, 1988.

Snead, James A. "Repetition as a Figure of Black Culture," in *Black Literature and Literary Theory*, edited by Henry Louis Gates, Jr., 59–80. London: Routledge, 1984.

Solie, Ruth. "The Living Work: Organicism and Musical Analysis," *19th-Century Music* 4 (1980), 147–56.

Southern, Eileen, ed. *Readings in Black American Music*. New York: W. W. Norton and Co., 1971.

Stefani, Gino. "Melody: A Popular Perspective," *Popular Music* 6 (January 1987), 21–35.

"A Theory of Musical Competence," *Semiotica* 66:1–3 (1987), 7–22.

Stratton, Jon. "Capitalism and Romantic Ideology in the Record Business," in *Popular Music 3: Producers and Markets*, edited by Richard Middleton and David Horn, 143–56. Cambridge: Cambridge University Press, 1983.

Stuckey, Sterling. *Slave Culture: Nationalist Theory and the Foundations of Black America*. New York: Oxford University Press, 1987.

Subotnik, Rose Rosengard. "Toward a Deconstruction of Structural Listening: A Critique of Schoenberg, Adorno, and Stravinsky," in *Explorations in Music, the Arts, and Ideas: Essays in Honor of Leonard B. Meyer*, edited by Eugene Narmour and Ruth A. Solie, 87–122. New York: Pendragon Press, 1988.

Developing Variations: Style and Ideology in Western Music. Minneapolis: University of Minnesota Press, 1991.

Tagg, Philip. *KOJAK, 50 Seconds of Television Music: Toward the Analysis of Affect in Popular Music*. Göteborg: Studies from the Department of Musicology, 1979.

"Analysing Popular Music: Theory, Method, and Practice," in *Popular Music 2: Theory and Method*, edited by David Horn and Richard Middleton, 37–68. Cambridge: Cambridge University Press, 1982.

"Open Letter: Black Music, Afro-American Music, and European Music," *Popular Music* 8:3 (October 1989), 285–98.

Taruskin, Richard. "Chernomor to Kashchei: Harmonic Sorcery; or Stravinsky's 'Angle'," *Journal of the American Musicological Society* 38:1 (Spring 1985), 72–142.

Tirro, Frank. *Jazz: A History*. Second edition. New York: W. W. Norton and Co., 1993.

Titon, Jeff Todd. *Early Downhome Blues: A Musical and Cultural Analysis*. Urbana: University of Illinois Press, 1977.

Tosches, Nick. *Country: Living Legends and Dying Metaphors in America's Biggest Music*. New York: Charles Scribner's Sons, 1985.

Twomey, Chris. *XTC: Chalkhills and Children, The Definitive Biography*. London: Omnibus Press, 1992.

Ulanov, Barry. *The Incredible Crosby*. New York: Whittlesey House, 1948.

Van der Merwe, Peter. *Origins of the Popular Style: The Antecedents of Twentieth-Century Popular Music*. Oxford: Oxford University Press, 1989.

Vulliamy, Graham. "Music and the Mass Culture Debate," in John Shepherd, Phil Virden, Graham Vulliamy, Trevor Wishart, *Whose Music: A Sociology of Musical Languages*, 179–200. London: Latimer, 1977.

Walser, Robert. "Eruptions: Heavy Metal Appropriations of Classical Virtuosity," *Popular Music* 11:3 (October 1992), 263–308.

Waterman, Richard Alan. "African Influence on the Music of the Americas," in *Mother Wit from the Laughing Barrel: Readings in the Interpretation of Afro-American Folklore*, edited by Alan Dundes, 81–94. Jackson: University Press of Mississippi, 1990. Originally published in 1952.

"'Hot' Rhythm in Negro Music," *Journal of the American Musicological Society* 1 (1948), 24–37.

Whitburn, Joel. *Joel Whitburn's Pop Memories, 1890–1954: The History of American Popular Music*. Menomonee Falls, WI: Record Research, 1986.

White, Cliff. Liner notes to *James Brown, the CD of JB: Sex Machine and Other Soul Classics*. Polydor 825 714–2, 1985.

Liner notes to *James Brown, the Second CD of JB: Cold Sweat and Other Soul Classics*. Polydor 831 700–2, 1987.

Discography in *The Godfather of Soul* by James Brown (with Bruce Tucker), 269–326. New York: Macmillan, 1986.

White, Hayden. *Tropics of Discourse: Essays in Cultural Criticism*. Baltimore: The John Hopkins University Press, 1978.

White, John. *Billie Holiday: Her Life and Times*. New York: Universe Books, 1987.

Wicks, Sammie Ann. "A Belated Salute to the 'Old Way' of 'Snaking' the Voice on its (*ca.*) 345th Birthday," *Popular Music* 8:1 (January 1989), 59–96.

Wilgus, D. K. "Country-Western Music and the Urban Hillbilly," *Journal of American Folklore* 83 (April–June 1970), 151–72.

Williams, Hank. *The Complete Works of Hank Williams: A 129 Song Legacy of His Music*. Nashville: Acuff-Rose, 1983.

Williams, Martin. *The Jazz Tradition.* New and revised edition. Oxford: Oxford University Press, 1983.

Williams, Roger. *Sing a Sad Song: The Life of Hank Williams.* Second edition. Urbana: University of Illinois Press, 1981.

   Liner notes to *Time-Life Country and Western Classics: Hank Williams,* CSL 3001 – CSL 3003, 1981.

Willis, Paul. *Profane Culture.* London: Routledge and Kegan Paul, 1978.

Willis, Susan. *A Primer for Daily Life.* New York: Routledge, 1991.

Wilson, Olly. "The Significance of the Relationship between Afro-American Music and West African Music," *The Black Perspective in Music* 2 (Spring 1974), 3–22.

Winkler, Peter. "Randy Newman's Americana," *Popular Music* 7:1 (January 1988), 1–26.

Wolfe, Charles K. Liner notes to *The Time-Life Bing Crosby,* SLGD–06, 1985.

Yeston, Maury. *The Stratification of Musical Rhythm.* New Haven: Yale University Press, 1976.

Select discography

American Popular Song: Six Decades of Songwriters and Singers. The Smithsonian Collection of Recordings, 1984.

Beatles, The. *Please Please Me.* Parlophone PCS 3042, 1963.
With the Beatles. Parlophone, 1963.
Rubber Soul. Parlophone, 1965.
The Beatles. Apple, 1968.
Abbey Road. Apple, 1969.

Berry, Chuck. *Golden Decade.* Chess Records, 1972.

Brown, James. *Live at the Apollo.* King K826, 1963.
Superbad. King K1127, 1971.
James Brown, the CD of JB: Sex Machine and Other Soul Classics. Polydor 825 714–2, 1985.
James Brown, the Second CD of JB: Cold Sweat and Other Soul Classics. Polydor 831 700–2, 1987.

Classic Country Music: A Smithsonian Collection. Second edition. RCA Special Products R 042 DML6–0914, 1990.

Costello, Elvis. *My Aim is True.* Columbia, 1977.
Stiffs Live. Stiff Records, 1978.
King of America. Columbia, 1986.
Spike. Warner Bros., 25848–4, 1989.
Mighty Like a Rose. Warner Bros., 1991.
and the Attractions. *This Year's Model.* Columbia, 1978.
Armed Forces. Columbia, 1979.
Get Happy. Columbia, 1980.
Taking Liberties. Columbia, 1980.
Trust. Columbia, 1981.
Almost Blue. Columbia, 1981.
Imperial Bedroom. Columbia, 1982.
Punch the Clock. Columbia, 1983.

Goodbye Cruel World. Columbia, 1984
Blood and Chocolate. Columbia, 1986.
Brutal Youth. Warner Bros., 1994.
with The Brodsky Quartet. *The Juliet Letters.* Warner Bros., 1993.

Crosby, Bing. *The Time-Life Bing Crosby.* SLGD–06, 1985.

Dylan, Bob. *Bringing It All Back Home.* Columbia, 1965.
Highway 61 Revisited. Columbia, 1965.
Blonde on Blonde. Columbia, 1966.

Holiday, Billie, with Eddie Heywood and his Orchestra. *I'll Be Seeing You.*
Commodore XFL 15351, 1980.
The Complete Decca Recordings. MCI Records, Inc., 1991.
The Quintessential Billie Holiday, Vols. 1–16. Columbia.

Lewis, Gary and the Playboys. "This Diamond Ring," on *Time-Life Superhits
1965.* Time-Life Records, 1990. Originally on *This Diamond Ring,*
Liberty Records, 1965.

Mitchell, Joni. *Blue.* Reprise, 1971.

Pickett, Wilson. *Wilson Pickett's Greatest Hits.* Atlantic CS 2–501, 1973.

Robinson, Smokey, and the Miracles. *Greatest Hits, Volume 1.* Tamla Records,
1969.

Sex Pistols, The. *Never Mind the Bollocks, Here's the Sex Pistols.* Warner Bros.,
1977.

Simon and Garfunkel. *Parsley, Sage, Rosemary, and Thyme.* Columbia, 1966.

Sly and the Family Stone. *Greatest Hits.* Epic 30325, 1970.

Taylor, James. *James Taylor.* Apple, 1969.
Mudslide Slim and the Blue Horizon. Warner Bros., 1971.

Williams, Hank. *Time-Life Country and Western Classics: Hank Williams.* CSL
3001–CSL 3003, 1981.

Index

Abbate, Carolyn, 207 n. 26
Abbey Road, 170
Abrahams, Roger D., 121, 122, 123, 124, 227 n. 51, 228 n. 53
"absolute" music, 19
"Ac-Cent-Tchu-Ate the Positive," 56
"Accidents Will Happen," 196
Acuff, Roy, 100
Adorno, Theodor: and culture industry, 219 n.10; and standardization in popular music, 205 n. 7
aesthetics: in analytical metalanguage, 20–21; legitimate, 13; in proportional analysis, 154; and repetition, 117–18; role of listening situation in, 17; in sixties rock, 168–71; *see also* Bourdieu, Pierre
aesthetics of reception, 6, 18, 55, 57, 206 n. 8
African-American literature, 116
African-American music: authenticity in, 109, 119; and essentialism, 109, 119; and "groove," 143; as historical discourse, 108–15, 216 n. 56; as musicological subject, 115–19; and religion, 111–13; repetition in, 117–19, 226 n. 38; as resistance, 114–15; and ring shout, 116–17; vocal style in, 195; and West African music, 136, 139, 143; *see also* Brown, James; Holiday, Billie; "Superbad"
African-American religion, 112, 225 n. 19
African-American urban folklore, 123
Agawu, Kofi, 30, 206 n. 15, 209 n. 39, 235 n. 40
"Alison," 164, 196
"All Day and All of the Night," 1

"Almost Blue," 236 n. 46
Almost Blue, 167, 236 n. 46
Alpert, Herb, and the Tijuana Brass, 5
American Society of Composers and Publishers (ASCAP), 101
"And I Love Her,"4
Andrews Sisters, The, 36, 56,
Angelou, Maya, 213 n. 19
Archies, 3
Armed Forces, 169, 170, 196
Armstrong, Louis, 37, 56
"Art" music, 19
art rock, 160
art school: and influence on British rock, 161–62
Astaire, Fred, 55
Attali, Jacques, 224 n. 14
Attractions, the, 164, 165, 167, 232 n. 4
audiences: for Brown, James, 108, 200; for Costello, Elvis, 169, 171, 197–98, 234 n. 29; cult, 162, 169, 198, 201–2; for Holiday, Billie, 62, 202; for "In the Midnight Hour," 7, 9; for "This Diamond Ring," 5, 7, 9, 202
Austin, Gene, 55
Austin, William W., 208 n. 34, 221 n. 43
authenticity: in African-American music, 109; and capitalism, 88–89; vs. commercialism, 19, 232 n. 9; in country music, 77, 78; and musical value, 219 n. 23; and Marxism, 219 n. 23; *see also* musical value; Hank Williams
authorial voice: in the Beatles, 16; in Brown, James, 124, 169–70, 229 n. 63; in classical music, 207 n. 26; in Costello, Elvis, 165–66, 169–71 197;

251

DON'T EVEN THINK ABOUT IT

Sarah Mlynowski

ORCHARD

ORCHARD BOOKS

First published in Great Britain in 2014 byThe Watts Publishing Group
This edition published in 2015 by The Watts Publishing Group

5 7 9 10 8 6

Text Copyright © Sarah Mlynowski, 2014

The moral rights of the author have been asserted.

A CIP catalogue record for this book
is available from the British Library.

ISBN 978 1 408 33156 9

Printed and bound in Great Britain by
CPI Group (UK) Ltd, Croydon, CR0 4YY

The paper and board used in this book are
made from wood from responsible sources.

Orchard Books
An imprint of
Hachette Children's Group
Part of The Watts Publishing Group Limited
Carmelite House
50 Victoria Embankment
London EC4Y 0DZ

An Hachette UK Company
www.hachette.co.uk

www.hachettechildrens.co.uk

For the ladies who lounge (and sometimes write):
Courtney, Jess, Adele, Robin and Emily
(and when I'm very lucky, Leslie, Joanna and Julia).

Thanks for the company and the cupcakes.

Chapter One
BEFORE

We were not always freaks.

Sure, most of us occasionally exhibited freakish behavior. But that's not the same thing.

Olivia Byrne, when she worried about something, picked the skin around her thumbnails until her fingers bled.

Cooper Miller sang badly. When he walked down the hall, when he studied, when he ate. He wasn't singing the Top 40 either – he made up tunes and lyrics about his everyday life. Walking to school. Being late to math.

Mackenzie Feldman, Cooper's girlfriend, hated needles. Not that any of us *liked* needles, but Mackenzie truly hated them. She hated them so much she'd never even gotten her ears pierced. She wore clip-ons to her own Sweet Sixteen. Or her Sweet, as we called it in Tribeca, our little downtown corner of Manhattan.

So yeah, we had certain quirks, but before October 2, which was eleven days before the Bloomberg High School carnival and eighteen days before Mackenzie's Sweet, Olivia, Cooper, Mackenzie, and the rest of us were pretty much just regular sophomores.

Even October 2, the day that changed everything, started normally enough.

We got ready for school. Most of us lived in Tribeca, within a few blocks from BHS, Bloomberg High School.

Tribeca is one of the wealthiest areas in Manhattan. Not that we were all wealthy – definitely not. Half of our parents owned our apartments; the other half rented. A bunch of us shared rooms with our siblings. If you lived in Tribeca and your parents were *really* rich or famous – like if your mom was Beyoncé or your dad ran an investment bank – you didn't go to BHS like us. You went to private school.

Anyway.

On October 2, we arrived at school, most of us on time. We locked our stuff in our lockers and headed to room 203, where 10B met for homeroom. Cooper didn't arrive on time – he was always late. He also didn't lock his locker, because he didn't bother having a lock. He could never remember the combination. And he trusted us. Back then, he trusted everyone.

We claimed our usual seats and chatted with our friends.

"Darren Lazar asked me if you were single," Renée Hinger said as she sat down beside Olivia in the middle of the room. Renée's leopard-print scarf fluttered behind her. She was also wearing a black hair band, earrings, and a silver bracelet crammed with charms. She was an accessories kind of girl. She was a busybody kind of girl. We're relieved she's not one of us. We have enough busybodies without her.

Olivia's heart skipped a beat. "What did you tell him?"

Renée laughed. "What do you think I told him? I told him you were. Unless you're involved with someone and keeping it a secret?"

Olivia had never been involved with anyone. Fifteen and never been kissed. She was afraid that when the time came she would barf all over the kisser.

Olivia did not have much confidence around boys or girls. One of the main reasons she hung around Renée was that Renée did 99.9 percent of the talking.

Of course, we didn't know the degree of her lack of confidence back then. We didn't know about her lack of kissing experience either. We didn't know any of each other's hidden thoughts or secret histories. Not like we do now.

"Do you think he's going to ask me out?" Olivia asked.

Renée twirled her scarf around her wrist. "Do you want him to ask you out?"

"I don't know." Olivia tried to picture him. He had light brown hair and red cheeks. Green eyes, maybe. Dressed well. Button-downs and the right jeans. He seemed nice. No one called him by his first name – he just went by Lazar. They had public speaking together. Her stomach clenched at the thought of the class. The next day she had to make a speech on Lyme disease, which was worth 40 percent of her grade.

There was nothing that terrified her more than speaking in front of others.

"I think you guys would be perfect together," Renée continued.

"Why?" Olivia asked. "Because we're both short?"

"No, because you're both nice. And smart. And cute."

Olivia didn't say no, but didn't say yes either. It wasn't that she didn't like Lazar. It was just that the idea of being on an actual date – where she would have to worry about what she wore, what she ate, and what she said – was incredibly stressful to her. She picked at her thumb.

Cooper came in at last, singing to himself. As usual, he looked slightly disheveled, like he'd woken up, picked up the green hoodie and jeans that were lying in a heap on his floor and put them on.

Which is exactly what he had done. Cooper was wearing his Yankees hat. He wore it all baseball season until they were out of the running. It brought out the blue in his eyes. Not that he'd be aware of something like that. Well, not without reading our minds.

Cooper cupped his ear with his open hand. "What's up, 10B, can I get a boo-ya?"

"Boo-ya," called Nick Gaw from the side of the room. Nick was one of Cooper's good friends.

Cooper sighed with exaggerated disappointment. "That was lame, people. Lame. Lame-o. The Yankees won last night! I said give me a boo-ya!"

Mackenzie responded with a "boo-ya." She had to. That

was her job as girlfriend, even if she occasionally found Cooper's antics a little embarrassing, like the time he insisted on giving her a piggyback ride down the hallway.

Cooper stood in front of Olivia's desk and wagged his finger. "Livvie, I did not hear you boo-ya. Why did I not hear you boo-ya?"

Olivia flushed. She gripped the sides of her desk. She did not like being put on the spot. Her heart sped up; her mouth felt dry. She debated. Would whatever she said sound stupid? Would she not make the right boo-ya sound? Would she sound too eager? Place too much emphasis on the *boo* and not enough on the *ya*?

But she liked Cooper. If he weren't totally out of her league and didn't already have a girlfriend, she might have a crush on him. He was one of those people who were always smiling. Always kind. Always inclusive. Like right then, when he was trying to get her to boo-ya.

She could do it. She could! She just had to push the words out with the tip of her tongue. "Booooo-ya?"

Cooper petted her twice on the head like she was a rabbit. When he was a kid he'd had a rabbit for a whole two weeks before his dad made him return it to the pet store. He'd gotten a turtle instead. Gerald. "Well done, Livvie. Thank you for playing."

Olivia turned bright red.

Cooper made a point of talking to Olivia. She was shy, but Cooper knew that she just needed some help breaking out of her shell. Like Gerald. When he'd first gotten Gerald, the turtle had barely ventured out of his bowl. These days Gerald strutted around the loft like he was the mayor of Tribeca.

Cooper got a few more of us to boo-ya as he zig-zagged his way through the desks to the empty seat in the last row by the window, right next to Mackenzie and her closest friend, Tess Nichols.

"Thank you, Cooper," Ms Velasquez said, closing the door behind her. "Now take off your hat, please."

Cooper gave our teacher a big smile. He had a small overbite from losing his retainer a month after he got it. "But, Ms V, I didn't have a chance to wash my hair this morning."

"Then you might want to consider getting up earlier in the future," she said, taking off her blazer and slinging it over her chair.

Cooper removed his hat, revealing slept-on hair, clutched it to his chest, and finally sat down. "Let's get this party started," he said, and leaned his chair all the way back so it kissed the wall.

"Let's see who's here," Ms Velasquez said, and called all our names. When she was done, she sat on the desk and swung her legs. "People, I have some good news and some bad news," she said. "I'll start with the bad news."

We waited.

"Those of you who are planning to get flu shots – and I think that's most of you – are scheduled to get them today at lunch," she told us.

We groaned.

Ms Velasquez cleared her throat. "So, the good news is…

Cooper made a drumroll.

Our teacher smiled. "You probably won't get the flu."

Naturally, we booed.

"What if I like the flu?" Cooper asked.

"Why would you like the flu?" Ms Velasquez asked.

"I'd get to stay home and watch baseball," he answered.

"I wouldn't mind missing a week of school," Nick said.

We understood. His mom was a biology teacher at school. If our moms taught at our school, we'd want to stay home too.

"I'm not getting the shot," Renée declared, playing with her headband. "I never get sick. And you know, I read an article that said that they don't even work. That the pharmaceutical companies are only interested in making money off us."

We all groaned and she crossed her arms and rolled her eyes. Renée was a conspiracy theorist. She thought the government was out to get everyone.

These days we're not so sure we disagree.

"I'm skipping it too," Mackenzie said.

Mackenzie had been born a preemie, at twenty-six weeks instead of forty. She'd required a lot of surgeries. Eye surgery. Kidney surgery. Heart surgery. She didn't remember any of it, but she knew she hated any kind of needle, and she assumed the two facts were related.

"You're going to make me get it alone?" Cooper asked. "We'll do it together. I'll hold your hand. It'll be fuuuuuun," he sang.

Mackenzie saw nothing potentially fun where needles were involved. But as usual, her boyfriend found the silver lining in everything. In coming to school. In the flu. In vaccinations.

Cooper lived in silver linings.

Ms Velasquez tapped her fingers on her desk. "So remember, everyone. Nurse Carmichael's office. Lunchtime. Bring your permission slips if your parents haven't already sent them back."

As Ms Velasquez continued to talk, Olivia continued to worry. Not about the vaccination. Needles didn't scare her. She was nervous about her Lyme disease speech.

She picked her thumb. *Everything will be fine*, she told herself. *Fine, fine, fine.*

Of course, it wouldn't be fine. Not at all. But Olivia couldn't know that. It's not like she had ESP.

Ha, ha, ha.

Not yet.

Maybe you think Olivia is telling this story. Or Mackenzie, or Cooper, or someone else in our home-room you haven't met.

It could be any of us. But it's not. It's all of us. We're telling you the story together. It's the only way we know how.

This is the story of how we became freaks.

It's how a group of *I*s became a *we*.

Chapter Two
IT HAPPENED HERE

At the beginning of lunch, we waited in line by Nurse Carmichael's office.

There were twenty-three of us. Most of homeroom 10B. 10A had gotten their shots the day before.

Adam McCall was missing – probably an ear infection. He always had ear infections.

Pi Iamaura went in and came out first. Her real name was Polly, after her grandfather Paul, but her nickname was Pi because she could tell you the first thirty-nine numbers of pi. They're 3.1415926535897 93238462643383279502884419, if you're curious.

BJ Kole went in next.

Yes, he called himself BJ.

His name was actually Brian Joseph, but he started going by

BJ in middle school. He thought it was hilarious. He was a bit of a perv.

He hurried into the nurse's office and closed the door behind him. He thought Nurse Carmichael was hot, and was always trying to come up with accidental ways to feel her up. He tried to feel everyone up.

Next in line was Jordana Brohman-Maizner. Jordana filed her nails while she waited. She kept a full manicure set in her locker. Base coat, top coat, clippers, and eleven different colors ranging from Bliss (shimmery yellow) to We Were Liars (fire-engine red).

Behind her were Olivia and Renée. Renée was still not getting the vaccination. She was only waiting in line so she wouldn't miss anything. She liked to know what everyone was up to at all times. She was the type of person who got email notifications every time her friends changed their Facebook statuses.

"Do you know that more people die from flu shots than the flu?" Renée asked.

"I'm not sure that's true," Olivia said. Actually, she was totally sure it wasn't true, because she had the Centers for Disease Control and Prevention website bookmarked on her laptop, and visited it frequently. In addition to having a lot of anxiety, Olivia was a hypochondriac.

"It's going to hurt," Renée said.

Her words didn't scare Olivia, but they terrified Mackenzie, who was right behind them. She'd decided to do it. She couldn't believe she was really going to do it.

Mackenzie was waiting with Cooper and Tess, although Tess was busy texting Teddy on her iPhone. Teddy was Tess's best guy friend. Tess also had a massive crush on him.

"Maybe I won't get it," Mackenzie said, suddenly unsteady on her feet.

"Oh, come on," Cooper said. "It's just a pinch. You don't want to get the flu."

"Everyone else is getting the shot. I won't get the flu."

"You might. It's going around. And your Sweet is soon. You don't want to be sick and have to cancel."

Mackenzie's parents would kill her if she got the flu.

It was all booked. Her brother and sister were flying in from Stanford. Her parents had spent a small fortune in deposits. They'd gone all out. They'd booked a hotel ballroom. Hired a DJ. Hired an event planner. Mailed out gorgeous invitations. Square, black, with cursive silver print.

The few of us who'd been invited had all RSVPed yes.

Mackenzie was excited for the party. Kind of.

Nothing was expected of her. All she had to do was dance and look pretty in her new black Herve Leger cocktail dress.

Mackenzie knew she was pretty. Ever since she was a kid, people had always told her as much. She had dirty-blond hair, dark blue eyes, a button nose, and a gymnast's body. She'd trained at the NYC Elite gymnastics studio for years. She'd tried competing back in middle school, but it wasn't for her. The night before one of her big matches, she'd stayed out late with her friends, broken curfew, been exhausted the next day, and tripped off the balance beam. Her parents had been furious. She had been relieved.

Outside the nurse's office, Cooper slung his arm around her and sang, "The needle will only hurt for a *secoooond*."

"But it's really going to hurt for that one second," Mackenzie snapped.

Cooper kissed her cheek. "I'll come in with you. And sing you a song."

He was always nice to her. Even when she wasn't nice back.

She knew she should be nicer to him. He definitely deserved it.

Mackenzie nodded to herself and to Cooper. She would do it. She would get the needle. She would do it because he wanted her to. She owed him, even if he didn't know it. The needle would be her punishment.

Back then, we didn't know she was punishing herself, or for what.

Now we know everything. Even the stuff we try to forget. Especially the stuff we try to forget.

Cooper squeezed Mackenzie's shoulder. "Then I'll get you a root beer float as a reward."

We were allowed to leave school for lunch. But we only had forty minutes, so we couldn't go far.

"Can we go to Takahachi instead?" Mackenzie asked. "I'm craving salmon rolls."

Japanese wasn't Cooper's first choice, since his mom ordered it every night. He was gluten intolerant, so there weren't too many options for him to eat – but he was a go-with-the-flow kind of guy. "Why don't we pick up Takahachi and then eat it at your place?" he asked, waggling his eyebrows. She lived a block away. No one was ever home.

"We're not going to have enough time for both after the vaccines," Mackenzie said. "Maybe tomorrow?"

Cooper was fine waiting until the next day. But he wondered if it was really going to happen then. They'd barely hooked up since he'd been back from camp. He wondered if Mackenzie was avoiding him. Although that didn't make sense – they hung out all day together at school. Why would she avoid him after hours? Did she not want to be alone with him?

The nurse's door opened. BJ came out. He had failed in his groping mission.

We all hoped Nurse Carmichael had stuck his arm with the needle really hard.

Jordana went in, barely bothering to look up from her nails. We waited.

A few minutes later she came out looking dazed. "That was miserable," she announced. She was holding a red lollipop.

Olivia was up. She stepped eagerly toward the door. She was a big believer in vaccinations. To prevent the flu. To prevent typhoid. If only they had one to prevent social anxiety, she'd be all set.

"You really shouldn't do it," Renée said to Olivia.

"I'll be fine," Olivia said. She usually followed Renée's lead, but she couldn't in this case.

Renée sighed, looking slightly confused that Olivia wasn't listening to her. "All right. If you insist. I'm going to the cafeteria. Meet me there and we'll talk to Lazar."

Olivia's stomach clenched. She wasn't sure she was ready for that. But she said okay and then went inside the nurse's office.

Mackenzie took a deep breath. She was next.

"Hey, Mackenzie," piped up Tess. "Do you need me to help you with any Sweet stuff after school?"

Unlike her bestie, Tess was no gymnast. Or dancer. Tess was a writer. Not a professional one – not yet – but she thought that maybe one day she could be. For now she volunteered for *Bloom*, the school's twice-yearly arts journal. Tess had wavy brown hair, olive skin, and brown eyes and was well aware that she was ten pounds – eight pounds on a good day – overweight. She was well aware because her mother told her daily and not so subtly. "Why don't you go to SoulCycle, Tess?" "Are you sure you should be having that ice cream sandwich, Tess?" "You should try your bagel scooped, Tess." "I'd give you my old cute Kate Spade dress but I think it would be too tight on you, Tess." Tess tried to think of her mom's incessant nagging as white noise. White noise that would one day give her more to write about.

For now Tess was looking forward to Mackenzie's Sweet. The party was going to be epic. She was proud that the first Sweet of their class was her best friend's. Mackenzie's birthday was earlier than everyone else's because her parents had held her back a year, since she was a preemie.

It was going to be at the SoHo Tower, which was one of those celebrity hotel hot spots constantly mentioned on *TMZ*. Tess was psyched. She had already bought a dress at BCBG.

"The event planner has it covered," Mackenzie said to Tess with a flip of her hair. "But you can come over if you want."

"Sure," Tess replied.

Olivia came out a few seconds later.

"We're up," Cooper said, turning to Mackenzie. "Ready to show the needle who's boss?"

Mackenzie hesitated.

"Come on," Tess said. "It'll hurt for a second and then you'll be done."

Mackenzie turned to Olivia. "Did it hurt?"

Olivia flushed.

Mackenzie waited for a response but eventually realized she wasn't getting one. *Weirdo.* She turned to Cooper. "Let's just do this," she said, and the two of them disappeared into the nurse's office.

Chapter Three
OUCH

Olivia looked at her reflection in the first-floor girls' bathroom mirror. When Mackenzie had asked her whether the vaccination hurt, she opened her mouth to say it was fine; great, even! But then she realized how insane she'd sound. Sure, she liked vaccinations – they made her feel safe and protected – but was she really going to announce that? That was not a normal thing to say. So she stood there, not responding. Which did not help in the looking-normal department.

Olivia sighed.

On the plus side, it had been nice to see Nurse Carmichael. Olivia and Nurse Carmichael were old friends.

Okay, not friends-friends. But in truth, Olivia felt more comfortable in the nurse's office than she did in the cafeteria.

She was in the infirmary a lot.

Like, a lot, a lot.

At least twice a week.

Anytime Olivia had a cough, or a stomachache, or a hangnail, she went straight to Nurse Carmichael. Just to make sure it wasn't cancer. Or a heart attack. Or lymphangioleiomyomatosis. Which, sure, only affected one out of a million people, but it started with a cough, and if you *were* the one out of a million, then you were done-like-dinner within the year.

Olivia's father had had a heart attack when he was forty-two. Olivia had been ten. One minute they were a happy family shopping at Roosevelt Field mall; the next minute he was clutching his chest and lying on the grimy food-court floor. He was dead by the time they got to the hospital.

After that, Olivia avoided food courts. And malls. And Long Island. Her mom felt the same way – they sold their house in the suburbs and moved a few blocks from her mom's job at American Express in downtown NYC.

Olivia found Nurse Carmichael's office, with the clean white walls and posters reminding us about the dangers of meningitis, comforting.

When she'd walked in to get her shot, Olivia had said hi, Nurse Carmichael had asked how she was, Olivia'd said she had a small headache but was otherwise fine, Olivia'd stuck out her arm, she'd gotten the shot, and Nurse Carmichael had slapped on a Band-Aid and told her she'd see her soon.

Olivia had no doubt that was true.

Then Olivia had chosen a green lollipop.

She waited until she walked away from Mackenzie and the rest of us before unwrapping it and popping it into her mouth. She hadn't wanted to look stupid sucking on it.

But now Olivia stared at her green lips and mouth in the bathroom mirror and realized she looked ridiculous. Why had she chosen green? Why, why, why? She looked like a sea monster. Or the Hulk.

She leaned over and rinsed her mouth with water. The green color stuck.

There was no way she was going to the cafeteria to talk to you-know-who. She wasn't going to talk to anyone that day. She wasn't even going to open her mouth that day if she could help it. Or the next day.

Oh no. No, no, no.

She had to open her mouth the next day. She had her speech! At eleven! What if the green didn't come out in time? What if it never came out? She held on to the edge of the sink, feeling dizzy, wishing she were anywhere but there.

Mackenzie watched as Nurse Carmichael and her giant needle crossed the room, heading straight for her.

"Cooper, you have to go first," Mackenzie said.

He pulled up his sleeve and made himself comfortable on the nurse's chair.

Nurse Carmichael aimed the needle at him. It was about to attack him. Any second. It was coming closer.

Mackenzie tried to look away. Must look away. Couldn't look away.

She definitely should have looked away.

"ARGH!!!!!"

That was Mackenzie, not Cooper. Cooper barely felt it. It was like a mosquito bite when you knew to expect a mosquito bite. And mosquito bites didn't get to Cooper. Nothing got to Cooper.

"Easy peasy," he said as the nurse pressed a Band-Aid onto his arm.

Mackenzie saw the room swim in front of her. "I don't feel well. If I'm sick, I can't get the shot, right?"

"Not if you have a temperature," the nurse said.

Mackenzie nodded. "I am pretty sure I have a fever."

Nurse Carmichael laughed. "I'll check it just in case."

The nurse pulled out the no-mouth thermometer she always used, the kind that scanned our foreheads, and took Mackenzie's temperature.

It beeped.

"No fever," Nurse Carmichael said.

"Damn it."

"You don't have to get the shot if you don't want to," the nurse said. "It's voluntary."

Mackenzie could have walked out.

We all could have walked out. Every single one of us could have turned around and walked right out the door and never looked back.

Would have, could have. Should have?

Didn't.

"No." Mackenzie took a shaky breath. "Just give me the

stupid shot." She flailed her right arm out.

The nurse rolled up the arm of Mackenzie's black cashmere sweater.

"Ow!"

The nurse laughed. "That was just the alcohol."

Cooper squeezed her knee. "Close your eyes. Imagine something good. Like lunch tomorrow."

Mackenzie could do that. She closed her eyes. Imagined Cooper's lips. He did have great lips. Pink. Like he was wearing lipstick even though he wasn't. Plump. The top slightly plumper than the bottom.

But then another pair of lips crowded into her brain.

Bennett's lips.

There was a stab in her arm. Ouch.

She deserved it. She deserved the pain.

"You're done," the nurse said.

Mackenzie didn't want to open her eyes. Didn't want to face Cooper.

"Babe?" Cooper said. "We're done."

We would be, she thought, *if you knew what I did. But you never will.*

She opened her eyes.

"Don't forget your lollipop," Nurse Carmichael said.

Chapter Four
OCTOBER 3

Today was the day. Not that Olivia knew it was THE day. At the time, she just thought it was speech day.

Three hours and forty-five minutes to go.

In the fifth grade, back on Long Island, Olivia had been cast as an extra in the school play. She only had one line. One single line. She practiced that line in the shower. In her room. In her backyard. But on the night of the one-liner, she stood onstage while expectant faces stared up at her, and her mind went blank. Empty. Wiped clean. She couldn't breathe. Black spots swam in front of her eyes. The rest of the cast tried to usher her off the stage, but she couldn't move. She'd just stood there. Frozen. Like a sad, melting Popsicle.

Clearly, there were no Tony Awards in her future.

As if she would ever voluntarily step on a stage

again. Thanks, but no thanks.

She rehearsed her speech in the shower. "In Ridgefield, Connecticut, Jamie Fields was innocently walking barefoot across her lawn. Little did she know that she was about to get Lyme disease."

Jamie Fields was a real person. A real dead-from-Lyme-disease person.

Olivia had chosen Lyme disease as her topic because after years of living with and being a hypochondriac, she was a champ at researching diseases, and this was one disease she was unlikely to contract, since she lived in downtown Manhattan.

She practiced while she got dressed.

She practiced on her way to the kitchen, clutching her notes.

"Morning!" her mom called. "Are you okay, honey? You look pale."

Her mother always thought she looked pale.

She *was* pale. She had straight dark brown hair and pale skin. You'd think while she was growing up, her favorite fairy-tale character would have been the similarly toned Snow White, but Olivia had never been able to relate to anyone who took food from strangers.

"I'm fine," Olivia snapped, but then she felt bad. "I'm fine," she said again in a softer tone.

"Are you sure you're feeling all right?" her mom asked. "The flu vaccine sometimes gives you symptoms."

Olivia's mom was a hypochondriac too. Her mom also had a not-so-mild case of OCD and severe anxiety. She washed her hands so often her knuckles bled. Olivia had inherited the hypochondria and anxiety but was thankfully still obsessive-compulsive free. She hoped it wouldn't come with age.

Olivia contemplated telling her mom that she was sick and staying home, but then she'd get dragged to the ER. And she knew she'd have to do the speech the next day anyway. She'd have to spend another entire day with the panic spreading down her body like an unstoppable rash. "I'm fine," Olivia said, her voice shakier than she intended.

"I poured you some juice," her mom said. "And put some banana in your granola. And put a vitamin on your napkin."

"Thanks," Olivia said, even though she was afraid that anything she ate would make her vomit.

Instead, she ran through her speech. *In Ridgefield, New York...*

Oh no. Not New York. Ridgefield was in Connecticut! She had forgotten where poor Jamie lived! If she couldn't remember where Jamie had contracted the disease, how was she going to remember the rest?

The clock said 8:02.

Two hours and fifty-eight minutes to go.

It was going to be a long morning.

She brushed her teeth, made sure the green tint really was gone, grabbed her bag – and notes! She had to remember her notes! Ridgefield, Connecticut! – ran to the elevator, and slid inside. There was a senior from her school already in there. Emma Dassin. Emma didn't say hi, so Olivia didn't either.

The rickety doors were about to close when Olivia heard, "Livvie! Livvie, hold on!"

Olivia pressed the *close* button, but it was too late.

Olivia's mom stuck her hands between the doors. "You forgot your hat." She held it out.

"It's October," Olivia grumbled.

"There's a breeze! And you're not feeling well. Take it."

She took it. Less embarrassing to just get it over with.

"Have a great day! Be careful crossing Broadway!"

At last the doors closed.

Olivia stared at her gray woolen hat. She didn't want a cold. But on top of everything else, she could not worry about having staticky hair.

She stuck it in her backpack just as the doors opened onto the lobby.

Homeroom. Two and a half hours before Olivia's speech.

"What's the worst that happens?" Renée asked her.

The worst? She saw it play out in her head. She would be standing in front of the class, everyone's eyes on her. Her heart rate would skyrocket. She'd be gasping for air. She'd see spots. She'd pass out and probably die.

Yes, die.

Olivia just shook her head.

"Why don't you imagine everyone in the class naked," Renée said. "Especially Lazar."

Olivia did not want to think about Lazar naked. She did not want to think about Lazar at all. Knowing there was a guy in her class who was potentially interested in her made everything worse. She picked her thumb.

BJ twisted back in his seat. "Did you say 'naked'?"

"Olivia has to present in public speaking," Renée said. "I think she should imagine everyone in the class naked."

"I *always* imagine everyone naked. I'm doing it right now." He looked from Olivia to Renée. "You both look pretty good."

"Oh, shut up," Renée said, but Olivia couldn't help noticing that she stuck out her chest.

Cooper sang his way in. "What's happening, 10B?"

"We're imagining each other naked," Renée said.

"Excellent," Cooper said, striking a He-Man pose.

Olivia smiled. Then she wished he were in her public speaking class. Not so she could picture him naked – just so he could make her laugh.

"All you have to do is focus on me," Renée said, since she was in Olivia's public speaking class. "Ignore everyone else."

Olivia was pretty sure that wouldn't help. Renée was an amazing speaker. She didn't even need notes. She just talked. And talked and talked and talked.

Ms Velasquez strolled in. "Who's here today? Adam? You're back. Good."

"I missed my vaccination yesterday – should I get it today?" he asked.

"Yes. At lunch."

Olivia looked at her watch. It read eight-forty-five. Two hours and fifteen minutes until her speech.

It was time. *Ridgefield, Connecticut. Tick bites. Bull's-eye rash.*

"Olivia Byrne, you're up," Mr Roth said. It didn't help that he was the scariest teacher in school both in attitude and physical appearance. He weighed about four hundred pounds, was over six feet tall, and had a permanent scowl on his face. He looked like a troll, if trolls were also giants.

Focus. Speech. Lyme disease.

She stood up. Her legs felt gummy. Her heart beat a gazillion miles an hour. She was 99 percent sure everyone could hear it.

Olivia remembered that irregular heartbeat was a symptom of Lyme disease. She definitely had an irregular heartbeat. Maybe she had Lyme disease after all. Maybe she'd willed it on herself. Was that possible? Was she contagious? Maybe she needed to be quarantined immediately.

The class was extra chatty. There were voices everywhere. She felt nauseated – like she was on a boat. The floor was swaying. Also, she was hot. And sweating. Her underarms were wet. Had she put on deodorant that morning? She thought she had. Yes.

She reached the front of the room. She turned around. She tried very hard not to look at Lazar, who was sitting two rows back and staring at her. He was definitely red-cheeked and cute.

Everyone in class continued to talk.

"It's so hot in here."

"Forgot my Spanish homework."

"Should have had a third cup of coffee."

"Why didn't I pee before class?"

Olivia didn't think she could do this. But she had to. Unless she refused. And failed the assignment and possibly the class.

She took a deep breath and waited for everyone to stop talking. She looked at Mr Roth, who nodded at her to go ahead.

She looked back at the class.

"This is going to be excruciatingly boring," someone said.

Olivia cleared her throat.

"Why is she just standing there?" Olivia heard.

They were still talking. Olivia closed her mouth, deciding to wait for everyone to shut up.

Renée looked right at her. "Come on, Olivia, you can do it," she said.

Except Renée's mouth wasn't moving. Her mouth was closed. Huh? Olivia was confused.

Oh no, she's looking at me strangely. Is she going to pass out?

Renée was talking, but her mouth wasn't moving. How was she doing that? She looked like a ventriloquist.

Lazar was looking at her too.

She doesn't look good, he said.

Why did he ask if she was single if he didn't think she looked good? And why wasn't his mouth moving either?

Was she hallucinating? Did anyone else notice what was happening?

Olivia looked around the room. Everyone was talking, but no one was moving his or her lips.

What's wrong with her?

She looks like she's going to barf.

Oh. My. God. They were not saying these things, Olivia realized. They were thinking them. She was hearing what people were thinking. And they were all thinking about her. The shock was so strong, she could barely breathe.

Voices were coming at her fast and furiously:

She's turning blue.

I really have to pee.

Why doesn't she start already?

The room began to spin. Olivia needed air.

She's going to faint!

What is happening? Olivia wondered. She saw Pi looking right at her.

I have no idea, Pi said.

Had Pi just responded to her thought? That made no sense. The room spun, like she was on the Tilt-A-Whirl. Olivia trained her eyes on Pi, a trick her dad had taught her when he took her to Disney World when she was a kid. Pick a point in the distance and stare and you won't get sick. But suddenly there were two Pis.

"Olivia!" Renée yelled.

That was the last voice Olivia heard before everything went black.

Chapter Five
I KNOW WHAT YOU'RE THINKING

We don't know why it happened to so many of us during third period. Not all of us. But a lot of us.

Eleven a.m. must have been the witching hour.

Mackenzie was sitting in calculus when it happened to her. She was thinking about Bennett. She didn't want to be thinking about Bennett. She tried to stop herself from thinking about Bennett. Did she even like Bennett? She wasn't sure.

He was a year older than she was. A junior. He went to Westside Academy. Private school. And he lived in her building.

They had spoken for the first time over a year ago, the summer before her freshman year, when she was single.

They'd met on the terrace on the eighth floor. It was August. She'd been tanning.

She tanned a lot. There were three lounge chairs on the

deck, and Mackenzie always took the one on the right.

He'd taken the chair next to her. Mackenzie hadn't noticed at first. She'd been listening to music on her iPhone, but then she opened her eyes to take a sip of Diet Coke – she drank a lot of Diet Coke – and there he was, the hot guy from the elevator.

He was tall, dark-haired, and shirtless. He was wearing aviator sunglasses and using a navy T-shirt as a pillow.

"Hey," he said.

"Hey," she said back. She wished she were wearing her black Michael Kors bikini instead of her green Milly one. And just like that, she was in love. Or at least in lust.

In October, he texted her at eleven to meet him on the deck, even though you weren't allowed on the deck past ten. He had a joint with him, and she smoked for the first time. Everything went fuzzy and they hooked up on the lounge chair. The lights were off by then, so no one could see.

They hooked up on and off: on the terrace, in her room when her parents and her sister were out, in his room when his parents were. They didn't have sex, but they did everything else. They met up at least twice a week until February, Valentine's Day, when Mackenzie had to know: What was going on between them? Were they just hooking up? Were they a couple? They hung out together in the neighborhood, but he never introduced her to his friends, who mostly lived on the Upper West Side. On the weekends, he went to his parties and she went to hers. Mackenzie's friends knew about him and his friends knew about her, but they weren't official.

Mackenzie liked things that were official.

When she was a kid she'd only been part of "official" fan clubs.

She never bought purses on Canal Street. If she couldn't afford the real thing, then she'd wait until she could. She didn't like fakes. She liked labels. And she wanted the label of girlfriend.

"I'm not looking for a girlfriend," Bennett told her. They were in his room, on his bed. She was putting her shirt back on and trying to look like she didn't care. He didn't want to be her boyfriend? Whatever.

Outside she could see the eighth-floor terrace. She realized he had probably watched her suntan the entire summer before he made his way out to meet her.

She had been lying there. Easy prey. Or just easy.

She moped for a week. She wouldn't tell her parents what was wrong. Cailin never even asked; she was too busy with her senior year. Mackenzie wasn't sure if she didn't notice or didn't care.

Mackenzie stopped texting him. She waited for him to text her, but he didn't. Since his school was uptown, he left an hour before she did, so she hardly ever ran into him in the elevator.

She avoided the deck.

A few weeks later, Cooper and Mackenzie kissed for the first time at Jordana's birthday party. She hadn't seen it coming – they'd known each other since they were in diapers. They grew up in the 'hood together. Cooper's parents, Mackenzie's parents and Jordana's parents used to triple-date, until Jordana's parents divorced and her dad moved to L.A.

Anyway, Jordana's party was the very first night Cooper and Mackenzie flirted. A lot.

The lights were low and they kissed in Jordana's mom's home office.

By the next morning they were a couple. Held hands. Talked every night. Hung out with each other's families. Mackenzie even invited Cooper's family to her Passover Seder. They were inseparable.

Until Cooper went to summer camp.

Mackenzie didn't mean for it to happen. Or so she convinced herself.

We aren't sure we believe her. Here are the facts: She went to the terrace. She sat in her chair. She wore her black Michael Kors bikini.

One hot August day Bennett came out and sat beside her. "Hi," he said.

"Hi," she said back.

That night he texted her to come upstairs and hang. She knew she shouldn't. She told herself, *Do not go, you know what's going to happen, you cannot cheat on Cooper*. But still she put on her cutest jeans, a lacy bra, a thong, and a tight black top Bennett had once said looked good on her. Then she went. Her heart thumped all the way up to his floor in the elevator.

They were in his bed thirty seconds after she knocked on the door.

Again, they didn't sleep together. Just everything else. In her mind, that made it less bad.

"What now?" she asked Bennett.

"What do you mean?" he asked, and she knew that nothing was different. Nothing had changed at all.

She wasn't sure what to tell Cooper. She wasn't sure why she'd done it. She loved Cooper, didn't she? True, she had felt some relief when she realized that hooking up with Bennett probably meant they were done. What she and Cooper had was too good, too easy. It was bound to end eventually.

But when Cooper showed up at her door a week later and smelled like home and hugged her so tight she thought she would burst – in a good way – she decided that she would only tell him one thing.

"I missed you" was all she said.

She felt guilty. Every day the guilt ate up a little more inside her, like a tapeworm.

That was why she'd gotten the flu shot. As punishment. She deserved it.

This was what Mackenzie was thinking about at eleven a.m. on Wednesday morning in Mr Gilbert's calculus class. Thinking very loudly, as it turned out.

She was not paying attention to Gilbert in the slightest. She was chewing on a pen cap and remembering. She turned to the window and realized that Tess was staring at her, eyes wide open in shock.

"What?" Mackenzie whispered.

"Did that really happen?" Tess whispered back.

Mackenzie had no idea what Tess was talking about. "Did what really happen?"

Tess leaned in closer. "You cheated on Cooper?"

Mackenzie's heart raced. "I did not." Had Bennett said something? He wouldn't. He wasn't the kind of guy to kiss and tell. Anyway, they didn't have any friends in common. And she hadn't breathed a word to *anyone*.

"You were just talking about it," Tess whispered. "Two seconds ago."

"I was not!" Mackenzie couldn't believe it. What was Tess trying to pull?

Tess shook her head. "I'm not trying to pull anything!"

"Girls," Gilbert said, turning from the whiteboard. "You're both excused."

Crap. Mackenzie was already in trouble with Gilbert for always handing in her homework late. She was in trouble with all her teachers, actually. "But—"

"Goodbye," he said. "Next time don't disrupt the class."

Mackenzie sighed. She and Tess collected their books and headed to the door.

At least, Mackenzie figured, she'd be able to find out how Tess knew about her and Bennett. Maybe Tess was just guessing. Although Mackenzie had been thinking about it. Had she been talking out loud? Mumbling to herself? No one else had heard her. Maybe she'd been mouthing the words and Tess had read her lips. Did Tess know how to do that? Mackenzie doubted it. Tess didn't have any secret skills.

The two girls stepped outside.

Tess's eyes were bugging out of her head. She definitely knew something.

This was not good. Not good at all. Mackenzie hadn't told a single person what had happened with Bennett over the summer.

No one was supposed to know.

Even Tess. She loved Tess, but she couldn't tell her something like that. Tess looked up to her. Mackenzie liked that Tess looked up to her. And Tess would think she should tell Cooper the truth.

Mackenzie couldn't tell Cooper. He'd break up with her. And then what? She'd lose him. He'd hate her.

We can't help wondering if she wanted to lose him all along.

Still, tears burned the backs of her eyelids. Her heart raced. Her head hurt. Her mouth was really dry. She needed a Diet Coke. Or one of Bennett's joints. No, no, nothing about Bennett. That was what had gotten her into this mess in the first place.

How had Tess found out?

I can't believe she hooked up with Bennett again. He's such a user.

"Excuse me?" Mackenzie asked, hands on her hips.

Tess took a step back. "I didn't say anything."

"Yes you did. You said Bennett was a user," Mackenzie said.

Not out loud! Tess thought.

What the hell is going on? they both thought.

At that second, just down the hallway, the door to Mr Roth's public speaking class was thrown open.

"Get Nurse Carmichael!" Lazar yelled as the entire class cleared out of the room.

Voices came from everywhere.

"Give her space!"

That must have hurt.

"She needs to breathe!"

She looks kind of dead.

Mackenzie grabbed on to Tess's hand. "I don't understand what's happening."

"Me neither," Tess said. "And it's so loud." They pressed their backs against the row of lockers to try to stay out of the way – of the people, of the voices. So many voices.

I'm hungry. Is it lunch yet?

I think I'm wearing different-colored socks.

Pi came out of the class last. Her eyes were shining as she walked by Mackenzie and Tess. She was muttering silently to herself. *I could hear her. I could hear what she was thinking. She could hear what I was thinking! How did that happen? Is she the only one?*

Mackenzie crossed her arms in front of her chest. *No,* Mackenzie thought. *She's not the only one.*

Pi stopped in her tracks and stared at Mackenzie. *You too?*

Me too.

And me, Tess piped up.

Pi started to laugh. *How is it that we can hear people's thoughts?*

We have no idea, Mackenzie and Tess thought at the same time.

Jinx, Mackenzie thought. *Now someone better buy me a Diet Coke.*

Chapter Six
IT'S A PUZZLE OUT THERE

Pi was the first one of us to get it. She got it before school, at seven a.m. We aren't sure why. She thinks it was because she's the smartest. We think it's because she was swimming at the time. Working out. More blood flow to her brain.

She was swimming in the downtown community pool on Warren, a few blocks from school. She swam every morning. It cleared her head. She'd read an article in *New York* magazine saying that daily exercise increased one's IQ by about ten points. She would not let ten points get away from her. She did all kinds of things that were supposed to increase IQ – ate fish with omega-3, practiced writing with her left hand, listened to classical music, taught herself chess and poker. Did sudoku. She did sudoku a lot. Sometimes she imagined boxes of numbers on white walls.

Pi had the second-highest GPA in our grade, just behind Jon Matthews. But Pi wanted to be number one. Harvard would never take two kids from one public school. And she wanted to go to Harvard. She wanted to study physics and be a physics professor. She wanted to understand the universe.

Her father was a doctor. Well, he was a researcher at Mount Sinai. He'd lost his license after a malpractice suit. It hadn't been his fault at all, but that was what happened in New York. Greed and bureaucracy got in the way of brilliance. Her mom had left him and taken a job at a hospital in Indiana when the whole thing went down. Pi had refused to move with her, deciding to stand by her dad. They didn't need her mom. She didn't need her mom. Pi would be fine – no, exceptional – without her.

On Wednesday morning, Pi was swimming laps when she kept hearing Black-Speedo Guy talking to himself about the memo he was supposed to send to his boss by noon. *Times or Arial? What says "promote me"?* She saw him there often; he always wore the same Speedo.

At first Pi stopped mid-stroke. "Excuse me!"

The guy ignored her and kept swimming.

But he also kept talking. *I need a raise. At least a hundred bucks a week. Then I could eat out more often and get cool stuff for my apartment. Like a high-def TV. Better speakers. A custom-made bobble head that looks like me and is wearing a Speedo.*

Everyone had the right to voice his ideas, Pi thought, but not when they intruded on someone else's personal space. And this was Pi's personal space. This was her morning swim.

When she reached the end of the pool, she stopped to tread water. She lifted her goggles. "Excuse me! Can you please stop?"

He didn't stop.

"Sir!" she said again, this time louder.

He stopped and turned to her. "Yes?"

"Can you please stop talking? It's making it difficult for me to concentrate."

"I'm not talking. I'm swimming."

"No, you're talking," she argued.

"No," he snapped. "*You're* talking to me." He shook his head and said, *Crazy chick. Her swimming cap is on too tight.* Then he dove under the water.

Pi held on to the edge of the pool and tried to figure out what had happened. He had said something, but his lips hadn't moved.

And on it went all morning. On the walk over to school. Getting her coffee – one cup of coffee was also rumored to increase IQ. Homeroom. She was starting to worry that she was working too hard when Olivia had her meltdown in class. It was then she realized what was happening. Olivia could hear thoughts too. Then, in the hallway, she discovered that the same thing was happening to Tess and Mackenzie.

As soon as she made that discovery, Pi moved Mackenzie and Tess down the hall so they could talk without anyone overhearing. Or without them overhearing anyone else. The farther they stood from the others, the quieter the voices in her head became.

Mackenzie hugged her arms to her chest. *What number am I thinking? Seven.*

"Seven," Pi said.

Tess's jaw dropped. "This is crazy. I heard it too. My turn." Tess closed her mouth. *Eight. No, ten. No, thirty-three and a half!*

"Eight, no, ten, no, thirty-three and a half," Mackenzie said.

"This is the coolest thing ever," Tess said, eyes dancing.

Pi glanced at the others in the hallway. "As far as I can tell, it's just happening to the four of us," she said. "You two, me, and Olivia."

"Where is Olivia?" Mackenzie asked.

"She fainted," Pi said matter-of-factly.

"From this?" Tess asked.

"Sort of," Pi said. "Not because of this, but because it freaked her out. She was doing her speech and then it kicked in and she passed out."

"Is she okay?" Tess asked.

"Probably," Pi said. She didn't want to talk about Olivia. She wanted to talk about what was happening to them.

"But what *is* happening to us?" Mackenzie asked, throwing her hands up.

"We can hear each other's thoughts," Pi said.

"Not just each other's," Tess said, looking at the crowd in the hallway. "I can hear everyone's thoughts."

"But why is this only happening to the four of us?" Mackenzie asked, her forehead wrinkling. "It's not happening to anyone else."

Pi was deep in thought. "We're all in the same homeroom." But what else did they have in common? Nothing, as far as she could tell. The other two definitely weren't as smart as she was.

"Hey," Mackenzie said. "Just because my GPA is low doesn't make me stupid." *I just don't try.*

"Whatever," Pi said with a shrug. "It's irrelevant. What do the four of us have in common?"

Mackenzie and Tess stared at her blankly.

Suddenly all the numbers aligned. Aha! "We all got our flu shots yesterday," Pi said.

"But everyone got their flu shots," Tess said. "Most of the school got their flu shots."

"That's true," Pi said. "I need to think about this."

Mackenzie rubbed the spot on her arm where she'd gotten the vaccination. "I didn't even want the shot!"

Pi rolled her eyes. "None of us *wanted* the shot."

"No, but I really, really didn't want to get it. I just did it because..." *I wanted to punish myself.*

Pi didn't understand what Mackenzie meant about the punishment thing. They had telepathy. This was amazing. They were exceptional.

"I wonder how long it will last," Tess said.

Not long, Mackenzie hoped.

They watched Nurse Carmichael enter the classroom. "Maybe we should talk to the nurse about it," Tess said.

Pi considered the options. Should they seek medical advice? What if the condition was dangerous? On the other hand, once they went public they couldn't take it back. Once they went public she would surely lose control of the situation. "If it really is telepathy, maybe we don't want everyone aware that we can read their minds," she said.

"People would freak out," Tess said.

"They'd cart us off to some mental institution," Mackenzie said, turning white. "Hook us up to all kinds of tubes." *So. Many. Needles. I don't deserve that. Do I?* "Maybe we shouldn't say anything. It might go away."

Tess nodded. *If I only have one day with this ability, I want to put it to good use.*

Pi was still weighing the options. There was no real rush to tell. She could always change her mind in the morning – if it was still happening. She might as well try to explore it on her own that day. It was like poker – no reason to show the rest of the world that she had a flush. "I think for now we should keep this just between us."

"I agree," Tess said.

Mackenzie nodded.

"I'll talk to Olivia," Pi said.

I'm going to find out everyone's secret thoughts! Tess thought.

Pi caught Mackenzie scowling. *I don't want Tess knowing my secret thoughts. I don't want anyone knowing my secret thoughts.*

"Why?" Pi asked. "What are your secret thoughts?"

"Nothing," Mackenzie blurted out. *Don't think about it, don't think about it.*

Tess shook her head. *She doesn't want the whole school knowing she cheated on Cooper.*

Aha.

"Tess!" Mackenzie yelled.

Tess clamped her hand over her mouth. "I'm sorry! I didn't mean to think it!"

As if Pi cared enough to keep up with her classmates' on-and-off-again relationships.

Mackenzie bit her lip. *Maybe I should talk to Carmichael. Maybe I want this mind reading thing to end as soon as possible. Before it ruins my life.*

"It won't ruin your life," Tess said quickly. "We won't tell anyone about the Cooper stuff. Swear."

"Swear?" Mackenzie asked.

Tess nodded.

Mackenzie turned to Pi.

"Whatever," she said. "I barely even heard anything. Don't worry about it." *Like I honestly care about her stupid relationship.*

"Hey!" Mackenzie said.

Pi rolled her eyes. "Sorry."

Tess linked her arm through Mackenzie's. "Let's go to the cafeteria. See what everyone's up to." *I want to find Teddy. ASAP.*

Pi had no idea who Teddy was and didn't care about that either.

"How do you not know who Teddy is?" Tess asked. "Teddy Russell? He's in our grade. He's my guy best friend."

Pi leaned against a locker. "I don't know. I just don't. You guys go. I'll wait for Olivia. What we should do is figure out if there are other people this is happening to. If so, round them up. Have a meeting."

Mackenzie nodded. "Where?"

"Club room 309. I have a key," Pi said. "I'm on the chess team."

Were we surprised by that? Not even a little.

Chapter Seven
THAT'S WHAT YOU THINK

When Olivia opened her eyes, she saw a white ceiling. She was lying on a floor. She closed her eyes again.

"Olivia?" she heard. "Can you hear me?"

"Yes," Olivia said. She opened her eyes and saw Nurse Carmichael – and then remembered what happened.

Oh. My. God.

She quickly closed her eyes again. She'd had a total breakdown. She'd hallucinated that she could hear people's thoughts! Who did that? The stress of speaking in public must have really gotten to her. She kept her eyes shut tight. "Is everyone watching me?" she asked.

"We cleared the class out. It's just you and me."

This was worse than she'd thought. "Did I faint?"

"Yes."

"How long was I out?"

"About a minute and a half. Your friend Renée caught you, so you didn't hurt anything."

"Sorry to bother you," Olivia said. "Again."

"It's no problem," Nurse Carmichael said, and Olivia finally opened her eyes.

Of all the kids who could have fainted, why does it have to be the one with the crazy mom?

Wait. What? Nurse Carmichael wasn't talking. Her lips weren't even moving.

Olivia decided she was still hallucinating. She tried to sit up, but Nurse Carmichael put a hand on her shoulder.

"Don't get up yet," Nurse Carmichael said. And then she thought, *If she passes out again, I'm going to call an ambulance.*

Olivia did not want an ambulance to come get her at school. Talk about embarrassing. "I'm fine," she said quickly. "Please don't call an ambulance."

Nurse Carmichael blinked. *Did I say that out loud?*

No, Olivia realized. But she didn't want to admit that. Because if she actually had heard it in her mind, Nurse Carmichael would definitely call an ambulance. And a shrink.

"Has this ever happened before?" Nurse Carmichael asked.

Had she ever heard voices in her head? No, she must have meant the fainting. "When I was younger," Olivia said.

"Let's go into my office," Nurse Carmichael said. *Maybe I should call an ambulance. If I don't and she faints again, that crazy Jennifer Byrne will sue. I'll lose my job! I'll have to go back to stripping!*

Agh! That was way more info than Olivia wanted to know about Nurse Carmichael.

Olivia rubbed her throbbing temples. No way had Nurse Carmichael been a stripper. Olivia was hearing voices in her head. Hallucinations. They would go away soon. Wouldn't they? Yes. They would. Of course they would.

"Would you like me to call your mom?" Nurse Carmichael asked. *I'd rather lick a cactus needle. No, I'd rather stick a cactus needle in my eye.*

"Why don't I just rest for an hour?" Olivia asked. "There's no reason to bother my mom yet. You know how panicked she gets. It's almost lunch. I'll rest in your office until then and we'll see how I'm doing, okay?"

"Oh. Okay." Nurse Carmichael stood up. "Let's go."

Olivia sat up. The room swayed, but she placed her hands firmly on the floor to steady herself. She probably had a concussion. *Oh my god, can I die from this? I probably can.*

Nurse Carmichael reached out to help her. "Let's go." *I hope Roth isn't still out there. He terrifies me.*

Not only was she dizzy and concussed, she was still hallucinating. It could be a stroke. Death could come at any second, if she didn't get help.

"Something weird is happening," she began as Nurse Carmichael opened the door.

"What?"

Olivia took a deep breath. She had to tell the nurse. What if she was having an aneurysm? "I hear something…strange."

Outside the door, the hallway was empty. Mostly. Pi was

leaning over and tying her shoes.

Pi looked up. "How are you feeling?"

"Um…fine," Olivia said. *Besides the fact that I'm probably dying.*

"Good," Pi said. *You're not dying. Don't tell Nurse Carmichael anything. Come with me and I'll explain.*

I imagined that, Olivia tried to convince herself. *I need to go to the hospital. It is my concussion talking. I'm going to need a CAT scan.*

Pi shook her head. *You're not imagining it. I can hear you. You can hear me. Tell Nurse Carmichael you're feeling fine and come with me to the chess room.*

Olivia didn't understand what was happening. "But—"

"Everything okay, Olivia?" Nurse Carmichael asked. "Let's go."

Tell her everything's fine and that you're coming with me instead.

Olivia didn't know who to trust. Was she going crazy? Were she and Pi going crazy?

Just tell her!

Okay! But if I die of an aneurysm, it will be your fault! "You know what, Nurse Carmichael? I'm feeling better. In fact, I think I want to get some lunch. Pi will look after me. If I have any issues, I'll go straight to your office." *If I'm not already dead.*

Nurse Carmichael looked worried. "You sure?" *I shouldn't let her go. But I really do need to run to the pharmacy to get more condoms for tonight.*

54

Pi and Olivia exchanged disgusted looks.

No, Olivia wasn't sure, but she nodded anyway. She needed to get away from Nurse Carmichael before she could never look the woman in the eye again.

I wonder if I have time to pick up a sexy French maid's outfit.

Olivia grimaced. Too late.

Chapter Eight
THE JUNGLE

Tess and Mackenzie had two minutes before the lunch bell. Mackenzie checked her phone and saw a text from Cooper:

Still on for my place?

No way. She could not go to Cooper's right then. She had to meet with Pi and Tess. And what if Cooper could hear her thoughts too? No, if he could, he wouldn't have sent that text. His text would have said something along the lines of *Holy shit, something weird is happening to me*.

True, he was in their homeroom. He'd gotten the same flu shot. But so far it was only happening to Pi, Tess, Olivia, and her. Maybe it was a girl thing?

Either way, they'd have to postpone their alone time until

this whole mind reading thing was cleared up.

Mackenzie texted back:

```
Can't today. Sorry.
```

"Let's do this," Tess said, eyes twinkling.

They stepped into the cafeteria. A cacophony of voices rushed at Mackenzie.

—five french fries today. Five. No more. My thighs are too—

—There's an empty seat at Jake's table! Should I take it? But Amanda said—

—Did I just get my period?—

As each thought hit Mackenzie's mind, so did a stabbing pain in her forehead.

She could hear people's thoughts. Could they hear hers?

Hello! she screamed in her head. *Can anyone hear me?*

"Yeah, me," Tess said, rubbing her forehead. "Don't shout."

"I meant besides you," Mackenzie said.

"Pi and Olivia," said Tess. "Duh."

Cooper waved to her from their regular table at the opposite end of the room. He was sitting across from Joel, one of his good friends. Joel was also one of Mackenzie's least favorite people. He'd nicknamed her Dumbie for most of second grade.

Where's Teddy? Mackenzie heard Tess wondering. *I need to find Teddy! This is my chance to find out how he really feels about me!*

Mackenzie looked at Cooper. What if he could read her mind? He'd know she cheated on him with Bennett. He'd hate her forever. There'd be nothing she could do.

I won't say anything, Tess thought back. *I swear.*

I know you won't. But what about Pi? What about Olivia? What about anyone else this is happening to?

They both looked over at Cooper. He was dipping french fries in ketchup. He didn't seem to be stressing about anything. He looked totally normal.

"He doesn't look like he has it," Tess said.

"Do I look like I have it?" Mackenzie asked. "How do you look when you have it?"

"You look freaked out," Tess told her.

We all did have a bit of a freaked-out look to us when we first got it. Which was understandable, since it was freaky.

Cooper, on the other hand, did not look freaked out at all. He looked completely at ease as he smiled at beady-eyed Joel.

"I don't think he has it," Tess said. "But look at BJ."

BJ was sitting one table behind Cooper and did in fact look freaked out. Instead of eating the pizza in front of him, he'd placed his palms flat on the table and was frantically looking back and forth at the people around him.

Tess giggled. "Should I put him out of his misery? Or let him wallow in it for a while? He's such a perv. I do not want to know what he's thinking at all."

"How are you going to put him out of his misery? By telling him that he probably has telepathy?"

"By telling him that he's not the only one."

"I guess," Mackenzie said. "And let him know we're meeting in the chess club room in ten minutes. But, Tess – can you check on Cooper? Make sure he's okay?" She wished she could hear what he was thinking from this end of the cafeteria. But it didn't seem to work like that. You had to be kind of close to people to hear them. Although if she could hear what he was thinking from here, then he'd be able to hear what she was thinking from *there*. If he could hear what people were thinking at all.

"You're worrying for nothing," Tess said. "Look at him, he's fine!"

Cooper waved to her again.

Mackenzie's heart sped up. "Please just check."

"Fine, give me a sec." Tess hurried over and sat down in the empty spot beside him. Mackenzie pretended to be interested in the lunch choice of tacos or grilled cheese, as she tried to digest what was happening.

A voice in her head sounded just like when the person talked out loud – but a bit muffled. Like there was a pillow over the person's mouth.

—*heard Olivia passed out* – thought Adam from homeroom as he walked by with a can of Diet Sprite.

—*the tacos might look like cat barf, but they taste really good* – thought a freshman who passed by her next.

She could only hear people in her immediate vicinity. As soon as Adam walked away and the freshman walked by, the freshman's thoughts kicked in.

The theme song from *Dora the Explorer* hit her next.

Unfortunately it was catchy. She couldn't help but sing along.

And then she heard someone's, *If I cover my nose with my hand, will anyone notice me pick it?*

Ew, really?

Mackenzie realized Tess was waving her over. Tess was too far for Mackenzie to hear what she was thinking, so she held her breath as she walked to the table. She gave Tess a look.

He doesn't have it! Tess thought at her before jumping over to BJ.

Mackenzie exhaled.

"Hey, babe," Cooper said. "What happened to our plans?"

"I'm sorry," Mackenzie said, sitting down beside him. "I forgot I have stuff to do. I'm just going to get some food to take with me." She hated that she was lying to him again. Hadn't she told him enough lies? But she had to talk to the rest of the crew and figure out what to do. Figure out what this was.

He looked right into her eyes. *I'm so bummed she canceled on me again. I miss her.*

Crap. She leaned over and kissed him gently on the mouth. He tasted like ketchup.

"Get a room, you guys," Joel hollered. He was chewing on an oatmeal cookie. *This sucks. I'm glad I swiped it instead of coughing up the fifty cents.*

"I was hoping to," Cooper answered him, "but I'll take what I can get." He kissed Mackenzie again but then pulled back. *Maybe I can change her mind.* "We still have time..."

"I can't," Mackenzie said. "I'll see you later." She stood up abruptly.

What a cold bitch. It was coming from Joel.

"At least I don't steal from the lunch lady," she barked.

He flushed. *She saw me?*

Mackenzie knew she probably shouldn't have said that. But c'mon. He'd called her a bitch.

What can we say? It wasn't the first time someone thought Mackenzie was a bitch, and it definitely wouldn't be the last.

Chapter Nine
US AGAINST THEM

Our first meeting took place in club room 309, the chess room.

It was small, and it had no windows since it was an interior room. It had brown carpet and smelled worse than the Chambers Street subway station in August.

Some of us sat on desks, some of us on chairs.

It was not the most organized meeting. Understandable, since on Day One we were kind of a mess. Half of us were talking out loud, the other half were thinking, and we all had headaches.

We'd rounded up eleven of us. We weren't sure if there were only eleven of us, or if we could only find eleven of us. But one thing was definite: all eleven of us were from homeroom 10B.

Who were we? We were Pi, Mackenzie, Tess, BJ, Jordana,

Olivia, Nick, Isaac Philips, Levi Jenkins, Brinn Ferrero and George Marson, who went by Mars.

The original eleven.

Pi and Olivia had walked by Nurse Carmichael's office and found Mars and Levi waiting for the nurse to get back from her condom run. Tess had found Nick, Isaac, and BJ disoriented in the cafeteria, and Olivia had found Brinn mumbling to herself in the bathroom.

I can't believe this is happening, thought Olivia now.

"It's happening," Nick said. *And my mom better not find out about it. She'll make me quit the baseball team. She'll think this is from the stress.* Nick was the only sophomore at BHS on the varsity baseball team. He glanced at the door as though his mom were about to sense something was up and run right from her biology class to the chess room.

Tess bit her lip. *Holy crap, this is ESP.*

"It's only one type of ESP," Pi said. "ESP is an umbrella term that includes all the extrasensory perceptions. We don't have clairvoyance or precognition. At least, I don't. Does anyone else?"

"I don't even know what those mean," Jordana said.

"Telepathy is when you can hear other people's thoughts. Clairvoyance is when you are aware of something happening in another location. Precognition is when you can tell the future. And then there's telekinesis, which is when you can move objects with your mind."

"No, I'm just having the first one," Tess said.

"Me too," Isaac Philips said, nodding his shock of gray hair.

Yes, gray hair. He looked like his head had been colored in by a lead pencil. He was also the only publicly gay guy in our grade.

Of course, within the next few days, we'd know about anyone who was still in the closet. There were no secrets from us.

"But why are we the only ones to have any of it?" Tess asked. "What's so special about us?" *Not that I'm complaining. This is going to make a great book one day. Not that anyone would believe it. I'll have to call it fiction.*

"It must have something to do with the flu shots," Pi said, pacing the room.

"We're not the only homeroom to have gotten the shot," Isaac replied.

Vaccines come in batches, Olivia thought.

Huh? Batches? Jordana wondered while filing her nails.

Olivia turned bright red. *Everyone heard me?*

"Get used to it," Mackenzie muttered. She was sitting in the corner, giving us all death glares.

What's her problem? Levi wondered.

"Me? You're the one who's always in a bad mood," Mackenzie snapped. *Although I'd be in a bad mood too if I had those teeth.*

Some of us gasped.

Mackenzie flinched.

Mackenzie wasn't wrong. He did have terrible teeth. Probably because his parents owned a candy store on Reade Street. He'd worked there since he was a kid. He ate a lot of candy.

"Sorry," Mackenzie added. *This whole thing is pissing me off. We should be pissed. Our brains were just contaminated by vaccines!* Brinn thought, not looking up from the notepad she was drawing in.

We all stared at Brinn. We'd never heard her talk coherently before. She was always in her own world, mumbling to herself and drawing in her notebook – usually while wearing fencing gear. She was on the fencing team but didn't seem to realize that the uniform wasn't supposed to be worn twenty-four seven. Brinn was our nerd. Sorry, Brinn, but it's true. She mumbled when she talked, her lips were so chapped they bled, and her hair looked like a bird's nest. Not that she seemed to care.

Mackenzie's not pissed because her brain's been contaminated, Jordana thought. *She's pissed because our brains have been. She doesn't want us all knowing her business.*

I don't want you all knowing my business either, Nick thought.

Pi slammed her fist against the table. "Can we try and focus, people?"

"What are we focusing on?" Levi asked. "I'm not exactly sure what we're doing."

I'm not sure why we're not in the emergency room, Olivia thought.

"I agree," Mars said. "We're hearing voices, people. That's messed up. Our brains might be melting." Mars was a piano prodigy. The day before the flu shot, he'd broken up with his girlfriend, Jill Clarke, because he didn't think they were a good fit. Jill had said she agreed. Mars was pretty hot. Dark hair, dark skin. Apparently he used to serenade her. He could sing, too, although unlike Cooper, he didn't force us all to listen to him.

"I'm not sure our best plan is to turn ourselves in immediately," Pi said. "We have to weigh the options. And I think what Olivia said about the batches was right. It was probably just our batch." *I would have realized that myself eventually.*

What a know-it-all, Mars thought.

And why is she acting like she's the boss? Levi wondered.

Pi spun around to face him. "Do you two want to run this meeting? Go ahead."

Mars cringed.

Levi rolled his eyes and sank back into his chair. Then he reached into his pocket and took out a multicolored bag of candy Runts.

"Can I have some?" Tess asked.

He passed the bag around the room.

"Let's review," Pi said. "All we know right now is that the eleven of us have developed some sort of telepathic capabilities."

We nodded.

"Let's discuss that capability for a minute, please." Pi tapped her pen against a desk. "What do we know about it?"

"The voices are like real voices," Nick said. "You hear them all, but it's hard to focus on more than one at a time."

"The closer you are to the person, the louder their voice," Mackenzie said. *I could hear Cooper really loudly.*

"You could? When? When you were getting it on?" BJ asked, arching his thick eyebrows.

Mackenzie rolled her eyes. "No. We were talking. But good theory."

"People are also louder when there's less in the way," Nick said. "Like right now, since Tess is sitting between me and Olivia, I can hear Tess's thoughts, but it's hard for me to hear Olivia's."

Good, thought Olivia.

Tess slumped in her seat. "Better?"

"Think something, Olivia!"

Olivia flushed. *My head hurts.*

Nick gave her a thumbs-up.

"We can't hear anyone outside this room," Pi said. "Maybe walls also act as interference."

BJ stretched his arms above his head. "Anyone want to test my 'thoughts are loudest when you're hooking up' theory with me?"

"No," the girls in the room said.

"Isaac?" BJ asked.

"You're not my type," Isaac responded. *He's so my type.*

Ha! BJ waggled his eyebrows. *I knew it! I'm everyone's type.*

You're not my type, Tess thought.

Olivia rubbed her temples. Her head was really killing her. She needed to go to the nurse's office to get some Tylenol. She closed her eyes. She wished she had gone home after all. The idea of everyone in the room knowing her every single thought filled her with dread.

She had dumb thoughts.

She knew she had dumb thoughts.

She didn't want everyone in the room to know all her dumb thoughts.

Wait a sec. She opened her eyes and heard—

Well, BJ, you hit on anything that moves and you're—

She closed her eyes again.

Silence.

Opened them.

—and your ears are kind of big—

Closed them.

Silence.

Opened them.

It stops when I close my eyes, Olivia thought.

Pi looked right at her. "Can you guys shut up so Olivia can talk?"

Olivia gulped. *I wasn't planning on talking.*

"Olivia," said Pi, sounding annoyed, "we're trying to learn from each other here. It doesn't help us if you hoard your discoveries. What were you thinking about your eyes?"

Olivia nodded. "I...I noticed that it doesn't work when you close your eyes."

"What doesn't work?" Pi asked.

"When I close my eyes, I can't hear you. The voices stop."

Why didn't I notice that? Pi wondered. "Let me try. Everyone think."

Mackenzie: *How much longer is this meeting going to last?*

Levi: *Who has the rest of my Runts?*

Pi opened her eyes. "Okay, enough. I couldn't hear any of you. Could you hear me?"

We shook our heads.

"Were you thinking things?" Nick asked.

"Of course I was thinking things," Pi huffed. "I'm always thinking things."

"So that's good news," Nick said. "If we close our eyes, we can stop listening to people and stop other people from listening to us."

He closed his eyes immediately. We all did.

"So we can still keep secrets," Jordana said. She heaved a sigh of relief. We all did.

"So what do we do now?" Nick asked.

We all opened our eyes.

That was the big question. Of course, all of us had different opinions.

Levi: *We spy on people!*

Nick: *I don't want to spy on people.*

Levi: *Then you're a moron.*

We should tell Nurse Carmichael, Olivia thought. The next thoughts came fast and furiously, ping-ponging around the room. It was hard to tell who was saying what. It was like all of us were talking at once in a stream of consciousness.

What's Carmichael going to do?... She could help us... How?... Maybe there's a reversal vaccine... Maybe it's not because of the vaccine... What else could it be?... Maybe she'll know how to get rid of it... Why would you want to get rid of it?... Why wouldn't I?... We have a superpower! Why would you want to reverse it?... I don't want to know what other people think!... I do! It's awesome!... Where are those candy Runts?... We should tell

Nurse Carmichael... Forget Nurse Carmichael. We should go to the emergency room... Or call the Men in Black... There's no such thing as the Men in Black... There's no such thing as ESP either... If we go to the emergency room, they'll put us all in a rubber room... And do experiments on us... If they believe us... They'd never believe us... It's not so hard to prove... True. We just tell them what they're thinking... No one's going to like that... No shit, Sherlock.

Brinn slammed her forehead on the desk and then mumbled something.

What did she say? we all wondered.

Can everyone shut up? My head is killing me.

"Me too," Mackenzie said, placing her hand on her stomach. "I feel like I'm going to puke."

"So have we agreed?" Pi asked, taking command of the room. "For now, we keep this among us?"

"I don't remember agreeing to that," Nick said.

"I think we should keep it quiet," Tess said. "Maybe not forever. But for now. Until we get a little more used to it." *Until I can use it to find out what Teddy thinks. Oops.* She looked around the room. Who had heard that?

Nick was looking right at her. He was one of Teddy's buddies. Had he heard?

Nick looked away. *Not getting involved*, he thought.

"We might as well see how we can use this," Mars said.

"Use this?" Mackenzie asked. "How do you use this?"

Tess gave her a look. "Aren't there things you want to know but no one will tell you?"

We all nodded. How could we not? Of course there were things we wanted to know.

"So let's see what we can find out," Pi said. "If we tell other people what we can do, they'll quarantine us. No one wants his or her secrets to be public knowledge. So we have to keep this between us. That means no telling anyone. Friends. Parents. Teachers." Pi looked at Nick. "Parents who are teachers."

Don't look at me, Nick thought. *My lips are sealed.*

"What about boyfriends who are in our homeroom but don't have ESP?" Mackenzie asked.

"Do not tell Cooper," Pi insisted. "Only tell those who develop it. And we must get to them before they tell anyone else."

"Who's not here from our homeroom?" Nick asked.

Tess counted those of us who were missing on her fingers. "Sadie, Isabelle, Courtney, Rayna, the twins. There are twenty-four people in our class. And we're only eleven."

"But two didn't get the shot," Mars said. "So that makes twenty-two."

"Unless someone from one of the other classes had the batch we got," Pi reasoned. She looked at us sternly. "We all have to be on the lookout for signs."

Or on the listen-out, Olivia thought, sinking into her chair. *That was totally dumb.*

Tess laughed. *Not dumb. I thought it was funny.*

Olivia sank even farther. *They can hear me worrying about my dumbness! And now they can hear me worrying about worrying about my dumbness. It's a friggin' house of mirrors.*

"It *is* a house of mirrors," Pi said. "And we have to watch from every angle. Especially the other people in our homeroom. Got it?"

We nodded.

"We have to be a team," Pi continued. "We'll meet again tomorrow at lunch."

"I have a *Bloom* meeting," Tess said.

"Skip it," Pi ordered.

Rude, Isaac thought.

"For all we know, we might not even have telepathy anymore tomorrow," Levi said.

Olivia nodded. *Fevers after vaccines only last a day or so. Why should this last any longer?*

Pi gave her a look that was part admiration, part annoyance. *For someone who has never spoken in class, you sure have a lot to say.*

Olivia flushed.

Mackenzie turned to Olivia. "So this could all be gone by tomorrow?" Her voice sounded hopeful.

Olivia nodded. *I hope so.*

"Thank God," Mackenzie said. *Life can go back to normal.*

Brinn shook her head. Her fingers were tinged with charcoal. *Normal is boring. Who wants that?*

"Okay, everyone," Pi said. "See you tomorrow at lunch. Keep your mouths shut. If you do discover someone else, please share our discussions with them and inform them about tomorrow's meeting."

We nodded. Pi had spoken: class was dismissed.

Chapter Ten
THE NON-DATE FROM HELL

Tess looked for Teddy all over school but couldn't find him.

She was psyched to finally find out if he liked her. No more wondering. She would just stand beside him and know if he felt the same or if she should move on.

But by the end of the day, Tess hadn't seen Teddy at all. Well, they'd crossed paths for a second on the stairs. Tess was going up; Teddy was going down. But there were like a hundred louder people between them, so she couldn't hear his thoughts.

She waved and tried to squirm her way toward him, but it was like rush hour on the subway, so no go.

Between sixth and seventh periods he was by his locker, so she thought maybe that was her chance, but he had some sort of French test and all he was thinking was *je pense*, *tu penses*, *il pense*, and that did not help her get a feel for if he liked her one bit, *malheureusement*.

By the time the bell rang, she knew she had to take matters into her own hands.

She texted him:

```
Hey, what are you up to later?
```

She stared at her phone. And waited. She knew in theory a watched phone never got a text, but she still stared.

Finally a text popped up – theory proven false!

```
Have practice. But want to see new
Death Valley movie with me and Nick
after that?
```

Tess did want to see *Death Valley*. She loved seeing horror movies, especially with Teddy. The scarier the better. When the movie was especially bloody, she had an excuse to press her face against his shoulder and breathe in his Irish Spring scent. Yum.

Usually Tess was happy to have Nick around too.

But not tonight.

Nick would hear everything she was thinking. Including thoughts about her signature sniffing-Teddy's-shoulder move.

So embarrassing.

But time could be running out. She needed to see Teddy soon. She texted back:

```
Sure.
```

She was extra pleased when she got out of the shower and saw:

```
Nick bailed. You still in?
```

Yes. She was still in.

Now, what to wear? She wanted to look pretty but casual. Not like she was trying. Normal, but really good normal. So he could see her and think she was pretty and not even notice the extra effort...or the extra few pounds. Or maybe even like them.

The weight was all her mom could think about. Seriously, her mom had been thinking about it as Tess ate dinner. *Maybe if she ate slower, she wouldn't be so hungry. Does she have to use that much salad dressing? Why is she taking more sweet potatoes?*

So what if she wanted a second serving of sweet potatoes? Sweet potatoes were vegetables.

She scrunched and diffused her hair and then zipped up her best jeans. Or what she thought were her best jeans.

We think her best jeans were actually the ones with the frayed bottoms.

Tess didn't know that at the time, though, so she called Mackenzie to make sure she looked good in them. "My James jeans don't make my ass look fat, do they?"

"No," Mackenzie said.

"Love you," Tess chirped. If Teddy felt the same way Tess

did, soon they'd be double-dating with Mackenzie and Cooper. She couldn't wait. "What are you doing?" she asked.

"Just thinking," Mackenzie said.

"About what?" she asked. She wished their telepathy worked over the phone. Then she wouldn't have to waste time with silly questions.

"Nothing. I gotta go. Good luck."

Tess put on her best bra. It was black lace and gave her great cleavage.

None of us had seen all her bras, so we can't make an informed decision on whether it was her best.

BJ had seen one of Tess's bras. He'd felt her up during a game of seven minutes in heaven in eighth grade while they were kissing. It was a cotton white one. It had been biggish back then, but now it fit perfectly.

As Tess put on a purple shirt, she thought about what it would mean if she found out Teddy didn't like her. What if he thought she was ugly? Or fat? Did she really want to know what he thought of her? Was she opening some sort of Pandora's box? Once she knew what he thought, she wouldn't be able to erase the knowledge. It was like reading someone's diary or overhearing a private phone conversation. Once you heard, you couldn't unhear.

Tess would die if anyone read her diary. She wrote religiously. Kind of. There was an entry for every day. But she back-wrote them about once a week. She fake-dated them and used a different pen for each day of the week to make it look legit.

So did she *really* want to know what he really thought?

Yes. She really did.

Tess waited for him at the entrance to the theater. Teddy grabbed her in a bear hug. "Tess! Are you ready to be terrified? There will be blood. And beheadings. Many beheadings."

"Awesome," she said. "Nothing like a good beheading."

Tess is the best. She's just such a cutie.

Of course he had no idea that she could hear him.

Why would he? Back then people didn't ever think about their thoughts being heard. These days it's a different story.

But Tess did hear. She was thinking, *Yes! Yes! Yes! He thinks I'm the best! He thinks I'm cute!*

For the record, we don't think "cute" and "such a cutie" are interchangeable. But anyway.

As they went to buy tickets, what Tess thought was this: *If he thinks I'm cute and we're already best friends, doesn't that mean he likes me? What else does he need?*

Teddy was looking as adorable as always. His eyes reminded Tess of hot chocolate. He was in great shape too – on the bigger side, and not too thin.

Tess and Teddy had met in a creative writing class back in seventh grade. He'd had a girlfriend then who lived in the West Village. Because he had a girlfriend, they'd been able to become fast – and best – friends. But he and the girlfriend had finally broken up – after three years! – just that summer.

Tess ordered herself one ticket and then Teddy got one for himself. She wished he had offered to treat her; that would have been a sign they were on an actual date.

But they had been to the movies lots of times before. They were just friends. Best friends. At a movie. Of course, a movie date could easily change into something more in a dark theater if the mood felt right. Right?

Right.

"I'll get popcorn," Teddy said. "You get us seats."

"Will do," she said. She smiled and then entered the empty theater. There was only a handful of people already there.

She chose a seat smack in the middle.

We think that was her first mistake, by the way. She should have sat in the last row. The last row says romance. Oh, well. Too late now.

The previews started as Teddy sat down a few minutes later. He was balancing one large popcorn and two large lemonades. They all looked precariously close to spilling.

Once he was seated, his knee was right next to hers. His arm too. They were so close. Any minute they could start kissing.

But was Teddy thinking about kissing? No. Teddy was thinking, *This preview looks awesome. I totally want to see* Iceman Revisited.

Maybe she needed more lip gloss?

Suddenly Teddy jerked in his seat. *She's here! She's here!*

Huh? She's here? Who's here? Tess looked over to see

Sadie Newman and Keith Asher climbing up the stairs. Ugh. *What are* they *doing here?*

"Hey, guys," Teddy said, "come join us!"

The other people in the theater gave him dirty looks, which

were accompanied by thoughts of *He better shut up!*

Tess wanted to scream, *Nooooooo! Sit somewhere else! Leave us alone!*

But she just smiled.

Sadie had curly brown hair, a big smile, a waif-like body, and huge doe eyes. You would not be surprised if you saw her on a teen book jacket, staring at the camera, looking wholesome while caught in a zombie-werewolf love triangle.

She waved and made her way toward them. She was in 10B too, but it didn't seem to Tess that any telepathy had kicked in.

Keith followed, looking vaguely annoyed.

We can't blame him. His night out with his off-and-on-again girlfriend had just become a group date with a bunch of sophomores. He was a senior. He played varsity baseball.

Keith cast a glance at Tess and gave her a brief smile. *What's her name again? Carrie?*

Tess was mortified. *He thinks my name is Carrie?* Was she that forgettable? But then Keith sat down beside Sadie, who was sitting beside Teddy, and Tess couldn't really hear anyone but Teddy. And she did not like what she was hearing.

Why is she with him? Teddy was thinking. *He's such a tool. And she's a goddess.*

Tess felt sick. Sadie was a goddess? *A goddess?!* She didn't like writing, or watching horror movies. She spent most of homeroom reading tabloids on her iPhone or picking her split ends.

"You didn't miss anything," Teddy said to Sadie. "Do you want some popcorn?"

"Sure, dude," Keith said.

I wasn't talking to you, jerkoff, Teddy thought. *I was talking to Sadie. Sadie, Sadie, Sadie.*

Tess wished he weren't talking to either of them. She wished they weren't there. She wished *she* weren't there. She wished she were at home writing in her diary.

Mmm. She smells so good, Teddy thought. *Like strawberries.*

Seriously? Tess thought. *Strawberries? He thinks it's good if a girl smells like fruit?*

We all know that if Teddy had thought that Tess smelled like fruit, any kind of fruit, even kiwis, she would have been over the moon. But as Tess sat in that movie theater, the only thing she wanted to do with strawberries was throw them at Sadie. Or maybe stuff them up Teddy's nose.

It continued.

When Teddy and Sadie both took popcorn at the same time, he wanted to hold her hand. He thought about her lips. He thought about what it would be like to kiss those lips. To kiss her neck. To unbutton her shirt. To lick those fingers. To—

Tess squeezed her eyes shut.

She did not want the visual, thank you very much.

Tess had no idea how she hadn't known this. They were supposed to be friends! Best friends! Why hadn't he told her he liked Sadie? And the three of them were in the same chemistry class together! How had she never noticed? The girl sat only four rows ahead of them. Was Tess that oblivious?

Tess felt crushed. Totally and completely annihilated. Like a truck had landed on her and then reversed and accelerated and then reversed and accelerated again until she was nothing but roadkill. She vowed never to open her eyes again.

She just couldn't believe it. Teddy didn't like her. He liked Sadie.

As if he had any chance with Sadie. She was dating a senior! She'd had sex with him, too! We all knew. Well, we were 99 percent sure. By the next day we'd have 100 percent confirmation just by sitting next to her.

Teddy tapped Tess's knee. "Don't close your eyes already! No one's even been beheaded yet!"

Tess wondered if she could volunteer to be the first. She opened her eyes.

Maybe Sadie will get scared and jump into my lap, Teddy thought.

Sadie turned to Teddy, looking startled. "Excuse me?"

Teddy beamed. *She's talking to me! Did you hear that, Keith? Huh?*

"Are you trying to talk to Keith?" Sadie whispered.

"Keith, Teddy has something to tell you."

Teddy recoiled. *I do?*

Keith leaned over. "What do you want, dude?"

Teddy shook his head. *I want to punch you in the face.*

"Teddy!" Sadie shrieked. "What's wrong with you?"

"SHHHHHH!" said the woman a few rows behind them.

Great, Tess thought. *Just great*. Sadie was getting ESP and it was Tess's job to help her. "Sadie, come with me to the bathroom?"

"Excuse me?" Sadie asked.

"Bathroom," Tess said, standing up. "Let's go."

What's she doing? Teddy wondered.

Carrie's weird, Keith thought.

Did Keith just say that out loud? Sadie wondered.

No, Tess thought. *Just come with me and I'll explain, okay?*

Sadie nervously picked at a split end. Then she nodded and followed Tess to the bathroom.

Chapter Eleven
PLEASE KEEP IT DOWN

Tess was not the only one with problems that first night.

Mars had trouble focusing on his piano lesson. It was hard to play Chopin when your teacher was making her grocery list. After his teacher left, Jill, his ex-girlfriend, dropped by his apartment to pick up a textbook she'd left behind.

"I can't stay long," she said. "I have plans." *I have no plans! I know I said it was a mutual breakup, but it wasn't! I lied! I miss you! Serenade me!* She picked up the textbook. "Later."

Levi had a shift at Candy Heaven after school, and not only did he have to listen to the kids' endless whiny chatter – "I want more gum!" "I want more chocolate!" "Ella got more jelly beans than meeeeee!" – but he had to listen to their nannies' thoughts too: *Does she never stop complaining? Why hasn't he called? Is it six o'clock yet?* He scooped a lot of gumballs with his eyes closed to block the noise. He also dropped a whole bunch on the floor by accident.

Olivia made her mom dinner. Olivia liked to cook. She made casseroles, risottos, stews. Tonight she made a chicken stir-fry. When she was done and was trying to do her math homework at her desk in the living room – there was no room for a desk in her tiny bedroom – she had to listen to her mom's OCD: *Did Olivia turn off the stove? I think she did. Maybe she didn't. I should just check. Oh, yes she did. I knew she had. But it's good to check.* Two minutes later: *What if I turned it on again by accident?*

Olivia retreated to her bedroom and spent some time Googling "flu vaccine reactions" on the family laptop. She found that most symptoms – normal symptoms, at least, like headache and sore arm – did in fact clear up on their own fairly quickly. So she had hope – *please, please, please* – that by the time she woke up the next morning, her homeroom's telepathy would be gone.

But we all agree Mackenzie had the worst evening. By far.

She knocked on her parents' door to say goodnight.

"Come in," they called.

Both her parents were sitting on their bed in their bathrobes.

"Night, guys," Mackenzie said, and gave them each a peck on the cheek.

"Night," her mom said. "Will you close the hallway lights?"

"Yes, I will *turn off* the lights."

Her mom was from Montreal and used weird Canadianisms

like "open and close the lights." Also "washroom" and "poutine".

In case you're wondering, poutine involves french fries, gravy and cheese curds. Those of us who have tried it claim it's delicious. Those of us who haven't are skeptical.

"Thanks, honey," her mom said. *Good thing Mackenzie is such a sound sleeper.*

Huh? Mackenzie wondered. *Why is it good I'm a sound sleeper?*

Her dad patted her mom on the leg. *I can't wait to take off Linda's robe.*

Huh? Oh no. Mackenzie slammed her eyes shut.

Her parents. Were. Going. To. Have. Sex.

Sex!

Imminently!

She backed slowly out of the room.

"Have a good sleep," her dad called.

Sleep? How was she supposed to sleep knowing what was taking place just a few feet away?

At least she wouldn't hear their thoughts once she was in her room.

She closed the door and got in her bed.

That feels soooooo good.

No. No, no, no.

They were on the other side of her wall! This wasn't supposed to happen!

She shut her eyes. Silence, thank goodness. Maybe she could just get a glass of water—

Mackenzie opened her eyes for a split second—but then heard *Her breasts look huge in that position* and immediately reclosed them.

Understandably, she refused to open them again until morning.

Chapter Twelve
THE MORNING AFTER

"Olivia? Time to get up."

Her mom was standing over her. "It's after seven. Didn't your alarm go off?"

Olivia remembered that something wasn't right, but she couldn't immediately place what it was.

Then she heard her mom think, *She looks strange*

Olivia stared. *No. No. No. No.* She could *still* hear things. Why could she still hear things? The ESP was supposed to disappear overnight! She was not supposed to hear things that morning. Would this telepathy never go away? Would she have it forever?

"Is something wrong?" her mom asked. "Are you sick?"

"Yes," Olivia said, pulling her covers over her head. "I'm sick. Very." *I am not going to school like this. I am not going to school until this ends.*

"Poor baby," her mom said, sitting on the edge of Olivia's bed and pulling the covers off her face. Her mom frowned. *The flu shot made Olivia sick! Or what if she was infected with the actual flu before the vaccine kicked in? She is not that diligent about washing her hands. Or what if it's something else entirely? There are a lot of terrible viruses going around. Didn't the health section in the* Times *say that SARS is making a resurgence? Is it SARS? I should take her to the emergency room.*

Oh God. Olivia did not want to spend the day in the ER with her mom. But she also did not want to go to school and deal with the fact that half her homeroom could hear her thoughts.

"Can I just stay in bed for now? Maybe take a day of rest and see how I feel? And if I'm not better by this afternoon, then we can go to the emergency room?" Oops. Her mom hadn't said the emergency room part out loud.

Her mother considered, not noticing the mistake. "Okay. I can stay home from work." *What if she collapses when I'm not here?*

"I won't—" She stopped herself. "I'll be fine here. I'll rest. I'll call you if I need anything."

Her mother hesitated. *I do have a meeting today. But what if she needs me?*

"I'll be fine. Promise." If her mom was staying home, then she was going to school. Her mom's crazy made Olivia feel even crazier.

"Okay, honey," her mom said finally. "Call me if you need

anything." *I'll call her every hour to check in. Maybe we can Skype so I can monitor her color.*

Olivia's phone buzzed next to her bed, and she twisted around to see what it said. She didn't usually get texts this early.

It was from Pi. She had started a group chat. It was to all of us. It said:

```
I'll assume nothing has changed?
Meeting still on for lunch.
Everyone be there.
```

Olivia thought the text sounded vaguely threatening.

We all thought the text sounded vaguely threatening.

"What's wrong?" her mother asked. "Who's it from?" She tried to sneak a peek at the message, but Olivia turned her phone over quickly.

She debated what to do. She really wanted to hide under her covers. But she needed to find out what was happening to her. "You know what? I'm feeling much better."

Her mother eyed her phone suspiciously. "Already?"

"Yeah. I must have had a nightmare or something. I'm fine. Really."

"Hmm." *I think she should stay home just in case. It could still be SARS.*

"Mom! I'm not sick. Feel my head."

Her mother pressed her palm against Olivia's forehead. Indeed, she had no fever. "You don't feel warm…"

"Because I'm not. I have a lot of work I shouldn't miss

today," Olivia rushed to explain. "If I need to, I'll stop by Nurse Carmichael's, 'kay?"

Her mom paused, considering. Then she nodded.

Sucker.

So we went to school.

By this time there were more of us. Twenty-one, to be exact. The telepathy had kicked in for almost everyone in our homeroom over the course of twenty-four hours.

Courtney Hunter got it while she was watching TV with her parents. She didn't have her own TV in her room, which was annoying. Her parents wanted her to bond with them over shows and have family time together. They liked to watch all the trendy shows about murdered teenagers and boys with paranormal powers on the CW and ABC Family. She sat in the middle.

I wish Stella would wear her hair like that, her dad thought.

Stella was her mom.

"What did you say?" Courtney asked.

Her dad kept his eyes on the TV. "Nothing."

I wish Gerry had abs like that, her mom thought.

"What did you say?" Courtney asked her mom.

"Nothing," her mom said.

Courtney started feeling sick. "Stop being weird!" she cried. But the thoughts kept coming.

Eventually she started screaming that she could hear what they were thinking, and they gave each other a look.

Is she on drugs? they both thought at the same time.

"I am not on drugs!" she yelled.

Her parents looked at each other in alarm.

"I think we need to check your room," her dad said.

"I am not on drugs!" she yelled again. Not at that moment. Even though she'd never had ADD she occasionally popped an Adderall. Just to help her concentrate when she had an exam. She took maybe one a week. Two, max. Luckily she was out, so her parents wouldn't find any.

They went to check her room while she watched the end of the show.

Isabelle Griffin got it during dinner. She was alone and had ordered pizza from Dean's, and when the food showed up, she could hear the delivery guy's thoughts. When her parents and brother came home, she could hear their thoughts too, and she freaked out. She started hyperventilating. Her mom didn't understand what was wrong – "What do you mean you can hear my thoughts?" And she called their doctor's office, which paged Dr Coven, who called back seven minutes later.

"She's hearing voices," Isabelle's mom told her, her voice trembling.

Dr Coven thought Isabelle was either on drugs or having a psychotic episode, and instructed her mother to take her to the ER immediately. The two of them took a taxi to St Luke's emergency room. While her mom was filling out paperwork, Isabelle texted her friend Jordana:

At hospital. Losing my mind.

Isabelle's phone rang two seconds later.

"You're not crazy," Jordana said, and explained.

Isabelle wasn't sure she believed Jordana, but then Jordana conferenced in Pi, and Pi explained how it all worked and about the eye closing and everything and ordered Isabelle to hightail it out of the ER.

Isabelle told her mom that she was feeling better, that the voices were gone, that all she needed was a good night's sleep, but the ER nurse was already calling her name, and so she had no choice but to get checked out.

Isabelle peed in a cup and got her blood drawn so they could run a toxicology report and do drug tests. Meanwhile, Jordana and Pi kept texting her.

Don't tell them anything.

Did they figure it out?

What's happening over there?

The tests all came back clean. The nurse couldn't find anything wrong with her.

Anojah Kolar got it over breakfast. She told her dad that she could hear his thoughts, but he didn't believe her. He asked her if she needed a new glasses prescription. LensCrafters was having a sale.

Dave and Daniel Zacow, the twins, both got it in the

elevator. They were the only ones in the elevator at the time, so at first they thought they were finally developing twin powers, which people were always asking them about. Anyway, when they stepped out of the elevator, they realized they could hear their doorman's thoughts too.

"Morning, Dave. Morning, Daniel," he said. *Good thing they're always together, because I never remember who's who.*

Edward McMann wasn't that surprised when he started hearing thoughts. He had always expected something paranormal to happen to him, but he'd always thought it would come in the form of him turning into a vampire. He watched and read a lot of vampire stuff. *True Blood*. Anything by Anne Rice. *Fright Night* – the original and the remake. He once put together a list of the top hundred vampire movies for his blog. He even read the Twilight books. He had to after he found out the lead guy was named Edward. He wanted to live forever and bite girls' necks and, well, sparkle.

Sergei Relov and Michelle Barak both got it on their way to school.

Sergei stopped in the park to call his girlfriend in Toronto. There were only a few people there that early and they weren't too chatty, so at first Sergei thought the extra voices were from cell phone interference. He hung up and called her again. It didn't help.

Michelle got it on the subway. Unlike most of us, she did not live in Tribeca. She lived in a small four-floor walkup in Midtown. But BHS was a better school than the one in her area and she had gotten in, so she took the subway there and back every day. When the telepathy kicked in, the subway got loud. Very loud. But hey – it was rush hour. Very loud was to be expected.

Rayna Romero got it right before homeroom while standing in the middle of the hallway. One second she was minding her own business, walking to class, and the next second voices were attacking her at full volume.

"Late night last night?"

He looks like shit.

"Wait for me one sec?"

I have a wedgie.

"Did you do your calc homework?"

She better let me copy.

"Will is such a loser."

Is everyone staring at my zit?

Rayna didn't understand what was going on. *Why is it so loud in here? Where are all the voices coming from?*

Rayna wanted to go to homeroom, but she couldn't move. She was *never* late for homeroom. She was never late for anything. She didn't like being late and she didn't like surprises. But that morning she just stood there. Suddenly she had a splitting headache.

The bell rang, making it worse.

Rayna, it's going to be okay, she heard from somewhere. She wasn't sure where the voice was coming from. She looked around. No one was talking to her. Tess was standing in front of her, but her lips weren't moving.

Rayna, we need to go to homeroom, the voice said – the

voice that was talking to her.

I don't want to go to homeroom! I want this to stop! Rayna's eyes were wild. Terrified. *But I can't concentrate. There are so many thoughts!*

"Excuse me!" a senior yelled as he stood behind her. "You're in the way!" *Honk! Honk! I wish I had a horn on my nose.* He eventually walked around her.

Rayna, close your eyes, the nice voice said. *Trust me, just close them.*

Rayna did what she was told, thinking maybe she was dreaming. She had a lot of weird dreams. Sometimes she flew through the hallway stark naked except for her days-of-the-week underwear.

As soon as she closed her eyes, the voices halved. *Better,* she thought. At least the real voices weren't so rude.

"It's going to be okay," the nice voice said, but this time it wasn't muffled and was accompanied by a hand on her arm.

She opened her eyes to see that Tess was talking to her. "What's happening? I really don't like surprises."

"Follow me to homeroom," Tess said. "We'll explain."

Unfortunately for Rayna, this wasn't the only shocker she would get that day. That night, while she downed a plate of cheese ravioli and breadsticks with her parents and younger sister, she would telepathically discover that she had been born with a sixth finger on her left hand, which had been promptly removed and never spoken of again.

Um, surprise?

Chapter Thirteen
SOMETHING FUNNY'S GOING ON AROUND HERE

Cooper sang to himself as he hurried up the stairs to school. As usual, he was late. This time he was late because Ashley, his three-year-old sister, would not let go of the leg of his jeans. She hadn't wanted him to leave. "Let's play Spider-Man!" she'd hollered. When she finally let go, she insisted on going with him to the elevator to press the button. He adored his sister, but she made it infinitely more difficult to leave the apartment.

He slept in by accident. He'd been up late the night before. The baseball game had gone into extra innings. Finally, the Yankees had beaten Baltimore in the eleventh, 4–3. They needed to win two more games to go to the American League Championship Series. After the game was over, he'd had trouble falling asleep. He'd been thinking about Mackenzie and trying to figure out what was going on with her. Something was up; he just wasn't sure what. When they'd spoken the night before, she had sounded distant.

"You okay?" he'd asked.

"Yeah. Fine," she'd said, her voice clipped.

It was with this in mind that he dumped his books into his locker and hurried to homeroom. He was looking forward to seeing her.

"What's up, 10B!" Cooper sang. "Can I get a boo- ya?"

Usually we responded to his chant. On this day, though, we just stared at him. No one said a word. Not even Nick or Mackenzie.

He tried again. "10B! I cannot hear your boo-ya!"

Again we didn't respond.

He looked confused. He was confused. Understandably. Every day for all of September at least some of us had responded to his boo-ya. That day we were all too busy mentally talking to each other.

And what we were saying was this: Everyone in our homeroom could read minds. Everyone except Renée, Adam McCall, and Cooper.

I get why Renée and Adam can't – they didn't get the vaccine. But why can't Cooper do it?

He got the shot, didn't he?

He did!

Did anyone see him get the shot?

Mackenzie did. She went in with him.

Mackenzie was in the back row. Tess was sitting to her right. Cooper would take the spot on her left.

Levi, BJ, and Courtney were all in the row in front of her.

Yes, Mackenzie thought. *I just hope it didn't work on him. Damn, I didn't mean to think that!*

Mackenzie's glad he doesn't have it! Courtney thought.

Why? thought BJ.

I don't know! replied Courtney.

Stop thinking about me! Mackenzie ordered.

Mackenzie always thinks everything is about her, Courtney thought.

Excuse me? I do not.

Why wouldn't you want Cooper to have it? BJ asked, twisting around to look at her. *Unless there's something you're not telling him. Did you lie to him? Did you cheat on him?*

The name *Bennett* popped into Mackenzie's head before she could stop it. She clenched her eyes closed immediately, but it was too late.

Way too late.

"Bennett who goes to Westside?" Courtney blurted out.

Oh no, oh no, oh no. Mackenzie didn't want to give anything else away, but she wanted – she *needed* – to know what the others were thinking. She opened her eyes.

"What about Bennett who goes to Westside? I know a Bennett who goes to Westside," said Jordana, who was sitting next to Courtney.

He's the guy Mackenzie cheated on Cooper with. He lives in her building. He's hot.

BJ shook his head in dismay. *Mackenzie cheated on Cooper with a private-school guy? Rough. Cooper doesn't deserve that.*

Mackenzie cheated on Cooper!

Why would she cheat on Cooper?

Slut!

Bitch!

Mackenzie gripped Tess's hand.

It wasn't me, I swear, Tess thought.

BJ was staring at both of them. *So it's true?*

Can you just stop thinking about this, please? Mackenzie begged. She spotted Nick in the front of the classroom. Nick was friends with Cooper. Not best friends, but good friends. Was he listening to this?

Don't worry, Tess thought. *Nick won't say anything. He's staying out of people's business. He didn't say anything to Teddy about me.*

Mackenzie put her head down on the desk and closed her eyes. She wanted this to stop.

"Hey, babe, what's wrong?" Cooper asked, finally taking the seat beside her. "Headache?"

She opened her eyes and stared at his trusting face.

"You have no idea," she said.

Chapter Fourteen
AND WE MEET AGAIN

Like the rest of us, Olivia walked out of homeroom with a pounding headache.

Unfortunately, she had public speaking next. She hadn't seen Mr Roth since the previous day's telepathy-induced panic attack. She had her speech with her, but she didn't think she could do it that day. She prayed her teacher would give her a break.

"Let's just stroll by Lazar's locker," Renée said. *They are going to be the cutest couple.*

Olivia was too tired to argue. And anyway, at this point she was happy to surround herself with people who could not read her mind. Homeroom had been one of the most stressful classes of her life. She was even too stressed to worry about Lazar. To worry what he thought of her. To worry if he thought she was cute. Or if he thought she was a total moron.

She'd felt awful for Mackenzie. Everyone in home-room had been thinking about her and Cooper. She felt bad for Cooper too, of course. The whole situation was miserable. If she'd been in either of their places, she would have just about died.

She hated that the people in her homeroom could hear her thoughts. She did not want them to know that the only kissing experience she had was with her pillow. She didn't want everyone knowing when she had to pee. Or when she had a stomachache. She had lots of stomachaches. At her next doctor's appointment she was going to ask them to check for Crohn's disease.

She didn't want everyone knowing anything.

She was planning on avoiding the other people with ESP at all costs. Since there were about two hundred people in her grade, only a few students in each of her classes would have ESP.

But she'd still have to listen to everyone else's thoughts, including Renée's. And all of Renée's Olivia-related opinions.

Olivia really should go out with Lazar. A boyfriend would make her so happy. She should also not tie her hair back in a half ponytail. It's so sixth grade.

"You should really wear your hair down," Renée said. "Have you thought about bangs?"

At least Olivia could trust Renée to say what she thought.

"There he is," Renée said. *I should get him to walk with us to public speaking!*

Olivia stopped in her tracks. *No! Wait!*

"Hey, Lazar!" Renée said. "Come walk with us!"

Argh.

Lazar looked up, first noticing Renée. *She is such a pest.*

Olivia tried not to laugh. She was a pest. But at least she was honest.

Then he looked at Olivia. *Oh! It's Olivia!*

Olivia stood up straighter. *Yes, it is. Thank you for noticing.*

I hope she's feeling better. What happened in class yesterday was insane. I've never seen anyone faint before.

Olivia felt her cheeks burn. Great. Just great. Now all he saw when he looked at her was a freak of nature.

"Hi," he said, looking into Olivia's eyes. He had splotches of red on his cheeks. "How are you feeling?"

"Oh, um—" Her throat closed up. She hated talking to guys. What if she said the wrong thing?

She looks better, he thought. *She looks good.*

Olivia blushed. *I look good? He thinks I look good! Wait, what was the question? Oh right –* "I'm feeling better. Thanks. Thank you."

"Good to hear. That was one scary fall," he said, still looking into her eyes. *She has great eyes. They're so expressive.*

He's complimenting my eyes! "Thanks," she said. Then she realized that he hadn't actually said that aloud. What had he said aloud? Oh! Her fall. That was one scary fall. "Yes," she said finally. "It was one scary fall. But I'll live."

He was still staring at her intently. *She's pretty.*

Hmm, Olivia thought. *Maybe hearing what people think won't be as bad as I thought.*

Tess also had a headache. And now she had chemistry class with Teddy and Sadie.

She would have to talk to Teddy. She would have to look at Teddy. She would have to listen to Teddy.

She would have to be lab partners with Teddy.

"Sorry you missed so much of the movie last night," Teddy said to Tess as she slid into the seat beside him. "Is everything okay?"

"Yup," she muttered.

Sadie walked in and waved.

"Hi," Sadie said, about to approach them. Sadie had texted Tess twenty times since the night before. And left five phone messages. It was super annoying. Tess would prefer not to chat with the girl who had stolen the heart of the guy she liked. She did not want to be best friends with her either. She wanted nothing to do with her. But since she wasn't a bitch, she'd had no choice but to help Sadie through her breakdown at the movies.

First she'd whisked Sadie away to the bathroom. "What is wrong with me?" Sadie had asked Tess, tears overflowing from her doe-like eyes.

So Tess explained. About how it was happening to everyone in their homeroom. That they were not the only ones. That they were meeting the next day to talk about it at lunch and to decide what to do.

Meanwhile Tess was thinking, *You better not like Teddy!*

And Sadie said, "What? Huh? Teddy?"

Then two other girls stormed into the bathroom and it got noisy. Tess had stepped back so that the other girls were between them and she could compose her thoughts while Sadie was distracted by the noise.

Tess did not want Sadie to know that Teddy thought she smelled like strawberries. She did not want Sadie to know anything about Teddy at all. He was *her* Teddy. Even if Sadie was dating Keith, it was still possible that she could fall madly in love with Teddy, right? Even if he was a sophomore and Keith was a senior? Unlikely, yes, but still possible.

Teddy was smart and funny and cute. No. Tess would not let herself think nice things about Teddy. Sadie would hear, and it would just encourage her to like him.

Other than physically putting other people between her and Sadie, or maybe hiding in the bathroom stall, Tess wasn't sure how she could stop Sadie from hearing her. She couldn't exactly close her eyes in the middle of a discussion.

The strangers went into stalls.

Tess decided to try something. "Everything is going to be fine," she said. "Don't worry. It's a little overwhelming at first, but you get used to it." Tess realized that if she kept talking, then Sadie would focus on what she was saying. Not on her thoughts. Also, if she forced herself to keep talking, then she wouldn't be able to think at the same time.

"And it stops when you close your eyes," Tess added.

Sadie slammed her eyes shut.

Tess took a deep breath. Ahhh. Free play. *You better not like Teddy! He's mine, mine, mine!*

Sadie opened her eyes. "I think I want to go to sleep."

"No worries," Tess said, backing away. "I'll tell Keith you're not feeling well. You can call me if you have any questions. Or text me."

Afterward, Tess had snuck back into the dark theater and told the boys that Sadie wasn't feeling well.

I can't believe she's making me miss the movie, Tess heard Keith think. *Then, I guess this means no sex tonight.*

Ass.

Oh no! Teddy thought. *This was our time together!*

Tess told Teddy that she had to deal with a family issue and spent the rest of the movie eating popcorn and sitting on the wooden bench outside the theater, reading and answering texts from Sadie.

```
Sadie: I can hear my parents too?
Tess: Yup.
Sadie: And my doorman?
Tess: Everyone.
Sadie: Do you think it'll be gone
by tomorrow?
Tess: I hope so.
```

Obviously it was not gone by the next day, because there they were in chemistry and it was still happening.

As soon as Sadie stepped inside the classroom, Teddy's brain went into overdrive. *She's here! Awesome. I hope she's feeling better. Her hair is so shiny.*

Barf, barf, barf, Tess thought, but then got nervous.

What if Sadie had heard her mentally barfing? Also, Renée was sitting in the front row. But Tess couldn't remember if Renée had gotten the shot. She didn't think so. She'd gone on and on about it all being some government conspiracy.

As Sadie stepped up to her, Tess started to panic. She did not want Sadie to know that Teddy was obsessed with her. No, no, no! She had purposefully kept as far away from Sadie as she could all morning so that she wouldn't accidentally give away Teddy's feelings. It hadn't been easy. After the previous night, Sadie thought Tess was her new best friend.

But as soon as Sadie walked down the aisle, she'd be standing next to Teddy and would know everything, because surely Teddy would blab on and on and on about the stupid strawberries.

Without thinking, Tess squeezed her way in front of Teddy so that she was between him and Sadie. Hopefully Sadie wouldn't be able to hear Teddy's thoughts over Tess's. And yeah, Sadie would still be able to hear Tess's thoughts, but maybe she could camouflage them better than Teddy could. "Excuse me," she said to him.

What's Tess doing? Teddy wondered.

Just go with it, she told him, even though she knew he couldn't hear. And now that she was between Sadie and Teddy, she gave Sadie a tight smile. "How are you?"

Sadie shrugged. "You know. Homeroom was crazy."

"No kidding."

Do you think it'll go away soon? Sadie asked. *I don't like it.*

Me neither, Tess thought.

Teddy's thoughts jumped into her head. *Why are they just standing there staring at each other?*

Oh, right, Tess thought. *This must look super odd.* "Let's chat at lunch," she told Sadie.

"But—" Sadie stopped. *I'm feeling so alone. I really want to talk.*

"We'll talk at lunch," Tess said.

"You guys are going for lunch together?" Teddy asked eagerly. "Want some company?"

Seriously? "We have a meeting at lunch," Tess said.

"What meeting?" Teddy asked.

Good question, Tess thought. She looked at Sadie. *Any ideas?*

Telepathy club?

Gee, thanks, Sadie. "Communications club," Tess said.

"Oh. Cool. Never heard of it," Teddy said. "Does it need new members? I'm looking for a club to join."

How about Pathetic R Us? Tess thought.

Why is he pathetic? Sadie wondered. *Aren't you guys best friends?*

Don't think it, don't think it, don't think it, Tess thought.

Don't think what? Sadie asked while Teddy thought, *It would be great to be in a club with Sadie. Get some quality time with her.*

Tess wished they'd both shut up.

Sadie blinked. *What's your problem?*

Tess couldn't take it anymore. *He likes you, okay? He likes you. Teddy likes you. Are you happy now?*

Sadie's jaw dropped. "I didn't know."

Teddy leaned against the table. "You don't know if they take new members?"

Sadie blushed. "No, I didn't know that—" Her voice trailed off. *But why are you so mad? Do you like him or something?*

Yes! I've liked him forever! And he's obsessed with you.

Her lips made an O. *I'm sorry!*

Me too. Tess turned to Teddy. "The club is by invitation only." *And you are not invited.*

Third period, Pi had a surprise quiz in precalc.

She was not prepared.

It was unusual for Pi not to be prepared. She was an over-preparer. She didn't have the second-highest GPA in her class for no reason. She had it because she had goals.

She wanted to get a perfect GPA.

She wanted to go to Harvard.

She wanted to be exceptional.

She wanted her mother to realize Pi was exceptional and to know she'd had nothing to do with it.

Second in your class was not exceptional.

First in your class was exceptional.

But Jon Matthews was number one, not her. It seemed to come easy to him too. He definitely wasn't as studious as Pi was. Plus he was in Glee Club. And he played in a band called Demon. And he had a girlfriend. How did he have time for all those things? And to still be number one? It was impossible to understand. Pi barely had time for anything except being number two. She studied all the time. Even having to play on the chess team stressed her out, but she needed *at least one* extracurricular to get into Harvard.

Jon barely seemed to break a sweat. Yet he was still number one.

Pi needed to study. Hard. That's why she wasn't prepared. She hadn't had time. Normally she reviewed her precalc notes at night. She practiced. But last night she'd been too busy exploring her new talent.

Anyway, who cared about a little math test when she could hear what people were thinking? Jon couldn't do that.

She could hear the person on her left: *X plus…no, that's not right*.

The person to her right: *Eight to the power of…*

The person behind her: *I'm never going to finish on time, must focus!*

She could even hear her teacher, Mr Irving: *What should I make for dinner tonight? Maybe a peanut butter and pickle sandwich? Or cream cheese and canned tuna?*

For the record, we all agree that both are absolutely disgusting dinner choices.

Anyway.

As far as Pi could tell, no one else could do what we could do. She had Googled and Googled and Googled some more.

She had read studies from medical journals. She had gone to the library.

She really *was* extraordinary.

Well, *we* really were extraordinary.

She'd debated telling other people. Like her dad. The world. Her mom. But if people knew what she could do, they would probably try to stop her from doing it. And they'd assume that her success was because of her telepathy and not because of her hard work. Perhaps it was better to use the ESP to give her a leg up, to help her be exceptional without anyone knowing how she was doing it.

She stared back at her test. She knew most of the answers. Even though she hadn't prepared, she was still smart. But she needed to get all the answers right.

Too bad she had surrounded herself with idiots. If she had sat closer to Jon, she'd have gotten every answer correct. Talk about giving herself a leg up. She looked around to see where her nemesis was sitting. He was a few rows behind her and diagonal. Maybe if she maneuvered a bit, she could get a straight line to him and there would be less interference?

She fidgeted and wiggled. She heard the girl in red. The guy in black. She never cared enough to remember anyone's name. She knew Jon's and her teachers' and that was enough.

She felt like she was playing with the antennae on a radio, trying to get the signals right.

If she angled her body to the left and tilted her head to the right, she could hear him more clearly...

Next, Jon thought. *Number fourteen*.

It worked! She could hear him!

Hold on – he was already on number fourteen? She was only on number ten! She shouldn't have wasted so much time.

He was staring at the equation. *Hmm. What's the value of y?*

And then he worked through the problem.

And Pi could hear him working through the problem.

She scribbled as he thought.

She knew he'd done it right. It was so effortless for him.

Fifteen.

All she had to do was listen.

Chapter Fifteen
MEETING NUMBER TWO

Our second meeting took place at lunchtime again, back in the chess room. We pushed desks and pulled out chairs so that we formed a circle. We could all hear each other. No interference.

Everyone in our homeroom who had gotten the vaccine was there. Everyone except Cooper.

"Are you sure he doesn't have it?" Pi asked Mackenzie.

"I'm sure," Mackenzie said. *I'd have heard it if he had it. Wouldn't I have?*

Yes, Pi thought.

"But why is he the only one not to have it?" Tess asked. "It makes no sense."

"What's different about Cooper?" Pi asked Mackenzie.

What's different about Cooper? Mackenzie wondered. *He likes to sing. He's nice to everybody.*

"He has a gluten allergy," Nick said. "Maybe that has something to do with it."

"Oh," Mackenzie said. "Right!"

Way to know your own boyfriend, Courtney thought.

Whoa! Tess thought. *Way to be bitchy.*

That could be it, Pi thought. "Does anyone else here have a gluten allergy?"

No one did.

"Different allergies could affect the processing time," Pi reasoned. "Maybe his system is slower to digest the vaccine."

"Or maybe he's not getting it at all," Mackenzie said hopefully.

"You're going to have to tell him," Jordana said while filing her nails.

"No one is telling anyone anything," Pi said forcefully.

"Not about us," Jordana said. "About you and Bennett. We all know."

The entire circle stared at Mackenzie. *Is this really happening? Am I really sitting on a desk discussing with practically my entire homeroom whether I should tell my boyfriend that I cheated on him?*

Yes, Brinn thought while drawing in her notebook. She was wearing her white fencing jacket over jeans. *It's really happening.*

"He's going to find out eventually," said BJ. "Wouldn't you rather he hear it from you?"

Tess put her arm around Mackenzie. "This is really between the two of them. It's none of anyone else's business."

"But now we're lying too," Courtney said. "We're involved.

I feel bad even looking at him."

"Gimme a break," Mackenzie snapped. "Are you saying I'm the only one here with a secret? You've never lied about something? Stolen something? Taken an Addie before a test?"

Courtney turned pink. *How did she know?*

Now we were all looking at Courtney.

"Taking an Addie is cheating," Tess said.

"Exactly," Mackenzie said. "I'm sure other people have cheated on tests too."

Pi turned red. *Like last period.*

Now we were all looking at her.

"You?" Tess shrieked. "Cheated? Aren't you like the smartest person in our grade?"

"The second smartest," Pi said in a small voice. "I didn't really cheat. I just…" Her voice trailed off.

Levi snickered. *Pi? Speechless? There's a first.*

"That just proves my point," Mackenzie said, looking meaningfully around the room. "We all have secrets. And they're all going to come out. So it's in all of our best interests to *keep* secrets."

"Are you threatening us?" Courtney asked. "One of us tells Cooper about Bennett, and you tell the principal I've taken an occasional Adderall to help me through an exam?"

"She didn't threaten anything," Pi said. "She was just informing us that that's the way it is. So it's agreed? Our secrets stay secret."

We all nodded. Some of us less convincingly than others.

Olivia was the least convincing of us all. *This is all getting a little crazy. Maybe it's time to call the CDC after all.*

"What's the CDC?" Courtney asked her.

Olivia flushed. "Centers for Disease Control and Prevention."

"Why would we call them?" Jordana asked.

Olivia cleared her throat. "They have a Vaccine Adverse Event Reporting System. Where people and doctors can call in to report possible side effects to vaccines."

Rayna nodded. "Then maybe they could make it stop." She was still shaken from her hallway experience that morning.

She would be even more shaken that night after her discovery at dinner. She would spend the next twenty-four hours wiggling her left hand.

"Why would you want to stop it?" Courtney asked.

"They'd want to stop it if they knew we had it," Levi said. He took out a paper bag with CANDY HEAVEN stamped across it and started munching on jelly beans. "No one would want us to use it."

Jordana smoothed the sides of her hair. "No one wants us using it on them."

"That's why I want to tell someone," Rayna said. "So they can make it stop."

Pi was clearly getting agitated. "Right now it's in our control. As soon as we tell someone, it's out of our control." She glared at Isabelle. "We almost lost control last night."

"Not my fault," Isabelle said. "No one told me what was happening until I got to the hospital."

"I think we should take a vote," Rayna said. "Who wants to tell and who doesn't?"

"Tell who?" Nick asked.

"The CDS or whoever," Rayna said.

"CDC," Olivia corrected her.

Pi gave them both dirty looks.

"Let's do it," Mars said. "Who wants to tell?"

On *tell*, twelve of us raised our hands. The twelve included Olivia, Mackenzie, Rayna, and Tess. On *don't tell*, nine of us shot up our arms.

"*Tell* it is," Levi said.

Pi glared at Tess, Mackenzie and Olivia. "What happened to you guys? I thought you agreed with me."

Mackenzie shook her head. "I want this to end. And we're not going to be able to end it without help."

She thinks she can end it before Cooper finds out.

Good luck with that!

He's so finding out.

"Well, I'm finding out all kinds of stuff I don't want to know," Tess said, looking sadly at Sadie.

"It's not my fault," Sadie whimpered.

What happened with them?

Tess is in love with Teddy, but Teddy's in love with Sadie.

Isn't Sadie still dating Keith?

Sadie nodded. "Exactly my point."

Pi looked at Olivia. "And what about you?"

"It's too overwhelming," Olivia said softly. She kept her eyes on the floor. "I can't handle all my thoughts being so public."

She's shy.

She'll have to get over that.

"I understand you're shy," Pi said. "But what do you think is going to happen if we go public? We're all going to be on display. No one will care if you're shy."

Jordana shrugged. "Can someone explain why we have to be in agreement? If some of us want to tell, we can tell. It doesn't hurt the others."

"Not true," Pi said. "If Rayna tells the CDC what's happening—"

"No one would believe her anyway," Jordana said. Pi paced around the inside of the circle. "They may not believe her at first. But eventually they would. She could prove it. And they'd figure out how it happened and they'd suspect all of us have it."

"But Rayna could say it's just her," Jordana added.

Pi shook her head. *And then Rayna gets all the glory?*

I don't want the glory, Rayna thought. *I want it to stop.*

Jordana looked at Pi. "I don't get it. If fame is the goal, we're better off telling people. We'd be on the news."

We'd be on 60 Minutes!

We'd be on the cover of Time *magazine!*

We'd definitely be on TMZ!

Pi looked around the room. "Is that the kind of fame we want? For everyone to think we're weirdos? For everyone to be afraid of us? No one will want to stand next to us. No one will want to talk to us."

Oh God, Olivia thought. *I don't want that at all.*

"Exactly," Pi said to her. "You're not evaluating this situation properly. You have to think about all the advantages we have."

Like cheating off of Jon Matthews and not getting caught? Brinn thought, still drawing.

Pi flushed. "Well, yeah. But I'm not talking about cheating on tests. Think beyond that. We can excel in our fields. We can be the best."

"I don't want to cheat to get ahead," Nick said. "My mom would beat me."

Does Mrs Gaw really beat him?

She does seem like a really strict teacher.

I wouldn't be surprised.

She also seems to love her wooden ruler.

Nick slapped his palm against his forehead. "She doesn't really beat me. It was a figure of speech."

Pi kept going: "It's not just about school. Think of the edge you'll have in everything. In relationships. You'll always have the upper hand. You'll always know if someone is about to break up with you. You'll always know what your parents are really planning. What they're thinking."

I had enough of that last night, Mackenzie thought. *Your breasts look good in that position? Seriously?*

BJ leaned in. "You and Cooper?"

"No," Mackenzie muttered. "Forget it." *My parents.*

Ewwwwwwww!

Your dad lucked out, BJ thought. *I've seen your mom and she's a MILF.*

Mackenzie closed her eyes. "Yes. I heard my parents. Having sex. In their room. Can we move on now?"

"You could hear through a wall?" Pi asked. "I thought we couldn't do that."

Mackenzie shrugged. "I did it."

Pi pursed her lips. *I can't do that. Why can't I do that?*

Jordana laughed. *Maybe Mackenzie has super ESP or something.*

Mackenzie opened her eyes. *Great. Just great. I want this thing gone.*

There is no way Mackenzie has more advanced ESP than I do. Maybe she had a hole in her wall or something. Pi shook her head. "You're not seeing the big picture. Let's think of our careers. We'll be the best at whatever we want to be. Anyone want to be a lawyer?"

Jordana raised her hand. Her nails were bright yellow.

"You will always know if your client did it. You will always know what the jury is thinking. Say you're a judge. You will always know the truth. Think about any job. This capability will give you an advantage."

What if I want to be a doctor? Olivia wondered.

Pi nodded. "You'll know your patient's symptoms without him having to say a word."

"Except if he's in a coma," Levi said.

"You can open his eyes," Pi said. "Check his vitals, read his thoughts."

"I could be an amazing psychologist," Courtney said.

Levi snickered again. *You want to be a shrink? Are you going to prescribe all your patients Adderall?*

F you.

"Does anyone have a pet? Has it worked on them?" Tess wondered.

I got a lot of barking from my dog.

"I do not want to know what my fish are thinking," Levi said. "I've killed five of them."

Sicko!

He probably fed them gummy bears.

I always knew he had it in him.

Levi looked offended. "Not on purpose! We have floor-to-ceiling windows! Our apartment is too cold!"

"Think about teaching," Pi continued. "You'd be amazing. You'd always know if your students were getting the lesson. And paying attention. Or cheating."

We were all quiet for a few minutes as we thought over the options. Even Tess and Olivia were nodding.

Slowly all of us were agreeing with Pi.

"We're assuming the telepathy isn't going to disappear," Jordana said.

"That's true," Pi said. "It might. I say we use it while we can."

Nick sat up straighter. "We could still use it to be awesome even if other people know we have it."

"Not if they're afraid of us," Pi said.

"Not if we're in a rubber room," Levi added.

"Should we take a revote?" Pi asked. "All in favour of keeping this a secret?"

Almost all of us raised our hands. Even Tess. Even Olivia. Everyone except Mackenzie.

"C'mon, Mackenzie," Nick said. "We have to all be in this together."

She doesn't have much bargaining power at the moment, does she?

You'd think she'd be afraid of pissing us off.

Pi stared Mackenzie down. "Mackenzie, are we a team or aren't we?"

I don't have much choice here, do I? Mackenzie wondered. *Anyway, even if we get rid of the telepathy, my secret is already out of the bag.*

Excellent point, Pi thought back. "One last vote. Are we all in it together?"

And we all raised our hands, Mackenzie included.

We would not tell.

Chapter Sixteen
JUST IGNORE ME

We didn't wait long to use our ESP to take over the world. Domination began during gym class.

At BHS, the gym classes were made up of two homerooms. We were combined with 10A.

The girls were playing volleyball inside the gym. The boys were playing a New York version of touch football in the park.

Even though we were matches in physical strength and coordination, they weren't exactly fair games. Not once we figured out how to position ourselves properly to minimize interference. Here's how volleyball went:

Leora from 10A prepared to serve. She looked across the court and tried to psych us out. *I guess I'll serve short to Olivia. She's the weakest.*

Olivia: *Ah! She's shooting it to me!*

Jordana: *I'll get it!* Jordana was our best player.

Leora served.

Jordana swooped in and popped it to Courtney, who slammed it back over the net.

One of them: *I'm hitting it to the open area between Brinn and Courtney!*

Brinn: *I got it!*

Jordana: *Hit it back to the area between Shoshana and Jill!*

Point!

Us: *Tip it!*

Point!

Us: *Cut shot!*

Point!

We kicked ass.

Our boys did just as well. We knew all of 10A's plays and kept intercepting the ball.

And sure, football was just football. Volleyball was just volleyball. Gym volleyball, and gym football, so even more irrelevant. But still. Our dominance over our opponents continued after school.

The BHS chess team had a match against Stuyvesant.

Pi's opponent was a senior named Rick. He was their best player.

Let's try a pirc defense, he thought, moving his pawn to the middle.

I don't think so, Pi thought. She laughed inside her head. Since she was the only one from 10B on the chess team, no one could hear.

Her opponent didn't stand a chance. Pi was able to block all his moves. She knew what was coming.

She won three games in a row.

Nick kicked ass at baseball practice.

Brinn kicked ass at fencing.

Dave and Daniel kicked ass at their wrestling practice. It was easy to block moves when you knew what they were. But when they had to wrestle each other, they ended up standing still, eyes locked, in a stupor.

Daniel: *I'm going for your legs.*

Dave: *Then I'm going for a whizzer!*

Daniel: *You suck at whizzers.*

Dave: *You suck at takedowns!*

Daniel: *You're ugly.*

Dave: *No, you're ugly!*

Daniel: *I'm kind of hungry, actually.*

Dave: *What do you think Mom is making for dinner?*

Mackenzie and Tess didn't have extracurriculars on Thursdays. Instead, they'd crossed the West Side Highway and were sitting on a bench in Battery Park sipping chocolate milk shakes from Shake Shack and gazing at the Hudson River. They could kind of see the Statue of Liberty from where they were, but it required some twisting. And they were too tired to do much twisting.

Tess took a big gulp of her shake and sighed. "This is not going to help me look good in my dress at your Sweet. It's already a little tight. You are a very bad influence."

Mackenzie took a long sip. "I've practically forgotten about my Sweet with all the insanity going on. So I think we earned these today."

"That was a rough lunch," Tess said, shivering. "This whole thing is crazy."

"I know."

"I'm glad you're going through it with me, though," Tess said. "We're lucky to have each other." She tried to imagine what it would be like if she had no one to talk to about what was happening. No, it would be too horrible.

"It really would be," Mackenzie said. Her phone buzzed with a text.

"Who is it?" Tess asked.

"Cooper," Mackenzie said. "He wants to know what I'm up to."

"Tell him to meet us."

Mackenzie shook her head. "I can't deal with him right now. Not in person. It's too stressful."

"I know what you mean," Tess said. "That's how I feel about Teddy."

Mackenzie sighed. *Not exactly the same thing.*

Tess felt like she'd been slapped. *I didn't say it was the same thing.*

Instead of answering, Mackenzie typed a text back into her phone. "I'm telling him I'm busy with you."

Poor Cooper, Tess thought.

"That doesn't help."

"Sorry," Tess said. "Are you going to tell him about Bennett?" Tess's feelings were still hurt that Mackenzie hadn't confided in her. Tess always told Mackenzie everything. About how weight-obsessed her mom had gotten since her dad dumped her. About how Tess had been bulimic for about ten minutes back in eighth grade. About how she stalked her dad's new girlfriend on Facebook.

I'm sorry. You like to share. I don't. "I guess I'll have to tell him," Mackenzie said eventually. "He's going to find out anyway."

"Not if he doesn't get it," Tess said. Maybe his gluten allergy had blocked it from appearing at all.

"Maybe. But with so many people knowing…" She stared into the water. "He's bound to find out."

"What do you think he'll do?" Tess wondered.

"I think he'll break up with me."

Yeah, Tess thought. *I guess so.*

Mackenzie flinched. Her phone buzzed again.

Tess heard Mackenzie read herself the message: *Are you guys in Battery Park? I think I see you.*

He saw them?

Mackenzie stiffened. *Damn, he's here.*

They both turned and spotted him waving from the other side of the grass, near the apartments.

Mackenzie waved back. *So much for avoiding him.*

He jogged toward them, a huge smile on his face. "What's up, laaaaadies?" he sang.

Tess felt suddenly out of place. *Do you want me to go?*

Please don't, Mackenzie thought. "Hi."

He kissed her on the lips. "Mmm. You taste like milk shake."

Mackenzie offered him her paper cup. "Want?"

"Yes, please." He took a big slurp. "Hey, Tess, what's shaking?"

"Besides the milk? Not much," Tess said. "Just enjoying the weather." It was a beautiful evening. But still, she felt awkward. *Mackenzie, are you sure you don't want me to go? Now would be a good time to tell him.*

Mackenzie's eyes widened. *No! Don't go! I can't tell him now!*

Okay, okay, I won't. Tess leaned back on the bench just as her phone rang. She looked at the caller ID. "It's Teddy."

"Tell him to come meet us," Cooper said. *Of course she will, she loves him.*

Tess's heart stopped. *How does he know that? Mackenzie, did you tell him?*

Oops. Will she know if I lie?

Mackenzie! Tess flushed. The phone rang again.

Tess ignored it. She wished Teddy didn't exist. She would not call him back. She was done with him. She looked at Mackenzie. *What should I do?*

Mackenzie leaned her head back against the bench. *Maybe he'd feel differently if he knew how you felt.*

I doubt it.

"You ladies are quiet today," Cooper said. He lay down on the bench and put his head on Mackenzie's lap. "Speaking of which, what was up with everyone in homeroom this morning?"

"What do you mean?" Mackenzie asked. She turned to Tess. *Why don't you just tell him that you want to jump him?*

I'm not going to do that! Tess cried. Well, she cried it inside her head. She picked up her legs off the ground and hugged them into her chest.

"Seriously?" Cooper asked. "You didn't notice everyone was acting weird? There was a lot of staring going on." *It was like a zombie invasion.*

"I didn't notice anything," Mackenzie said.

Mackenzie, Tess thought, *if I jump him, then he'll know I like him. What's the point of that if I know he doesn't like me?*

"Then you'd know for sure," Mackenzie said.

Cooper blinked in confusion. "Then you'd know what for sure?"

Mackenzie!!!! Tess wailed.

Sorry, sorry. "Just talking to myself," she said. *This is too confusing. I can't keep up two conversations at the same time. Can we discuss this later?*

Tess sighed. *Whatever. I should probably go.*

"No!" Mackenzie yelled.

Cooper blinked again. "No, what?" *What is up with her today?*

Mackenzie shook her head. "No, I didn't realize what time it was. I have to get home."

"Already?" Cooper asked. "It's only five." *She's definitely acting weird. Maybe she has her period?*

Tess rolled her eyes. *I hate when guys blame weird moods on periods.*

Mackenzie sighed. *They're usually right, though. I'm a bitch when I get my period.*

You can be bitchy even when you don't have your period, Tess thought.

Mackenzie blinked. *True. I didn't know you thought so, though.*

Tess bit her lip. *I didn't mean that. You're not bitchy. Only a little bitchy. To everyone. Including me. Crap. I didn't mean that either. Yes I did. No I didn't. All right, I did. I just didn't want you to know I did.* "I'm starving," Tess said, desperately wanting to think of something besides Mackenzie's bitchiness. "I think I'm going to go back to Shake Shack and pick up a cheeseburger."

That's not going to help with the dress, Mackenzie thought.

Tess froze. *See? Bitchy.*

I really did not mean to think that out loud.

Tess shook her head. *You just meant to think it to yourself? Best friends aren't supposed to think you need to diet.*

You said you were having trouble fitting into the dress! Eating a cheeseburger isn't going to help! That's not a secret! And a best friend isn't supposed to call you a bitch either!

I called you bitchy, not a bitch!

We agree. Like cute and cutie, bitch and bitchy are not the same thing.

"I'm going to finish this unless you stop me," Cooper said. He took the top off the milk shake and downed what was left, giving himself a milk shake mustache.

"I'm off," Tess said. *This whole conversation is upsetting.* "I have a ton of homework," she lied.

"Me too," Mackenzie said quickly. *I'm a horrible person.*

No you're not, Tess thought.

Cooper sat up. "I'll walk you both back. Unless you want to watch the baseball game with me?"

"So much homework," they both said. *Boring*, they both thought. They looked at each other and smiled.

"Where's your team spirit?" Cooper asked.

"I have to finish an English essay," Mackenzie said.

"When's it due?" Cooper asked.

Mackenzie shrugged. "Yesterday."

Cooper laughed.

Tess knew Mackenzie wasn't kidding. Mackenzie handed in everything late. Even when Tess offered to help.

All three stood up. Mackenzie put her hand on her friend's arm. *Tess, I'm sorry. Let's both get cheeseburgers. My treat.*

I'm sorry I called you bitchy.

I am occasionally bitchy. But you're not fat.

Swear?

Yes! You're not skinny, but you're not fat.

The thought felt like a kick to Tess's stomach. But could she blame Mackenzie? She wasn't wrong.

I'm sorry! I didn't mean to think that! You're very pretty! If you went to the gym twice a week, you'd be gorgeous! Shit, shit, shit. I'm sorry! I can't help it!

Tess knew that Mackenzie was gorgeous. Everyone knew that Mackenzie was gorgeous. But Tess had always hoped that Mackenzie had thought Tess was gorgeous too. As is.

Mackenzie looked straight at Tess. *I'm sorry. Really. You're a much better friend than I am. I don't deserve you.*

"I said, where's your team spirit?" bellowed Cooper.

When did I ever have team spirit? Tess thought. *Go home, Cooper!*

Mackenzie giggled, which made Tess start giggling too.

Cooper took Mackenzie's hand and smiled. *Now she's in a good mood. Maybe she doesn't have her period after all.*

Which made Mackenzie and Tess laugh harder.

Chapter Seventeen
SWEET WHISPERS IN YOUR EAR

Mackenzie's phone rang at eleven-thirty. She was fast asleep. She'd made sure to go to bed and shut her eyes long before her parents even started looking sleepy.

"Hello?" she whispered.

"You're not going to believe what just happened," Cooper said.

"New York lost?" Mackenzie asked.

"No. They won. Three to two. Go Yankees. It was something weird. Really weird."

Mackenzie jackknifed in her bed. "What?" She prayed it was something innocuous. Like his TV wasn't working.

"Ashley woke up and came into my room and I walked her back to bed. She kept talking about which princess she should be for Halloween — Cinderella, Belle, or Aurora — but her mouth wasn't moving. It was like I was reading her thoughts. I'm losing it, huh?"

She didn't know what to say. She had to tell him. She had to tell him about the telepathy. She had to tell him about Bennett. She had to tell him everything and pray that he loved her enough to forgive her.

She couldn't tell him part one without part two, could she? No. Because if she told him part one, about the telepathy, he would want to know why she hadn't told him to begin with. He had called her as soon as he noticed something strange. He'd wonder why she hadn't called him.

He would hate that their whole homeroom knew about Bennett. Everyone but him.

He wouldn't be mad. He would be hurt.

She had to tell him. She opened her mouth to tell him.

Then she closed it.

She didn't want to be the one to hurt him. She didn't want to be the one to burst his the-world-is-wonderful bubble. She was thankful that thoughts could not be heard over the phone. She said, "Yup. You're losing it. But I'm impressed you know the names Belle and Aurora."

"Of course I do. I have a three-year-old sister. She's obsessed with them. Also with trick-or-treating." Mackenzie heard him take a short breath. "So what do you think about the fact that I hallucinated hearing my sister's thoughts? Do you think my neighbor was smoking pot in his bathroom again and the fumes were leaking into my room?"

She forced a laugh. "That guy is such a stoner."

"It's like I was in a science fiction novel or something."

"I can tell my mom," she said, trying to keep her voice light. "It sounds like a perfect TV show." Mackenzie's mom was an exec at NBC.

"Prime time?"

"Definitely."

"Will I get a producer credit?"

"Greedy, aren't you?"

"Did I wake you up?" he asked. "I know I said goodnight an hour ago."

"Yeah," she said. "But I don't mind. Are you in bed?"

"Not yet."

Since Cooper wasn't dwelling on his newfound power, Mackenzie assumed he didn't believe it had really happened. He didn't know the truth yet. He'd find out – but not tonight. "Wanna fall asleep on the phone?" she asked. They hadn't done that in a while. Since before the summer. This might be their last time. She felt a tightening in her chest.

" 'Kay," he said. "I just need to brush my teeth. Should I call you back in five?"

"No," she said, afraid of losing the connection. "Don't hang up. I don't mind hearing you get ready for bed."

"Then here we go," he said.

She heard the water run and then the sound of his electric toothbrush.

"ARGH ARGH ARGH," he said.

She laughed. "Am I supposed to understand that?"

"I ran out of toothpaste the other day and found an extra

tube under Ash's sink. It has Cinderella on it and is bubble gum flavored."

She laughed again. "Is it delicious?"

"Very. Frankly, I don't know why anyone uses anything else."

"I like my Crest Extra Whitening."

"And you do have a beautiful smile."

"Why, thank you." Would he still think she had a beautiful smile the next day?

She heard the sound of tinkling. "Are you peeing?" she asked.

"Why, yes I am. You said you didn't mind if I got ready on the phone."

"I didn't realize that included peeing."

"It's part of the bedtime routine."

She could still hear the tinkling sound. "That is the longest pee in the history of mankind," she said. Maybe it would go on forever. Then they'd never have to go to sleep, and they'd never have to wake up and face the rest of the world.

"Ashley and I had to have our glass of warm milk before bed. It's also part of the routine."

"What's the rest of your routine?" Mackenzie asked.

"Milk, potty, teeth brush, change into pajamas, book, bed. Well, that's Ashley's. Mine is just teeth, pee, take off pants and shirt, bed, mind read."

There was another opening. She took a deep breath. "Maybe you really can read minds."

He snorted. "Yeah, right. Hallucinating seems more likely

now that I've said it out loud. What's your bedtime routine? Wait. Let me guess. Change into sexy lingerie, teeth, pee, bed?"

Opening closed. She felt a whoosh of relief. "You forgot face wash. Don't you and your sister face wash?"

"No, we do not. I wash my face in the shower. She washes hers in the bath. We have good skin. We're lucky."

I'm lucky, Mackenzie thought sadly. *Lucky to have you.*

"Are you ready yet?" she asked.

"One sec. Turning off lights. Getting into bed. Finding comfy spot. Okay. Ready. Hi."

"Hi," she said. She felt a weight on her chest. This could be their last phone call. Unless he didn't really have telepathy. Maybe it was a fluke. Maybe he really was hallucinating. Maybe he hadn't really heard his sister.

Poor Mackenzie. Now she was the one hallucinating.

She knew she should tell him. She had to tell him.

She didn't tell him.

"Love you," she said instead.

"I love you too," he replied.

Mackenzie fell asleep with the phone in her hand.

When she woke up the next morning, the phone was dead.

It was late already – after eight.

She got out of bed, her heart thumping. This was the day. She knew this was the day. She charged her phone while she showered.

She had to talk to Cooper. Why hadn't she told him the

night before? She should have told him everything the night before.

We can't help but agree. She should have told him everything when she had the chance. Could have, should have, didn't.

Mackenzie's cell only had a few bars, but she called him anyway. It went straight to voice mail.

His phone had died too.

Shit, shit, shit.

She had to get to him before he got to homeroom. Where should she find him? Should she sprint to his apartment or find him at his locker?

She ran the five blocks to school. She'd meet him at his locker. Then she'd tell him. She'd tell him everything.

Chapter Eighteen
START SPREADING THE NEWS

Cooper was late. So late he didn't even have time to go to his locker. He went straight to homeroom.

It was warm for October anyway, so he didn't even have a jacket.

It was a beautiful day.

The Yankees had won.

He and Mackenzie had had one of those perfect nighttime conversations that they hadn't had since before the summer. The kind when you talked late into the night with someone and the whole world but the two of you disappeared. The night before, everyone but them had disappeared.

Sure, the thing with his sister had been a bit weird. He could have sworn she was talking to him but her lips weren't moving. It was like there was a recording of her playing from somewhere in the room.

Maybe it had been one of her dolls talking? A lot of them did weird things like clap and dance. Maybe they talked too.

His alarm had gone off that morning and he had hit the sleep button a million times. He'd looked briefly for his cell but hadn't been able to find it. It was probably dead somewhere under his duvet. No biggie. He'd thrown on a pair of cleanish-looking jeans, a gray shirt, and his Yankees hat, then brushed his teeth and grabbed an apple.

His mother and sister were already up by then. His dad was in Chicago for work. Or maybe it was Denver. He was always somewhere.

"Coop, Coop, Coop," his sister cheered. "Come sit next to me."

Cooper's sister had dimples and corkscrew curls, and a cute personality to match. She was always smiling and singing to herself. Just like her big brother.

"He's already late," his mom said. She worked, but only half days now. She dropped Ashley off at school just before nine, went to work, and picked her up at one.

"What's up, my favorite ladies?" Cooper sang. He kissed his mom on the cheek and then his sister on the forehead.

I'm fucking exhausted, he heard his mom say.

He looked back at her in surprise and laughed. "Mom, Ashley heard that."

"Sorry?" His mom poured herself a cup of coffee.

"She repeats everything," Cooper said.

"What are you talking about?" His mom took a long

sip, no milk, no sugar.

"I repeat everything," Ashley said.

"Never mind," Cooper said. "I gotta go. I'm late!"

"Have a good day!" his sister cheered. "Good day, good day, day, good day!"

"You guys, too," he said.

I'll try to stay awake, his mom said.

Huh? He turned back to her. "Mom, you okay?"

"Yes, honey, I'm fine." She gave him a smile. "See you later."

He knew he should probably run to school, but he was enjoying the sky. And the red and orange leaves on the trees in Washington Market Park. There was nothing better than fall in New York. It was so crisp and colorful and full of life.

Maybe he could take Ashley apple picking that weekend. Maybe Mackenzie would even want to come.

Everyone was chatting as they walked down the streets. Other students, parents, toddlers, nannies, babies in strollers. People were even singing to themselves. It was a merry, lively, louder-than-usual morning. He had a bit of a headache, but he was in too good a mood to let that bother him.

He stepped through the school doors just as the bell rang. He said hello to people as he walked through the hallways, and they said hello back. It was louder than it normally was, but he didn't really notice.

"What's up, 10B!" he cheered as he stepped into homeroom. He looked around for Mackenzie, but she wasn't there yet.

Everyone stared at him.

Does he have it yet?

I wonder why he doesn't have it.

"Have what?" Cooper asked.

He heard that!

He has it!

Cooper looked around the room, but no one was talking. It sounded like they were talking. But their mouths weren't moving. He was thoroughly confused.

He must have just gotten it.

He doesn't know what's going on.

Someone should tell him.

Where's Mackenzie?

He's not going to want to talk to Mackenzie in about five seconds.

Does she know he has it?

Cooper grabbed hold of a nearby desk. He felt woozy. Something strange was happening, but he wasn't sure what. Why was he hearing voices? He looked at Isaac and Nick and Pi, and they stared back at him.

It seemed to him like everyone was watching him.

He was right. We *were* all watching him.

"It's so quiet in here. Has anyone read any good books lately? I need a rec," Renée piped up from her desk.

Poor Renée.

Maybe she'll get it too. Cooper did.

Yeah, but Cooper got the vaccine, she didn't.

Right.

So now she's the only one?

Adam McCall didn't get it either.

He's not here again.

He's sick.

He's always sick.

Well, then, maybe he should have gotten the vaccine.

Voices were coming from everywhere. Who was talking? Where were they coming from? Where was Mackenzie? He didn't understand what was happening.

Olivia, who was sitting next to Renée, stood up. "Cooper, why don't you sit down?" *My turn to be kind. And brave.*

She held on to his arm and brought him to the back of the room, where he always sat. "Don't panic," she said.

"I don't understand," he said. "What's going on?"

Olivia looked right into his eyes. *We can't talk about it here in front of Renée. She doesn't know. But you can hear me, right? Nod if you can hear me.*

He nodded. He didn't know how he was hearing her when she wasn't talking, but he heard her.

We're not sure what happened or why, but we think there was something in the flu vaccine that is giving us telepathy. Nod if you got that. And don't talk. Just think.

He nodded. *But what does that mean?*

Nick's desk was the seat right in front of him. *We can hear each other's thoughts*, Nick thought.

Just each other's? Cooper asked.

No, Olivia told him. *Everyone's. We can hear everyone's thoughts.*

Voices, voices, everywhere.

It's so cool, another voice added. *You're going to love it.*

You can make it stop, too! If you close your eyes, you can't hear. If someone else closes their eyes, you can't hear them either.

It's like if you're listening to the radio in your car and you close the window. No one can hear it.

Cooper wasn't sure what he could hear. He was insanely overwhelmed. Thoughts were swirling around him, everywhere.

Who has this again? he wondered.

Us!

Who's "us"?

Just our homeroom.

Mackenzie too?

Yes, Mackenzie too.

Mackenzie can hear through walls.

That's bullshit.

It's true! I can a little bit too. If I'm pressed up against them.

Cooper's hands were fists. *But why didn't she tell me? Why didn't anyone tell me?*

The room was silent. "BJ, shut up," Nick barked.

Everyone who was sitting next to BJ gave him a look.

"I didn't hear him," Cooper said.

He's blocked by other people, Nick said. *You can hear the people around you best.*

"But what did he say?" Cooper asked. He looked at BJ, who had the desk in front of Nick.

He's going to find out anyway, BJ thought, leaning to one side.

Cooper heard him that time. "I'm going to find out what?"

Renée stood up and glared. "Have you guys all been taken over by aliens or something? Cooper, what are you talking about?"

Cooper shook his head. "I have no idea."

Ms Velasquez walked in and closed the door. "Morning, everyone."

We were all still watching Cooper. And BJ.

Cooper looked at Olivia for help. *What are they talking about?*

Don't think about it, don't think about it, don't think about it, Olivia repeated to herself. Then she closed her eyes.

He stood up and surveyed the room. *You mean there's more? Mind reading isn't all that's going on?* He looked at Nick. *Someone better tell me what's going on. C'mon. Tell me!*

Nick sighed. *Mackenzie hooked up with some tool this summer.*

Cooper gripped the sides of his desk. *No she didn't.*

Nick shrugged. *That's what everyone's saying. Sorry, man. We're all on your side.*

She's a bitch.

Slut.

Give her a break. She's sorry.

Cooper's head hurt. *Mackenzie wouldn't do that.*

She did it.

"Can everyone sit down, please?" Ms Velasquez asked. "Cooper, please take off your hat. No song for us today?"

Cooper didn't want to sit down. He didn't want to sing. He didn't want to take off his hat. He wanted to go home. He wanted it to be the day before. He wanted to be back in bed

with Mackenzie's voice on the phone. Quiet. Just them.

The door opened and Mackenzie was there. We all looked up at her. She looked back at Cooper.

She didn't need to hear it to know that he knew.

Chapter Nineteen
FLIRT

We felt terrible about what had happened to Cooper.

We loved Cooper.

But we couldn't spend too much energy thinking about him, because we all had our own stuff to deal with.

In Olivia's case: public speaking class.

"Olivia," Mr Roth barked, waving her over to his desk. "I'm expecting you to redo your speech next week. Thursday."

Argh. She had to try again? Hadn't once been enough? "If you want me to," she squeaked.

Poor girl. She's clearly terrified. But she has to keep trying. It's like falling off a bicycle. Or in my case, learning to tango. At first I was terrible. But now I'm the Monday night king of Calesita's. "Yes," he said sternly. "You must."

Aw. We hadn't realized Mr Roth was secretly a

softy. Or a dancer. Olé!

Renée had already taken a seat in front of Lazar but then gone to chat with a friend at the back of the room. Olivia took the empty seat next to her.

She could feel Lazar watching her as she sat down. She told herself to be bold. She looked back and gave him a smile.

"Hey," he said. *She looks great today.*

She did? She was wearing her regular jeans but had spent a few minutes putting on some blush, eyeliner, and pastel pink eye shadow that morning. "Hi," she said back, but then realized that her voice was really low, so she said it again but louder. "Hi."

Lazar straightened his shoulders. *Do it. Do it. Do it.*

Olivia wondered what he was going to do. Was it possible he wanted to ask her out?

He looked down at the floor. *What if she's busy?*

He was going to ask her out! He was!

She probably has plans. It's already Friday.

She wanted to shout at him that she had no plans. Ever. *Ask me out! Ask me out!* For a second she wished he could read minds. Or that she could implant her thoughts into someone else's head.

Unfortunately for Olivia, we didn't figure out how to do that until much, much later.

"Hey, all," Renée said. "Olivia, what was going on in homeroom today? Why did you tell Cooper not to panic?"

Olivia swiveled back to Renée. "I didn't say that," she lied.

"Yes you did. Didn't you? Class was seriously weird. Did

something happen between Cooper and Mackenzie? They both looked like they wanted to cry." *I wonder what happened,* thought Renée. *Maybe it's about her Sweet? I don't understand why I wasn't invited. It doesn't make any sense. Maybe my invitation got lost in the mail. It happens all the time. I should tell her I never got it.*

Olivia was embarrassed on her friend's behalf. But all she said was "I don't know what happened." She hadn't been invited either. She didn't really care – it wasn't like she and Mackenzie were friends. And anyway, parties gave her major anxiety. On the other hand, it would be fun to slow dance with Lazar.

Mr Roth banged his fist on his desk, signaling that they'd all better shut up.

I'll talk to her after class, Lazar thought.

Yes! Olivia thought. *You should!*

So at the end of class she waited.

I should ask her now, he thought. *Before she leaves.*

"Come on," Renée said, standing up.

"You go ahead," Olivia hurried to say.

"Are you talking to Mr Roth again?" Renée asked. "Do you need me to talk to him for you?" *I'm so his favorite.*

"Oh, um, I'm okay, thanks."

"I can wait with you."

"I'm good."

Renée looked from her to Lazar. *Maybe she wants to talk to Lazar. Should I stay and facilitate? She might need my help.*

I'm not going to ask in front of Renée, Lazar thought.

Renée put her hands on her hips. *Is it possible she wants to talk to him alone? That's so unlike her.*

It was unlike her. Or unlike the old her. The old her would have avoided him altogether because the anxiety of a date would have made her pick her fingers apart. ESP was making her brave. "Goodbye, Renée!" Olivia said more forcefully. "I'll meet up with you later." Olivia wasn't sure how else to get her friend to take the hint.

Renée smiled. *She does want to talk to him alone!* "Okay! See you later!" She sashayed out.

Finally.

Olivia waited.

Lazar cleared his throat. "Olivia?"

"Yes?" Olivia said. She turned around to face him. She tried to look surprised.

Oh no, she looks like she doesn't want to talk to me.

No! No! I do want to talk to you! She tried to make her face look unsurprised. Expecting.

She looks like she's in a hurry.

Ahhhh! What was wrong with her face?

Maybe I shouldn't ask her out. He stood up. "Have a good weekend."

No, no, no. That was not how this was supposed to go. "Um, you too," she said. But then she added, "Wait!"

He stopped.

She took a deep breath. "What are you doing this weekend?"

"Oh, I have tickets to see *Men of Paris* on Saturday. They're great seats. Fifth row." *She's probably busy.*

*I'm not busy! I'm wide open! I have no idea wh*at Men of Paris *is, but I like Lazar, I like men, and I like Paris – in theory, anyway, since I've never been – so what's not to enjoy?* "Is that a…play?"

"Uh, yeah. It's a play. It's Off Broadway. Jacob Irvinston directed?" *How could she not know that?* Time Out New York *gave it five stars!*

"Oh," she said. "I know it. *Time Out New York* gave it a five-star review, right? I really want to see it."

"You do?" He eyed her skeptically.

"Yes. I wish you had an extra ticket. I would love to go. This weekend. With you." She couldn't believe she'd just said that. But she had. The words had flown from her mouth.

He blinked. "You would?"

She nodded.

It's like she's reading my mind. "Well, I have an extra ticket. Would you like to come with me?"

"Yes!"

In truth, she was dying to know if it was a musical, because she really did love musicals and was kind of bored at non-musicals, but she decided not to ask. Either way, she was going to a play. With a guy. *Oh my goodness, I just asked a guy out.*

As they collected their books and walked out of class, Olivia felt a wee bit guilty that Lazar didn't know she was reading his mind. But not too guilty. It wasn't like she asked to be able to read his mind.

And she wasn't trying to trick him. She was trying to date him.

Chapter Twenty
THE TRUTH HURTS

Cooper avoided Mackenzie all morning.

At lunch she cornered him by his locker. "Please talk to me."

He shrugged. "What's there to say?"

"I'm sorry. It was a totally horrible thing to do."

No kidding, thought Jordana. She was filing her nails one locker over.

"Can we go somewhere private to talk?" Mackenzie asked. *Please don't shut me out.*

We had decided not to have a meeting at lunch that day. Pi and a few other 10Bers had an American history test and they wanted to prep then.

Instead, we were all meeting after school at Sadie's apartment on Duane Street.

He shook his head. "Sure, now you want to go somewhere private."

"Let's go to my place," she offered.

I can't be in your room. It would hurt too much.

His thought pierced her heart.

"Let's go to the gazebo."

The gazebo was in Washington Market Park, only a few blocks from school. They walked out together, him a few steps ahead, not looking back.

They were both quiet. All she kept thinking was *I'm sorry, I'm sorry, I'm sorry.* All he kept thinking was *I can't believe this is happening*, over and over again.

When they got to the gazebo, they sat beside each other, not speaking.

Finally he turned to her. "Did you sleep with him?"

"No," she said quickly. *No! I didn't!*

"What did you do, then?"

"I…" She wanted to lie, but she couldn't. He would know.

"So your first instinct is to lie to me? Great." *Does she always lie?*

"No! I don't! I just…I don't want to hurt you."

"But you did hook up with him," he said. *How could she do that?*

"Yes." *I'm sorry.*

"While we were together." *Why would she do that?*

"Yes." *I'm sorry.*

"And you didn't tell me." *Liar.*

"No." She felt tears well up in her eyes. Was their relationship really going to end? Just like that?

"Why?"

She shook her head. Was he asking why she had hooked up with Bennett or why she hadn't told him? She wasn't sure she knew the answer to number one, but she definitely knew the answer to number two. "I knew you'd break up with me, and I didn't want that to happen."

He sighed. "Too late now." *It's so over. I can't even look at you.*

Pain exploded in her chest. "Please, Cooper. We don't have to break up. It was months ago." She put her hand on his arm. "Please. Don't. We are so good together. I screwed up."

We agree. She really did screw up. Big-time. Huge-time.

"I would change it if I could," she babbled. "I would go back and change it." She would change everything. She didn't want to be the kind of girl who cheated on her boyfriend. She didn't want to be a bitch. She wanted to be sweet. She wanted to be worthy. She couldn't lose him. She just couldn't. She loved him. She really did. "I love you."

He shook his head. *I still love you.*

"See! You do! I know you do!"

"Stop it," he said, and closed his eyes. "I don't. I *loved* you."

The past tense crushed her.

He opened his eyes and said, "Mackenzie, we're done."

"No, don't say that! You can't say that." She wanted to push the words back into his mouth. His beautiful mouth, with the top lip slightly plumper than the bottom. They couldn't break up. She couldn't not see him. Her Sweet was in two weeks. Would he not even come?

He knocked the back of his head against the gazebo pole. *So this is about your Sweet?*

"No! I don't care about my Sweet. I just care about you being there with me."

The idea of having a huge party without him by her side – maybe without him even there – was beyond depressing. She'd cancel it if he wanted her to. She really didn't care about it. She didn't think she ever had.

I can't stay with her. I can't.

She put her hand on his knee. "Yes you can," she whispered. "You can."

He shook his head and closed his eyes again. "I don't want you reading my mind."

She hated being shut out. "Cooper, please. We can get over this. Together."

He kept his eyes closed. "Can you go? I want to be alone."

"I don't want you to be alone. I want us to be together."

"It's not up to you."

Okay, I'll go. She stood up. *But I love you.*

His eyes were still closed. He didn't hear.

Chapter Twenty-One
PEEKABOO

That afternoon was the American history test. Pi sat down in the front row, like she always did.

Courtney came in and sat down next to her – for the first time ever.

Two seconds later, Daniel came in and sat on the other side of her. When Dave came in next and sat directly behind her, Pi blew up.

"Seriously?" she asked. "None of you have ever sat next to me before."

Dave laughed. *Might as well use what we got.*

I studied for this! Pi felt indignant.

I studied too, Courtney thought. *But you're smarter than me.*

Pi glared at her. *Taking an Adderall doesn't count as studying.*

Courtney shook her head. *I'm out. And anyway, I'm too afraid to mix them with the telepathy. I don't want any more side effects. I could start speaking in tongues or something.*

Pi crossed her arms over her chest. *I'm not letting you cheat off me. It's not right.*

Um, excuse me, thought Dave, *didn't you cheat off Jon Matthews just yesterday?*

Pi wasn't sure what to say to that. It was true.

Dave continued: *If you're allowed to cheat, why aren't we?*

Rationally, Pi knew he had a point. But still. It didn't seem fair.

Mr Johnson burst into the room. "Morning, everyone!" he chirped. "I hope you're all ready. It's a tough one."

Good thing we have a secret weapon, Daniel thought.

Pi narrowed her eyes. *You do not have a secret weapon!*

As Mr Johnson passed out the papers, Pi tried to block hers with her arms. As if that would help.

She looked at number one: *Which state was one of the original American colonies? A. Ohio. B. Vermont. C. Rhode Island. D. Maine.* She marked C.

Way to go, cheered Dave.

Thanks, Pi, thought Courtney.

Pi was annoyed. Very annoyed. She read number two and then tried to close her eyes before the answer came to her. *D. Battle of Fort Charlotte!* But it was too late.

Thanks again, thought Courtney.

Pi couldn't work like this. Not with the chorus commenting on her every move.

Daniel coughed. *Actually, I think the answer might be C.*

Wasn't it the Battle of Cape Spartel?

She looked back down at her paper. *No. You're wrong.*

Pi wondered if maybe she should think about the wrong answers on purpose.

Daniel coughed again. *That's a real asshole thing to do.*

It totally is, thought Courtney. *What happened to us against them? Being a united front?*

Don't you want to help us? asked Dave. *We're all Espies here.*

Espies? Pi asked.

People with ESP? It has a nice ring to it.

It did have a nice ring to it. But still. *No,* Pi thought. *I want to get the highest grade in the class. If we all hand in the same thing, that isn't going to happen. Don't you think Mr Johnson will be suspicious?*

So I'll get some wrong, Dave thought. *There are twenty multiple-choice questions and two short essays. You normally get perfect, right?*

Pi straightened her shoulders. *Almost.*

Out of the corner of her eye she could see Daniel twirling his pencil between his fingers. *We'll dumb down our essays. Make some spelling mistakes. Use our own words. You'll still get the highest grade in the class. It'll be fine.*

Pi gave a small shake of her head. *It'll mess up the curve. Don't you normally fail?*

No!

Cs, then.

Daniel was now thumping his pencil against the desk. *I'll get two of the multiple choice wrong, then, 'kay? Happy?*

Pi sighed. Did she have a choice? What was she going to do, complain? *Fine. Copy if you want. But stop annoying me. I need to focus.*

With an audible sigh, she tried to block out our voices and looked back down at the test.

We cheered. *Thank you, Pi! We love you, Pi!*

As a token of our appreciation, she received *The Big Book of Sudoku* the next day.

Chapter Twenty-Two
WE KNOW EVERYTHING

It took us a while to file into Sadie's apartment.

She lived on the ninth floor, and there was only one elevator.

There were twenty-two of us.

It was one of those elevators that opened directly into the apartment. And it was a really nice apartment. Like *really* nice. It was the whole ninth floor, plus a wraparound outdoor terrace. Terraces in New York are rare but coveted. Sadie even had a barbecue on hers.

While we waited for everyone to come upstairs, we gossiped.

Because after three days of being Espies – yup, Dave's nickname stuck – we had accumulated a lot of secrets.

Emma Dassin, the senior who lived in Olivia's building, had missed her period and was going to get a pregnancy test after school. She hadn't told her boyfriend. She had told her best friend. Her best friend thought it was Emma's own fault for not using a condom. Meanwhile all the best friend had eaten all day was half an apple. She was seriously anorexic.

There was the freshman who dropped his retainer in a toilet in the second-floor school bathroom and then – wait for it – put said retainer straight back into his mouth.

The other freshman who still wet his bed. He had an appointment with a urologist on Wednesday.

The junior who had walked in on his stepmother taking a shower.

The sophomore who had stolen a glitter pen from the Duane Reade pharmacy on Greenwich. She stole something every day. Sometimes from Duane Reade, sometimes from Whole Foods. Her dad ran a hedge fund, so it definitely wasn't because she couldn't afford the stuff.

Hey, Rayna, do you ever shoplift? Six-finger discount!

So not funny.

A little funny.

We passed around secrets like trading cards until everyone arrived.

All twenty-two of us. Even a sad-looking Cooper. Even Mackenzie.

We sat in as much of a circle as we could. We were on couches, the carpet, chairs; some of us even sat on the glass coffee table, which was probably not a great idea. A buzz of comments – out loud and in our heads – flew around like we were in a real-life Twitter.

"We have an hour," Sadie said.

What happens then?

Keith coming over for some lovin'?

"My parents come home," Sadie said.

Was Sadie the first one of us to lose her virginity?

I think she was!

"Do you mind?" Sadie asked, turning red.

The first girl, maybe. Wasn't it BJ?

"Of course it was," BJ said. *I wish.*

I bet they have a lot of sex.

Who?

Keith and Sadie.

"I have a lot of sex. A lot," BJ says. *At least a little.*

Anojah fiddled with her glasses and thought, *But Sadie hates kissing Keith because he has bad breath.*

"Omigod!" Sadie yelled. "Can you guys shut up?"

Anojah blushed. "I'm sorry! I heard you thinking about it this morning!"

"Thinking about what?" Jordana asked, moving in closer. "Did I miss something?"

Sadie fidgeted in her chair. "Can we talk about something else, please? Anyone want a drink?"

"I'll take a beer," one of the twins said.

"Um, no," Sadie said. "My parents would shoot me. We have Vitaminwater."

"Do you have any chips?" Nick asked.

"Salt and vinegar."

"Perfect."

"I could use something sweet," Courtney said.

Levi pulled a paper bag out of his backpack. "I have gummy bears."

"No, I want chocolate." *Maybe we should send someone on a brownie run to Tribeca Treats.*

"So go, Courtney," Mars said. "You're the one who wants something sweet."

I don't want to miss anything.

"It's just down the street," Sadie said.

"I have a Twix," Tess said. "You can have that." She glanced at Mackenzie. *Since apparently I should be on a diet.*

Mackenzie gave her a look. *I never said that!*

Tess shrugged.

"I thought we made up," Mackenzie whispered.

"We did," Tess whispered back. "Don't worry about it." *I'm still pissed. I can't help it.*

Pi stood up. "Now that the all-important snack issue is settled, let's get down to business. How is everyone feeling?"

"I'm still getting headaches," Courtney said, chomping on the Twix.

Levi nodded. "Me too."

"Mine are getting better," said Courtney.

Anojah reached behind her glasses and rubbed her eyes. "My voices are really loud. And my head is still killing me."

Pi tilted her head to the side. "I wonder if it has something to do with your glasses."

"What do you mean?"

"Well, we can't hear other people's thoughts if our eyes are closed. And no one can hear us if our eyes are closed either.

So it seems transmission is coming through the eyes. Have you noticed a difference when you take your glasses off?"

Anojah pushed them on top of her head like sunglasses. "Someone think something."

Hey, babe!

How vile was the lasagna in the cafeteria today?

Not as vile as the chicken potpie.

Anojah blinked repeatedly. "That was so much better. Quieter. Much."

Pi smiled smugly. "There you go."

Anojah rubbed her eyes again. "But what am I supposed to do? Walk around blind?"

"Speaking of blind," Mars said, "have any of you tried hearing Keren Korb's thoughts? I couldn't. She was a dead zone."

Interesting, thought Pi.

Keren was the only vision-impaired kid at our school. She was a senior and had short bright pink hair and wore pitch-black sunglasses everywhere she went.

"I noticed that," Jordana said. "I guess her blindness is shutting us out."

Anojah waved her hand. "Can we get back to me and my blindness? Pi, what should I do?"

"I can't fix everything," Pi barked.

She's grumpy because of what happened in American history.

Heard about that.

Lucky.

I wish Pi were in my classes.

Pi put her hands on her hips. "Speaking about what happened in American history, we have to be extra careful. We don't want to get caught."

"We won't," Dave and Daniel said simultaneously.

Maybe they did have twin powers.

"I'd like to talk about something," Cooper announced.

We all swiveled to face him.

Is he mad at us for not telling him about Mackenzie?

He must be so embarrassed.

I'm surprised he even showed up.

From his seat on the couch, Cooper looked around the room. "I don't understand why we're keeping this a secret."

"Because we're not ready for other people to know about it yet," Pi said, sounding impatient.

"But it's wrong," Cooper continued. "We're lying."

Haven't we already had this discussion?

He's just pissed because of Mackenzie.

Mackenzie blushed.

"This isn't about Mackenzie," Cooper said forcibly.

"Although it does suck that every one of you knew and no one told me. I don't like living a lie."

"Well, you're too late," Pi said. "We voted and that's what we decided to do."

Cooper got up. "I think I'm going home."

Way to be a baby.

"I'm just tired, okay? It's been a long day." *I want to watch the game. I don't want to be here.*

We nodded. We understood.

Pi crossed her arms. "You're not going to say anything, right?"

"I won't say anything. I just need to think." *In private*, he added. He pressed the button to the elevator and it opened immediately.

Mackenzie got in with him. The door closed.

He's never going to forgive her. Would you?

No way.

I don't know. If it was really a mistake, maybe.

People do make mistakes.

And she's pretty hot.

"Is there anything else we need to discuss?" Sadie asked, glancing at the clock on the DVR. "It's getting late." *Keith is going to be here in fifteen minutes.*

"Do we really need to have so many of these topsecret meetings?" Jordana asked. "My friends think I'm ditching them."

I'm surprised more people haven't been suspicious.

What are they going to suspect?

That we're up to something.

We are up to something.

"We don't have to meet this weekend," Pi said.

Daniel stretched his arms above his head until they popped. "Good. What's everyone up to?"

"Olivia has a date," BJ said.

Olivia blushed. *How does he know?*

Seriously? You've been thinking about it all day.

"I can't believe he's taking you to *Boys of Paris*," Courtney said. "Snore."

"It's *Men of Paris*, and it got a rave in the *Times*," Sadie said.

Tess stood up and glanced at Olivia. *I'm not a play person.*

Me neither, Olivia admitted. *But I'm excited for the night.*

Good luck, Tess thought. *Can't wait to hear how it goes.*

Thanks. Good luck with Teddy. I hope he realizes how awesome you are.

The intercom near the elevator door buzzed.

Sadie pressed a button. "Hello?" she said.

"Keith is here," said the doorman. "Should I send him up?"

Shoot! He's early! "Oh! Tell him I'll come down in a minute?"

"He says he needs to use your bathroom."

Classy.

Sadie pressed the intercom button. "I guess...send him up?"

We felt the vibration of the elevator moving back up the floors.

"Won't he wonder why we're all here?" Jordana asked.

Sadie pulled on a split end. "I told him I was taking a nap. He's gonna wonder why I lied."

"Is there another way out?" Tess asked.

Her eyes darted around the room. "There's a fire exit out the back of the apartment. Do you guys mind taking the stairs?"

"Of course not!" Olivia said.

I mind! We're nine floors up!

Come on, let's move.

Sadie opened the door to the stairwell for us and we silently followed Pi and filed out.

The staircase was grungy. Since there was only one tenant

per floor, every landing seemed to be used for recyclables and storing oversized suitcases. We snaked down and around the staircase.

"I'm getting dizzy," Courtney complained.

"It's too dark in here," Jordana said.

"*Shhh!*" Pi ordered.

This is so creepy.

Do you think we're the first people to ever use this staircase?

Hopefully. It's in case of fire.

Or sneaking your homeroom out to hide your secret ESP meeting.

Tess tripped over a tricycle and into Olivia, who fell against Mars.

"Sorry!" Tess whispered.

This could turn into a really unfortunate game of dominoes.

Don't even joke.

Couldn't Sadie have just told him we have a homeroom project?

That would have been easier.

They're so hooking up right now.

Then I hope he brought breath mints.

A few of us giggled. Pi pushed the stairwell door open and led us into the light.

Chapter Twenty-Three
THE BIG NIGHT OUT

Lazar picked Olivia up at six. They were going to get pizza first and then take the subway to the theater district.

Olivia was a nervous mess. She had never been on a real date before. She had never even been on a pretend date.

She'd spent the day trying to distract herself with television. She'd started with repeats of *House*, *Grey's Anatomy*, and *Mystery Diagnosis*, but then somehow ended up watching hours of the OWN network. She admired Oprah but found the woman a mystery. How did anyone have so much confidence that they could tell other people how to live their *best* life? How did she not doubt herself? How could she stand the entire world watching and gossiping about her every move? How did she know what to wear on TV?

Wait a sec. Did Oprah have ESP?

Olivia turned off the TV and went through her closet, eventually settling on a light green dress and black heels. She definitely looked like she was going on a date. She hoped she wouldn't trip walking down the subway stairs.

She doubted Oprah worried about tripping down subway stairs.

We doubt Oprah ever takes the subway.

"He goes to school with you, right?" Olivia's mom asked.

"Yes, Mom."

I don't understand who this Lazar character is. She's never mentioned him before. What if he tries something? Should I call his parents?

A half hour later there was a buzz from downstairs. "I'm coming down!" she called into the intercom.

Her mom popped up beside her. "No way. Tell him to come up."

Olivia pressed the intercom again. "Actually, can you come up?"

"Sure."

"You're not wearing those heels, are you?" her mom asked.

Olivia twirled her foot. "I am. What's wrong with them?"

"Aren't you taking the subway? That's a lot of walking. And a lot of stairs. I don't want you to trip."

"I won't trip, Mom. I know how to walk." It was one thing when Olivia worried about it, another thing when her mom did.

As she waited, her heart beat hard, too hard, in her chest.

Was she having a heart attack? Could teenagers have heart attacks? She wasn't sure. She wished she had time to Google it. Maybe she should make an appointment with a cardiologist.

She quickly opened the door when Lazar knocked.

"Hi," he said. *Oh, so pretty.*

She blushed. "Hi."

"This is my mom," Olivia said, motioning behind her.

He nodded. "Hello, Mrs Byrne. Nice to meet you."

"You too," Olivia's mother said. *At least he's polite. Short, though.*

"Mom!" Olivia yelled.

Startled, Olivia's mom asked, "What?"

Oops. "Nothing. Um, we're going."

"Okay, have fun. Be careful on the subway. Especially in those heels."

They all looked down at her shoes.

I wish she was wearing flats, Lazar thought. *I don't want her to be taller than me.*

Oh. Olivia hadn't thought of that. "You know what?" she said. "Mom, you're probably right. Be right back." She ran to her room, changed into her boots, and ran back, praying that her mom hadn't said anything too embarrassing.

Better, Lazar thought, and opened her front door.

Hey! The date was going to be easier than she'd thought. All she had to do was listen.

He better not try anything too advanced for her, thought her mom. *He looks like a nice boy. But it's always the ones who look*

clean-cut who end up being the sociopaths. Hmm. She's not wearing a sweater? Does she want to get pneumonia? "Olivia, don't forget to take a—"

"Goodbye, Mom," Olivia sang. She blew her mom a kiss and closed the door behind her.

Chapter Twenty-Four
IT ALL SUCKS

Cooper was depressed.

It was Saturday night and he was lying on his bed, watching the baseball game on the TV above his desk.

The Yankees were losing 3–0. It was the bottom of the ninth. Jeter was at bat with two outs. He needed a home run.

If they lost this game, the Yankees were out of the series.

Strike one!

Damn.

"Come on!" he yelled. "Do it!"

Cooper's iPhone rang. It was Mackenzie. Again.

He didn't answer. He didn't want to talk to her. He didn't know what he wanted.

No, that wasn't true. He wanted his world to go back to normal.

He wished Mackenzie had never cheated on him. He wished she had never lied to him. He wished he had never gotten a stupid flu shot. He wished the Yankees were winning.

But it wasn't just Mackenzie who was a liar.

Everyone was full of shit.

The day before, he had arrived home after the meeting feeling numb. When he'd unlocked the door, he'd felt a flood of relief at the sight of his mom and sister.

"It's good to see you," he said.

But Ashley didn't even look up from the TV. She was watching *Cinderella II*. She was thinking, *Funny mousies funny mousies*.

"I'm home," he said. "Do I get a hug?"

Ashley motioned to him to be quiet. "Shhh!"

His mother looked up briefly from her laptop. "Hi, honey," she said, and then returned to the screen. *I can't believe how high this bill is. How am I going to pay for it?*

When he strolled over to the kitchen to get a snack, his mom slammed her laptop shut. *Not for his eyes.*

Huh? What bill couldn't he see? Was his mother keeping secrets from him, too?

She looked up and smiled. "How was your day?" *What should I make for dinner? Can we order in Japanese again or does that make me a bad mom?*

"Fine," Cooper said. "Do you want to order Japanese?" Might as well make life easy for her. He grabbed a cheese stick from the fridge. "Is Dad back tonight?"

"He has to stay over the weekend," his mom said.

"Again? How come?"

His mom traced her fingers along the table. "His project," she said, but then she thought, *His floozy*.

Cooper almost choked on his cheese stick. "His what?"

"Project," his mom repeated. "Some big deal he's working on in Chicago."

Cooper hadn't known what to do with himself. He kept standing up and sitting down, standing up and sitting down. His mother had definitely thought *floozy*. Was his father having an affair? No. It couldn't be. There was no way he was finding out that both his girlfriend and his father were having affairs. That was too insane.

He couldn't think about it. If he didn't think about it, it wasn't happening.

Except he couldn't *stop* thinking about it.

He told his mother he wasn't feeling well, and had spent most of the past twenty-four hours in bed.

His life was falling apart. His girlfriend had cheated on him. His father seemed to be cheating on his mother. And his mother...well, she was hiding something.

Everyone was a liar. Except Ashley. And Gerald. But turtles couldn't talk. All Cooper could hear from him was a low squeaking sound.

At least Ashley had told it like it was. She didn't want to be interrupted during her movie, so she'd told him to be quiet.

But she was only three.

Strike two!

One day he'd woken up happy and the next day everything

was fake. Everything was a lie. He was surrounded by liars.

And he was no better. He was pretending he couldn't hear his mom. He was a fake, just like them.

Cooper watched Jeter get ready for the next pitch. His phone buzzed.

    Please forgive me. I love you.

Strike three!

The Yankees' season was over.

Most of us were bummed by the news, but Cooper was the only one to throw his phone at the TV.

Chapter Twenty-Five
BRAVO

The date went perfectly. How could it not? Olivia didn't have to worry about screwing up. Every concern Lazar had, Olivia heard.

If she doesn't walk faster, we're going to be late.

Olivia walked faster.

She has a pretty smile.

Olivia smiled more.

What did she just say? She speaks so softly.

Olivia spoke up.

I wonder what her favorite band is. I hope she likes Delivery.

"I just love Delivery! They're the best."

"Did you like the new Thomas Allen movie?" *It was so amateur. I hope she didn't like it.*

"No way," Olivia said. "It was so amateur."

We know — we can't believe she used the word *amateur* either.

But Lazar nodded, his eyes wide. *It's like she's taking the words right out of my mouth!*

Which she was.

He thought she was amazing — which she knew because, well, she could hear what he was thinking.

His thoughts weren't the only ones she could hear.

The man sitting in the row in front of her at the show: *Did I gain weight or are these seats getting smaller?*

The tourist beside her: *Sleeping with my psychiatrist may have been a bad idea.*

One of the actors onstage: *Maybe I should try out for* American Idol.

The twelve-year-old sitting diagonally from her: *This is so boring. Is it almost intermission?*

Olivia agreed. Five stars or not, *Men of Paris* was excruciatingly boring. She couldn't help wondering if the five had been out of ten.

Listening to the people around her was much more entertaining.

Lazar especially. *That guy is too tall to play Pierre. He's a giant. Couldn't they have found someone shorter? He can barely stand up straight. He's like the Leaning Tower of Pisa.*

And then even more interesting: *I want to kiss her.*

Oh! Yay!

But did he mean now? Or did he mean he wanted to kiss her later? Like when he was walking her home?

He wasn't going to kiss her right now, was he? When they were still at the show? That seemed like a strange thing to do.

Olivia peered at the other members of the audience. No one else was kissing. It was an Off Broadway theater, after all. That seemed disrespectful. Worse than chewing gum, and she knew she wasn't supposed to do that. She had thrown hers in the garbage bin outside.

By the way, we agree: making out at an off Broadway show is unacceptable. Even if you're in the back row.

But Olivia wanted Lazar to kiss her. She was pretty sure. He was nice. Or nice-ish. At the very least, he was the first guy to show interest in her.

Maybe I'll take her hand first, Lazar thought.

That sounded like a decent idea. She realized her hands were in her lap, so she tried to subtly lift the one next to him and rest it on the arm of her seat.

He took the bait and grabbed her hand. His fingers were colder than she had expected. And long. They were nice fingers. She liked the way they held hers.

His hand intertwined with hers – the way he moved his thumb in circles on her palm every now and then – made the boring second half of the play go by much faster. They were walking back from the subway stop. They were holding hands again. Hers aligned perfectly with his, since she was wearing flats.

I'm going to do it, he thought.

Olivia cheered silently.

I should wait until we're outside her building.

Good idea, she thought.

Or maybe I should do it now.

She swallowed. Hard. *Now?*

Right now. Olivia's heart raced in a way that could not have been healthy.

They were on the corner of Church and Murray waiting for the light. *Now! I'm going to do it now!*

Seriously? she wondered. There was no one else waiting at the light with them, but there were definitely people on the streets. She wasn't really a make-out-in-the-streets kind of girl. She wondered if she should stop him. Did she want him to kiss her? Did that mean they were a couple? Did she even like him? Did she want her first kiss to take place while waiting for the light?

He put his arm around her shoulder and pulled her toward him. *Here I go!* He closed his eyes and his lips pressed against hers.

She closed her eyes too.

Suddenly they were kissing. His lips were soft and sweet.

They stayed there for a few minutes until he pulled away and she opened her eyes.

She did it! She had her first kiss! And it was nice!

He was smiling. *That was good*, he thought. *Although I wish she'd use more tongue. Two stars*.

Olivia felt herself turn red. Two stars? She was a bad kisser! She finally had her first kiss at the age of fifteen and she wasn't even good at it! She'd failed! Was she going to get another chance? Or was that it? She tried to hear his thoughts, but all he was thinking about was the best way to get to her house. *Around the block or cut through the park?*

Oblivious to her panic, Lazar took her hand and led her across the street. They didn't say anything until they got to her door.

"I had a really great time," he said.

"Me too," Olivia responded.

I guess I should kiss her again, he thought.

Yes! Olivia thought. *You should!* But she wondered, what did that mean to use more tongue? She knew what it meant, technically, but how was she going to do it? Just stick it in there?

He leaned in toward her and then closed his eyes as his lips pressed against hers. She opened her mouth and gently let her tongue trail into his mouth and meet his. His tongue was sandpapery, but she swirled it back and forth. Was that right? She opened her eyes in case his eyes were open and then she'd be able to hear, get a progress report maybe, but no, his eyes were closed.

But then they opened.

Why are her eyes open?

Oops. She closed them.

A few minutes later, when her tongue started to get tired, she pulled away and opened her eyes.

That was awesome, he thought. *Five stars*.

Now, that's a rave review.

Chapter Twenty-Six
NEW PLAN

Pi called an Espies meeting for Monday before school. She texted us all the night before, instructing us to meet her in the chess room at seven-thirty. It was early. Very early.

But we all showed up – all except Cooper.

We weren't surprised. He was never on time, and anyway, he kind of hated us right then.

"He doesn't hate you," Mackenzie said, sipping a Starbucks pumpkin spice latte. "He hates me."

We nodded.

"He just needs some alone time," Nick explained.

Pi paced the room. "Okay, people, I want to chat about our booth at the carnival on Saturday. We have a bit of a problem."

Once a year, BHS students put on a carnival in the gym to

raise money for the library. Every homeroom had a booth. The entire neighborhood came by to support the school.

"What?" we asked.

We're supposed to do the fortune-telling booth.

We laughed. We couldn't help it.

"So what?" Courtney asked.

"We can't tell people their fortunes," Pi said. "We'd give ourselves away."

Nick shook his head. "Am I missing something? Did we develop clairvoyance when I wasn't paying attention?"

"No, we didn't," Pi said. "At least, I didn't. No one else did, did they?"

We shook our heads.

Pi looked at Mackenzie suspiciously. *I bet she can't really hear through walls.*

I can.

Whatever, thought Pi. "The fortune-telling booth is still too risky. Reading minds. Telling fortunes. Too close. We should do something else."

She gives us a few test answers and she thinks she's in charge?

"I *am* in charge," Pi said huffily. "I don't see anyone else taking the leadership role. And we need a leader. If someone else thinks he or she could do a better job, please feel free to step up."

We looked at each other and shrugged.

"We should have a nail-polish booth," Jordana chirped.

"11C is doing nail polish," Sadie said. "Keith's homeroom. They're also doing back massages."

Good thing they're not doing a kissing booth. Keith would scare everyone away.

Shut up!

BJ groaned. "A kissing booth! Why didn't we think of that?"

"What about bobbing for apples?" asked Anojah, squinting at the rest of us. She was always squinting without her glasses.

Brinn mumbled something.

"What?" Pi barked. "Can you just think, please? I can't understand you when you talk."

Brinn rolled her eyes. *Whatever you say, Polly. Do you know that your real name means "bitter"?*

I'd prefer you call me Pi, thank you very much.

"Who gave you that nickname, anyway?" Levi asked.

"My fourth-grade teacher," Pi said, but first she thought, *I gave it to myself.*

We all smirked.

"What I was trying to say," Brinn said super-slowly, "is that we already got approval for the fortune-telling booth. It's too late to change."

"Argh," Pi groaned. "Well, then, our fortune-teller needs to be someone who can't read minds. So we don't give ourselves away."

We all thought it at the same time – Renée. There wasn't much choice.

"So we're settled?" Pi asked. "Someone tell Renée."

I guess that's me, Olivia thought.

Pi banged her fists on the table. "Good."

Were her eyes always purple?

Pi turned around. "What was that?"

Dave stared more closely at Pi. "Your eyes are looking purplish."

She motioned to her blue shirt. "They're blue. Maybe it's the shirt."

Daniel looked at her a little more closely. "No, I don't think that's it."

"You know," Levi said, "I've noticed that my eyes are getting a little purple too."

Maybe you've been eating too many purple jelly beans, Courtney thought.

"Does anyone have a mirror?" Pi asked. "Jordana?"

What, I'm so vain that I must have a mirror?

Yes, thought Pi, *exactly*.

My money's on Jordana having a mirror.

What's the big deal? Anojah wondered. *I have a mirror.*

But does Jordana?

I really want to say I don't, Jordana thought. *But I do.* She pulled out a silver Kate Spade compact mirror and handed it to Pi. *Just in case I ever have spinach in my teeth.*

If she'd had spinach in her teeth, we would have noticed. And she would have heard us noticing it. But anyway.

Pi studied her reflection. *My eyes are vaguely purple. How did I not notice that?*

You clearly don't spend enough time in front of a mirror, Jordana thought, and a bunch of us giggled.

"Some of us have more important things to worry about

than how we look," Pi snapped. "Is this happening to anyone else?"

We checked out each other's eyes. Tess's were still brown. So were Olivia's. She stopped at Mackenzie's. "Yours have a purplish glint."

"They do?"

"The purple eyes must have something to do with the ESP," Tess said.

Pi snorted. *Thank you, Captain Obvious.*

I knew we were turning into vampires, thought Edward.

"We are not turning into vampires!" Jordana screamed.

"We'll see," said Edward.

"I don't want my eyes to turn purple," Rayna whined. "I like my eyes the way they are."

Purple eyes are seriously weird.

Creepy.

I think it's cool.

Better than the boring brown color I have now.

I was thinking of getting colored contacts, but this is free.

Pi needed time to think about it. "I guess there's nothing we can do but—"

Keep an eye on it? Olivia thought.

BJ and Tess laughed.

Pi gave a tight smile. Having purple eyes was highly unusual. It would certainly set them apart from everyone else.

Mackenzie's next thought said it all: *It means we won't be able to keep this a secret.*

Chapter Twenty-Seven
SLAMMING DOORS

Mackenzie was not having a good week. No one was talking to her, at least not out loud.

It had started on the way to homeroom on Monday. Tess was wearing her favorite jeans and a new pair of boots.

No tall boots with those jeans, thought Mackenzie. *Why can't she see it makes her thighs look huge?*

It was involuntary. Mackenzie would never have said such a mean thing in a million years. But Tess snapped, "You really do think I'm fat, don't you? You think it all the time."

"I do not!"

"You think I should lose ten pounds! You know I'm a perfectly healthy weight, but you think this kind of crap all the time. It's like you're siding with my mom."

"Your mom is crazy. I'm not siding with her," Mackenzie

said, but she couldn't help thinking, *Eight pounds, maybe.*

"You are such a liar," Tess said, shaking her head. *At least my mom tells me what she thinks, ugly as it is.*

Instead of sitting with Mackenzie in homeroom, Tess went to the front of the class and sat next to Olivia, of all people. When had she ever spoken to Olivia?

At least Olivia doesn't think I'm a pig, Tess barked.

"I don't think you're a pig!" Mackenzie yelled. Of course we all heard.

And then weighed in.

No pun intended.

She's definitely not a pig. I think she's pretty.

She's okay.

She could lose five pounds.

But what if it was five pounds of boobs? That would be a travesty. She has good boobs.

You could lose five pounds.

Me? I'm a growing boy.

Leave her alone.

Can't you judge a girl on her brains? Or her sense of humor?

Do you want her to become anorexic?

Then she'd definitely have no boobs. Or ass. And her ass looks hot in those jeans. She's bootylicious.

You are an animal, BJ.

I'm a healthy, normal, growing boy.

Was that a double entendre?

Double what? Think English.

Gross.

Tess was horrified.

Mackenzie sat through homeroom by herself.

Now everyone thought she was a horrible slut *and* a bad friend.

And Mackenzie couldn't help agreeing. She was a terrible friend. She was a terrible girlfriend. She missed Cooper so much she ached. She never thought she'd miss him this much. How could she have cheated on him? How could she have been so careless about their relationship? Why hadn't she told him – fought for him – when she'd had the chance?

When she got back her English essay during sixth period, she was reminded that not only was she a bad friend and girlfriend, she was dumb too.

C-.

With the note: *More effort, please! And hand it in on time!*

The only thing Mackenzie was good at was being pretty.

By the end of Tuesday, Mackenzie was exhausted and miserable. Plus it was raining.

She staggered back to her apartment and into her elevator. She pressed the *close* button so she wouldn't get stuck listening to the French thoughts of one of the many Parisians who lived in her building. Nothing was more annoying than listening to someone rant in a language she couldn't understand.

The door started to close when a knapsack swung inside.

A gray knapsack.

She knew that knapsack.

It was Bennett's. Which meant—

"Hey," he said, his voice husky.

"Hey," she replied, heart instantly in her throat.

He raised an eyebrow. "Haven't seen you in a while."

She tried to sound cool. "I've been around."

"We must keep missing each other."

She felt him checking her out. *She's looking hot. Maybe she'll come over?*

"So what are you up to today?" he asked.

Was he serious? Did he really think she was going to run into his arms after what had happened the past summer? "Not hanging out with you," she snapped.

He laughed. "Am I that obvious?" He reached over and tugged at her sleeve. The touch made her jump.

"Yes?" she said.

She seems mad at me.

Was she? It wasn't his fault that she'd hooked up with him. It wasn't his fault she was weak. He never made her any promises. He was single. He'd never done anything wrong, really.

The elevator stopped on her floor. "Wait – it missed you. Aren't you on fifteen?"

He glanced at the panel. "Oops. Forgot to press it. I was distracted by your beauty."

"What a charmer," she said, stepping out.

I'm not giving up yet. This time I won't blow her off for Victoria. I'm done being played by that crazy chick. He held the elevator open with his hand. "What are you up to tonight?"

Victoria? Who was Victoria? Had he blown her off because he'd been pining after some girl? "Test tomorrow," she said eventually. It wasn't a lie. She did have a physics test. Too bad Pi wasn't in her class. But Jon Matthews was. She refused to sit next to him, though.

She was done with cheating.

We must admit, we were impressed with her ethical resolve. Even if it was too little, too late.

Bennett held the elevator door open. "And this weekend?"

"Carnival," she said.

The elevator banged against his hand and then reopened. "Right. And next weekend is your Sweet. I got your invite."

Oh God. She'd forgotten that she'd sent him an invite. She'd done it weeks earlier, before everything had happened.

Why had she sent him one? It wasn't long after they'd hooked up. She'd already started to feel guilty, so why had she invited him? Had she wanted him to show up? What had she thought would happen?

Mackenzie felt like crying. And now her Sweet was next week. The event planner was coming over later to go over details. Her sister and brother were coming in. Her mom had booked them a million spa appointments that weekend.

They'd bought her a Louis Vuitton clutch too. The one she'd wanted forever, with the classic design. They hadn't given it to her yet – it was a surprise – but it wasn't like they could keep secrets from her. Not anymore.

She didn't deserve it. She didn't deserve any of it. She was a horrible person.

The Sweet was supposed to be the best night of her life, or at least one of the best nights of her life, and it was all a hot mess. Cooper wasn't talking to her. Her best friend wasn't talking to her. What if no one showed up? She looked back at Bennett. Would he show up? "Are you coming?"

"Maybe," he said. *Depends what I have going on.*

He was such a jerk.

"I'll see you when I see you," she said, and walked away.

I think I—

The elevator door closed and she had to wonder how he'd finished that sentence.

She wondered if it was *I think I made the biggest mistake of my life.*

Then they'd be thinking the same thing. In his case, letting her go. In her case, letting him in.

Chapter Twenty-Eight
PARTY ON

Olivia was having a great week. Really great. Possibly the best week ever.

Before she'd gotten ESP, she'd spent a lot of time and energy worrying about what people thought of her, but to her relief, she was discovering that most people – well, the non-telepathic kind, anyway – didn't think about her at all. Plus she had a boyfriend. A cute boyfriend! They weren't soul mates just yet, but Olivia knew that a true connection took time to build. Time and telepathy.

For the first time in a long time, Olivia also had a ton of friends. Tess had sat next to her in homeroom. Even Jordana and Courtney said hi to her between classes.

It might have been rough for some of us, but for Olivia, having the Espies was the besties.

Ha, ha.

Of course, Olivia didn't ditch Renée. She would never do something like that. At least there were no surprises with Renée – her internal thoughts weren't that different from what she said aloud. Both were overconfident and self-deluded.

"I'm going to be an amazing fortune-teller," she'd bragged to Olivia on Wednesday morning in home-room. She stood up and tossed her striped red-and-orange scarf over her shoulder. *I think I'll have a real gift for it.*

Renée really thought she knew what was best. At all times.

Renée knew what Olivia should order for lunch in the cafeteria. "Do not get the chicken burger. The cook never cooks the chicken properly." *One day the whole school is going to get food poisoning.*

Renée knew what colors looked best on Olivia. "You should buy more green. It's very flattering on you." *I'm lucky I can pull off almost every color.*

And of course, Renée had known that Olivia would make a good couple with Lazar. In that case, Olivia was grateful for her friend's overbearing know-it-all-ness.

Life was good.

Not for everyone, though.

Olivia watched a sad-looking Mackenzie enter the class by herself.

Slut.

Bad friend.

Cheater.

Olivia couldn't help feeling bad for her.

Mackenzie sighed. *Even Olivia feels sorry for me now.*

Olivia blushed.

"Sorry," Mackenzie said. "I didn't mean it the way it sounded."

Renée looked back and forth between them. *Did she just say something to us?*

"Don't worry about it," Olivia said to Mackenzie.

Why's Olivia being nice? thought Renée. *She wasn't even invited to the Sweet! Neither of us were! Unless my invitation really was lost in the mail.*

Mackenzie flushed. *Oh, man. Olivia, did I not invite you?*

Well, we've never actually spoken before, Olivia thought.

Mackenzie nodded. *Right. There's that. Do you want to come?*

Too much pressure. Too much anxiety-producing activity. Small talk! Dancing! Walking in heels! Food between her teeth!

Oh come on, Mackenzie begged. *Please?*

Olivia hesitated. *Can I bring my boyfriend?*

Mackenzie's mouth opened in surprise. *You have a boyfriend?*

Olivia heard a tsk from a few seats over. *Mackenzie is so self-absorbed*, Courtney thought. *How does she not know who Olivia's boyfriend is? She's been thinking about that kiss all week!*

This time both Olivia and Mackenzie blushed.

I've had a lot going on, Mackenzie thought.

Jordana shook her head. *What, and the rest of us haven't?*

It's Darren Lazar, Olivia thought. She wasn't sure if Mackenzie would know who he was.

Oh! He's the short guy, right? Of course you can bring him. I like Lazar.

Courtney tsked again. *Not enough to have invited him in the first place.*

Mackenzie spun around. "Can you mind your own business?" *I'm kinda wishing I hadn't invited Courtney.*

Courtney gave her the finger. *If I hadn't just bought a dress, I wouldn't come.*

Levi banged his fist against his desk. *Catfight! Catfight! Catfight!*

Renée twisted her scarf around her wrist, obviously confused.

Mackenzie looked pained. *Am I going to have to drop out of school? Or at least cancel the party? It's going to be a disaster.*

"It won't be," Olivia said.

"What are you talking about?" Renée asked. "Did I miss something?"

"Do you guys want to come to my Sweet?" Mackenzie asked Olivia and Renée. "I'm sorry I didn't invite you earlier, but you can bring a date if you want, and it would be really fun if you came."

Renée smiled. *Hurray!* "Fantastic. We'd love to come!"

Olivia wasn't exactly sure she wanted to go, but the look on Mackenzie's face broke her heart. "Lazar and I will be there. Sounds fun."

"I'll bring you a printed invitation tomorrow. In fact, I should make sure everyone in 10B gets an invitation." *I don't need anyone hating me any more than they do already.*

Levi smirked. *Doing us all a favor, are you?*

Mackenzie rolled her eyes. *Give it up, Levi. You know you're coming.*

Cooper walked in, late as usual. He sat in an empty seat near the wall, diagonally from Olivia.

Olivia turned around and gave him a sad smile. *What you're going through sucks.*

You don't know the half of it, Cooper thought.

I do, Olivia thought, feeling her face go pale. *I think everyone knows.*

It's not just about Mackenzie.

I know, Olivia thought. *Your dad too, right?* She did not want to be the one to tell him, but someone had to.

"I think I'll wear my orange dress," Renée mused.

Cooper froze. *Everyone knows about my dad?*

Olivia nodded. *If you're thinking about it, so are we.*

Cooper put his head down on the desk. "Terrific," he said aloud.

Renée smiled at Cooper, completely oblivious. "Thanks, Cooper!"

"You're welcome," he said. *I have no idea what she's talking about.*

Don't worry about it, Olivia thought, but he had closed his eyes and she knew he couldn't hear.

Chapter Twenty-Nine
NOWHERE TO HIDE

When Cooper walked into economics, he looked for a spot that was Espie-free. He tried to avoid us whenever he could. He couldn't stand our sympathy.

He saw an empty seat in the back corner and took it. The only one of us who was nearby was one of the twins, Dave – but he was a few seats away. Hopefully there would be enough interference between them that Dave wouldn't be able to hear him.

The sympathy was everywhere. In the halls. In the cafeteria. In class. All from us Espies. We knew everything.

By the time Cooper's dad had come home on Sunday night from Chicago, Cooper had convinced himself that the truth couldn't be as bad as he feared. His mom was probably imagining the affair. She was tired and lonely and that was it.

But then they sat down for dinner. "How's everything going?" his dad had asked, his voice booming across the table.

The four of them were sitting at the kitchen table, eating takeout Haru.

"Everything's okay," Cooper lied. He certainly wasn't going to tell his parents about the ESP thing. He wasn't ready to talk about Mackenzie either. He wasn't sure what to say. He couldn't tell them that she'd cheated on him. His parents were good friends with her parents. His whole family was going to her Sweet.

Halfway through the meal, Cooper's dad took out his iPhone and scrolled through his messages.

Ooh, from Mandy, he thought.

Cooper's spine straightened.

I miss you already, his dad read. *When can I see you again?* His dad took a break for some tuna tartar and then typed back, *Wednesday at one. I'll book a room at the Westin. Wear what I bought you at La Perla.*

Cooper almost vomited his edamame.

"Can you put the phone away?" his mom asked. *He couldn't be reading his whore's emails right at the dinner table, could he?*

He could, Cooper wanted to say. *He is.* But Cooper kept quiet.

"It's family time, family time, family time," Ashley sang. "Then can I watch *Cinderella*?"

"I don't think so," his mom said. "It's late."

I'll ask Daddy. He never says no. "Daddy, can I watch *Cinderella* after dinner?"

"Sure, honey," he said absentmindedly.

"Yay! I love you so much!"

Way to undermine my authority, Cooper's mom thought. *This is exactly what I told Newton about.*

Newton? Who was Newton? Was his mom having an affair too?

"Can I have cookies after dinner?" Ashley asked.

His mom sighed. *I can't believe I thought having Ashley would save our marriage.* "One," she said.

"Two!" *Twooooooooo.*

Save their marriage? Before the ESP Cooper hadn't realized their marriage was in trouble.

We think Cooper must have been walking around with serious blinders on. Even Mackenzie suspected their marriage was in trouble. Cooper's mom and dad always looked vaguely pained to be in the same room.

That night after his parents went to bed, Cooper looked through his mom's Internet history and found out who Newton was.

One of Manhattan's top divorce lawyers.

His father was having an affair and his mother was suing for divorce.

He didn't tell his mom that he knew about the affair. He didn't tell his dad about the divorce attorney.

And he didn't tell either of them that he and Mackenzie had broken up.

Because he missed her. He knew it was stupid. He missed her voice. He missed her smell. He'd had a crush on her since his cubby was next to hers in nursery school. One day she'd taken his hand and taught him how to do a somersault. He'd begged his parents to make playdates with her after school.

Did he have to lose her? He didn't have a say in his family's falling apart, but he did have a say in what happened between him and Mackenzie.

Cooper, don't take her back, man, Cooper heard, the thought immediately pulling him back to the present. He jumped in his chair and looked around the classroom. Dave was looking at him and shaking his head. *Don't be pathetic*.

Not only did we all have sympathy, but we listened to everything. And we all had opinions.

Cooper moved to an empty seat in the front of the room.

Chapter Thirty
THE FUTURE IS BRIGHT

Olivia took a long sip of water. The carnival hadn't even started yet and she was already exhausted.

"Is everyone ready?" Pi barked.

The doors to the gym opened in ten minutes. We all congregated at our Madame Tribeca fortune-teller booth. Adam McCall had an ear infection.

And Renée was sick.

"Sick?" Pi sounded incredulous. "She's sick? She can't be sick!"

Olivia nodded. "She texted me that she was barfing all night." Olivia had resisted the urge to tell her friend that maybe she should have gotten the flu shot after all. Instead, she texted back:

> You didn't eat the chicken burgers,
> did you?

"We need someone to take over." Pi looked around our group. "Olivia, you're up."

Olivia's breath caught in her chest. No way. She did not want to play fortune-teller. *I can't talk to that many strangers!*

"That is a ridiculous reason," Pi said. "You'll be fine. Go get dressed."

"Why me?" Olivia wondered.

"You're the least likely to say something stupid."

"But I don't know what to do," Olivia said, her heart racing. "Or say."

"I'll help you."

"Okay, I guess. I'll do it."

"Good," Pi said. "Go inside the tent and put on your costume. The doors are about to open."

The booth looked amazing. The twins had brought an old tent they used for camping and we covered it with dark purple scarves. A desk outside the tent was covered with a dark purple tablecloth. It was lined with lava lamps. We were going to charge five tickets per reading.

At Pi's insistence, we divided the inside of the tent in two. In the main part, we taped up glow-in-the-dark stars, set up a small table, covered it with a midnight-blue scarf, and placed a crystal ball in the center. It wasn't really a crystal ball – it was actually one of Levi's old fishbowls. In the second part, we dragged over a chair for Pi to sit on while she helped Olivia.

After climbing inside the tent, Olivia put on the black robe that made up her costume and sat down, adjusting to make herself comfortable.

Pi came in a minute later and set herself up in the second compartment. Her goal was for no one to see her but for her to be able to help Olivia. First she unzipped the small mesh window above her head so she could continue to hear the words and thoughts of people outside. No reason for her to miss out on anything important that happened outside the tent. Then she set up the partition, which was an old brown sheet she duct-taped to the tent's ceiling. She'd cut the sheet down the middle and made sure it was a bit open so she and Olivia could hear each other and the people in the booth. *I know Mackenzie said she could hear her parents through a wall, but I'm not sure I believe her*, Pi thought.

She can't lie, Olivia said. *We'd know.*

So I guess you can hear me?

Yes.

Good. I'm here if you need me. "We're all set!" she hollered. "You can send in our first customer!"

The first person inside was a girl, probably around eleven years old. She was extremely pretty. She had shiny brown hair and bright eyes. Her mom, also gorgeous, bent to enter the tent behind her.

"Hello," the mom said, sitting down. "My daughter wants her fortune told. This isn't going to be scary, is it?"

"No," Olivia said quickly. Her hands were shaking.

Say hello, Pi told her.

"Hello," Olivia said.

Use a spookier voice.

They don't want me to be scary!

There's no way you're going to be scary. Just do it.

"Helllllo," Olivia said again. Instead of deep and mysterious, she sounded like a monkey.

The girl laughed. "Hi."

The mom gave Olivia a fake smile. "So tell us what you see. I hope it's good." There was a warning to the mom's voice. *She'd better be nice! I don't want her freaking my kid out!*

Olivia pretended to look deep into the crystal ball. *Now what?*

Just make stuff up, Pi said.

Olivia contemplated the ethics of what she was doing. What would happen when the things she promised didn't come true? Wouldn't they feel ripped off?

Olivia, Pi thought. *They paid five tickets, each worth a dollar. They don't really think you're psychic.*

Oh. Right. "Is there anything specific you want to know?" Olivia asked.

The mom nodded. "Is my daughter going to be a famous pianist one day?"

Olivia didn't need to be a fortune-teller to know what the right answer for that question was. "Yes," she said. "Absolutely. It will take many years of toil and hardship, but she will one day become a concert pianist!"

Uch, the daughter moaned. *I hate the piano.*

Good, the mom thought. *Maybe she'll stop being lazy and start practicing again.*

Olivia heard a small snort from Pi.

Olivia's cheeks heated up and she looked back down at the crystal ball. "Hmm, maybe I misread it."

The girl leaned toward the table. "You did?"

"Yeah. It's, um, not piano."

"It's not?" she asked hopefully.

What are you doing? Pi wondered.

"What is it?" the girl asked.

"It's…um…it's…" Olivia rubbed her temples. She was about to close her eyes to look like she was channeling something, but realized that wouldn't help matters. She was listening hard and hoping that the girl would give something away.

The girl leaned even closer. *Is it the drums? Am I going to be a famous drummer?*

Aha!

"I definitely see music," Olivia said. "But it doesn't appear to be the piano. It's louder. It has more of a rhythm."

The girl's eyes widened.

"Yes!" Olivia cheered. "It's the drums. You're going to be a successful drummer…in a band! I think I see Grammys in your future!"

Olivia, didn't I tell you not to use the telepathy to tell their fortunes? Pi asked. Were you not listening?

This is ridiculous, the mom thought. "How did you know she wants to take drum lessons?" She turned to her daughter. "Did you tell her?"

You see! Pi yelled. *She's getting suspicious!*

"I didn't say anything, Mom! You were with me the whole time!"

Olivia gave a slight shake of her head. *Suspicious that I'm really psychic! Not that our homeroom has telepathy!*

We agree with Olivia. Pi was being majorly paranoid.

The mom glared at Olivia. "Did she put you up to this? Do you two know each other?"

Olivia tried to look as innocent as possible. She shook her head. "We don't. I swear."

"Mom, the fortune-teller is amazing!" the girl exclaimed. "She really knows her stuff! Mom, ask a question about you!"

Ella was probably drumming her fingers against the table or something. That's how the girl knew.

"So what about you?" Olivia asked the mother. "What would you like to know about your future?"

The woman just stared at her, her mind blank. Not helpful.

Olivia glanced at the woman's ring finger to see if she was still married.

She was.

Hmm. "Any questions about the future at all?"

Blank.

"About your career?"

"I don't work," the mom said.

She doesn't do anything, Ella thought. *Except bug me.*

Olivia pretended to look into the crystal ball.

Olivia looked up. "Even if you don't have a paying job, I can see you're going to be very busy this fall."

No kidding, the mom thought. *The Seaport committee is going to be the death of me. I don't know why I agreed to help with the Winter Wonderland. Geena totally roped me in. What a time suck. And I'm not even her co-chair.*

Aha! "It's something to do with seasons," Olivia began. "Summer…no, spring…no! Winter."

I know I'm supposed to be mad at you, Pi said, *but this is funny.*

The mom wasn't even listening. Instead she was thinking, *I really need to fix my highlights. And get more Botox. Maybe I should just get a face-lift. Why not? Geena did it. She can afford it, though. Her husband is about to make a fortune with all his Tableau stock. I don't know why Dave wouldn't buy any. Insider trading-shmading.*

Interesting, Pi thought. *What stock did she say?*

Tableau or something? thought Olivia. *Why?*

I want to write it down! I guess now that I'm sitting here I might as well be taking notes. Where's my notebook?

"Anything else?" the girl prompted Olivia.

It had been a full minute since Olivia had spoken. She had to find something, stat. She peered into the crystal ball. She squinted to make it look more authentic. "I also see some major work being done in your future. Renovations, maybe?"

The mom's jaw dropped.

Pi snorted.

"You're doing something to your apartment? No. I don't think it's the apartment. I see your face featured very clearly."

The mom touched the side of her face. *Holy moly. How did she know?* "Would you mind telling me, then, if, well, if the renovations look good? Are they worth doing?" *I do not want to end up with one of those stretched-out faces like Romy Brohman.*

Olivia gazed back into the ball. "Honestly, you regret them. You wish you had left everything the way it was."

The mom's head bobbed up and down. "Thank you."

Olivia smiled. "Any time."

"You have really unusual eyes," she continued. "Are they purple?"

"They're colored contacts," Olivia said quickly. She'd noticed they started turning that morning.

I should buy some, the mom thought. *Cheaper than a face-lift.*

Maybe, Olivia thought. *But they're certainly not without baggage.*

She wondered who was next.

Chapter Thirty-One
WORKING THE BOOTH

Tess was collecting tickets at the fortune-telling booth with
BJ when Teddy popped up in line.

His homeroom was hosting a bake sale and he smelled like
chocolate. *There she is. She can't get away now.*

Tess pretended to be very busy counting change.

"Have you been avoiding me?" he demanded.

"What? Me? No."

BJ coughed. *Bullshit.*

Tess glared at him. *None of your business.*

You can't be mad at him for liking someone else, BJ thought.
He made change for a freshman and then looked pointedly at
Tess.

Um, Tess was pretty sure she could. She couldn't stand
listening to his lovesick thoughts. Sadie was so gorgeous. Sadie

was so hot. Look at Sadie's awesome perky breasts. Yes, that was what he'd been thinking about during chemistry the day before. Tess had almost puked into her beaker.

You have better tits than Sadie, BJ thought.

She flushed.

Teddy leaned toward her over the table. "I've left you a million messages."

"I know, I'm sorry. I've been really busy." She shot a look at BJ. *Please don't use the word tits.*

I didn't say it. I thought it. Anyway, it's true. What would you rather me call them?

How about breasts?

Point taken. You have better breasts than Sadie.

Tess looked down at her chest. *I do?*

Yup. I've felt hers – and yours – so I know.

Oh, shut up.

Don't tell me you've forgotten about our time together in the closet? Do you still have that sexy white bra?

Tess's cheeks heated up. *Eighth grade. Seven minutes in heaven. Unsexy white bra. I haven't forgotten. So when did you feel up Sadie?*

He smiled smugly. *Eighth grade. And it was sexy. On you, any bra would be sexy.*

You had a very busy eighth grade, she fired back.

Teddy placed a chocolate cupcake in front of Tess. "For you."

"Aw, thanks," she said. *Too bad cupcakes aren't on my diet.*

Oh, please, BJ thought. *You do not need to be on a diet.*

Don't listen to Mackenzie.

Maybe if I was as skinny as Sadie, Teddy would like me.

If you were as skinny as Sadie, you would have no boobs. And I like your booty too.

"I'll get out of your way," Teddy said, "but do you want to get coffee after the carnival?"

"Oh, um, I don't think I can today. I have plans."

His face fell. "Oh, that's too bad. Tomorrow?"

"Maybe. I'll call you if I can, okay?" she said.

He nodded. "Okay. Have fun. See you soon." He waved and walked away.

"What plans?" BJ asked.

"I'm going to try a SoulCycle class," she said.

"Is that the spin class?"

"Yup."

"Ouch," he said. "Sounds painful."

She nodded. *Maybe if I lose five pounds, Teddy will like me.* She eyed the cupcake. The moist-looking cupcake. It was calling to her. *Eat me. Eat me! I am delicious!*

BJ laughed. "Just eat it. A guy doesn't fall for a girl because of five pounds."

Tess shrugged. "Ten pounds, then. Can you eat it? It's taunting me."

"Let's share it," he said, picking it up and offering her half.

She couldn't resist. "But tell me this. If it's not the five – maybe ten – pounds, then what is it? I know he thinks I'm cute, I know he likes spending time with me. According to you I have better—" *Breasts.* "So what is it?"

"Have you ever heard him thinking about your weight?" BJ asked.

"No," Tess admitted.

"Then it's not that."

"But maybe he just doesn't see me as sexy because of the extra weight. It's subconscious."

BJ shrugged. "Maybe he's just never thought of you that way. Maybe he'd change his mind if he knew how you felt."

"That's what Mackenzie said. When we were talking to each other."

"You won't know unless you try. Throw down the gauntlet. What do you have to lose?"

My dignity?

BJ laughed.

Tess flushed. *Like you know anything about dignity.*

"Ouch!" He held his hand to his heart. "I'm not the enemy here."

He was right. He wasn't the enemy. Teddy was the enemy. Sadie was the enemy.

"Just cover yourself in chocolate frosting and show up naked at his apartment."

Tess smacked him on the arm as a group of junior guys approached their booth.

All you think about is sex, Tess thought.

All anyone thinks about is sex. All the guy in front of us thinks about is sex, and he's thinking about sex with his stepmom. Now, that's wrong.

Tess laughed. *Not everyone thinks about sex all the time. I don't.*

Oh, please. Don't tell me you don't think about Teddy when you're alone at night.

Tess's jaw dropped. She did not! *Only sometimes! Omigod.*

BJ smirked.

She turned her back to him. *Agh! Stop listening to me!*

You're a good kisser. You should just kiss Teddy. See what happens.

I am?

He nodded. *One of the best kissers I've been with.*

Her heart swelled. She couldn't help it. *Swear?*

Swear. His eyes brightened. *Do you know what you should do?*

What?

Kiss me right now.

Are you crazy?

Think about it. How jealous would Teddy be if you kissed me?

Not jealous at all. He doesn't like me.

He just doesn't think of you in that way. But if he sees you making out with me, he'll start.

You just want to make out with me. Or any other girl with a beating heart.

He shook his head. *Not any other. But you, yes. It's true.*

This whole conversation was ridiculous. Tess saw BJ's point, but she was not just going to make out with him.

You've probably made out with a hundred girls since eighth grade.

Forty-two.

She rolled her eyes. *Yeah, right.*

It's the truth.

Liar.

You can't lie in your thoughts.

You can if you want to.

He smiled. *Point is, we kiss. Teddy realizes he loves you. I win, you win.*

Tess stood on her tiptoes and looked around the room. She spotted Teddy near the balloon booth. "I'll think about it," she said. Incidentally, BJ wasn't altogether repulsive.

Why, thank you. BJ made a small bow. "I'm at your service should you need me."

"Hey, guys," Mackenzie said. "I'm up. Who am I replacing?"

Here she is, BJ thought. *The scarlet* M.

"I heard that," Mackenzie said.

"I know you did. I'm sure you've heard worse. And scarlet is my favorite color. I still think you're hot."

Case in point, Tess thought at BJ. *You'd hook up with anyone.*

Mackenzie looked hurt. *Hello? I thought we were friends.*

We are friends. But I'm still mad at you about the weight thing.

I'm sorry! I'm a moron! That isn't news!

You're not a moron. But I'm not ready to forgive you yet. She didn't look at Mackenzie while she thought it. "You can stay with BJ."

Mackenzie peered into the tent. "Who's inside?"

"Olivia and Pi."

"I think Levi is switching with me at some point," BJ said.

"Oh, joy."

"Is Cooper here?" BJ asked.

"I don't think he showed," Mackenzie said.

"Can't really blame the guy," Tess said.

We couldn't blame him one bit.

Spotting Mackenzie across the gym made Cooper even more miserable. She was talking to BJ as though everything were fine with the world.

Everything was not fine. Everything was a mess.

"Can I get my face painted now?" Ashley asked him, pulling his hand.

"Yup." He hadn't wanted to come, but he knew Ashley would enjoy it, and he wanted to make his sister as happy as possible before her world imploded.

He took her to get her face painted by two senior girls. She sat on a bar stool trying to stay perfectly still as the girls painted cat whiskers on her cheeks. After this Cooper planned to take her to hair braiding.

Truth was, Cooper was enjoying spending the day with her. She was the only person he wanted to be around, since she was the only person who didn't lie. She said what she thought. She thought what she said.

Hey, Cooper, in defense of us and the rest of the world, Ashley was only three. She hadn't fully learned how to filter her thoughts yet.

Cooper just couldn't stand being around liars.

He knew he was sounding a little Holden Caulfield-esque

calling everyone a phony, but he really did think everyone was a phony.

The senior taking his twenty bucks to get in the door? A phony. "Hey, man, how are you, good to see you. Glad you could come." *What's that kid's name again?*

The junior who sold him and Ashley cookies: "I hope you like them! I made them myself!" *I bought them at Crumbs, but no one will know.*

Cooper knew. We all knew.

Oops, thought the girl painting on a whisker. *Messed that up a little. Oh well.*

"You messed it up," Cooper blurted out. "Please fix it."

"What's wrong?" Ashley asked him. "Is it pretty?"

"Very pretty," Cooper said, "once she fixes her mistake." He glared at the girl and said, "Make it perfect, will you?"

The girl blinked. And then blinked again. *He wants me to make a perfect cat face?*

Yes. That was exactly what he wanted. A perfect cat face. Was that too much to ask? Did everything in life have to be messed up? He took a deep breath. He was overdoing it. It wasn't the face painter's fault that everyone was a liar. It wasn't her fault that Mackenzie had cheated and lied to him. It wasn't her fault that his parents' marriage was falling apart. He sighed. "Just make it as good as you can, okay?"

The girl nodded. She took a paper towel and wiped away a small line.

"That's better," Cooper said. Honestly, he couldn't tell the difference. But he appreciated the effort.

Cooper looked back across the room. Mackenzie was collecting money from a junior who was going into the Madame Tribeca tent.

She'd left a message on his phone that morning, asking if he was going. "I miss you," she'd said. "I heard what's happening with your parents. I'm here if you want to talk."

He missed her too. A lot.

He wondered if they should get back together. Sure, on the surface, breaking up seemed like the right thing to do. Girl cheated on guy, guy broke up with girl.

But now he saw that things weren't so black-and-white. Everyone lied. Everyone cheated. Everyone was full of it. At least Mackenzie knew she'd made a mistake. At least her lies were on the table. And he really could use someone to talk to.

Ashley jumped off her chair. "Meow!" *Meow meow meow meow!*

Someone who wasn't three.

"Can my brother go next?" Ashley asked the senior. "Can you paint Spider-Man on him? Or Superman? Or maybe Wonder Woman?"

"Sure," the senior said. "Is your brother a super-hero?"

"He is," she said proudly.

"I can do Spider-Man," the girl said.

"Go for it," Cooper said, and sat down in his chair. Cooper did not feel like a superhero. But what the hell.

Chapter Thirty-Two

I HEAR YOU

Pi stretched her arms above her head.

Olivia had done a fantastic job at the fortune-teller booth.
And thanks to Olivia, Pi had never felt more powerful. In her
little hot hands, she now had everyone's secrets.

She'd gotten the goods on everything that was happening at
our school. Crushes, college dreams, whatever. And it wasn't
just the kids' secrets she knew. Grown-ups too. Bankers.
Lawyers. Psychologists. Mostly parents who'd come with their
kids, but still, the parents in Tribeca ran a lot of New York. She
now knew about drug addictions, affairs, abortions, investment-
banking deals, and more.

What could she do with all that information? How could
she use it? Without, you know, resorting to bribery? Before
she'd become an Espie, she'd barely bothered to learn people's

I told you, Olivia responded. *My boyfriend.*

The voice continued: *Maybe that's why no one has come forward. Or maybe they're keeping the ability a secret.*

The hairs on the back of Pi's neck stood up. She didn't recognize the voice. It sounded older. It definitely wasn't one of us. *Is she talking about us?* Pi needed to see who it was. Immediately.

Pi tried to lift the side of the tent, but it was fastened down. She pressed her face against the small mesh window but couldn't see anyone. Pi had to find out whom those thoughts belonged to before the woman got away.

She dropped her notebook into her knapsack – no way was she misplacing that – slid the bag over her shoulder, broke through the sheet, pushed her way past Olivia and a surprised-looking Lazar, and stormed out of the tent. The light made her blink. It was busy out there. Really busy. But whose voice had she heard?

She circled the tent, listening for voices and thoughts of the people swarming around her.

Why does my son always smell like BO? I know he showers.

Can anyone tell how high I am? Cupcakes! Want cupcakes! More cupcakes!

I think I have lice.

Pi circled around and around the tent, trying to find the woman. Who was it? She'd definitely sounded like she knew about the vaccines. How did she know? Had someone spilled the beans? No. Pi would know if one of us had. We wouldn't be able to keep it from her.

names. Now she alone knew everything.

Olivia too.

But Olivia was hardly a threat.

Although Pi knew secrets would spread to the r[e]
pretty fast. Not for the first time she wished she were
one with telepathy.

"Hi!" she heard Olivia say now.

"Hey there, pretty," the guy said.

Pi opened her eyes. *Who is that?*

It's Lazar, Olivia thought.

Who?

My boyfriend.

"So what does my future hold?" he asked. "Does i[t]
going to another play tonight?"

"Should it?" Olivia asked.

"I think it should. Because I got tickets to *Night Wal[k]*

Another play? Olivia thought. *Can't we go out for dinn[er]*

What's wrong with plays? Pi wondered.

Nothing. But the ones he gets tickets to are so boring. Mu[sicals I can]
get, but these are the talking-talking-talking-about-nothing[?]
And the seats are really uncomfortable.

Then tell him you don't want to go, Pi thought.

I can't do that!

"So?" Lazar asked. "Does it? *Time Out New York* g[ave it]
five stars!"

Maybe no one at Bloomberg was affected, a new voice th[ought]
from the other side of the tent window. A woman's voice.

Pi's back stiffened. *Who was that?*

This was not part of her plan. Not at all. She was in charge here. She would have to figure out who else knew what, and soon.

Chapter Thirty-Three
ONE MORE CHANCE

After an exhausting day at the carnival, Mackenzie wobbled home.

Just as she was unlocking her front door, she saw a text from Cooper.

```
Meet me at that bench in Battery
Park at 9 tonight if you want to
talk.
```

Yes. Yes, yes, yes, she did want to talk. She wanted to do more than talk. She wanted to wrap her arms around his neck and kiss him until he forgave her.

Now here she was, sitting on their bench at Battery Park in front of the water, still waiting for him. He was going to show, wasn't he?

A few minutes passed before she heard his footsteps behind her. She also heard, *She's here*.

"Of course I'm here. I miss you," she said, and turned around. She couldn't help laughing. He had red paint all over his face.

I miss you. "I'm Spider-Man," he said instead.

"I figured. Listen, Cooper, I am so, so, so sorry about what—"

In the moonlight she saw that tears were dripping down his cheeks through the paint.

She hadn't seen him cry since...well, since second grade when he fell off the seesaw and had to get stitches. It broke her heart right in half. "Oh God, Cooper, I can't believe I did that to you." Her voice cracked. *I'm sorry, I'm sorry, I'm sorry.*

"It's not just you," he said slowly. He wiped the tears away with his sleeve, staining it red. *It's my parents. Everyone. The Yankees.*

"The Yankees?"

He hiccup-laughed. "Yeah." He stood beside her and stared at the water ahead. "It's everything. Do you want to walk?" he asked.

"Sure." As she stood up, she took his hand. He didn't stop her.

As they walked south, following the railing, he told her about his mother and father and about how everywhere he went he heard lies, and it was killing him.

"I'm sorry you had to learn such crap stuff about your parents," she said.

"Have you heard things about yours, too?"

"I heard them having sex," she said. "But that was it."

At least they're having sex with each other. "Lucky," he said.

"It didn't feel lucky at the time," she replied. From where they were standing, they had a perfect view of the Statue of Liberty.

"Let's run away," she said.

"To where?"

"Anywhere but here." She took a step closer to him. "Do you think you can ever forgive me?"

He looked deep into her eyes. *I don't know.*

You don't?

No. But I'm willing to try.

"You are?" she asked. Her throat choked up.

"Yeah."

She gulped, and the next thing she knew, tears were streaming down her cheeks too. She threw her arms around him. "I just love you so much." *I'll never take you for granted again.*

"I love you too," he said. "I just hate everyone else right now."

"Me too," she said. "Especially the other Espies."

"I know."

"And they listen to everything. With their beady little purple eyes. Let's ignore them. What do we need them for?"

"They're hard to ignore."

"We can do it," she said, lacing her fingers through his. "We can make our own little bubble. It'll be us against them."

"Us against the world," he said.

She leaned toward him. *Can I kiss you?*

You're going to get red face paint all over you.

I would love to get red face paint all over me.

I hope I don't regret this, he thought, and then closed his eyes and kissed her.

Chapter Thirty-Four
STILL GOING

We were so over it the next week.

We were used to our parents pretending to listen to us while they were really thinking about meetings, or what to make for dinner, or in Mackenzie's case, her dad's new Viagra prescription.

And we were getting increasingly annoyed with each other.

Homeroom was the worst. Renée and Adam – on the rare occasion he showed up – were suddenly the most popular people in the class. They were a wall of interference. Otherwise our thoughts spread through the room like germs after a sneeze.

Still taking those Addies, Courtney?... Levi, why don't you go to a dentist?... Are Cooper and Mackenzie back together?...

Clearly – they're sitting in a corner together... What about Bennett?...I guess Cooper forgave her... I wouldn't have forgiven her... Good thing I'm not you... Cooper, ignore them... I'm trying to, but they're so loud... Hey, Olivia, how's Lazar?... Did you have to go see another boring-ass play?... They're not that boring... Don't lie. You were just thinking about how boring they are... Is something up with BJ and Tess?... Why?... She's ignoring him... Tess is in love with Teddy... But Teddy likes Sadie... Is he using mouthwash yet, Sadie?... It was only one time! He had souvlaki for lunch... Hey, Tess, are you fantasizing about me yet?

Tess froze. Then she slammed her eyes shut. She might have spent a few minutes reminiscing about her seven minutes in heaven. But BJ could never, ever know.

He knew. We all knew.

We all closed our eyes for as much time as we could, but Ms Velasquez was starting to get frustrated.

"Are you guys not getting enough sleep? Next person I find napping in class is getting detention!"

Just what we wanted – more time in school. At least in our apartments no one could hear us.

Except for the twins. We all felt bad for the twins, who shared a room.

The rest of our classes weren't as bad. Every hour of every day was a barrage of other people's thoughts – their secrets, their lies, their stupidities – but we didn't have to worry about being heard ourselves. We put multiple non-Espies between us as buffers. We needed space.

Except at test time. Then we all parked ourselves next to the smartest person in the room. Pi hated it. She hated it more when Jon was in our class and we all crowded around him. Jordana and Courtney even got into a telepathic fight about who sat next to him. Chair grabbing was involved. Jon thought it was because of his new cologne.

Lunchtime was awkward too. Cooper and Mackenzie left school for lunch. Olivia sat with Lazar. Tess avoided BJ. And Sadie. And Teddy, obviously, although he wasn't one of us. She started to skip lunch entirely and spend the time studying in the library. She only lost two pounds, but she aced all her work that week. She didn't even need to sit next to the smartest person in the class.

And Pi? Well, Pi was watching us. Pi was definitely watching everyone. Pi was always watching. She was watching the redheaded fake nurse who was wandering our hallways.

Olivia had been the first to see her. She'd gone to the nurse's room on Wednesday with a headache. She'd ignored it until eleven but then realized she needed some Advil or she'd have to go home. So she'd made her way down to Nurse Carmichael's office and knocked on her door.

"Hi there!" the woman said in a voice that was way too cheerful. "What can I help you with?" *Does she have it?*

Olivia wondered what this woman thought she had. Was something contagious going around school? The flu? Meningitis? "Where's Ms Carmichael?"

"She's on vacation," the woman said. *Permanent vacation. Screwup.* "I'm Suzanna."

What screwup? What Olivia wanted to know was what

Carmichael had screwed up, but of course she couldn't ask.

"Come on in," Suzanna coaxed.

Olivia did not want to get exposed to meningitis. "Oh, never mind. I thought I had a headache, but I feel fine now. It's gone."

She's panicking. Maybe she has it. The woman took hold of her arm. "Are you sure? Why don't you come in for a few minutes? And chat?"

Olivia was officially freaked out. "I should get to class."

"Wait. What's your name? What grade are you in? You have very unusual eyes," the woman said. *That's the color!*

Oh. She knew about the ESP. How did she know about the ESP? Olivia took a step back.

Olivia's mom had noticed her eyes the night before. "Are your eyes itchy? They look strange. Do you have pinkeye?" she'd asked.

"No," Olivia had answered, avoiding her gaze. "I'm just wearing purple eyeliner."

In theory, purple eyes were cool. But in reality, it was supremely creepy when one day our eyes were brown and the next they had a lilac tint. It was like we were turning into vampires or something.

"We're becoming undead!" Edward had cheered.

Olivia ran away from Suzanna without answering any questions. She recounted the story at our next Espies meeting.

"Who do you think she was?" Tess asked.

Do you think she knows about us?

Is she the person Pi heard by the tent?

Definitely seems like it.

She's spying on us.

Why would a substitute nurse spy on us?

Maybe she's not a substitute nurse!

I bet she's from the CDC!

She wants to round us up and have us quarantined!

She wants to take away our telepathy!

What should we do?

We should confront her.

"No," Pi said. "Even if the nurse suspects something, she doesn't know anything for sure. If she did, she would have said something to us. If we approach her, we're just going to look suspicious."

Jordana pointed a lime-green nail to her eyes. "We already look pretty suspicious."

"She's probably gathering evidence against us," Levi said.

"Maybe she is," Pi admitted. "So let's not give her any. Avoid her. And we all have to be on our best behavior. In school and outside of it."

We nodded.

Pi stood up. "That means in school no one visits the nurse's office. If you see her coming, walk the other way. Keep your distance. Don't blow it out of school either. Stay in control. No drinking."

No one spike the punch at Mackenzie's Sweet.

No pot either.

Or Addies.

Why would you take an Addie at a Sweet?

You guys are no fun.

"Just stay under the radar," Pi repeated. "Got it?"

We nodded. Once again we had a plan.

If only all of us had stuck to it.

Chapter Thirty-Five

TWO DAYS UNTIL THE SWEET

"Olivia, it's your turn," Mr Roth said.

Here it was. The moment of truth.

Speech time.

Again.

Lyme disease, Lyme disease, Lyme disease.

She could do this. She was not the same person she had been two weeks earlier. She was different. She had a boyfriend. She could hear people's thoughts. She had confidence.

Or, at least, more than she'd had before.

She stood up. Slowly.

Is she going to pass out again?

She looks nervous.

Olivia tried to smile. *Lyme disease, Lyme disease, Lyme disease*. Did she have Lyme disease? No, she did not.

She turned around to face the crowd.

She definitely looks nervous.

Lazar gave her a thumbs-up.

She's going to do it, Renée thought. *Go Olivia!*

Yes! She could do this! She knew how her speech started: *In Ridgefield, Connecticut!* She looked at Lazar and smiled.

He smiled back. *She's not going to fall again, is she? That would be so embarrassing.*

Olivia narrowed her eyes. Embarrassing for her? Or embarrassing for him?

The room started to sway.

"Olivia?" Mr Roth asked. "Are you okay?"

She didn't feel okay. She felt sick. Her headache was back and it was a bad one. Oh God. She was going to pass out again. She was going to pass out and hit her head, and this time she really was going to die.

"You know what?" she said. "I think I need to sit down." Without looking at her teacher, she returned to her seat and slumped into her chair. Mission unaccomplished. Olivia felt like crying.

Lazar gave her a puppy-dog face. *At least she didn't pass out.*

Wow, Pi thought, *Olivia, your boyfriend is a real asshole.*

That's it, Renée thought. *She needs my help. I'm practicing with her after school.*

"Olivia, we'll need to discuss this after class," Mr Roth said sternly.

When the bell rang, Olivia slumped her way over to Mr

Roth. "You're getting one more chance. That's the best I can do. Or you fail the assignment. Next week. Got it?"

She got it, all right.

Teddy cornered Tess after class. "You're coming with me to the ball fields to watch the baseball game. No excuses. Let's move."

"Fine," she said. It was a nice day. It wasn't a terrible idea to get some fresh air. Sit outside. Cheer on Nick. Support BHS against Millennium.

Most of us were going to the game. It was the semifinals. We wanted to support Nick. We might not all have been friends before this, but there was nothing like having ESP to bond you to a person.

Tess looks really good, Teddy thought.

Was he noticing her because of the two pounds she'd lost? Probably not. His attention was more likely because of her new V-neck that showed off her cleavage. BJ had been thinking about her breasts all through homeroom. And so had other boys, actually, as the day went on. Not one of them had said a word. Without ESP, Tess would never have thought a single one of these guys found her sexy. Maybe they always had, and she never knew?

They climbed up the stands. Nick was walking toward the mound. Teddy and Tess cheered loudly.

From where they sat, Tess could kind of see the catcher making those weird finger signals to the pitcher. When she focused on the catcher's thoughts, she heard: *Try a fastball*.

Then Nick's thoughts as he held the bat: *Fastball. Got it.*

The pitcher threw the ball; Nick swung and sent it over the fence.

"Home run!" the umpire yelled.

"Go, Nick!" Tess hollered along with everyone else.

"He's been playing so well this week," Teddy said. "I knew he could do it."

Yeah, he'd been playing well. With a little help.

Tess smiled. Nick was doing great. She was here with Teddy and he thought she looked good. In fact, lots of boys did. Life was good. Tess felt the sun on her face. She closed her eyes and enjoyed the moment.

Then she opened them and heard Teddy think, *There she is!* Her heart plummeted. Of course that was why Teddy had wanted to come. Keith was on the team, so Sadie would be there. Why hadn't it occurred to her?

A text dinged on her phone. BJ.

```
You look like you're about to kill
him.
```

Tess looked up and spotted BJ sitting high in the bleachers. He waved. She typed:

```
He's thinking about her again.
```

BJ looked down at his phone and wrote back:

```
He only likes her because she's
unavailable. You have to show him
that you're unavailable.
Tess: And how do I do that?
BJ: Come kiss me.
```

Ha. She shook her head. Did he really think she was going to cross the field and kiss him in front of everyone?

```
Tess: Yeah right.
BJ: I'm coming over.
```

By the time she looked up, he was already walking toward them.

Oh God.

"Hi there," he said, and squeezed onto the bench beside her. "What's up, peeps?"

You are not going to kiss me, Tess thought.

You so want me to, he thought back. With a totally straight face, he put his hand on her knee.

She wanted to punch him. Kind of.

I'm growing on you, aren't I? He winked, then turned to Teddy. "Hey, Teddy, my man, what's happening?"

Teddy looked back and forth between Tess and BJ's hand on her knee. *What the hell is that?* "Not much," he answered. "Just watching the game."

He's freaking out, Tess told BJ.

Of course he is. Can I touch your breast now? That would really freak him out.

You are not to touch my breast.

Not even the left one?

No breast-touching at all. She laughed. She couldn't help it.

"Uh, what's new with you, BJ?" Teddy asked.

"Nothing much. Trying to convince your friend here to go out with me sometime, but she keeps turning me down."

BJ!

What? I'm helping you!

"She does?" *She never told me that.*

"She thinks she's too good for me, but she'll come around. It's only a matter of time."

Teddy clenched his jaw. *She's thinking about it? She cannot go out with that sleazeball.*

What's he thinking? BJ wondered. *You're right between us. You're blocking his thoughts.*

Tess smiled. *He's thinking you're a sleazeball.*

He turned to look at her. *Do you think I'm a sleazeball?*

Tess gave the question some thought. *I used to. But I guess... well, everyone else is thinking the same things as you. At least you're saying them.*

BJ raised an eyebrow. Then his hand began to creep slowly up her leg.

I spoke too soon.

He gave a slight nod. *Let's play chicken.*

She put her hand on his. Then she leaned over and very

slowly gave him a long kiss on the cheek. "Thanks for coming to visit."

BJ laughed. *Am I being dismissed?*

I don't like this one bit, Teddy thought.

Holy crap. He's jealous! It's working!

BJ stood up and saluted them. *Good luck. The offer is still good if you want me to keep going.*

She shook her head. *Goodbye!*

"You're going to Mackenzie's Sweet, right?" BJ asked.

"Yeah," Tess answered. Things with her and Mackenzie were definitely strange, but she wouldn't miss the Sweet. That would be unforgivable. Plus there would be dancing.

BJ jumped down the stairs. "Save me a slow dance!"

"I'll think about it!" she hollered back.

The girls in the row in front of her were buzzing. *Does BJ like Tess?*

Tess could feel Teddy's eyes on her. "We can go to the party together if you want," he said.

Huh? She turned to him.

I can't believe BJ was sleazing up my Tess.

Seriously? Since when was she his Tess?

He squirmed in his seat. "You're not really going to go out with him, are you?"

She tried to sound flippant. "I might. He's funny." *And honest.*

"Funny-looking," Teddy said. *She's so not his type. Although she is looking sexy.*

She was looking sexy? She preened in her seat.

"He's not funny-looking," she finally answered. BJ was a lot of things, but funny-looking wasn't one of them. He was hot. He had great shoulders. Really big hands. She felt herself flush. She was suddenly very, very, very glad that he wasn't sitting next to her right then.

Mackenzie and Cooper skipped the baseball game. They went to dinner instead. Like they had every night that week.

Cooper had been spending as little time as he could at his apartment. "I miss you!" Ashley cried, wrapping her arms around his leg. *Why does Cooper not take me with him all the time?*

He felt bad for Ashley. He missed her too, but he just couldn't take being at home. He couldn't face anything. Except Mackenzie. If he could just focus on Mackenzie, everything would be okay.

He was dreading Saturday.

"Gee, thanks a lot," Mackenzie said as they waited for a table at Kitchenette. "Aren't you excited to see me all dressed up?"

"You are going to look amazing," he said. "It's just everyone's going to be there, lying. My parents too."

"Sorry about that. My parents insisted on inviting some of their friends whose kids are coming. I didn't know, so…" She kissed Cooper hard on the lips. "I'm sorry they're coming. But I think it'll be okay," she told him. "As long as we're together. A team. It's us against them."

They thought they could hide. They thought they could separate themselves from us.

Impossible.

There was no escaping us.

Chapter Thirty-Six
PARTY PREP

The big day was finally here.

Sweet day.

We spent the afternoon getting ready.

Some of us got manicures. In Manhattan, there's a nail place on every corner, but most of us went to Beauty Charm on Chambers. It had the best massage chairs. Courtney and Jordana went to Drybar. Courtney got the straight-up blowout while Jordana got the just-got-out-of-bed look. Mackenzie, Mackenzie's mom, and Mackenzie's sister, Cailin, spent the day at Bliss SoHo getting everything done: hair, nails, pedicure, and makeup.

Mackenzie had been excited to spend the day with her sister.

But the excitement ended about five minutes into the appointment.

"So, how's school?" Mackenzie asked.

"Fine," Cailin said. *I can't believe Mom made me come in for this stupid party when I should be in the library.*

The appointment didn't improve.

"You have the most incredible eyes," the makeup artist told Mackenzie. "I'm going to use a teal green to really bring out the violet. They're so unusual."

Come tonight and you won't think they're so unusual, Mackenzie almost said.

"Did you get colored contacts?" her mom asked, peering at her face.

"No, they're just changing color. Puberty, I guess."

Under the circumstances, we thought that was a decent excuse. Tess's hair had been straight until her fourteenth birthday, when it had gone wavy, right? These things happened.

Cailin sighed. *I got zits and Mackenzie got exotic eyes. How is that fair? Ugh.*

Mackenzie wanted to tell her to shut the hell up, but she closed her eyes instead.

"Do we really have to go to this Sweet Sixteen party?" Lazar asked as they walked up West Broadway. "I could get us tickets to *The Eiffel Tower* at the Atlantic Theater."

If Olivia were being honest, she'd admit that she didn't really feel like going to the Sweet either. She was depressed. Her epic fail in public speaking class had been a punch to her stomach. "I promised Mackenzie I'd be there," Olivia said.

She'd bought a gift. A set of cute mini metallic nail polishes. She'd "overheard" Mackenzie admiring Jordana's nail color one day in homeroom and had asked Jordana where it was from. Olivia had also borrowed a green dress of her mom's and a pair of sparkly flats. She even did her makeup just the way Lazar said he liked it on the day he'd finally asked her out. Well, not said. Thought. "It should be fun," she added. More fun than *The Eiffel Tower*, anyway.

"I don't dance," Lazar said.

"Oh, don't worry," Olivia said. "I'm not a great dancer either."

Such a waste of time. Why does Olivia care about Mackenzie? She's kind of a bitch. Olivia cares too much about what stupid people think.

Olivia stopped in her tracks. Maybe she should turn around and go home. She didn't want to drag him against his will. "Do you want to just go home?"

He turned to her, surprised. "I thought you wanted to go."

"I do want to go. But not if you're going to complain the whole time."

He blinked. "We can go," he said finally. "I'm just not really a party type of person." *I never know what to do with myself. I never know what to do with my feet. I should have taken dance lessons when I was younger or something.*

Aw, Olivia thought. Her heart melted. *He's shy. Just like me.*

Olivia laced her fingers through his. "We don't have to stay long."

They walked the last few blocks, hand in hand.

Mackenzie was in the bathroom at SoHo Tower reapplying her lipstick. It was seven-fifty-eight, which meant the party was starting in two minutes.

She wasn't sure how it was biologically possible, but her heart was pounding inside her head, her neck, her fingers. She was nervous. Very nervous. Not about one thing specifically. She was nervous about it all. Would someone think something they shouldn't? Would Cooper change his mind and decide he hated her after all?

Everything was set up. Her parents and siblings were there, the DJ was organizing his stuff, the bartenders were ready – no alcohol for anyone under twenty-one. She was sure some of the non-Espies would smuggle in booze, but she knew none of us would drink. Too risky. The waitresses had their hors d'oeuvres ready to go: mini pizzas, mini lobster rolls, spring rolls. The room looked fun, flirty and modern but not cheesy, just the way the event planner had promised – white leather couches and chairs, glass bar tables, white candles in square silver candleholders, white roses in silver vases. No balloons. No streamers. A silver square dance floor in the middle of the room.

Everything was going to be fine, Mackenzie told herself.

Completely fine.

The Espies will behave themselves. I have Cooper. He's all I need.

Mackenzie pushed open the bathroom door and headed down the hallway to the hotel ballroom. People had already arrived. Olivia. Lazar. Jordana. Isaac. No sign of Tess, but most of the rest of us were there. Even Brinn, in a slightly ill-fitting black dress. Even Pi. She was wearing a navy blue dress, a navy blue jacket, and matching navy pumps. She looked like she was interviewing for a job on Wall Street.

Jordana clucked her tongue. *Way to make fun of your own guests.*

Oops. Maybe Mackenzie would tell the DJ to make the music loud. Really loud. *So loud the Espies won't be able to hear themselves think, never mind each other.* Would that work?

Mackenzie spotted her parents chatting with Cooper's parents. Both dads were wearing black suits. The moms were wearing cocktail dresses. But where was Cooper?

He was alone at the bar, wearing non-wrinkled black pants, a black jacket, and a gray shirt. He looked swanky. He looked beautiful.

Mackenzie approached him from behind and put her arms around his waist. "Hey."

He turned and kissed her on the forehead. "Hi. Happy birthday."

She loved the fact that it was her actual birthday. How often did that happen? That a party celebrating your birthday really fell on the right day? For the first time in weeks she felt lucky. It was meant to be. Everything had been messed up until that day, but now everything would be fine. Magical.

"Sorry I couldn't be here earlier," Cooper said. "Ashley was throwing a fit."

"You should have brought her."

"She wanted to come. She put on a party dress and her party shoes."

"Aw, that's so sad. I wish she were here."

"I think my mom wanted a night out."

They both looked at his parents.

Cooper's father had his arm around his wife's waist. Was it possible Cooper had been wrong? Maybe he'd misunderstood?

Cooper shrugged. *Let's not talk about it tonight.*

You sure?

"Yeah. But…" *They seem happy, right?*

Absolutely. Mackenzie hugged him. Everything was going to be fine. Everything was going to be great. "Wanna dance?"

He took a sip of his Coke. "Boo-ya. Let's doooo this," he said, and Mackenzie could have sworn his words sounded like a song.

Tess and Teddy arrived together, her arm linked through his.

If we were surprised by the turn of events, Tess was even more surprised.

He'd called her earlier that afternoon and asked if they were still going together.

"Sure," Tess said. "Whatever." So he was going to walk with her? Big whoop. It wasn't a real date.

But then he offered to pick her up at her apartment. And he didn't ring from downstairs. He came up to get her.

"Let me get some pictures," her mom said when she saw them both in their fineries. It felt like a prom.

Did she lose a few pounds? her mom thought. *It's still not enough. She needs to lose at least another seven.*

That thought had almost ruined Tess's night, but she kept on her game face. Still, she sucked in her stomach.

Anyway, Teddy's reaction made up for her mom's. *She looks hot. And those eyes... Did she always have such gorgeous eyes? She has great boobs.*

Is he staring at her boobs? her mom wondered. *He definitely is. I wish I had boobs.*

Ha! If she lost another seven pounds, she'd have no boobs. *Take that, Mom!*

They'd walked arm in arm to SoHo Tower. By the time they arrived, the room was packed.

"Let's go say hi to Mackenzie," Tess said. Their arms were still linked. Did it mean what she thought it meant? Was getting Teddy to notice her really that easy? Step one, show that other guys were interested? Step two, get dressed up and show cleavage? Was that all it took?

She found Mackenzie on the dance floor with Cooper. Cooper was a great dancer. He'd always been a great dancer. Maybe the two of them would be okay. She squeezed Teddy's arm. Maybe they'd all be okay.

She hugged Mackenzie tightly. "You look amazing," she said. "Happy birthday."

Does this mean you forgive me? Please forgive me? I'm sorry. I miss you. And you look amazing too. And happy. You came with Teddy! Is that on?

Tess blushed. *We'll see. All signs point to positive.*

I'm so happy for you. I want to hear everything. I know I haven't always been a great friend but I do—

Tess squeezed Mackenzie's shoulders. *We'll get through it. Good.*

"What up, Coops?" Teddy said, and they gave each other one of those boy handshakes involving loud palm smacks.

"Come dance with us," Mackenzie insisted.

For a few minutes that's what they did. The four of them dancing, just the way Tess had always imagined. The music was pumping; she was moving, her hair flying all over the place.

For the next song, the music went old school and Marvin Gaye's "Sexual Healing" came on. Teddy and Tess moved closer together. His arms were around her waist and hers were around his neck, and they were dancing and kind of rocking back and forth.

Me and Tess? Teddy thought.

She could feel his hands on the small of her back. Was this really, finally, happening? Her heart was thumping so loud she could barely hear anything except the music. His eyes were closed, so she couldn't hear his thoughts, but she didn't need to. She could feel him pressed against her. She knew something had changed. Shifted. Even though they hadn't *done* anything, or said anything, they had crossed over from " just friends" to something more. This was going to happen. This was finally going to happen.

* * *

"It's so loud in here," Lazar whined.

It *was* loud. But still, Olivia was having fun. She hadn't expected to have fun, but she was. All her friends were there. Look at that! She had friends! And after reading everyone's minds, she knew two things: one, she was looking cute, and two, she didn't have food in her teeth.

Olivia felt brave. "Come on. Let's dance."

He shook his head stubbornly. "I told you I don't dance."

"One song," she begged.

He sighed. "Fine."

They squeezed their way onto the dance floor.

It's so hot in here, he thought.

She couldn't help wondering if he ever stopped complaining. "Why don't you take off your jacket if you're hot?"

He scowled. *How did she know I was hot? Am I sweating? I must be sweating*. "Where would I put it?"

Close call. "On a chair?"

"What if someone takes it?"

Was he serious? Did he really think someone here was going to steal his jacket? He was the smallest guy here – it wasn't like his jacket would fit anyone.

She tried to ignore him and focus on the music. The last time she'd danced in public was…well, she couldn't remember. The truth was she liked to dance. A lot. She knew she wasn't the best dancer or anything, but it was fun. She danced in her room with the blinds closed, and while she was cooking dinner. In public she'd always worried people were staring at her – but now she *knew* no one was watching her. No one cared. Everyone was feeling the music and no one was looking. No one was judging her. She could do whatever she wanted to do. She lifted her arms above her head. Wahoo!

She's getting a little crazy, Lazar thought.

Olivia froze. Yeah, no one was judging her. No one except Lazar.

Pi was watching.

She sat on a bar stool in the corner and monitored the room. She'd come to make sure no one did anything foolish.

She'd stopped at least three of us from trying to sneak alcohol. She didn't understand why we would take risks at a time like this.

She watched Olivia dance with that jerk boyfriend of hers. Tess was dancing with that guy she was obsessed with. Mackenzie was dancing with Cooper.

Everything was under control. Just the way Pi liked it.

She took a sip of her water and a bite of miso cod. At least the food was good. Nobu had catered.

Pi had surprised herself by going to Bloomingdale's and buying a new outfit for the party. She knew her suit was conservative, but she felt sophisticated and smart.

She'd bought some makeup for the event too. But when she opened the packages, she realized she had no idea how to use eye shadow or eyeliner. She wished she had someone to teach her.

Instead she watched an eye-makeup tutorial on YouTube and tried to follow along. When she was done, she studied herself in the mirror. She looked like a raccoon. She scrubbed the color off and hid the makeup in the back of a drawer.

Aw. Poor Pi.

She was about to take another bite of cod when she saw her. The redhead. The fake nurse. Suzanna. What was she doing here?

She was wearing black pants and a black blouse, and she was sitting at a table across the room.

Pi had spent the past week ducking in the hallway whenever the woman was near. We all had.

Pi pushed her chair back and snaked her way to the other side of the room. She wanted to get close enough to the woman to find out who she was and what she wanted, yet stay far enough away that the woman didn't see her.

There were many people in her way. Pi struggled to get close enough to hear without being obvious and without being interrupted by random party-goers' dumb internal and external thoughts.

Suzanna: ...*at least fifteen of them seem to have it...*

"This party is the best!"

...*I think Sadie forgot to wear a bra...*

Suzanna: ...*eyes are definitely turning...*

She was definitely referring to the Espies! She had to be!

...*shouldn't hug people when he's so sweaty. It's disgusting!...*

"I love this song!"

"Why aren't you dancing?"

...*have some vodka in my purse...*

...*I think I just swallowed a toothpick...*

Pi's schoolmates were officially driving her crazy. She squeezed her way closer to the woman and heard:

At least we should have more of the antidote by Thursday.

Pi steadied herself on a table. Was the antidote for them? Would it get rid of the telepathy?

The woman turned around and saw Pi. *Why is she staring at me? Oh! Her eyes are purple! She's one of them! If she's one of them, she can hear me. Hello? You can hear me, can't you?*

Pi felt numb. Then, without thinking, she turned and ran out of the room.

Mackenzie was pretty sure it was the best party ever. Everyone was having a great time. The dance floor was packed. Even Olivia was dancing. Olivia! She'd never seen Olivia get down before, but there she was, partying it up.

"I am so sweaty," Cooper said. "Am I smelly?"

"You are not," Mackenzie murmured. "Trust me."

I wish I could. Cooper froze.

Mackenzie froze. She deserved that. She put her hand on his shoulder. "You will. Maybe not today. But you will."

He looked into her eyes. *I hope so.*

"Let's get something to drink?"

He took her hand and they walked back to the bar. *I'm going to get over it. I'm going to get over it. I need her.*

I need you, she thought. "I'll have a Diet Coke, please," she told the bartender. "Coop? What do you want?"

Romy Brohman, Jordana's mother, approached her. "Happy birthday, sweetie. I haven't seen you in ages! You look all grown-up and gorgeous!"

"Thank you! Thank you for coming," Mackenzie said. The woman's cotton candy perfume was overwhelming and almost choked her.

The woman motioned to Cooper. "Is that your boyfriend?"

"He is. Cooper, do you know Romy? Jordana's mom?" *We had our first kiss in her office.*

"Of course," he said. "How are you?"

"I haven't seen you in years! You're so handsome. You look just like your dad." A smile danced on her lips. *I haven't seen him in ages either. Since that time I bumped into him and his wife at Odeon. He was so smooth too. Considering our history.*

Mackenzie bit her lip. She prayed Cooper hadn't heard that.

Cooper's eyes flashed. He had definitely heard.

"Cooper, let's go dance," Mackenzie snapped. She wanted him out of there before he heard anything worse.

His hand gripped his glass like he was trying to squeeze the life out of it. "Not yet. I have a few questions." He was definitely not singing now. His voice was cold. "What exactly is your relationship with my dad, Romy?"

Romy's eyes widened and she shrugged her thin shoulders. *Does he know about our affair?* "What do you mean?"

Cooper was about to blow. His face was turning red and it wasn't from the colored strobe lights.

"Cooper, let's get some air. Now." Mackenzie yanked his arm, causing his Coke to splash over the edge of his glass and onto her dress. It didn't matter. She needed to get him outside.

"I want to talk to her," Cooper protested as she pulled him through the room.

"No you don't. You want to talk to your dad."

"I want to punch my dad, not talk to him. Do you know what this means? The Chicago person isn't even the first time he cheated. He's such a bastard. I'm glad my mom's divorcing him."

He looked back at the bar, but the woman was now approaching Cooper's parents. *I can only imagine what she'll say. Or what she'll be thinking about. What my dad will be thinking about. What my mom won't know.*

"I'm sorry," Mackenzie said. She didn't know what else to say.

I hate them all. I hate his father for being a dick, I hate Jordana's mom for sleeping with him, and I hate his mom for divorcing him.

Mackenzie pulled open the door to the room and stepped into the hallway just as someone else was coming inside.

Bennett.

Mackenzie gasped. *Oh shit. Shit shit shit.*

Cooper turned to her. "What?"

She looks hot. Even hotter than she did in that black bikini, Bennett thought.

Cooper looked at Bennett and then back at Mackenzie. *Who is that?*

Mackenzie didn't want to say. She didn't want to think. Didn't want to move.

I guess that's the boyfriend, Bennett thought.

Shit, shit, shit.

"Is that him?" Cooper asked, his voice rising. "Bennett?"

"The one and only," Bennett said.

Cooper's fists tightened. *Are you freaking kidding me?*

And then, surprising us all, he punched Bennett in the face.

Tess and Teddy were holding hands and on their way to get a drink when they ran into Sadie. Sadie, who was looking gorgeous.

She was wearing a loose silver dress and silver heels. Her hair wasn't even done; it was just tied back. It screamed, *Look how pretty I am and I don't even have to do anything.*

Teddy stopped walking. *Sadie! And she's alone.*

Tess looked around for Keith but didn't see him.

"Keith's not coming," Sadie said. *We broke up.*

"You guys always break up," Tess said, tightening her grip on Teddy's arm.

"This time it's for real." *I just couldn't stand kissing him anymore. Or listening to him. You know what I mean.* She looked at Tess meaningfully.

Tess did know what she meant. Because right then she was listening to Teddy.

She's single? Does that mean there's a chance for me?

He let go of Tess's hand.

Tess couldn't stand hearing Teddy think about Sadie right then. *She* was the one who was supposed to be with him. Tonight, Sadie was not getting in the way! Tess gave Sadie a look of desperation.

I'm not getting in the way, Sadie thought back. *I don't like Teddy!*

But he likes you!

But I don't like him! So it doesn't matter! I'll just walk away and you guys can be together!

I don't want to be someone's second choice!

Sadie shrugged. *I don't know what I'm supposed to say to that. Can you just go?*

Sadie nodded. "I'll see you guys later." Before Teddy could react she disappeared into the crowd.

Now what? Tess looked at Teddy.

Teddy looked back at Sadie.

It's never going to happen with Sadie, he thought. *But maybe...well, maybe Tess and I can...I don't know. Tess is the best. We like so many of the same things. She gets me. Should I see where this is going?*

Yes! Tess almost screamed. *Yes, you should. Let's see what happens.*

Another slow song came on.

Her heart hammered in her chest and she tried not to think about what she was about to do. She was going to kiss someone she knew didn't feel the way she did.

She hated the stupid telepathy. If she didn't have it, then she would never have known Teddy had feelings for Sadie. They'd have had their dance and they'd be walking off into the sunset. She should just pretend that she hadn't heard his thoughts. That was what she should do. They would kiss and to hell with Sadie. Who cared if Tess wasn't his first choice?

"Let's go dance again," she said. She pulled him back onto the floor, and before she had a chance to think things through, she pulled him closer.

She smells good. Like vanilla, she heard him think. *I should kiss her. No. Yes. No.*

Yes. It's a good idea. It's a very good idea and it's going to happen right now. She pressed her body firmly against his. The music coursed through them both. It was going to happen. It was definitely going to happen.

The back of her head was against his neck, but she turned so she was facing him, facing his neck. If she opened her mouth, she could lick it. Not that she would lick his neck — that would be weird. But she opened her mouth a little so he could feel her breath.

His heart beat louder. *I should do it*, he thought. *Why not?*

Exactly, Tess thought. *Why not! Do it! Do it! You should do it!*

Ever so slowly, he lowered his head down to hers. A second more and their lips would be touching. *Don't think about it*, he thought. *Just do it.*

She agreed a hundred percent. She closed her eyes, waiting.

His lips touched hers. Soft at first. She pressed back. So soft. She hadn't expected his lips to be so soft. Sweet, even. It was weird to have known someone for so long, to know him so well, but not know what his lips felt like. To not know such an important part of him.

They were kissing, their lips opening and closing, so soft, so sweet, so gentle. It was all she had expected and nothing she had expected wrapped together in one feeling. It was everything.

When the song ended, he pulled back, blinking.

She was about to burst with happiness. "Hey," she said shyly.

And then he thought, *I hope Sadie didn't see.*

Tess's heart exploded.

Murmurs of a fight spread through the party, and we all went to see what was going on.

"Cooper!" Mackenzie yelled as she watched Bennett go flying back.

"What the fuck?" Bennett yelled from the floor.

"What do you expect?" Cooper yelled. "You hook up with my girlfriend and then show up here and don't expect me to punch you in the face? Are you an idiot?" Cooper was furious. He wanted to do more than hit the guy. He wanted to kick him. He wanted to kill him.

"I didn't know you knew, asshole." Bennett stood up and rubbed the side of his face.

Cooper lunged to hit him again.

Mackenzie grabbed his arm. "Stop it. What are you doing?"

"Why the fuck is he here? You invited him?"

"I invited him before!"

"Before what? Before you hooked up with him or before I found out?"

"Before...anyone found out." *I'm sorry. I shouldn't have invited him. I don't know why I did.*

Cooper couldn't take it anymore. "I picked out the invitations with you! I picked them out and then you sent one to him!

What were you thinking?" He heard his voice crack.

"I'm sorry," she whimpered. *Please, Cooper, not here.*

"You're always sorry. Just not sorry enough."

To make things worse, that was when Cooper's mother and father walked over to them, looking stern.

"Cooper, what's going on?" his dad asked.

"Are you fucking serious?" he yelled. He knew he was losing it. He knew, but he couldn't stop. He felt like the Hulk just as he was about to turn green. "I'll tell you what's going on!"

Mackenzie grabbed his arm. "Cooper! Stop it!"

"Calm down," his father said. *What the hell is wrong with him?*

"Nothing is wrong with *me*. Something's wrong with all of you. I don't want to calm down. I want everyone else to stop being such fucking liars."

Is he drunk? his mother worried.

"No, Mom, I am not drunk. I am pissed off. At this jerkoff for showing up. At Dad for screwing Jordana's mother and some woman in Chicago. And at you for calling a divorce lawyer. Although Dad definitely deserves it."

His mom gasped.

We all gasped.

His dad shook his head. "I don't know what you're talking about."

"Yes you do. I know what's going on. Mackenzie knows what's going on. Everyone in this whole fucking room knows what's going on, because we can hear everything you're all thinking."

Shit.

Uh-oh.

Here we go.

He's definitely drunk.

Everyone at the party who wasn't us looked around in confusion.

"I think he's high," one of the party guests said. "Do you see his eyes? They look weird."

Nick and Isaac came up beside him. "Hey, man, let's go outside and get some air, okay?"

Cooper looked around at all of us. And then he deflated like a popped balloon.

Mackenzie reached out to try to touch him, but he stepped back. "No. Everyone leave me alone."

He pushed his way through everyone and into the stairwell. He ran down the one flight and ended up in the hotel lobby. He stood still for a minute, trying to calm down. No one even wanted to hear what he had to say. No one cared. His father had practically dismissed him.

"Cooper," said a woman behind him. He turned.

She had her red hair pulled back and was wearing black pants and a black blouse. She looked familiar, but he couldn't figure out from where.

Yup. His eyes are purplish. "I heard what you said up there," she said. "About hearing other people's thoughts. I want to talk to you."

Cooper took a step toward her. At least she wanted to listen.

* * *

"What a freak," Lazar said, shaking his head.

Olivia, who, like the rest of us, had witnessed the whole scene, felt her heart break for Cooper. "He's not a freak. He's just overwhelmed."

"He's a loser," Lazar said. "Can we go now?"

Suddenly, Olivia realized that Lazar *wasn't* like her. He wasn't shy. He was antisocial. She had always liked being around people – but she just didn't know how to talk to them. He didn't like people. He liked judging them.

"Go without me," she said.

"What do you mean?" He took a step back. *I must have heard that wrong.*

"You didn't hear that wrong. I want to stay. If you want to go home so badly, go home."

He shook his head. *I don't need this attitude.* "We came together. We should leave together."

"But I'm not ready to leave yet. And you're clearly miserable, so go."

"You want me to leave by myself?" He looked incredulous.

"Yes. Goodbye! No one's keeping you here!" She wanted to forcibly shove him out the door.

Bitch, he thought. Then he stormed out.

For the first time all night, Olivia breathed a huge sigh of relief.

She spotted Tess, Sadie, Mackenzie, Jordana, and Levi in the corner and hurried over to find out what was going on.

Mackenzie was shaking.

"What happened to Cooper?" Olivia asked.

"He just blurted everything out," Mackenzie said. "And then he ran off."

"It's not like anyone believed him," Jordana added.

"Has anyone seen Pi?" Sadie asked. "She'll know what to do."

"I think she left," Levi said.

"I'll text her and see where she is," Tess said. *Stupid jerk.*

"Who's a stupid jerk?" Jordana asked her. "Cooper?"

"Not Cooper." Tess shot a look at Sadie. "I don't want to talk about it."

"I saw you and Teddy making out," Levi said to her. "What's up with that?"

"Nothing's up with that," Tess muttered. *Don't wanna talk about it.*

Mackenzie was still shaking. "I think I want to go home."

"You can't leave," Tess told her. "It's your party."

"I don't care," Mackenzie said. Her face was bright red. "I can't breathe. I need to get out of here."

Olivia put her arm around her. "Take deep breaths, okay? Let's just step outside and get some air. Someone tell her parents where we are. Someone get us some water."

Olivia led Mackenzie out the door and into the stairwell, leaving the rest of us behind.

"That was some Sweet," Jordana said.

Levi shook his head. *It was more of a sour.*

We couldn't help but groan.

Chapter Thirty-Seven
WE'VE BEEN MEANING TO TELL YOU

They called us early the next morning.

7:02 a.m. *Ring!*

Mackenzie woke up immediately.

"Who the hell is calling so early?" barked her dad, *We did it three times last night! I am loving my Viagra prescription!*

Cooper's house line rang at 7:11 a.m. He was already awake and pouring his sister a bowl of cereal. He had barely slept all night.

"Nobody get that!" Cooper's mom yelled, storming into the kitchen and glaring at the phone. It went to voice mail. *No way I'm getting that. It's definitely Harry calling from his hotel.* She listened to the message two minutes later.

It was not Cooper's dad. It was Nathan Michaels, the school's principal.

The message requested Cooper's family to please call back immediately. They would be having an emergency meeting in the BHS auditorium at seven p.m. regarding their son's homeroom, and it was imperative that he and his parents go.

7:22 a.m. *Ring!*

Olivia heard her mom pick up and wondered who it could be. *What happened? Who died?* In Olivia's mind, all middle-of-the-night or early-morning calls were to report heart attacks, brain aneurysms, or plane crashes.

"But why?" she heard her mother ask. "What's this about? Is my daughter sick?"

Pause.

"Is she in any kind of danger?"

Pause.

"What about the flu shot?" Olivia's mom shrieked.

Pause.

"Unusual neurological symptoms? Are you kidding me?"

Of course, Olivia's mom ran right into Olivia's room.

"Wake up!" she yelled, throwing open the door. "What's going on? Are you okay?"

Olivia was already sitting up in her bed and waiting.

"What's going on?" her mom continued. "What happened with the flu shots? What aren't you telling me?" *Principal Michaels called! I thought someone died! You have complications from a tainted flu shot! They told us not to tell anyone!* Her face was red and she was out of breath.

At first all Olivia could think was, *I can't deal with her now*, but when she saw the panic in her mom's eyes and heard her think, *If something bad happens to my daughter, I'll kill myself*, Olivia reached out her arms to hug her.

"I'm fine," Olivia began. "Sit down. I'll tell you everything. I'll show you what I can do."

And she did.

We all did.

We texted back and forth like crazy.

> Levi: What happened? How did
> Michaels find out?
> Jordana: Does the whole school
> know?
> Nick: School admin knows, teachers
> don't. Except my mom.
> Isaac: That new nurse was at the
> Sweet. Maybe she told Michaels? Pi?
> Daniel: We saw Cooper talking to
> her in the lobby.
> Courtney: Cooper, did you talk to
> her?
> Jordana: Cooper?
> Levi: Cooper???
> Tess: Pi, what do we do?
> Pi: We go to the meeting and hear
> what they have to say.

What choice did we have?

* * *

We were all early.

Even Cooper. He showed up with both his parents, which was a bit awkward, considering his father had moved into the Conrad Hotel the night before. Cooper sat on the opposite side of the room from Mackenzie. He gave her a sad smile when he saw her, but quickly looked away.

"Thank you for coming," said the man on the stage. He'd introduced himself as Hank Soporic, executive director of the Centers for Disease Control and Prevention. He was tall and wore a blue suit and a traumatized expression. *I can't believe this is happening. This makes no sense. This is impossible.*

No kidding.

Suzanna sat by his side.

Hank coughed. "As I'm sure your children have informed you, they seem to have developed some, um, complications from their flu shot."

Complications! Ha!

A sore arm is a complication. We've become mutants.

It's true. We're like the X-Men.

You know, the Espies would make an awesome comic book series.

We hear thoughts and fight crime!

I am so not wearing a leather catsuit.

Hank rubbed his forehead and continued. "It appears that the flu vaccine has caused your children to develop..." His voice trailed off and his face flushed with embarrassment. *I can't believe I'm saying these things out loud. They make no scientific sense.* "To develop headaches. Headaches and…a form of telepathy." He shook his head. *This is insanity.* "It appears that they can read other people's thoughts."

Our parents:

She wasn't kidding?

Impossible!

Oh dear, oh dear, oh dear.

"They've really been hearing everything we've been thinking?" Levi's mom asked.

"Yes," Hank said, still shaking his head. "That seems to be the case."

Everything?

Even the swearing?

Oh shit.

"How many people have been affected?" Isaac's dad asked.

"We can't share that information with you at the moment" – *because we have no idea* – "but we can tell you that we've traced at least three contaminated batches."

Contaminated?

Batches, plural?

There are others with telepathy?

Oh God. I hope it's not my French tutor. She's so hot.

"Were all the batches given to New York City students?" asked Courtney's mom.

"No. One of the contaminated batches was delivered to a nursing home in Jacksonville, Florida. One was delivered to a family clinic in Cleveland, Ohio, and one was delivered here, to Manhattan. To Bloomberg High School."

At least no one else at school is reading my thoughts secretly.

At least it's not my French tutor. She's so hot.

Olivia's mom thought she might hyperventilate. *What if this causes brain tumors?* "Are those the only complications? Telepathy and headaches?"

"No." Hank rubbed his forehead again. *It gets scarier.*

Scarier?

Now I'm nervous.

You're only nervous now?

"We've also noticed a slight pigment change in the subjects' irises. You might notice that your children have a purplish tint to their eyes."

Our parents all stared into our eyes.

I did notice that.

I thought she looked good.

I thought he was tired.

I thought he was on drugs.

"We're not sure what's causing the pigment change, but we believe it's related to the telepathy. We believe headaches may be another side effect. Symptoms tend to be severe immediately following the vaccine and tend to clear up. The risk of pigment change seems to increase as time goes on." *As does the risk of death.*

Huh?

"Death?" Olivia repeated.

"Are you kidding me?" Jordana called out. "We're going to die?"

A startled Hank nearly jumped off the stage. "Oh! I

forgot you could…hear me."

Our parents started panicking.

"Death?"

"Who said anything about dying?"

We should have moved to Canada. This would never happen in Canada!

Hank cleared his throat again. "One patient who received the contaminated vaccination suffered a stroke and…er… expired."

Our parents:

Expired? As in died?

The vaccination killed someone?

My poor baby!

Us:

My mom's a lawyer!

We should sue!

We can't sue if we're dead!

I can't believe I'm going to die a virgin!

"But," Hank continued, his voice shaky, "he was also eighty-one. The stroke may have been unrelated. The autopsy was inconclusive."

"Why weren't we notified about this situation immediately?" Cooper's dad barked. "Did you know that contamination was a possibility when our kids were vaccinated?"

"Absolutely not," he said. *It's not like we believed the complaints. Telepathy? Gimme a break.*

"So there were reports of telepathy," Nick called out. "You just didn't listen to them."

Hank reddened. "Er, right. There were reports. Three weeks ago a clinic in Ohio contacted us. They'd had complaints from patients who'd received their flu shots and seemed to have developed...unusual neurological symptoms."

"You mean telepathy," Olivia's mom said.

"Right," he squeaked. "Telepathy. Patients claimed to have developed telepathy. We were, um, doubtful at first." *That's the understatement of the year. We joked about it over cappuccinos. Oops. They can hear that. Just kidding! We didn't joke about it! We don't drink cappuccinos! We work in a government building! We can't afford a cappuccino maker! I should just keep talking. Yes. Continue talking.* "In addition to the, um, unusual neurological symptoms, the patients in Ohio complained of headaches and changing eye color. We instructed them to monitor their symptoms..." *How were we supposed to know that they weren't crazies? They sounded like crazies. This whole thing makes no sense. I miss SARS.* "Then we received some calls from a retirement home in Florida with reports of similar symptoms. By the time we followed up, the death had already occurred. The retirement home patients had in fact received their vaccinations before those in Ohio, but the nurses believed the patients were suffering from age-related dementia. It wasn't until there was a cluster of symptoms that the health practitioners took them seriously and informed us. Now we're tracing the batches we believe to have been contaminated. We thought one might have been sent to Bloomberg High School, but we didn't know which students had received the infected batch. Unfortunately,

Nurse Carmichael improperly tracked them." *Idiot*.

"Why didn't you ask everyone who'd gotten flu shots if they had telepathy?" Jordana asked.

He flushed again. "It just…well, it seemed like a loony thing to ask. And we didn't want to cause a panic. We thought surveillance was a better idea. We removed Nurse Carmichael and installed one of our own agents – Dr Dail – at Bloomberg, hoping that she would be able to find the affected parties."

Agents?

Suzanna!

Suzanna is CIA?

Who said anything about CIA?

This is so cool.

No it's not! We're going to die! Dying is not cool!

"Didn't the school have a responsibility to tell us?" Isaac's dad asked.

Hank shook his head. "The school didn't know. We didn't know. We suspected that an infected batch had been sent here, but we didn't have confirmation until last night."

Well, duh. If the school had known, we'd know they knew.

You're missing the point. Someone gave us up!

It was so Cooper!

We saw him with Suzanna!

It wasn't me.

Liar!

"But somebody died," Olivia's mom said. "You should have been cautious and called us immediately."

"There's no proof that the death was a direct result of the

vaccination. It was likely just old age." *Although we can't say for sure*. "But! We have good news," he rushed to add. "We've been able to isolate the compound in the vaccination that has been causing the, um, irregular neurological condition. It's a reaction to a new preservative we've been using to stabilize the vaccine, called NFG. And now that we know what caused it, we've developed an antidote."

A what?

A reversal vaccine.

We can make it stop?

"It's one hundred percent effective. We've used it on the group in Jacksonville and in Ohio, and both groups' symptoms have disappeared. The telepathy, the purple eyes, everything."

Our parents all heaved sighs of relief.

We weren't sure how we felt.

We didn't want strokes, obviously.

But were we ready to give up our telepathy for good?

"Can our children get the antidote today?" Olivia's mother asked.

"The next batch will be ready on Thursday," Hank said. "One last thing to discuss is discretion. I'm sure you can all understand the need to keep this quiet. We want to avoid public panic. We don't know how many other batches have been affected. We'd like to steer clear of mass paranoia and conspiracy theories. The vaccination manufacturer is requiring everyone who receives the antidote to sign a confidentiality agreement."

"Why would we sign anything?" Tess's dad asked. "They

have to give our kids the antidote, since they're responsible for this mess in the first place. We'll sue if we have to."

"You could," Hank said. *Please don't sue. What a pain in the ass that would be.* "The problem is that legal action takes years. And we don't know what the short- or long-term effects of the reaction to the NFG will be. Symptoms might progress. We're concerned about the potential for stroke. One of the Ohio patients also reported vision problems. We're apprehensive that eventual blindness might be a complication. We don't know what our time frame is here. We don't know what we're dealing with. We don't want you – a group of minors – to be our guinea pigs. Also, we can only imagine the media frenzy that would take place if this went public. We would not be able to shield your children from that. The pharmaceutical company has agreed to settle with you all now, with an immediate check for fifty thousand dollars to every affected person."

We all took a collective breath. That was a lot of money.

"But what if something goes wrong with the antidote?" Courtney asked. "What if we develop more 'unusual neurological symptoms'" – she made air quotes – "or our eyes turn orange?"

"There is a provision in the pharmaceutical company's agreement that if the antidote doesn't work, or if there are any additional unusual symptoms – besides nausea and a low-grade fever for twenty-four hours after the vaccination – the agreement is null and void."

Our parents made their decisions.

Where do we sign?

She could use that money for college.

I'm not risking him having a stroke.

But we weren't as sure.

I don't want to die.

Only one person died.

But still – he died!

Fifty thousand is a lot of money.

It's not that much. My family spent more than that on our last trip to Cannes. We flew private.

Won't you miss it?

I'd miss being able to see more than I'd miss hearing your thoughts.

We turned to Pi. She'd know what to do. She always did.

Do we sign? we asked.

Pi nodded. *Yes, it's the only option. We can't risk our lives.*

If even Pi thought we should get the antidote, then we figured we really should.

So we agreed. We would take the antidote.

Chapter Thirty-Eight
LAST CHANCE

It was a week of weirdness.

Levi's parents had him working overtime at Candy Heaven, listening for shoplifters. Over the course of the week, he was able to stop twenty jelly beans, three Blow Pops, and one bag of circus peanuts from disappearing from the store.

Courtney's mom and dad avoided her. They stayed out of her room. They even let her stretch out on the couch and watch all her CW and ABC Family shows by herself.

Isabelle's dad hosted his monthly poker game. With Isabelle by his side, he won six hundred and eighty bucks.

Mackenzie's parents attempted celibacy. Yes. Attempted.

Olivia's mom panicked and Googled stuff.

Tess's mom spent extra time at the gym.

Cooper's mom and Cooper had a long, long talk.

And the twins' parents...well, they pretty much just laughed and gave up.

In class, and in our spare time, we hung out together. We thought of it as our last hurrah.

We're going to have to start talking to each other again when this is done.

And studying.

At least we'll have some privacy.

So I can start imagining you all naked again?

As if you ever stopped, BJ!

Mackenzie was leaving school when Cooper caught up with her. "Can we talk?"

Mackenzie and Cooper hadn't spoken since he'd punched Bennett, except for across the room at the meeting the night before. He'd been avoiding her all day.

She wasn't sure she wanted to talk. *Talk* sounded ominous. Like he was going to break up with her again. Maybe it wasn't a breakup talk? Maybe the talk wasn't about her at all?

He sighed. *It's a breakup talk.*

Fuck.

"Can we walk?" he asked.

They waited for the light to change and then crossed the West Side Highway.

I don't want to have the breakup talk, Mackenzie thought at him.

I know.

So let's not.

We have to. He sighed. *We have to break up.*

She stopped in the middle of the street. *No.*

He put his arm on her elbow and led her to the sidewalk. *Yes.*

"No!" she yelled. "I'm sorry about what happened with Bennett! I'm really sorry!" Her chest hurt. Her feet hurt. She couldn't move off the sidewalk. Cars zipped by her. "I don't want to break up!"

He led her away from the street, closer to the water. "I think you do," he said. *At least, you did.*

She shook her head. *No, no, no.* "I didn't. I don't. I love you."

"Maybe you do. But we're not breaking up because of what you did with Bennett." He shook his head. "Well, not just because of that. I've been thinking a lot about this and... well, you do stuff like this all the time."

She didn't understand what he was talking about. "I cheat all the time?"

"No. You ruin things."

It felt like there was an elastic band tightening around her chest. "What does that even mean?"

"You self-sabotage."

"No I don't." *That's crazy.*

"Yeah, you do. You never study, so you get bad grades. You hand in homework late for no reason. Like that English essay. Mackenzie, why'd you quit gymnastics?"

"I don't like competing!" *I was afraid to lose!*

"No, you're afraid of winning. Of trying. And why'd you

invite the guy you cheated on me with to your Sweet?"

I wanted you to know, she realized. Her eyes stung. She had invited Bennett so Cooper would find out what she'd done. So he'd break up with her. What was wrong with her? The tears spilled down her face.

"I can't… It's hard to hear what you're thinking when you cry," he said after a few minutes.

It's true. Crying garbles incoming and outgoing telepathy. Too bad we can't all cry on demand.

"I'm sorry," Mackenzie said, wiping her eyes with her jacket sleeve. "I'm fucked up."

"We're all fucked up," he said softly. "And what's happening to us is fucked up. And my life is really fucked up right now. And I just don't think we're the right people to help unfuck each other up. Am I making any sense?"

She shrugged, still crying. Now her nose was running too. She knew she was an ugly crier. She was glad she couldn't hear him noticing.

"I think I want to walk on my own." She hiccuped and dried her eyes again.

He shifted his weight. "You sure you're okay?"

"I'm fine." *And fucked up, apparently.*

I heard that.

She bit her lip. "So…" *We're really over?*

He nodded. *Do you want me to walk you home?*

Always a gentleman. No. Go. I'll be fine.

All right. Goodbye, Mackenzie. He turned and recrossed the street. She watched him walk east. At first he moved slowly, but he moved faster as he got farther away.

She didn't want to go home yet, so she walked into Battery Park and kept going south. She walked until she could see the Statue of Liberty.

Maybe Cooper was right about the self-sabotage. Because now that she was truly free, she felt miserable.

Tess wasn't sure if she was avoiding Teddy or if he was avoiding her. Either way, it was Tuesday morning and they hadn't spoken since the Sweet.

After the kiss at the party, she'd run. She couldn't take it. They had finally had their perfect kiss and he was still thinking about Sadie. She couldn't deal.

Since he hadn't chased after her, she assumed he thought the kiss was a mistake. And she…well, she thought it was a mistake too. How could she be with someone who liked someone else? She couldn't. She wanted more. She deserved more.

You totally do, BJ told her in homeroom. He'd started sitting next to her in the back row.

But we were best friends and now that's ruined.

It's only ruined if you want it to be ruined. He's confused. It's not that he doesn't like you, he just doesn't like you enough. He doesn't want to lose you. He doesn't want to hurt you. He doesn't know you know about Sadie. If you want to stay friends with him, let him off the hook.

She suspected BJ was right, so just before lunch, she texted Teddy to meet up and grab a bite.

When they met at the school door, he gave her a stilted hug. *She wants to talk about the party. I'm not sure what to say. We're best friends. She's cute. Why am I not into her? I should be into her.*

Tess died a little death with every unspoken word.

But still, she agreed with BJ. It was like the kids' song "We're Going on a Bear Hunt." The only way over this was through it. As they walked down the street, she said, "Teddy, I'm sorry about what happened. It was a mistake. See, the thing is, I like you. I've liked you since we became friends. Even when you had a girlfriend, I've had feelings for you – more than friendship feelings."

He nodded. "I guess I knew that."

"So I wanted what happened at the party to happen. But I know you don't like me like that."

His eyes widened. "But—"

"No. Don't say you do. I know you don't. I know how you feel about Sadie."

He blushed. "You do?"

She nodded. "I do. And I don't want to be the person you hook up with just because I'm there. I want to be someone's Sadie."

"I'm sorry I kissed you." *Not that sorry. It was a good kiss.*

It really was. She took a deep breath. "Good. Now that that's settled, where should we go for lunch? I'm starving."

"What are you in the mood for?"

"Shake Shack?" To hell with the five – no, seven – pounds. She wanted a cheeseburger, and a milk shake, and bring on the fries! She was absolutely sure she deserved it.

"Olivia?" Mr Roth asked. "Are you sure you want to try your presentation again?"

"Yes," Olivia said, standing up.

She's totally going to bomb, thought Lazar. *She thinks she's too good for me. She's not even that pretty.*

Screw you, Olivia thought, and oddly, that gave her the burst of confidence she needed. Olivia pushed Lazar's thoughts out of her mind and focused on her notes. "I have a new topic."

"What is it?" Mr Roth asked.

"It's about Oprah."

He nodded. "All right, go ahead."

She could do this. She would not forget what she was talking about. She would not faint. She would not die. She would not care about what Lazar – or anyone else – thought. She cleared her throat. "Oprah was born…"

She focused on her own words and her own thoughts and didn't stop until she reached the end.

On Wednesday, BJ winked at Tess when he sat next to her in homeroom. *What's happening, gorgeous? How's Teddy?*

It's over.

Well, I'm not going to pretend I didn't know that already. You know he's not good enough for you, right?

I guess. I want to be someone's first choice.

Even though she was looking down at her notebook, she could feel him watching her.

You're my first choice.

She smiled. *I am not.*

You are too. Can I be your first choice?

That's it? You're throwing down the gauntlet?

He inched his seat closer to hers. *I'm throwing down the gauntlet. Putting it out there. You and me. What do you think?*

She wasn't sure. *What about Teddy?*

I thought it was over with Teddy.

It is over. But I, you know, can't pretend I don't still have feelings for him.

Do you know what would really help you forget about Teddy?

What?

Me.

Ms Velasquez walked in and closed the door.

Tess smiled to herself. *I'll think about it.*

Does that mean you'll fantasize about me tonight?

Courtney turned around and glared at them. "You know we can still hear you, right?"

Oh, right.

One more day.

Pi could hardly wait.

She stood in the bathroom and checked under the stall doors to make sure she was the only one there.

She was.

Her shoulders relaxed. She was alone. Finally.

She exhaled a big sigh of relief. Controlling her thoughts all week had been exhausting. But she had no choice if she was going to do what she wanted to do.

After Suzanna had approached Cooper at the Sweet and he had shrugged her off, Pi had decided that she had to control the situation. The authorities already knew about the telepathy. The cat was out of the bag. Pi had to find out exactly what Suzanna knew.

Pi had approached her in the lobby. She had asked Suzanna to join her for a cup of coffee.

"Sure," Suzanna had said while thinking, *She must have received one of the vaccines. Her eyes are definitely purple. She must have ESP! She wants to talk.*

"I do have ESP, and I do want to talk," Pi announced.

Holy crap, she can really hear me! She's it! She's it! I found one! She's real! This is actually happening! Holy shit!

When they sat down across from each other, Pi began the meeting by saying, "How did you get into the party?"

"Mackenzie's parents invited me," Suzanna answered smoothly. *I slipped the doorman a hundred bucks.*

"You slipped the doorman a hundred bucks. Got it. But why were you there?"

She blinked repeatedly. *How am I supposed to keep things classified if she can hear everything? I guess I can't.* "I figured out that most of the students with probable ESP were from your homeroom. I was instructed to follow you all as much as possible."

"But how did you know that most of us were in the same homeroom?"

"I spotted four students with purple eyes. I tracked who they were and what grade level they were in and discovered that they – you – were all in homeroom 10B."

Pi kept on. "Why did you come to the party?"

"We suspected that a group of students had telepathy. But we didn't know for sure. We needed someone to admit it before we could move on."

"Move on? What does that mean?" Pi pressed.

Suzanna went on to tell Pi that once they knew who the affected students were, they planned to debrief our parents. Pi also learned about the other tainted batches, the other infected populations – including the old man who'd had a stroke – and the antidote. And she learned that they expected us all to take it. That everything would go back to normal. That there would be financial compensation.

"No," Pi said, sipping her coffee. "I'm not taking an antidote."

What? She has to! "But – but it's dangerous," she sputtered. "Someone's already died."

"Please. He was over eighty and in a nursing home." Pi dismissed Suzanna's concern with a wave of her hand. "What happened to me is exceptional. I am not getting rid of it. You can't force me."

"We can't take that risk with twenty-four students."

"We're only twenty-two students."

"The batch had twenty-four vaccinations in it. The additional two were given to other students. We're looking for them. We'll be offering them the antidote as well."

"So offer it to them. Don't risk their lives. Risk mine only." Her plan began to formulate. *I'll get everyone else to take the antidote. I'll remain the only one with telepathy. I'll be the last remaining Espie.*

I'll truly be exceptional.

She would need her father's permission, of course, but he would give it. He valued brilliance. Plus he could monitor her behavior and symptoms in case there was any real risk. Her mom would miss out on everything. She didn't deserve to be a part of it.

Is she crazy? I think she's crazy.

"I'm not crazy," Pi said. "Think of this as an incredible opportunity. I'll tell you everything you want to know. Plus I'll meet with you once a month so you can do whatever tests on me you want. I don't mind the risks. Imagine all you can learn. It would be brilliant research."

It would be fascinating...but there's no way they're going to go for it.

Pi slammed her coffee cup on the table. "Make them go for it."

She is hard-core. "I have to talk to my supervisor."

Pi nodded. "Do that."

Suzanna bit her lip. *Could we do this? Yes. No. Maybe. But what if the others find out that she's not taking the antidote? They could all decide not to take it. We'd have a major issue on our hands.*

"I won't tell anyone. You have my word."

"But they can hear what you're thinking!"

Pi smiled. "Not for long."

Keeping her plan a secret hadn't been easy. But if anyone could do it, Pi could. It took focus. And she had focus. She just could not let her mind wander. She hid. She discovered that humming helped block her thoughts. So she hummed at all times. She closed her eyes a lot. Plus she wore really, really uncomfortable shoes all week. Shoes that gave her blisters. That way she could focus on the pain.

Do you need a Band-Aid?

Why do you keep wearing them if they hurt so much?

Just get new shoes already. This is ridiculous!

She wished she could just stay home, but she feared it would be way too obvious, since she had a perfect attendance record.

She tried to teach herself to cry on demand, but unless she waved onions under her eyes, she couldn't quite master it.

Pi had made an interesting discovery one day when she'd bumped into Keren Korb in the bathroom.

Keren had taken off her dark glasses and was splashing water on her face.

Ahhh. My skin feels so oily today.

Pi almost laughed out loud.

We hadn't been able to hear Keren not because she was blind – but because she wore dark sunglasses. They stopped transmission. But Pi had worn sunglasses outside, hadn't she? Yes, she had. It hadn't stopped her from hearing other people's thoughts, had it? She didn't think so.

Maybe her sunglasses weren't dark enough.

After school, she went straight to the closest Sunglass Hut and tried on a few pairs. She bought the ones that blocked the most light.

It worked. She couldn't hear anyone in the store's thoughts. She assumed that meant we wouldn't be able to hear hers.

The problem was she wanted to hear our thoughts.

Plus, wearing dark sunglasses to class would make us too suspicious. Although Suzanna and her people might be able to use them. We were already suspicious of them.

Pi took the sunglasses off.

She'd figure it out.

It was a test. And Pi liked tests. She wanted to be number one.

Chapter Thirty-Nine
WE MEET AGAIN

We were told to be at the nurse's office early, at seven a.m.

Our parents were asked to stay home so as not to raise suspicion among arriving students or faculty. We thought three men and one woman in dark sunglasses and navy suits surrounding us in the hallway might set off some alarm bells, but what did we know?

Hank Soporic greeted us in the hallway. "Good morning, everyone." He adjusted his dark glasses first and then his tie. "There are donuts for you in the cafeteria, so as soon as you're done, you can relax until your classes begin. Suzanna will be done setting up in just a minute."

What's up with the dark sunglasses?

They're trying to look like government agents.

They are government agents.

I can't hear what they're thinking.

Me neither!

Is it because of the glasses?

It must be!

How did we not know that earlier?

Too late.

It's disturbing.

Let's just get this over with.

"Who's going first?" Levi asked. We all looked at Pi.

"I don't mind." *Hum, hum, hummmmmm.*

Olivia was behind Pi. Behind Olivia was Mackenzie, and behind her were Tess and BJ.

They couldn't stop flirting.

"We should just kiss now," BJ said.

"Why now?"

"Don't you want to see what it's like? To kiss with ESP? We'll keep our eyes open and everything. It'll be wild. It's our last chance. C'mon, you know you want to."

She laughed. "I'm not making out with you in front of the entire class!"

"Why not? No one cares." He turned around and addressed the rest of us. "Would anyone care if we made out?"

Go for it!

Please don't!

I haven't even had coffee yet.

Tess shook her head. "I'm sure we'll have time later. The vaccination took a day to kick in."

"The antidote might work right away," BJ warned. "We

just don't know. Why take a chance?"

Tess put her arms on his shoulders. *I would do it if we were alone.*

He stood up straight. *Have you ever been in the guys' bathroom? Let's go.*

Gross, thought Mackenzie. *I'd go to the girls' bathroom if I were you.*

Tess put her hand on her hip. *I shouldn't. I know I shouldn't.*

Oh, just do it, Mackenzie thought. *Why the hell not?*

BJ nodded eagerly. *We have at least fifteen minutes.*

Tess laughed. *We're not kissing for fifteen minutes!*

There's other stuff we could do. Are you wearing the white bra? He waggled his eyebrows.

"Don't push your luck," she said. Then she added, *All right, let's go!*

His eyes lit up. He grabbed her hand and practically galloped down the hall, dragging her behind him.

Suzanna came out and smiled. "You're up, Pi!"

Pi went in.

We looked around at each other.

This is it. This is really it.

I can't believe how different everything is now.

"I'm going to miss the ESP," Olivia said.

Jordana nodded as she filed her nails. "Me too. To be honest, I'm not exactly sure why we're getting rid of it."

Olivia turned back to Jordana, wondering the same thing. Why were they getting rid of it?

Levi snorted. "Because it's going to kill us?"

But would it? "We don't know that," Olivia said, her heart speeding up. "Maybe we should keep it," she said quietly.

Everyone looked at each other.

The two men in navy still outside shifted uncomfortably.

"Isn't it a little late?" Isaac asked. "We already signed the forms. I have plans for the cash."

Olivia felt her confidence – the confidence that had come from the ESP – build inside her. "So we won't take the checks. We'll rip up the forms. We don't have to do anything we don't want to do."

"But my eyes are purple," Courtney said. "And I don't want to have a stroke. Aren't you the one who usually worries about strokes?"

"Only one person had a stroke," Olivia said. "And he was eighty-one." Her heart was beating hard against her chest. Was she really suggesting keeping the telepathy? Staying an Espie? What would that mean for her future?

"We need that money," Dave said. "My family needs that money."

"So do I," said Michelle. *I don't have a fancy down-town apartment like the rest of you. We have mice.*

"We don't have to be unanimous," Olivia said. "We can each do what we want."

Courtney put her hands on her hips. "No way am I giving it up if I know some of you are keeping it. I don't want you reading my mind when I can't read yours."

"Me neither," added Levi.

"But what would we tell our parents?" Anojah asked, squinting.

Olivia stood up taller. Her mother was definitely going to have a heart attack. "It's not up to our parents. It's up to us."

"I'm with Olivia," Courtney said.

Levi nodded. "Me too."

Mackenzie wasn't sure. She thought about what Cooper had said about self-sabotage. Was keeping something in your brain that might kill you self-sabotage? Or was getting rid of a skill that could make you amazing self-sabotage? She decided it could probably go either way. "Me too," she said. "You all know how I feel about needles."

"But what if we get sick?" Anojah asked. "What if we do start to go blind? I can barely see as it is!"

Olivia definitely did not want to go blind. But losing her mind-reading abilities would also feel like a type of blindness. "I guess I just don't see what the rush is. We can still get the antidote. We just don't have to get it today. Can't we wait and see?"

We all started to nod. What was the rush? Why were we in such a hurry to get rid of something that was so incredibly awesome?

Everyone in line was nodding, even Michelle. Everyone except Cooper.

Olivia looked up at him. "Not you?"

He shook his head. "I just want this to stop."

She nodded. She understood. He'd had a rough few weeks. "I know it's been tough for you—"

He laughed. "My whole world fell apart."

Olivia took a step toward him. *Not because of the telepathy, though. Your whole world was already cracked. You just didn't realize it.*

No one said anything. Including Cooper.

"We all have to do what we have to do," Nick said. Just then the door opened and Pi came out. "All done," she barked. "Who's next?"

Oops.

We forgot about Pi!

It's too late for her!

Pi's eyes narrowed. "What's going on?"

Olivia cleared her throat. "We decided – well, most of us decided – that we're not taking the antidote."

Her face paled. "What are you talking about?"

"We want to keep the telepathy," Jordana said.

Pi's eyes flashed.

She's pissed.

Her hands clenched. *Of course I'm pissed!*

How did she hear us?

"The antidote takes a day to kick in," Pi snapped. "I don't have time for this. Go get your shots. Now. Olivia, you're next."

Olivia stood her ground. "I'm not getting it."

"Yes you are."

"No I'm not. We're not."

Pi grimaced. *No! This isn't happening!* "We already came to a decision."

Olivia did feel bad about that. "Pi, we're so sorry we made a new decision after you already took the antidote, but—"

No! Pi stomped her foot. *I'm supposed to be the only one left!*

"Huh?" Jordana wondered out loud, putting down her nail file. "Left of what?"

"Left of...left of..." *Crap, what do I say?*

Left with telepathy?

Did she get the shot or not?

We circled closer to her.

Pi, take off your blazer.

She shrugged and removed it.

She's wearing a Band-Aid.

She could be faking it.

Why would she do that?

Why else? So she could be the only one.

"Care to explain?" Levi asked.

Pi took a step back. "There's nothing to explain. I got the shot. Now it's your turn." *Hum, hum, hum, hummmmmm.*

Without a word, Jordana reached over and ripped off Pi's Band-Aid.

Ouch!

Pi's arm was needle-mark-free.

"You are such a liar!" Anojah yelled.

"This is totally worse than giving us the wrong answers on a test," Daniel said.

Pi shook her head. "You don't understand. They don't want all of us to keep it. It's too risky. It makes the most sense for it to be only me."

The door opened. Suzanna smiled. We could see our

reflection in her dark sunglasses. "Can the next person come in, please?"

She's in on this with Pi!

The sunglasses are blocking us from hearing her!

She's blocking us from hearing her!

They all are!

"We're not coming in," Olivia said.

"We know Pi didn't get it, and neither are we," Daniel announced.

Suzanna turned to Pi. "What are you talking about?"

Pi's arms shook. *I didn't tell them! They decided on their own!*

She can't hear you.

But we can.

Olivia stepped forward. "We're sorry, Suzanna, but we're breaking the deal."

Her smile faltered. "You can't," she said. "It's too risky. We don't know what will happen to you. You could have a stroke. You could go blind. Hank! Come out here!"

"What we want," Olivia began, "is to not ignore this opportunity. What's the rush, anyway? We can always change our minds later, can't we?"

Hank stepped out of the office. "What's going on here?"

"They're refusing to take the antidote," Suzanna explained. She turned back and shook her head. "We don't know what the window is. What if you change your mind and it's too late?"

We exchanged glances.

"I don't think a few weeks will kill us," Mackenzie said.

"It might," snapped Pi.

Daniel laughed. "Says the person who wasn't getting the antidote anyway."

Hank shook his head. "You get the check when you get the shot. Don't you want the money?"

There goes my college tuition.

There goes my motorcycle.

There goes my pet pig named Pillow.

"Kids," Hank said in a cooing voice, "we're going to have to call your parents. They'll want you to take the antidote."

My parents are going to kill me.

They'll understand.

No they won't.

We'll make them.

It's our lives. Our choice.

I think mine were kind of disappointed I was giving it up.

"The school won't like it either," Hank continued.

They're not going to let us go to regular classes now if we can hear everyone.

And cheat.

They'll figure something out. They'll have to.

They're not going to tell the rest of the students, are they?

"This doesn't have to be a unanimous decision," Suzanna said. "If there is anyone who wants the antidote, I can still give it."

Cooper stepped up. "I do."

What?

Are you sure?

Don't do it, man!

He nodded.

"I'm calling your parents," Hank grumbled. He took off his sunglasses and rubbed his temples. *This is going to screw up everything.* "This isn't over." He stalked off in the other direction.

Suzanna took off her sunglasses too. "If any of you change your mind, I'll be here for the rest of the day. Cooper, come with me." *Lucky kids. If I were them, I wouldn't get rid of it either.*

The door closed behind them.

"You're all a bunch of morons," Pi snapped, and marched down the hallway.

"What do we do now?" Daniel asked.

Courtney licked her lips. "Get a donut?"

Brinn mumbled something.

"What did you say?" Jordana asked.

Brinn wrinkled her nose. *Maybe we should skip the donuts. In case they put the antidote in there.*

"Good call," said Dave. "But I'm starving."

Me too.

Me three.

We're all starving.

"Let's raid the vending machine," Courtney said. We waved goodbye to the two remaining and useless bodyguards and followed her to the vending machine in the cafeteria.

That's our story.

How we became a *we*.

And that's what we are these days. A we.

When you're a group that can hear each other's thoughts, the line between *I* and *we* gets kind of blurry.

Along the way to the vending machine, Olivia stopped in the bathroom. She pushed the door open and interrupted a kissing BJ and Tess.

Can we do this forever?

We may have to eat at some point.

I think I can go without food.

Olivia jumped back. "Oops! Sorry!"

The couple pulled apart.

"Omigod, Olivia, you have no idea," Tess gushed. "Kissing another Espie is the most insane thing ever."

BJ motioned to Olivia. "You two should totally give it a try. I'll watch."

Tess punched him in the arm. "I guess it's our turn for the antidote, huh?"

"Actually," Olivia said, "there's been a bit of a change in plans. Some of us – most of us – changed our minds. We're not getting it. We're keeping the telepathy."

"Oh!" Tess said, her hand still on BJ's arm. "Cool."

"More Espie kissing!" BJ cheered.

"How long do we have until homeroom?" Tess asked.

"About twenty minutes," Olivia said. "I'm going to get a snack."

BJ waved. "We'll be here if you need us."

Olivia guessed she would have to find another bathroom.

She backed out and let the door swing behind her. When

she turned around, she saw Cooper.

She couldn't help feeling sad for him. "You're done? Did it hurt?"

"No," he said.

"Well, that's good, at least."

"No, I mean I didn't do it." He smiled.

"You didn't? Why not?"

"I don't know. I just thought…well, Ashley already calls me her superhero. Imagine what she'd think if it were true."

Olivia laughed.

"I guess I just hated finding out that everyone was lying to me. But now no one will be able to lie to me, right?"

"Right," she said.

"And you were great out there," he said. "I was impressed."

Olivia blushed and smiled. "Thanks."

She's really cute, Cooper thought.

She blushed even more. *I think you're really cute too*. She didn't see Courtney, Jordana, and Levi approaching from behind, candy bars and gummy bears in hand.

Omigod, did you hear that? Olivia is hitting on Cooper!

Does he like her?

Olivia spun around. "I…we…"

Ten bucks they're hooking up before the end of the month… By the end of the month? By the end of the week!… They'll make such a cute couple… Mackenzie is going to freak.

What can we say? We know everything.

ACKNOWLEDGMENTS

Thanks to my awesome agents, editors, publishers, colleagues, and friends: Laura Dail, Tamar Rydzinski, Wendy Loggia, Krista Vitola, Beverly Horowitz, Lauren Donovan, Colleen Fellingham, Trish Parcell, Tamar Schwartz, Rachel Feld, John Adamo, Dominique Cimina, Adrienne Waintraub, Deb Shapiro, Brian Lipson, Jess Rothenberg, Emily Bender, Anne Heltzel, Farrin Jacobs, Eloise Flood, Targia Clarke, Bonnie Altro, Brahm Morganstein, Judy Batalion, Lauren Kisilevsky, Alison Pace, Susan Finkelberg-Sohmer, Corinne and Michael Bilerman, Adele Griffin, Leslie Margolis, Kristin Harmel, Maryrose Wood, Tara Altebrando, Sara Zarr, Ally Carter, Jennifer Barnes, Julia DeVillers, Alan Gratz, Penny Fransblow, Maggie Marr, Susane Colasanti, Lauren Oliver, Aimee Friedman, Jen Calonita, Gayle Forman, Jennifer E. Smith, and everyone at *Justine* magazine.

Extra special thanks to Courtney Sheinmel, Elissa Ambrose, Lauren Myracle, Anna Kranwinkle, Avery Carmichael,

E. Lockhart, Robin Wasserman, Jess Braun, and Elizabeth Eulberg, who read early drafts of this book and showed me how to make it so much better.

Love and thanks to my family: Aviva, Mom, Robert, Dad, Louisa, Gary, Lori, Sloan, Isaac, Vickie, John, Gary, Darren, Ryan, Jack, Jen, Teri, Briana, Michael, David, Patsy, Murray, Maggie, and Jenny.

Extra love and extra thanks and lots and lots of kisses to Anabelle, Chloe, and Todd.

One year + one beach house + zero parents =

TEN THINGS
WE
SHOULDN'T
HAVE DONE

Sarah Mlynowski

Pbk: 978 1 40830 979 7 £6.99 / eBook: 978 1 40831 376 3 £5.99